VISUAL QUICKSTART GUIDE

Palm

Organizers

FOURTH EDITION

Jeff Carlson and Agen G.N. Schmitz

 Peachpit Press

Visual QuickStart Guide
Palm Organizers, Fourth Edition
Jeff Carlson and Agen G.N. Schmitz

Peachpit Press

1249 Eighth Street
Berkeley, CA 94710
(510) 524-2178
(800) 283-9444
(510) 524-2221 (fax)

Find us on the World Wide Web at: www.peachpit.com
To report errors, please send a note to errata@peachpit.com
Peachpit Press is a division of Pearson Education

Copyright © 2005 by Jeff Carlson

Editor: Nancy Davis
Production Editor: Lupe Edgar
Copyeditor: Liane Thomas
Proofreader: Ted Waitt
Indexer: Jan Wright, Wright Information Indexing Services
Cover Design: The Visual Group

Notice of rights

Notice of liability

Trademarks

ISBN: 0-321-28766-5

9 8 7 6 5 4 3 2

Printed and bound in the United States of America

Praise for *Palm Organizers Visual QuickStart Guide*

If I had to describe this book in one word, it would be "meaty." ...While each of the Palm-Pilot books to date has unique value, this book is a diamond in the rough and one of my favorites. I highly recommend it.

— Scott Sbihli, *Pen Computing Magazine*

What a great book! If you're a Palm device user, you're going to get a lot out of this book. Jeff Carlson's writing style makes everything easy to understand, yet deep, chock full of valuable information.

— David Gewirtz, Editor-in-Chief, *PalmPower Magazine* (www.palmpower.com)

One strength of the book is in Carlson's outstanding use of the Visual QuickStart Guide format, illustrating each point with plenty of screen shots and examples from the Palm, Windows, and Macintosh operating systems. I can't wait to try some of the new tips and procedures in this terrific book.

— John Nemerovski, Book Bytes Columnist and Reviewer, *My Mac Magazine* (www.mymac.com)

Carlson—clearly an avid Palmist with some accumulated wisdom on the topic—goes beyond merely rehashing the Palm's own documentation.

— David Wall, Amazon.com

Dedication

For Kimberly, who understands Jeff more than he realizes.
For Parie, who says she loves Agen more. We'll see about that.

Special Thanks to

Nancy Davis, for getting this book project started in the first place, for remaining flexible and cheerful, and for simply chatting when our brains required a much-needed break.

Liane Thomas, for being a kindred spirit and succinctly nailing the way we both tend to work (despite our best efforts): "think, think, think, plan, plan, think, oh yeah...write!"

Ted Waitt, for slaving away at the tiny details and consistently catching us when our focus ebbed.

Jan Wright, for coming to our aid in the nick of time and creating a thorough, and thoroughly humorous, index.

Rosie Pulido, for providing us with Palm information and hardware when needed.

Glenn Fleishman, Jeff Tolbert, Larry Chen, Kim Ricketts (plus the various long-distance inhabitants) at the Greenwood compound, for their invaluable advice, experience, and sense of fun.

Nancy Aldrich-Ruenzel, Connie Jeung-Mills, Lupe Edgar, Gary-Paul Prince, Marjorie Baer, Kim Lombardi, Lisa Brazieal, Megan Lynch, Rebecca Ross, Mimi Heft, and **Paula Baker** at Peachpit Press. They genuinely make the book-creation process a pleasure.

Our Wives and Loves of our Lives, Kim Carlson and Parie Hines, for making a little extra coffee and understanding that book projects do, in fact, finish.

Soundtrack

BBC's The Blue Room (hosted by Rob Da Bank and Chris Coco); **Bent**, *Ariels*; **Finn Brothers**, *Everyone Is Here*; **Kings of Convenience**, *Riot on an Empty Street*; **Mull Historical Society**, *This Is Hope*; **Wilco**, *A Ghost Is Born*; **Badly Drawn Boy**, *One Plus One Is One*; **Future Loop Foundation**, *A Very English Summer*; **Telemann**, *Tafelmusik*.

TABLE OF CONTENTS

Chapter 5: Contents   149

TABLE OF CONTENTS

INTRODUCTION

Jeff bought his first handheld, a PalmPilot Personal, in 1997 for a number of reasons. Of course, the gadget factor was pretty high. Plus, the PalmPilot was getting raves for its ability to store volumes of formerly paper-based contact and scheduling information in a device slightly larger than a deck of cards, as well as its capability of synchornizing with a desktop PC.

For Agen, the gadget factor was the top draw. But as he followed Jeff into the world of full-time freelancing, he soon discovered the same truth that Jeff found with this cool gadget: it helped provide a greater measure of control over a myriad of overlapping tasks and time commitments.

This is part of the appeal of a Palm OS organizer. Yes, it's a cool gadget. Yes, you can accessorize it to your heart's content with styli, cases, and custom flipcovers. Yes, it piques people's curiosity and makes complete strangers walk up and ask, "What's that?" But it's also an efficient, well-thought-out organizational tool that performs its tasks exceptionally well. Instead of being a self-contained computer in a smaller container, it's an extension of the information that millions of people rely on every day.

Excerpted from an interview with Bill Gates, CEO and Chairman of Microsoft Corporation, on the television show "Charlie Rose," March 4, 1998 (used with permission).

Bill Gates: The future of the PC is to be a tablet-sized device or perhaps larger than a tablet.... But then you also have a lot of other devices, things like—I think I've got one in my pocket.

Charlie Rose: A Pilot is in his pocket.

Bill Gates: No, no, no, no. This is the competitor to the Pilot. Don't say "Pilot." Geez. This is the—

Charlie Rose: Does that look like a Pilot? I rest my case.

Palm Organizers: Visual QuickStart Guide

This book is meant to be a compact, functional extension of a Palm OS organizer. Not just a how-to approach to using an electronic tool, this Visual QuickStart Guide is a primer on how to effectively get control of your schedule, contacts, and all the data that used to occupy reams of papers and Post-it notes.

Our aim for this book is to show you what's possible with Palm OS devices, from their basic features to tips and tricks for using them smarter and faster. At times we'll personally recommend a product or a technique because it's what we've found useful. As a result, and to keep this book from becoming ten times larger than the device it covers, we don't list every product on the market—we want you to have fun exploring what's available.

In fact, with millions of Palm OS devices in use today, it's impossible to cover every detail. For example, the Preferences screen on a Tungsten T is different than a Tungsten C, which differs from devices that came before them—but the preferences themselves are similar.

Also in the name of generalization, you'll find that we'll often mention a shortcut Graffiti stroke (for example, ✓-B), knowing full well that some devices such as the PalmOne Treo use a thumbpad keyboard instead of Graffiti. (Here's your first tip: use the Treo's Menu key, then the shortcut letter.)

People who swear by their handhelds also tend to integrate them into their lives, moving beyond business meetings to birthdays, home finances, electronic books, and the occasional game of solitaire. It continues to be an invaluable part of our everyday lives.

We'd love to know how your handheld helps (or hinders) your life. Feel free to email us with feedback at palmvqs@necoffee.com.

The Hand(held) of Progress

As we were finishing up this fourth edition, PalmOne was gearing up to release new models in the Fall 2004 timeframe. However, due to scheduling, we weren't able to incorporate those new models into the book. (At press time, the model names, operating systems, and release dates were still undisclosed.)

Since there wasn't time to incorporate the new information into this edition, we'll cover the changes in a new appendix, and post it as a PDF file at the companion Web site for this book: www.necoffee.com/palmvqs/. We'll also post news tidbits we come across and new software discoveries, so please check back from time to time.

Part 1
Using Palm Organizers

The Handheld Portal to Your Information

You've probably read articles about them, or seen them in advertisements. More likely, you know someone who has one, and his or her enthusiasm was infectious. That's how we were introduced to Palm organizers, and now it's hard to find us without one.

Chapter 1, **Palm Basics**, introduces you to Palm OS-based organizers, discussing the different families, their hardware controls, battery usage, and available accessories.

Chapter 2, **The Palm OS**, covers the handheld's most undervalued feature: the powerful, yet minimalist, operating system. We'll explore system-wide preferences, memory management, and learn how to write Palm's celebrated—and simple—Graffiti alphabet.

Chapter 3, **HotSync**, examines the feature for synchronizing information from your handheld with the desktop software, including infrared synchronization and using other programs to tie your data into your Personal Information Manager (PIM) software.

Chapters 4–6 (**Calendar**, **Contacts**, and **Tasks, Memos, and Notes**) deal with the main built-in programs, showing you why a tiny screen can be so much better than crumpled pages of scribbled appointments and Post-it notes tucked into a bulging "personal organizer."

Chapter 7, **Calculator, Expense, and Clock**, delves into the number-crunching applications provided by Palm, plus the simple but useful Clock application.

PALM BASICS

The ancestry of today's Palm organizers can be traced to the Pilot, the original creation of inventor Jeff Hawkins. It began as a block of wood that Hawkins carried around the hallways of Palm Computing. It was the essence of the term "hardware"—no buttons, no batteries, no screen (certainly no backlight, though a fluorescent highlighter might have worked), no software.

It was also simple. The device in Hawkins's mind didn't take a modern PC and cram its guts into a smaller case, or try to woo consumers with its multimedia capabilities. Instead, the handheld machine focused on performing a handful of essential tasks well, in tandem with the computers and data that people were using at the time.

As an evolutionary surprise, today's Palm devices can do much more than their founder's intent: wireless Internet access, color photos, global positioning, and more. And yet, despite the wide array of software and hardware add-ons you can get for them, today's handhelds remain true to Hawkins's original vision: simple to use and simple in scope (though not limited, as you'll discover). They also have become simply essential for millions of owners.

PalmOne Device Families

Like any product, the Palm organizer evolved over time; there are still thousands of people using even the earliest Pilot models. As more companies have licensed the Palm OS, multiple variations of devices have appeared, to the point where it's impractical to list them all here. Instead, let's look at the major families of devices that are shipping as of this book's publication date (Fall, 2004).

PalmOne Zire series

Before introducing the Zire, Palm had seen considerable success with handhelds, adding capabilities as users' needs grew. But Palm also discovered that a large number of its customers were using just the basic features: keeping track of schedules, storing addresses, making lists of to do items, and taking short text memos. Seeing an opportunity, the company created the Zire, a handheld that stuck to the basics. The first Zire included 2 MB of memory, no backlight, and the core Palm applications in an attractive white enclosure. Oh, and it cost $99. It was an unexpected hit.

The Zire 21 (**Figure 1.1**) is the next generation device, sticking to the same basics but now including 8 MB of memory and a much faster processor (but still no backlight). For synchronizing to your computer, both the original Zire and Zire 21 use a USB cable instead of a cradle, which is good for travelers but means they won't work with third-party devices, like keyboards, that require Palm's Universal Connector.

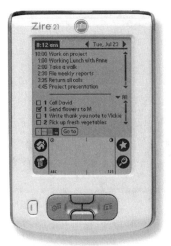

Figure 1.1 The Palm Zire 21 is a bare-bones organizer, but at $99 it's all that many people need in a Palm.

Palm OS, PalmOne, and PalmSource

In 2003, with the handheld market consolidating in a tough economy, Palm purchased Handspring and renamed the joint company PalmOne. It then split off the part of the company that developed the operating system (OS), calling it PalmSource. Thus, your PalmOne handheld is powered by the Palm OS, which is developed by PalmSource. *Alles klar?*

Figure 1.2 The $300 Palm Zire 72 is a multimedia hand-held for the masses, incorporating a color screen and a built-in digital camera.

In mid-2004, PalmOne released two new handhelds—the Zire 31 and Zire 72—boasting color screens and multimedia capability. They both also include a five-way navigator on the front of the case, headphone jacks (for listening to MP3 audio files), an expansion card slot, and Palm OS 5.2.8 (the most recent release of the Palm operating system as of this writing).

The Zire 31 is the immediate successor to the Zire 21 in both numerical progression and step-up features (as they say in the industry), bringing a 160 by 160-pixel color screen and 16 MB of memory to the party.

The snazzy Zire 72 (**Figure 1.2**) doubles those specs to 320 by 320 pixels and 32 MB of memory, and improves upon its Zire 71 predecessor with a 1.2-megapixel digital camera built into the back of the handheld. (The Zire 71 clunkily required you to slide open its back panel to reveal the camera.) And it includes a digital voice recorder, accessed via a button at the top-left side of the case. The Zire 72's big claim to fame is that it's the first PalmOne handheld geared to the consumer (and not the business professional, as the Tungsten series is) to incorporate Bluetooth wireless connectivity. This enables you to communicate with other Bluetooth-enabled devices, from sending a contact to your cell phone to performing a wireless HotSync with your laptop.

PalmOne Tungsten series

Okay, so maybe these handhelds aren't actually made out of tungsten, a hard element with the highest melting point of any metal. But the Tungsten line certainly looks shiny and impressive. Featuring bright color screens, fast processors, expansion card slots, and multimedia features, the Tungsten models represent the middle and the high end of PalmOne's handhelds.

The midrange Tungsten E (**Figure 1.3**) is simple but svelte, and is the logical successor to the m500 series. The Tungsten T3 introduces Palm's first rectangular screen (**Figure 1.4**). Like the previous T2, the bottom portion of the case slides down, but in this case it reveals more active screen area—320 by 480 pixels to be specific. (When using many applications, a software silkscreen Graffiti area appears.) For applications that can take advantage of it, the T3 can be used horizontally as well—turn it sideways and read more text of an ebook, view spreadsheets, or even watch mini-movies in widescreen mode.

The specialized Tungsten C is equipped with Wi-Fi (802.11b) wireless networking, such as is found in an increasing number of offices, homes, coffeeshops, and airports. Not only can you access the Internet, you can do it at broadband speed.

All Tungsten models are stacked with memory, with up to 64 MB in the T3 and C, and the T3 includes built-in Bluetooth wireless networking, an internal microphone, and a headphone port for listening to digital music or voice memos.

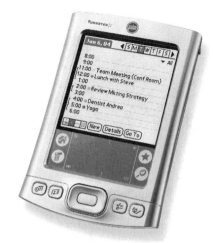

Figure 1.3 The Tungsten E is the current workhorse of the Palm line of organizers.

Figure 1.4 The bottom section of Palm's Tungsten T3 slides down to reveal more active screen area instead of a static silkscreen area.

Figure 1.5 The PalmOne Treo 300 is a Palm OS handheld that doubles as a cellular phone.

Figure 1.6 The Treo 600 is smaller than many cellular phones, but still packs a full Palm organizer inside.

PalmOne Treo

Bear with us for a moment as we go through a bit of Palm OS history. In 1998, the creators of the original PalmPilot—Jeff Hawkins, Donna Dubinsky, and Ed Colligan—formed Handspring, Inc., licensing the Palm OS and developing a low-cost handheld called the Visor. In 2001, Handspring shifted its focus and introduced the Treo "smartphone" that incorporated a PDA with a cellular phone. Unlike bulky phone hybrids that came before it, the Treo is slightly smaller than most other Palm devices. It can be used against the ear like most phones, or with an included hands-free adapter (which lets you also use the Treo as an organizer as you talk).

With the 2003 purchase of Handspring, PalmOne became the manufacturer of the Treo, and it continues to offer two of the earlier models: the Treo 270 and Treo 300 (**Figure 1.5**). Both feature color screens and built-in QWERTY keyboards, but the Treo 270 works with the worldwide GSM/GPRS cellular formats while the Treo 300 uses CDMA (which is supported by Sprint).

PalmOne's focus is the relatively diminutive—compared with other PalmOne handhelds—Treo 600 (**Figure 1.6**), which comes in both GSM/GPRS and CDMA flavors. It includes 32 MB of memory, a memory card slot, the five-way navigator (which vastly improves one-handed operability), as well as a 640 by 480-pixel camera and MP3 audio capability.

For more on using the Treo, see Chapter 9.

PALMONE DEVICE FAMILIES

Other Palm OS Devices

When we say "Palm organizer," you probably think of devices like those on the preceding pages. But the Palm OS is used for several other variations, a few of which we want to note here.

Kyocera Smartphone

Although the Treo has made a big splash, it wasn't the first phone/PDA combination device to hit the market. The Qualcomm Smartphone integrated the functions in one unit; unfortunately, it was enormous and expensive. Qualcomm sold their wares to Kyocera, and now the third generation Smartphone 7135 is a much better hybrid (`www.kyocera-wireless.com`).

Opening the clamshell reveals a Palm OS organizer at the phone's heart (**Figure 1.7**). The Palm OS is actually a part of the phone's inner workings, allowing you to find someone in your Contacts and dial their number with one tap, or easily check your email and other online information.

Figure 1.7 The Kyocera 7135 Smartphone integrates a Palm device and a cellular phone.

✔ Tips

- In addition to being a phone/PDA combination, the Smartphone has a few other helpful features. The Voice Dial application lets you record a spoken word or phrase and associate it with a number, so you can press a button and say a person's name to dial their number. This is a great feature if you have to make a call when driving or are otherwise occupied.

- The Call History application (**Figure 1.8**) offers a detailed breakdown of your calls, without relying on the phone company's records.

- The Smartphone 7135 is a little behind the times, using Palm OS 4.1.

Call History			▼ All
Who	**When**	**Length**	
Data Call	7/20	03:52	
Data Call	7/16	03:49	
Carlson, Kim	7/16	00:55	
Data Call	7/10	01:42	
Tolbert, Jeff	7/10	00:08	
Schmitz, Agen	7/10	00:53	
Data Call	7/10	07:59	
Data Call	7/2	01:46	
Data Call	6/21	01:21	
Data Call	4/3	01:36	
5088659888	4/3	01:05	

Figure 1.8 Don't wait until the phone bill arrives to see your cellular usage.

Figure 1.9 Find your way back with Garmin's iQue 3200 and 3600 handhelds, featuring an integrated GPS receiver.

Samsung SPH-i500

Another well-regarded smartphone device is Samsung's SPH-i500 (www.samsungusa.com/wireless/), which is smaller than the Treo and Kyocera 7135.

Garmin iQue

Garmin's iQue 3200 and 3600 (www.garmin.com) offer an integrated GPS receiver in a device that's chock-full of features: voice guidance commands, a tall 320 x 480-pixel color screen, memory expansion slot, MP3 audio playback, voice recorder, and Palm OS 5.2 (**Figure 1.9**).

Alphasmart Dana

Alphasmart's Dana (www.alphasmart.com) at first seems like a PDA on steroids because it boasts a large screen and full-size keyboard. Used primarily in education settings (though some news reporters use it in place of a laptop on assignment), the Dana is an energy efficient, ruggedized word processor that also happens to run whatever you can throw at a typical Palm OS device.

Symbol devices

Symbol Technologies (www.symbol.com) has been creating Palm devices since the early days of the PalmPilot, incorporating barcode readers and other in-the-field technologies for specialized uses.

Where's the Sony CLIÉ?

Sony announced in June 2004 that it would no longer develop and sell its CLIÉ ("clee-ay") handhelds to the U.S. market (though it would continue selling CLIÉ devices in Japan). Sony will continue to support all current customers worldwide for the life of the warranties on their handhelds.

This is disappointing, as Sony really pressed PalmOne to innovate with their own handhelds. Without Sony, the five-way navigator, MP3 audio, and image capture might not be the standard-issue features they are today.

OTHER PALM OS DEVICES

PalmOne Device Overview

No matter which handheld you use, they all share the following characteristics.

Power button

Every device has a power button that turns the organizer on and off (**Figure 1.10**). The handheld will automatically power down after two minutes (you can change the time delay; see Chapter 2).

The power button often has a secondary function on many handhelds. On some color devices, holding the power button activates the screen brightness control. On others, like the Zire 72, holding it activates a keylock feature. On the Treo, holding the power button initiates a connection to your cellular provider.

Screen

The average handheld's screen accounts for most of the device. Some models, such as the Zire 21, feature a liquid-crystal display (LCD) that is black and white only (or, more accurately, black on a gray-green background) and measures 160 by 160 pixels.

Increasingly, organizers feature active-matrix color screens that display anywhere from 256 to 65,000 colors. PalmOne is moving to devices that have a higher screen resolution of 320 by 320 pixels (such as on the Zire 72 or Tungsten E). PalmOne and Garmin have also released devices with a vertical 320 by 480-pixel screen resolution (with the Tungsten T3 featuring a slide-out screen).

Most importantly, every screen is touch sensitive, which is why you can interact with it using a stylus. However, not every screen (namely the Treo 600) understands the Graffiti method of handwriting.

Power/backlight button

Figure 1.10 The power button doubles as the backlight control on many devices.

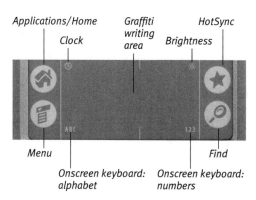

Figure 1.11 Use the silkscreened area to input text using Graffiti. It's also jam-packed full of triggers for launching certain functions, from accessing the home Applications screen to performing a HotSync.

Silkscreen Graffiti area

This is where you input text using Graffiti, the Palm method of handwriting (see Chapter 2). It's usually referred to as the "silkscreened" area, because the Graffiti input area and the buttons on either side of it are printed on a layer of glass by a silk-screening process.

The silkscreened area also features two button icons on either side that trigger certain functions. Current PalmOne models include the Applications (also known as Home) and Menu buttons on the left, and HotSync and Find buttons on the right. The Graffiti writing area also includes buttons for accessing the clock, brightness controls, and onscreen keyboard (**Figure 1.11**).

A few devices, such as the Tungsten T3, incorporate the silkscreen area in software, making the space available to other applications (see the sidebar on the next page).

✔ Tip

■ To take care of your screen, just wipe it with a clean cloth occasionally. Since the Graffiti area tends to get the most use, one low-tech solution to protecting it is to put strips of tape over it (Scotch 811, in the blue box, is the preferred variety). Other people have used Post-it notes, tape flags, and transparency film.

Keyed Up

Two PalmOne handhelds—the Treo and the Tungsten C (see **Figure 1.10**)—have built-in keyboards, eschewing the silk-screened area altogether. (The Tungsten C does allow Graffiti input on its screen, while the Treo accepts only keyed input.) In addition to using a Shift key to capitalize characters, both handhelds offer an option key that's used in combination with other keys to access secondary characters (such as numbers or symbols).

The Tungsten T3's Electronic Status Bar and Silkscreen Area

Because of its streched 320 by 480-pixel screen, the Tungsten T3 doesn't use the traditional, static silkscreened Graffiti area. Instead, it offers a first in the PalmOne universe (as well as a sneak preview of the upcoming Palm OS 6, dubbed Cobalt): an electronic status bar that can transform into an input area. The status bar collects a variety of shortcuts and functions (**Figure 1.12**):

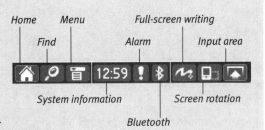

Figure 1.12 The full lineup for the Tungsten T3's electronic status bar.

◆ The first three buttons—Home, Find, and Menu—mirror those found in the typical silkscreened area, and their functions remain unchanged.

◆ The System Information button displays the current time. Tapping it brings up a screen that collects the remaining battery life, available memory, screen brightness, and alarm volume controls.

◆ The Alarm button blinks when a Task or Calendar event becomes due. If you select snooze when a reminder comes due, the button icon continues to blink; tapping it brings up the reminder screen.

◆ The Bluetooth button lets you enable or disable Bluetooth connectivity, and access preferences.

◆ Tap the Full-screen Writing button to enable Graffiti input anywhere on the screen—and not just within the boundaries of the input area. The screen is invisibly divided into sections that mirror the input area: letters are written on the left half of the screen (the a-b-c side), uppercase letters in the middle, and numbers on the right half (the 1-2-3 side).

Figure 1.13 Tap the Input Area button to select one of three modes from the popup: keyboard (top), traditional Graffiti input with icons (bottom), and icon-less Graffiti input (middle).

◆ The best part about having a 320 by 480-pixel screen is the ability to rotate the screen's orientation (which is quite handy for reading ebooks). Tap the Screen Rotation button to toggle between landscape and portrait modes.

◆ The Input Area button brings up one of three electronic input area screens: one with the typical silkscreened icons, one without, and one with the onscreen keyboard (**Figure 1.13**).

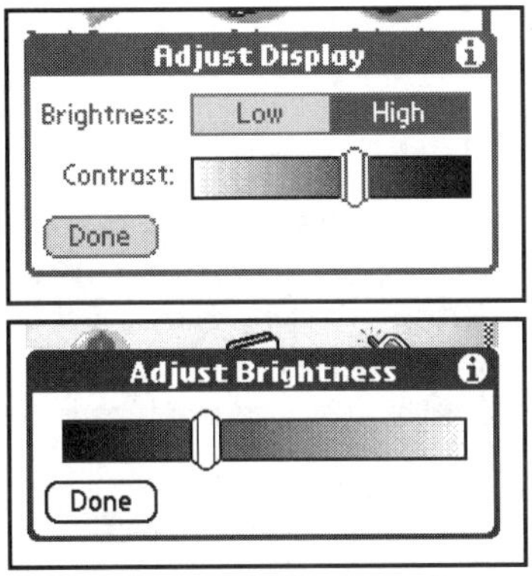

Figure 1.14 Some devices can adjust both contrast and brightness (Zire 31, top), while others only have a brightness control (Zire 72, bottom).

Figure 1.15 The World Clock shows current time in up to three time zones.

Figure 1.16 Use the onscreen keyboard as an alternative to writing Graffiti.

Contrast/brightness control

Adjust the screen's contrast or brightness using the button in the upper-right corner of the silkscreened area (**Figure 1.14**).

✔ Tips

- The default brightness setting for color devices is set at about 25-30 percent of maximum. Although you may be tempted to crank it to the highest level, you'll get more battery life out of a lower setting.

- Some handhelds offer only the brightness control.

Clock

Tap the clock icon in the upper-left corner of the silkscreened area to view the current time in the World Clock application (**Figure 1.15**). See Chapter 7 for more about using World Clock.

✔ Tip

- With Palm OS 5.2.8, you'll also see the current time displayed in the upper-left corner of the Applications screen.

Onscreen keyboard

When using a text-based application like Memos (see Chapter 6), the onscreen keyboard is a good alternative to writing Graffiti, especially if writing a long note (**Figure 1.16**). Tapping the ABC button opens the keyboard's alphabetic portion, while the 123 button accesses numbers and calculator-related symbols. See Chapter 2 for more on using the onscreen keyboard.

✔ Tip

- You can only access the onscreen keyboard when viewing a screen with a text input field.

PALMONE DEVICE OVERVIEW

Stylus

The stylus is your main method of interacting with the handheld, though just about anything that isn't sharper than a No. 2 pencil can work (that includes fingers and toes too!). Where original Palm handhelds came with a stylus made of a metal barrel (with plastic tip and end pieces that screw in at each end), most of today's PalmOne devices come with a plastic unibody stylus.

Application buttons

The plastic buttons on the case activate a pre-assigned application. On most devices these are Calendar, Contacts, Tasks, and Note Pad (**Figure 1.17**). Wireless devices tend to substitute an Email button for Tasks and a Web button for Note Pad. We rarely launch the main programs any other way.

✔ Tips

■ Pressing one of the application buttons when your handheld is powered down will turn it on and launch that program.

■ You can launch any program—not just the built-in ones—by pressing one of the application buttons. To remap their functions, tap the Buttons section of the Preferences application (see Chapter 2). (You can also remap the silkscreened HotSync button icon within the Buttons section of Preferences.)

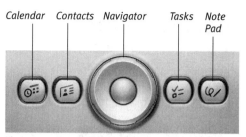

Calendar Contacts Navigator   Tasks Note Pad

Figure 1.17 The plastic application buttons take you directly to the built-in programs. The scroll buttons or Navigator (shown here) are often a better substitute for tapping the scroll arrows in many applications.

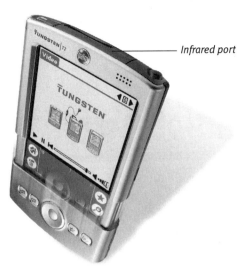

Infrared port

Figure 1.18 The infrared port can be used to beam information between Palm organizers, and for synchronizing with an infrared-equipped PC.

Scroll buttons/Navigator

The Zire 21 continues the tradition of adding two up and down scroll buttons on the front of the plastic case, which is a handy way to scroll through text and other information.

But most newer devices use what PalmOne calls the Navigator, a five-way controller that is quite useful (in addition to the four compass points, the fifth direction is a middle button used as a selector in some applications). It's great for looking up addresses, for example (see Chapter 5).

✔ Tip

- On handhelds equipped with the Navigator controller, press the center button when the power is off to display the current date and time briefly. Press and hold it in any program to go to the Applications list.

Infrared port

Every handheld includes an infrared port that enables you to "beam" information from one device to another (**Figure 1.18**). See Chapter 2 for more information about beaming applications, and program-specific chapters (such as Chapter 4) for more on beaming individual records and categories.

✔ Tip

- Infrared is slowly making way for wireless Bluetooth connectivity (included with the Zire 72 and Tungsten T3), which enables you to communicate with other Bluetooth-enabled handhelds, laptops, or peripherals (like printers) within a 30-foot radius. See Chapter 2 for more about Bluetooth networking.

PalmOne Device Overview

Reset button

There will probably come a time when something has happened that renders your handheld unusable (it will stop responding to your input). To get back to business, locate the tiny reset hole in the back of the unit. Use the reset pin located in the stylus (in older handhelds), or straighten part of a paperclip, and insert it into the hole to reset the Palm OS (known as a *soft reset*—it won't erase your data). See Appendix A, *Basic Troubleshooting*, for more on performing a reset.

✔ Tip

■ Device makers are finally getting wise and making the slots for accessing the reset button big enough to accommodate the stylus tip itself (such as on the Zire 72).

HotSync cable

The ability to synchronize information between the handheld and a desktop computer is one of the reasons for Palm's success. All PalmOne devices include synchronization software for your PC called HotSync Manager. Older models used to include a cradle with a connecting cable (USB or serial). To minimize cost (and improve portability), many of today's current PalmOne models come only with a USB synchronization cable.

To begin synchronizing on current models, tap the HotSync icon in the silkscreen area. (If a cradle was included with your handheld, you'll find a HotSync button on the front of the cradle.)

Universal Connector

The Tungsten T3 and C still use the universal connector, PalmOne's attempt to standardize accessory connectivity. Other models with this feature include the Zire 71, i705, Tungsten T, T2, and W, and m500 series handhelds. If you own one of these devices, you can still use the optional Universal HotSync Cradle (in both USB and serial flavors) and Mini Cradle accessories. See PalmOne's online store (`store.palmone.com`) for more information.

Figure 1.19 Most current PalmOne handhelds accept postage-stamp–sized Secure Digital/MultiMediaCard expansion cards.

Expansion Cards

The latest Palm organizers have begun offering slots for expansion ports, enabling you to add removable memory or peripherals without occupying a device's serial port. For information on transferring data to and from cards, see Chapter 2.

Secure Digital/MultiMediaCard

The most common expansion cards on handhelds are Secure Digital (SD) or MultiMediaCard (MMC) expansion cards (www.palmone.com/products/accessories/expansioncards/). The formats use the same physical specification, which is only about the size of a postage stamp (**Figure 1.19**). Cards add more memory or include reference materials like electronic books or other data, but the format also supports devices such as digital cameras, GPS receivers, and wireless modems.

✔ Tips

- Shortly before this book went to press, PalmOne released a Wi-Fi SD card (compatible with the 802.11b standard) that enables you to connect to your email or browse the Web while at a wireless hotspot (such as a neighborhood coffee bar). It's compatible with the Zire 72 and Tungsten T3 models and supports either 64- or 128-bit WEP encryption security.

- You must purchase an optional memory card in order to take advantage of the Zire 72's video recording feature. See Chapter 11 for more about using the Zire 72's built-in camera.

- Sony CLIÉ devices use Sony's proprietary Memory Stick, a card that's literally about the shape and size of a stick of gum.

Battery Use

The era of the AAA battery is over, as today's PalmOne handhelds are powered by built-in rechargeable lithium ion batteries. Because battery use is minimal (the CPU is asleep most of the time, even when powered on), you can experience a battery life of up to several weeks. Where previous rechargeable devices were recharged using the included cradle, today's PalmOne devices now include a separate AC adapter. The battery icon found at the top of the Applications screen changes to denote that a charge is being received (**Figure 1.20**); some handhelds (like the Zire 72) have a small LED indicator on the case.

AAA batteries

For older handhelds that use replaceable batteries, a new set of two store-bought AAA batteries gives you 3 volts of power (**Figure 1.21**). When their capacity approaches 2 volts, the device will begin to warn you that it's time to install a fresh pair. Although some people go ahead and swap out the old batteries after the first warning, you can probably get several more days of moderate use before switching.

Charging battery

Figure 1.20 The battery level is shown at the top of the Applications screen; if it's charging, you'll see a lightning bolt icon.

*Remove the battery door, then replace
the batteries, first one, then the other.*

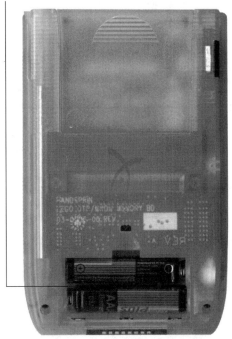

Figure 1.21 Older devices (including this Handspring Visor) use replaceable batteries versus the built-in rechargeable lithium ion batteries found in current PalmOne handhelds. When it's time to replace the AAA batteries, you have about 60 seconds after removing them to swap them out before your data is lost.

✔ Tips

- It only takes a few minutes each day to refill a rechargeable battery with the included AC adapter. Some PCs (though not all laptops) can provide a "trickle charge" to your handheld through the USB connection, but it's recommended that you rely on the AC adapter.

- If you've just opened your brand new device with a rechargeable battery, stop! Be sure you charge the unit for three or four hours before first use to ensure that the battery is fully charged. Not following this simple step can cause the battery to hold less of a charge over the long run.

- If, for some reason, your internal rechargeable battery is losing charge, don't open the case to try and replace it—doing so would void your warranty. Instead, contact PalmOne technical support.

- You can conserve battery life with a Bluetooth-enabled device by turning this feature off when you don't plan on using it. See Chapter 2 for more on using Bluetooth.

- It's almost inevitable that at some point you'll find yourself without power. If you have a rechargeable device, use the included USB power cable to siphon power from your computer (or buy an additional cable for business trips). If you have a PalmOne handheld with a universal connector (see previous sidebar), Keyspan offers a Sync + Charge cable for Palm that retracts into a compact hub (www.keyspan.com).

BATTERY USE

Accessorizing

A characteristic of a successful product is how well you can accessorize it, so it's not surprising to find a cottage industry that caters to handheld accessories. These range from stylish styli to screen protectors to clothing specially designed with PDA-ready pockets.

Styli

As you might expect, you can buy replacement styli, ranging from brass styli that fit into the stylus slots to hybrid pens such as the Cross DigitalWriter (`www.cross.com`). The LandWare Floating•Point stylus has a special nib that replicates the feel of writing on paper (`www.landware.com`) (**Figure 1.22**). For more variations, see PDA Panache (`www.pdapanache.com`).

Cases

There are numerous case variations on the market, ranging from Palm's Slim Leather Case (**Figure 1.23**) to RhinoSkin's classy yet tough aluminum hard cases (`www.saunders-usa.com/rhinoskin/`). There are also varieties of belt-loop cases, zippered pouches, and carriers with shoulder-straps. For a good resource on cases, check out The Gadgeteer (`www.the-gadgeteer.com`).

Other accessories

Depending on your needs, a variety of other helpful goodies can be ordered. Examples include extra HotSync cradles and cables, travel kits, and chargers.

Figure 1.22 Replacement styli range from simple substitutes to pen/stylus combinations to traditional pens with PDA nibs. The LandWare Floating•Point stylus is shown here.

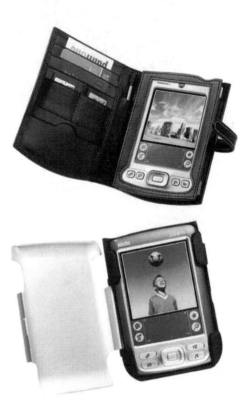

Figure 1.23 Handheld case manufacturers have taken advantage of this niche market—you can buy a style of case customized for your needs (slim leather case on top; hard case on the bottom).

ACCESSORIZING

Figure 1.24 The Palm Ultra-Thin Keyboard is a full-size keyboard that folds up to a size slightly larger (and much slimmer) than a Palm device.

Figure 1.25 Palm's new wireless keyboard variation uses infrared to work with any Palm device, no matter what type of connector it uses.

Keyboards

The Palm's pen has proved mightier than the chiclet keyboards on many other PDAs, but there are times when a real physical keyboard can come in handy. Anyone who has tried to work on a regular-sized laptop computer in an airplane's coach seat knows that space is at a premium.

Although perhaps overkill for everyday handheld usage, keyboards excel at typing long memos, emails, and especially for taking notes during a meeting. Plus, they're great for grabbing attention; Agen always made an impression at meetings when he fluidly flipped open his keyboard and attached his handheld.

The Palm Ultra-Thin Keyboard (designed by Think Outside; www.thinkoutside. com) is a full-size keyboard that folds into a compact rectangle not much larger than a Palm device (**Figure 1.24**). In addition to being small and light, it has special keys that launch applications and access Palm OS features such as command shortcuts. It's compatible with handhelds with the universal connector.

PalmOne has also introduced a wireless keyboard that interfaces with any handheld via infrared. A swiveling arm ensures that the IR port is lined up properly, and lets you use devices horizontally, as well (**Figure 1.25**). It's compatible with a wide range of handhelds, including the Zire 31 and 72.

Both keyboards are available at the PalmOne store (store.palmone.com).

Palm Desktop

Most of this book concerns the Palm OS and the handhelds that use it, but there's also another very important component to the organizer: the desktop software. A Palm OS handheld is primarily intended to be an extension of your personal data, so the desktop software acts as the core.

You also have the option of using other PIM programs like Microsoft Outlook or Lotus Notes. But Palm Desktop is the one that most closely resembles what you find on the palmtop.

Palm Desktop makes it easy to access your data when you're working on your computer, printing information, installing software on the handheld, or just needing to enter a lot of data without cramping your fingers writing Graffiti. At the very least, Palm Desktop provides the framework for keeping backup copies of the data on your handheld.

Throughout the book, we'll cover specific features of each module in their respective chapters (such as Chapter 4, *Calendar*).

Palm Desktop for Windows

Most of the functionality found on the Palm translates directly to the Windows version of Palm Desktop (**Figure 1.26**). On the desktop, however, you get the advantage of a computer's larger screen size, so you can see more information at a glance than on a handheld.

Palm Desktop is also the place to access archived data (which you've deleted from the handheld but want to store on the PC).

And Palm Desktop for Windows has kept up with the move to embrace multimedia, with built-in tools for editing images and video (**Figure 1.27**).

Figure 1.26 Palm Desktop for Windows replicates most of the Palm OS's functionality, but puts most of the information on the same screen.

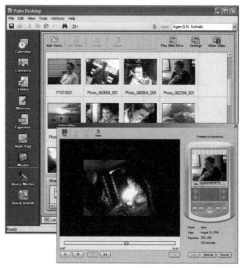

Figure 1.27 View your handheld's collection of images (and videos, with a Zire 72) as well as edit them in Palm Desktop's Media application.

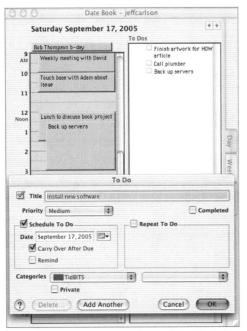

Figure 1.28 The Palm Desktop for Macintosh includes the features of the late Claris Organizer, upon which it was based.

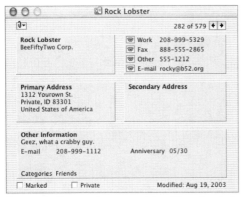

Figure 1.29 You can store more data, although not all of it will transfer to the handheld.

Palm Desktop for Macintosh

The first incarnation of the Macintosh Palm Desktop only synchronized the built-in applications, with no way for developers to write additional conduits (software bridges between the Palm OS and the desktop). For a few years, Pilot Desktop 1.0 remained the only choice for Palm-owning Macintosh users. Eager to reestablish contact with its Mac user base, Palm made an interesting choice when updating the desktop software: it bought Claris Organizer from Apple. Rather than build something new from scratch, they built upon Organizer.

The result is a vastly different desktop PIM from both Pilot Desktop 1.0 and the Windows counterpart (**Figure 1.28**). Although it shares basic functionality with Palm Desktop for Windows, there are notable differences: Some features, such as support for a second address field (so you can store home and work addresses, for example), exist only on the desktop, not under the Palm OS (**Figure 1.29**); you can assign sub-categories to records; and, of course, the interface is quite a bit different.

✔ Tip

- PalmOne announced in early 2004 that it would no longer support synchronization tools on the Mac. Luckily, Mac developer Mark/Space has stepped into the void to provide The Missing Sync, which offers improvements over HotSync Manager and aids in synchronizing multimedia content as well as using Apple's iCal and Address Book applications instead of Palm Desktop. See Chapter 3 for more on using The Missing Sync to perform your HotSync duties.

THE PALM OS

Much is said and written about the portability of Palm organizers and the ease of synchronizing data with a desktop PC. When the attention is turned to the software running inside it, though, the focus usually shifts to how many events can be stored, or how quickly one can look up an address.

We would argue that the Palm Operating System (Palm OS) is actually the strongest, and most overlooked, of the Palm device features. Like a well-scored movie soundtrack, which adds to the atmosphere of a film without drawing attention to itself, the Palm OS provides a lot of power while remaining essentially invisible to most owners. If you're used to the shaded buttons and colors of Windows, the Palm OS probably looks sparse and boring (and if you're a Macintosh user, you may think you've returned to the early days of System 6!). As a result, using a Palm device for the first time is surprisingly easy.

Yet it isn't just ease of use that makes the Palm OS notable. Beneath the uncluttered interface lies an operating system that's been designed with an emphasis on efficiency and usability. After using the Palm OS for only a few hours, you'll realize that your stylus is only tapping its surface.

Navigating the Palm OS

There are four basic methods of interacting within the Palm OS, three of which depend on the stylus. The fourth, on some models, is a scroll or "jog" wheel. Since the screen is touch-sensitive, there's no need for a proxy device such as a mouse.

Tap

Tapping a record with the stylus selects it by either opening up a new window or placing a cursor within the text. You also use taps to manipulate the following interface elements (**Figure 2.1**):

- **Icons.** In the Applications screen, tapping a program's icon or name launches it. Smaller custom icons, such as the alarm clock and note, are also used.

- **Buttons.** Similar to the buttons found under Windows and the Mac OS, these rounded-corner boxes are used to activate commands or confirm actions.

- **Menus.** When you tap a title bar or the silkscreened Menu icon, drop-down menus become visible at the top of the screen. Tap to select menu items.

- **Scroll arrows.** When data spills beyond the size of the screen, tap the up/down scroll arrows to move the active information up and down. You'll also encounter left/right scroll arrows, like the Calendar arrows that move between weeks (see Chapter 4).

- **Popup menus.** Whenever you see a small triangle pointing down next to a word, it indicates that more options are available via a popup menu.

- **Checkboxes.** Tap on a checkbox to mark or unmark it, toggling the action that is assigned to it (such as the Private indicator in most records' detail screens).

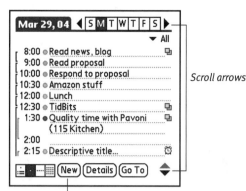

Scroll arrows

Button

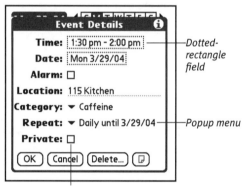

Dotted-rectangle field

Popup menu

Checkbox

Menu

Icon

Figure 2.1 Tapping just about any interface element in the Palm OS evokes a response.

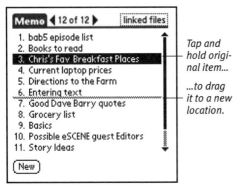

Tap and
hold origi-
nal item...

...to drag
it to a new
location.

Figure 2.2 Memos provides one
example of dragging a list item to a
new location.

| Memo ◀ 12 of 12 ▶ | linked files |

Top Grossing Movies - 23-25 July

```
1    The Bourne Supremacy Uni.
$52,521,865
2    I, Robot Fox $21,728,525
3    Catwoman WB $16,728,411
4    Spider-Man 2 Sony $15,015,872
5    A Cinderella Story WB
$7,834,289
6    Anchorman: The Legend of Ron
Burgundy DW $6,974,614
```

(Done) (Details)

Figure 2.3 Tap to set your cursor, then
drag through letters to highlight them.

◆ **Dotted-rectangle fields.** These fields
display the information that has been
selected for them, but also indicate that
tapping the field allows you to change it.

Drag

In a few cases, you will want to drag an item
using the stylus. The most common examples include (but are not limited to):

◆ **Scroll bars.** If you have more than 11
memos displayed in Memos, a vertical
scroll bar appears at the right side of the
screen. Tap and hold on the solid scroll
bar area, then drag it vertically.

◆ **Custom ordered memos.** In Memos
and some applications, you can "grab" an
item and drag it to a new position within
a list (**Figure 2.2**). A thick dotted line
indicates where the item will be placed
when it is "dropped" (i.e., when you lift
the stylus from the screen).

◆ **Highlighting text.** To select a series of
letters or words, tap to place your cursor,
then drag to select the text (**Figure 2.3**).

Write

Using the silkscreened Graffiti area, you can
use the stylus as a pen and write letters that
appear within text fields.

Scroll

Some models include a scroll wheel or a
multi-directional controller to navigate data.
Pressing the wheel can also act as a tap,
depending on the application.

✔ Tip

■ Under Palm OS 3.5 and later, double-tap
to select a word; triple-tap to select a line.

Accessing Menus

Although hidden to conserve valuable screen space, drop-down menus similar to those found in Windows and the Mac OS are available for most applications. Access menus to take advantage of commands not displayed on the current screen, and to edit text using Cut, Copy, Paste, and Undo commands.

To access menus in applications:

◆ Tap the program's title bar to make the menus appear.

Or

1. Tap the Menu icon located in the lower-left corner of the silkscreened area of the screen. You'll see a row of words appear at the top of the screen such as Record, Edit, or Options.

2. Tap a word to see a drop-down menu of related commands (**Figure 2.4**). You don't have to maintain contact with the stylus; these menus are "sticky" and will stay visible until you tap the stylus on a command or elsewhere on the screen.

3. Tap the desired menu item to perform its action.

✔ Tip

■ If you're *still* using a handheld running a Palm OS version earlier than 3.5, you can't tap the title bar to access menus. However, you can get the same functionality by installing the HackMaster extension MenuHack (www.daggerware.com/mis-chack.htm).

To make menus visible...

...tap this icon first.

Figure 2.4 It may not make much sense to jump from bottom to top to access menus, but it's nice that menus are normally hidden to save space.

ACCESSING MENUS

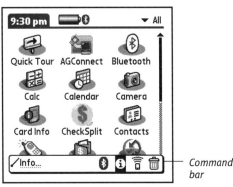

Command bar

Figure 2.5 In Applications, the command bar provides access to common features, like the Info or Delete screens.

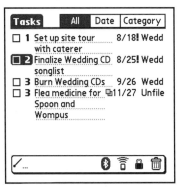

Figure 2.6 With nothing selected, the command bar offers few choices. However, a Bluetooth-enabled device displays its icon.

Figure 2.7 With a record selected, the command bar displays icons for commands which work in that context.

The Command Bar

Palm OS 3.5 and higher take the concept of command strokes one step further with the command bar (**Figure 2.5**). When you write a command stroke, the command bar displays icons for actions that are usable depending on the current context.

For example, with no records selected in Tasks, the only icon to appear is the Security icon (**Figure 2.6**). However, with a task selected, the Beam Item, Paste, and Delete Item options appear (**Figure 2.7**).

If you don't act within three seconds, the command bar disappears until invoked again.

To access the command bar:

1. Draw a diagonal line from the bottom-left to the top-right corner of either Graffiti area (╱).

2. Tap an icon on the command bar to perform an action. You can tap and hold on an icon to see its description; when you lift the stylus, the action is executed.

✔ Tips

- The command bar is an addition to the Palm OS's command-stroke function; if a command isn't represented by an icon, you can still invoke it by writing the command shortcut letters found in the application's menus.

- If you've tapped an icon but decide not to invoke its action, drag the stylus away from the icon before lifting it from the screen's surface.

Onscreen Help and Tips

Nestled within the tight memory confines of the Palm OS exists a handy location for accessing onscreen help and application tips. Most dialog boxes (windows that are identified by a thick outside line and a black title bar at the top) include a "circle-i" information icon in the upper-right corner (**Figure 2.8**). Tapping this small icon displays a screen titled Tips, which often provides instruction or pointers for using an application's features (**Figure 2.9**). It's often worth poking around the dialog boxes of a new program to see if any "hidden" features may be revealed on the Tips screen.

Figure 2.8 Tap the "circle-i" icon in the upper-right corner of dialog boxes to access help and other information.

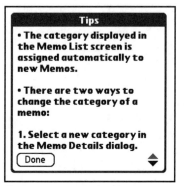

Figure 2.9 It's worth checking out a new program's Tips screens—often you'll find real tips, not just online help.

Figure 2.10 If you'd prefer to tap on letters instead of write them, bring up one of the onscreen Keyboard layouts. This is often the best way to access symbol and international characters.

Using the Onscreen Keyboard

The Palm OS includes two methods for entering information: Graffiti, the style of lettering you use to write individual letters (see the next section), and a virtual keyboard for tapping letters on the screen. The keyboard can be accessed only when your cursor is in a text field. Activating it brings up a new window containing the text field (or as much as can be displayed in the smaller space), with the keyboard located below (**Figure 2.10**).

Three separate keyboards are available: the abc keyboard, which is laid out in Qwerty format (like most computer and typewriter keyboards); the 123 keyboard, which gives you access to numbers and common symbol characters; and the Int'l ("international") keyboard, which creates common letters with diacritical marks (such as é) as well as characters like ß, ¿, and æ. Switch between layouts by tapping the corresponding button beneath the keyboard.

To activate the keyboard:

◆ There are three ways of accessing the keyboard: Tap either the abc or 123 section in the lower corners of the Graffiti area; select Keyboard from the Edit menu (when available); or write ╱-K in the Graffiti area. Tap Done when finished.

✔ Tips

■ If you like the onscreen keyboard but find the Qwerty layout difficult, install Fitaly (`www.fitaly.com`), which arranges letters based on frequent usage.

■ If you don't mind Qwerty, but don't like tapping the small letter squares, install DotNote (or ".Note") (`www.utilware.com`) to display larger keys.

Graffiti

One of the few things that makes potential Palm organizer buyers hesitate before purchasing is the prospect of hand-writing letters on the screen. Some are concerned that they'll have to learn a new "language." Others are gun-shy after hearing about the difficulties with handwriting recognition that plagued other handhelds (notably Apple's discontinued Newton MessagePad). In the Palm OS, you use the stylus to write the Graffiti 2 alphabet, which translates those written gestures into proper text characters.

After your first attempts at writing a "k", you may be a skeptic. But we're here to reassure you that: (a) Graffiti is simpler than you think (you'll pick up the basics in the first few hours, we promise); and (b) because it doesn't technically do any handwriting recognition, your chances of writing something like "The quack bruin fax junked over the hazy fog" are fairly minimal (unless that's what you meant in the first place).

Graffiti 2

In 2003, Palm switched to using Graffiti 2 instead of Graffiti due to a lawsuit by Xerox, who claims Graffiti was misappropriated. A version of Graffiti 2 was previously available as a third-party utility called Jot, which Palm purchased. If you've been using a Palm V and are now just updating to a new PalmOne device, Graffiti 2 will be familiar with many pen strokes remaining the same from the original version. However, some are different, requiring two strokes to complete a letter (**Table 2.1**).

Some rules have changed, too. You don't have to write a Caps Shift stroke to make capitals, for example, and some characters are made by writing one stroke on the left side and one on the right.

Table 2.1

Graffiti 2 Letters and Numbers			
LETTER	GRAFFITI	LETTER	GRAFFITI
A	∧	N	N
B	ß	O	O
C	C	P	p
D	ᴅ	Q	q
E	Ɛ	R	R
F	Γ	S	S
G	G	T	+̇
H	h	U	U
I	i²	V	V
J	J	W	W
K	ʼk²	X	X²
L	L	Y	y
M	m	Z	Z
1			8	8
2	2	9	9
3	3	0	O
4	4	backspace	←
5	5	return	/
6	6	shift	↓
7	7	space	⟶

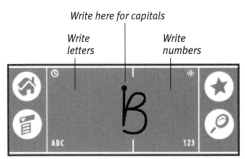

Write here for capitals

Write letters

Write numbers

Figure 2.11 Create Graffiti letters on the left side of the Graffiti area; write numbers on the right. Capital letters are written in the space dividing the letter and number sections.

Writing Graffiti

Here's the big secret about Graffiti: Nearly every character can be written with only one stroke of the stylus (the exceptions being I, K, T, and X). The identity of the character is determined both by the shape of the stroke, and by the combination of the stroke's origin point and direction.

The Graffiti area

One of the key differences between traditional handwriting recognition and Graffiti is that you don't write directly on the active portion of the screen using Graffiti. Instead, you form letters in the silkscreened Graffiti area, where they are interpreted and displayed wherever your cursor happens to be.

The Graffiti area is split into two sections: Write letters on the left side, numbers on the right. This is an important distinction, because some characters, such as B and 3, can be written using identical strokes.

With Graffiti 2, write uppercase letters in the middle of the Graffiti area, overlapping both the letter side and the number side (**Figure 2.11**).

✔ Tips

■ Devices running Palm OS 5.2 and higher now let you write Graffiti anywhere on the screen. See "Writing Area" later in this chapter for details.

■ You'll notice that the first letter you write in a Contacts field or a memo is automatically capitalized, and subsequent letters are in lowercase. When you begin a new field, or write an end-of-sentence punctuation such as a period or exclamation point, the Palm OS assumes that you want a capital letter.

To write basic Graffiti characters:

1. First, you need to be in an application where you can write text. Press the Memos button on the front of the handheld, then tap New to create a new memo. Place the tip of the stylus at the left side of the Graffiti area.

2. Write the Graffiti stroke for C (Ĉ), starting at the dot. Make sure you write the complete stroke without lifting the stylus until the end. You should see a capital C.

3. Using the same side of the Graffiti area, write the stroke for A (/\), again starting at the dot. Repeat the process for K (⅄), and E (Ɛ) (**Figure 2.12**).

Writing numbers is exactly the same, only you write strokes in the right side of the Graffiti area.

To write special characters (such as $, #, %):

1. Write a Punctuation Shift upstroke (|); the symbol appears in the lower-right corner of the screen.

2. Write the character on either side of the Graffiti area.

3. Write another Punctuation Shift upstroke to finish the character.

✔ Tip

- For more Graffiti 2 characters, see the decals that came with your organizer, or choose Graffiti 2 Help from the Edit menu in any application where you can enter text (**Figure 2.13**).

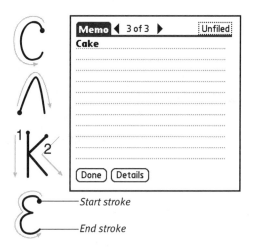

Figure 2.12 Most characters can be written using one stroke of the stylus in the Graffiti area (the exceptions being I, K, T, and X). Start at the dot (but don't try to draw the dot), and lift the stylus at the end of your stroke. For letters requiring two strokes, start the second motion as soon as you can after lifting the stylus from the first stroke.

Figure 2.13 How do you write an @ symbol? Hang on, help is on the way—just choose Graffiti 2 Help from the Edit menu for a quick refresher.

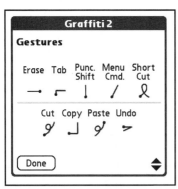

Figure 2.14 Use Graffiti navigation and quick command strokes to speed up your data entry.

3	Catwoman WB $16,728,411
4	Spider-Man 2 Sony $15,015,872
5	A Cinderella Story WB $7,834,289
6	Anchorman: The Legend of Ron Burgundy DW $6,974,614
7	Fahrenheit 9/11 Lions $4,759,921
8	The Notebook NL $4,268,634
9	King Arthur BV $3,036,114
10	Shrek 2 DW $2,316,663

✓Graffiti 2 Help   🔘 📶 ↶ 🗑

Figure 2.15 Use the command stroke (/) to open the command bar; write the Graffiti stroke for the menu item you want to activate (such as G for Graffiti Help).

Simple tips for improving Graffiti recognition

- **Write large.** Feel free to use the full Graffiti area to write your letters—that way, more touch-sensitive sensors are registering your strokes.

- **Write at a natural speed.** If you write too slowly, you can confuse the sensors and generate errors.

- **Don't write on a slant.** Try to keep vertical strokes vertical, and horizontal strokes horizontal.

Navigating using Graffiti

You can move your cursor within a field or to an adjacent field without erasing the letters you've already written using Graffiti navigation strokes (**Figure 2.14**).

Command strokes

There's a better way than tapping menu items to access commands. Rather than use three taps to access a menu item (tap the Menu icon, tap the menu name, tap the menu item), it's much easier and faster to write a command stroke. Draw a diagonal line from the bottom-left to the upper-right of either side of the Graffiti area (/). You'll see the command bar (see earlier in this chapter) appear at the bottom of the screen. Write the stroke that activates the menu item you want (such as /-C for Copy) (**Figure 2.15**).

✔ Tip

- Graffiti 2 provides four quick strokes for cutting, copying, pasting, and undoing (see **Figure 2.14**).

WRITING GRAFFITI

Using the Treo's Keyboard

Eschewing all things Graffiti, the Treo uses its built-in keypad for all character input (**Figure 2.16**). The touchscreen enables you to tap buttons and menus, but doesn't allow for writing.

Treo keypad operation

◆ The command strokes are represented with the same icon (╱) in the menus, but the keypad's Menu button (at the bottom-right corner) replaces this stroke. Thus, to copy a selection of text to memory, press Menu-C.

◆ Press the Shift button to type a capital letter, or press it twice to turn on Caps Lock. Press it again to turn it off.

◆ The Option button is used to type both numbers (denoted by dark keys with numerals sitting above letters) and punctuation (also found sitting above a key's letter). Press Option twice to create a lock effect; press it a third time to turn it off.

◆ To type special characters (such as those with an accent or umlaut) or symbols, first type the corresponding character found on the keypad, then press the Alt/0 button. A popup menu appears with choices for that character (**Figure 2.17**); use the up and down buttons on the five-way navigator to make a selection, then press the center button to accept it. Refer to your Treo manual for the complete mapping of symbols and special characters.

✔ Tips

■ Press Option then Shift to open the Find dialog.

■ Some application views (like the Phone's dial pad) and fields (such as a phone number in Contacts) automatically default to an Option lock.

Option button ... Menu button

Shift button ... Alt/0 button

Figure 2.16 Text entry is all thumbs (in a good way) with the Treo.

Figure 2.17 Type a letter on the keypad then press the Alt button to view its special character options.

Tungsten C Keyboard

The keypad for the Wi-Fi Tungsten C is similar to the Treo's, substituting the Function key for the Option key to access secondary characters on the keys and combining the Function and spacebar (Symbol) keys to type special characters.

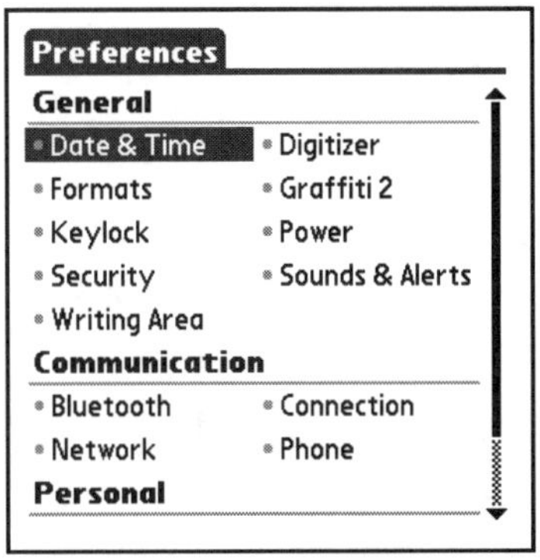

Figure 2.18 Palm OS 5.2.8 collects all the individual preferences into one screen (and sorts them thematically); tap titles to open a preference's settings.

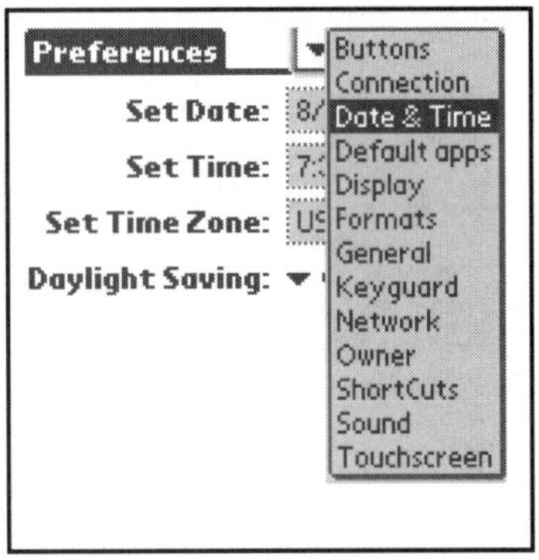

Figure 2.19 Palm OS 5.2.1H, found on the Treo 600, collects all preferences within the popup menu.

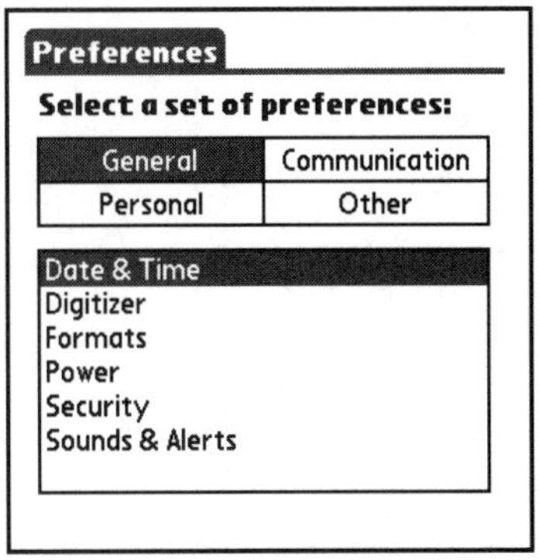

Figure 2.20 The Preferences screen can vary between device models (Palm OS 5.0 on a Tungsten T shown here).

General and Personal Preferences

The Prefs application looks mundane at first, but closer inspection reveals that the rest of the OS hinges upon the settings you choose here. In previous versions of the Palm OS, you accessed individual preferences from a popup menu in the upper-right corner of the application. Palm OS 5.2.8 collects all the preferences into one screen and divides them thematically—General, Communication, and Personal (**Figure 2.18**).

The examples that follow come from Palm OS 5.2.8 (found on the Zire 72 and 31). We'll also note some differences found in Palm OS 5.2.1H (used by the Treo 600 and modified from its Handspring roots), which has a previous version of Prefs that requires you to select individual preferences from the popup menu (**Figure 2.19**).

✔ Tips

- Palm has modified the Preferences screens several times during the progression of the Palm OS—including some early Palm OS 5 devices (**Figure 2.20**). If you don't see something where we're describing it, our best advice is to check another screen. As long as it works, consistency isn't important, right?

- If you have a device with a five-way navigator, use the up/down and left/right buttons to move through the Preferences list, then press the center button to open a selected item. When finished making modifications, press the center button again to save changes and return to the main list.

Date & Time

An organizer without the correct time can't do a good job of organizing. Get started by setting your temporal status (**Figure 2.21**).

To set the date and time:

1. Tap the Set Date field to select today's date from a calendar.

2. Tap the Set Time field to configure the hour and minute values.

3. From the Location popup menu, choose a city located closest to your own.

4. If you don't find a city within the default list, select Edit List to bring up its dialog, then tap the Add button (**Figure 2.22**). In the Locations dialog, choose a city that's within your time zone (you might not find your exact geographic location from this short list). Tap OK.

5. The Edit Location dialog appears, enabling you to give this time zone a specific name (such as a city not appearing in the list or someone's name) (**Figure 2.23**).

6. Tap the dotted Time Zone field to select the exact time zone.

7. Marking the Daylight Saving Time checkbox brings up the default behavior for the city selected from the Locations dialog. If your location has a different behavior, tap the dotted Start and End fields and make your modifications.

8. Tap OK, then tap Done on the Edit List to return to the Date & Time preferences.

Figure 2.21 Time keeps on slippin', slippin', slippin'...sorry, having a Steve Miller Band moment.

Figure 2.22 If your city isn't in the default list, tap the Add button from the Edit List to find a location within your time zone.

Figure 2.23 You don't have to use the name selected from the Locations dialog—personalize it!

Figure 2.24 The Treo presents actual time zones (and not city names within time zones).

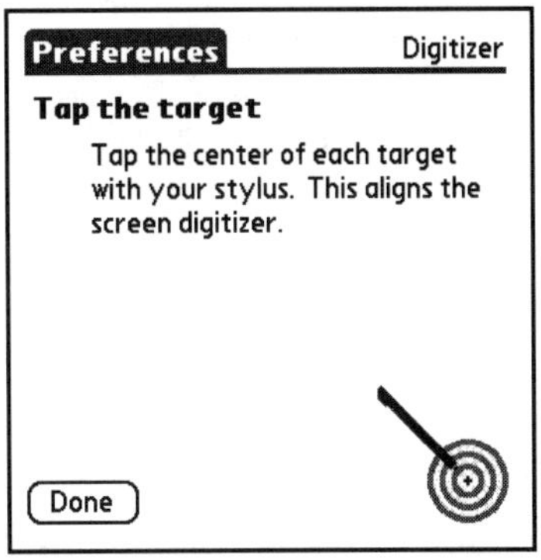

Figure 2.25 Tapping the targets ensures that your touch-sensitive screen is accurately registering the tap locations.

✔ Tips

■ Select the time zone (not a city name) from the Set Time Zone field in Treo's Date & Time preferences, then choose to turn daylight saving time on or off (**Figure 2.24**).

■ Be careful about changing the time to reflect new time zones on your handheld and laptop when traveling. Since the time and date stamps are referred to when you perform a HotSync, having your organizer and your PC living in separate zones can cause data to be overwritten incorrectly.

Digitizer

Due to temperature variations, repeated use, and the general passing of time, the digitizer can gradually slide off track. If your pen taps don't seem to be working the way they used to, run the Digitizer.

To calibrate the Digitizer:

1. Choose Digitizer from the Preferences popup menu.

2. Tap the center points of the target shapes that appear (**Figure 2.25**). This process ensures that the pixels you tap on the screen correspond with the pixels that the Palm OS thinks you're tapping.

✔ Tip

■ This preference is called Touchscreen on the Treo.

DATE & TIME, DIGITIZER

Formats

If you dream of traveling abroad, select Formats from Preferences and tap the Preset to popup menu to select the country in which you'd like to reside. Otherwise, it's probably a better idea to choose your current location.

To change time, date, week, and number formats:

◆ The formats have already been configured for each country, but you can adjust them individually by tapping each setting's popup menu (**Figure 2.26**).

Graffiti 2

Getting frustrated with the method for writing a T? The Graffiti 2 preferences let you customize the way you can write four characters: P, T, Y, and $.

To customize a character:

1. Tap one of the character buttons to open the Graffiti 2 Tuner dialog.

2. Mark the checkbox to use the displayed writing form, then tap the Done button to save it (**Figure 2.27**).

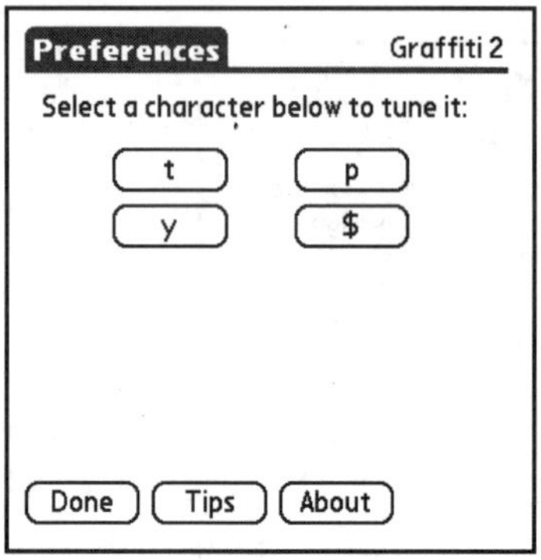

✔ Tip

■ If you select T, you'll also modify the procedure for writing a space followed by an L (**Figure 2.28**).

Figure 2.26 The Formats screen offers preconfigured settings for 24 countries.

Figure 2.27 You can modify how you write four Graffiti 2 characters: T, P, Y, and $.

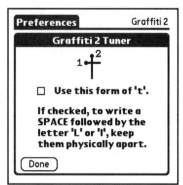

Figure 2.28 Choosing the alternate method of writing a T brings with it its own consequences.

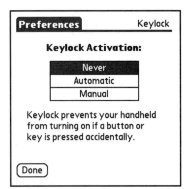

Figure 2.29 Prevent unexpected turn-ons (of your handheld) by locking its buttons.

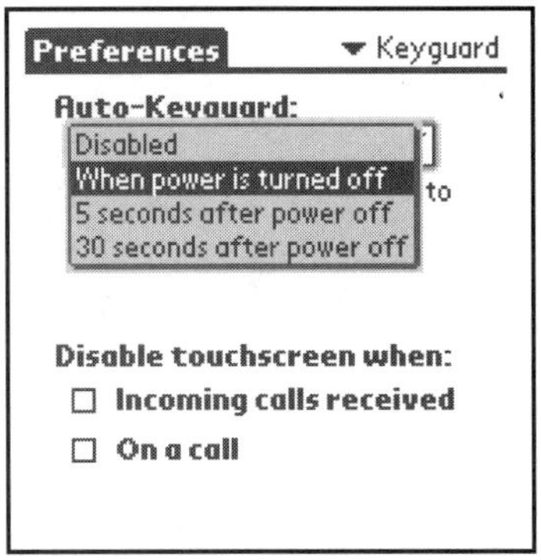

Figure 2.30 The Treo's Keyguard preference performs the same task as Keylock.

Figure 2.31 Don't wait for the Treo to power down—press the Option and Screen buttons to manually lock the keyboard.

Keylock

Have you ever found your handheld's batteries drained after, say, taking a flight where your device kept getting turned on while in your carry-on bag? In addition to the on/off button, PalmOne devices can be turned on by pressing any of the application buttons on the front of the case. Keep your handheld's battery level in check with the Keylock preferences.

To configure handheld locking:

◆ Tap one of the three levels of Keylock Activation (**Figure 2.29**).

▲ **Never:** Turns off the Keylock feature.

▲ **Automatic:** Locks your handheld every time it is turned off.

▲ **Manual:** To activate the Keylock feature, you'll need to press and hold the power button for two seconds.

Keyguard (Treo)

The Treo has a similar preference called Keyguard. If activated, this setting requires you to press the five-way navigator's center button to turn the Treo on; if you don't oblige, the Treo screen turns off after a few seconds.

To customize locking settings:

1. In the Auto Keyguard popup menu, choose to turn on this preference immediately after shutting off or after a delay of 5 or 30 seconds. To turn it off, select Disabled (**Figure 2.30**).

2. Select to disable the touchscreen during a call or when receiving an incoming call to avoid accidentally hanging up.

✔ Tip

■ As noted in the Keyguard screen, pressing Option and the Screen button (⊛) manually locks the Treo's screen and buttons (**Figure 2.31**).

Power

Use the Power preferences to further conserve handheld energy (**Figure 2.32**).

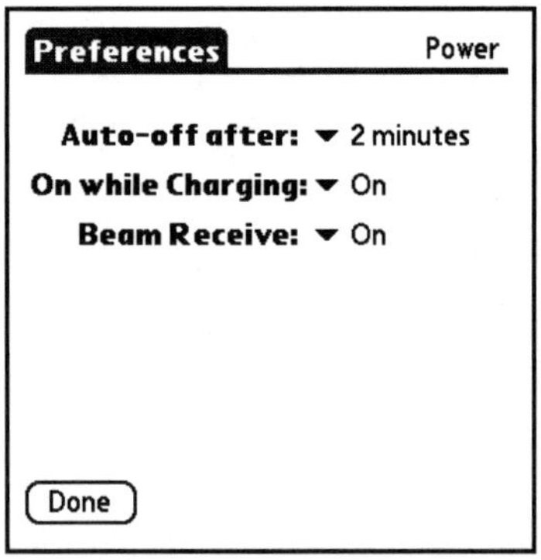

To customize power settings:

1. Your device will shut itself off after a period of inactivity. Tap the Auto-off after popup menu to choose from four preset delays.

2. Choose whether to keep your device on or off while charging.

3. Specify whether people can beam data to you using the Beam Receive popup menu.

✔ Tip

- Leaving Beam Receive on can drain your battery at a higher rate. However, returning to Prefs each time you wish to receive something can be a pain. Instead, write ℛ . I (ShortCut stroke, period, I) in any text field to turn on Beam Receive for a single instance. See more about ShortCuts and Beaming later in this chapter.

Figure 2.32 Conserve your battery power by selecting to turn Beam Receive off until it's needed.

Figure 2.33 Security controls whether records marked as private throughout the Palm OS are shown, hidden, or masked.

Masked record

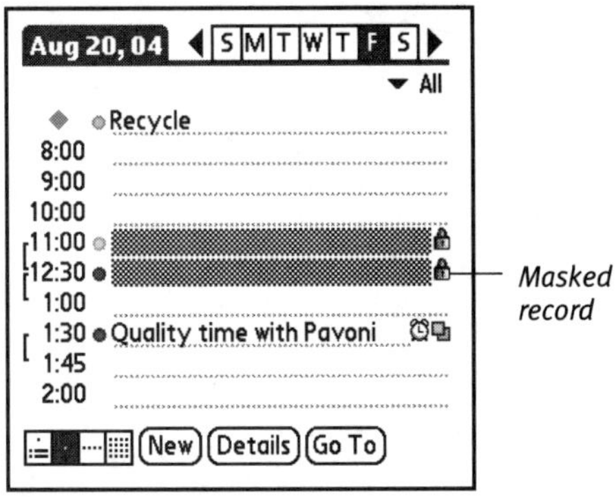

Figure 2.34 Masking records can be preferable to hiding them, as it's a reminder that you have private records.

Security

You're probably carrying around your most important information in a device no bigger than your hand. Although you're no doubt careful with your organizer, there's a half-decent chance that it may get swiped, or even left on top of your car as you're rushing off to work. The Palm OS's built-in security features provide a first line of defense in case your Palm is picked up by the wrong person.

The Security preferences control whether or not records marked as private—no matter which program they reside in—are shown, hidden, or masked (**Figure 2.33**). You can also change the global security setting within individual programs, saving a trip to the Security application itself (**Figure 2.34**).

If you own a Treo, you'll find a separate Security application (as found in previous versions of the Palm OS) that handles these settings.

To set up a password:

1. Tap the dotted Password field, which should read Unassigned if this is your first time using Security.

2. Enter a password (by writing it or tapping the numbered keypad) and a hint, then tap OK.

3. Re-enter your password to verify it.

To change or delete a password:

1. Tap the dotted Password box, which should read Assigned.

2. Enter your current password.

3. Write a new password to change it; tap the Delete button if you want to not have an assigned password at all.

4. If you changed your password, re-enter it to verify it.

SECURITY

To access a forgotten password:

1. If you've forgotten your password, you can remove it, but at a price. Tap the Password field, then tap the Lost Password button in the Password screen.

2. If you wish to proceed, tap Delete Password (**Figure 2.35**). The state of the Password field will revert to Unassigned.

✔ Tips

■ You don't have to set up a password if you don't want to. Setting Security to hide or mask records without specifying a password still makes private records unreadable. You won't be asked to provide a password if you switch to Show Records.

■ Don't use easy passwords: birthdates, addresses, family members' names, and especially pet names. The best password is a combination of letters, numbers, and symbols. And it's always good to create a descriptive, yet oblique password hint (**Figure 2.36**).

■ Security passwords are case-sensitive, recognizing upper- and lowercase letters.

Locking your handheld

In addition to hiding records, you can lock access to your handheld, which then requires your password to get access to its contents.

To lock your handheld manually:

1. Tap the Lock button.

2. The Lock dialog opens, asking you to verify this action. Tap the Lock Device button.

   The System Lockout dialog appears. You can now turn off your device, or enter your password to gain re-entry (**Figure 2.37**).

Figure 2.35 If you've forgotten your password, your private records will be deleted until the next HotSync.

Figure 2.36 Leave yourself some bread-crumbs along the memory trail when you forget your password.

Figure 2.37 If you want to see your data again, write your password in the blank provided.

Figure 2.38 Be diligent about securing your data by enabling the Auto Lock Handheld feature.

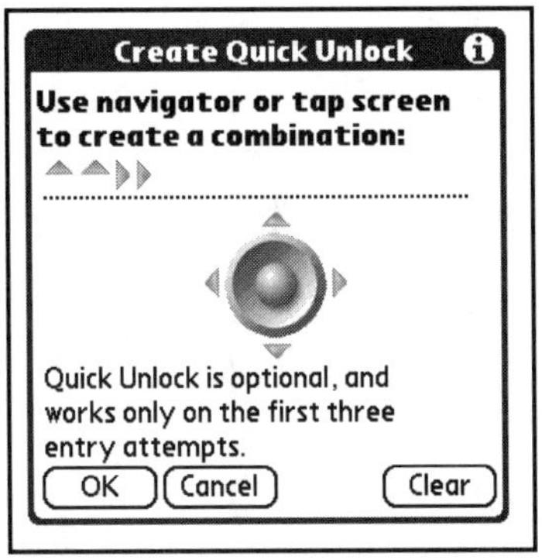

Figure 2.39 Creating a Quick Unlock enables you to set a combination of the five-way navigator's buttons to enter your locked handheld.

✔ Tip

■ The Treo's Lock & Turn Off button does the same thing, but automatically turns the device off.

To automatically lock your handheld:

1. Tap the Auto Lock field.

2. Select a time period to have Security automatically lock your device. The default is Never, but you can choose to engage the feature whenever the handheld is turned off, at a specific time of the day, or after a delay of several minutes or hours (**Figure 2.38**). Tap OK.

When you assign a password, Palm OS 5.2.8 adds the ability to access a locked handheld with a combination sequence of the five-way navigator's buttons.

To use the Quick Unlock feature:

1. Tapping the Quick Unlock field opens the Create Quick Unlock dialog (**Figure 2.39**).

2. Press the five-way navigator's up/down and left/right buttons (or tap the navigator image on screen) to create a combination. You can have up to 12 button presses.

✔ Tips

■ If you set a Quick Unlock combo, you'll be asked to enter it when your handheld is locked. Your full text password will be required only for viewing masked or hidden records.

■ The Owner screen can be accessed from a locked Palm OS 5.2.8 handheld, so your lost (but locked) device can be identified.

■ If your Treo is locked, you can still make a 911 call by tapping the Make Emergency Call button.

SECURITY

Encryption

Palm OS 5.2.8 also adds some heavy-duty security measures, including record encryption and a self-destruct feature!

To set Security options:

1. From the main Security screen, tap the Options button (**Figure 2.40**).

2. Mark the Encrypt data when locked checkbox. If you want to only encrypt masked or hidden records, mark the Encrypt private records only checkbox.

3. Tap the Choose Applications button, then mark those applications you want encrypted (**Figure 2.41**). Tap OK.

4. Choose your encryption type—RC4 or AES (FIPS), both of which offer 128-bit security.

5. Tap the dotted field under Intrusion Protection to enable this feature.

6. In the Intrusion Protection dialog, write the number of attempts before the feature will kick in (**Figure 2.42**). Choose how much data you want destroyed from the Delete popup.

7. Tap OK. The next time you lock your handheld, your selected data will be encrypted and your device will be protected from unwanted intrusion.

✔ Tip

■ If you have a lot of stored data, choosing to encrypt only private records will make the process go faster.

Figure 2.40 Secure your data with one of two 128-bit encryption options: RC4 or AES (FIPS).

Figure 2.41 Minimize the encryption process by selecting only your most sensitive data.

Figure 2.42 Intruder alert! Set a number of failed attempts to unlock your handheld before the data is wiped out.

SECURITY

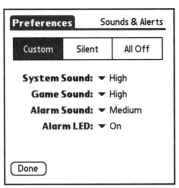

Figure 2.43 Remember to go silent when you're at the opera.

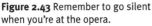

Figure 2.44 The Treo provides volume settings as well as the ability to customize tones for different actions.

Sounds & Alerts

Your cell phone isn't the only device in your pocket that can turn an entire movie theater against you. Open the Sounds & Alerts preferences and modify your alerts to suit your environment.

To set sound volume levels:

1. Tap the Custom button to make modifications to individual settings (**Figure 2.43**).

2. Specify the volume settings for the System, Alarm, and Game default sound levels as High, Medium, Low, or Off.

3. If your device has an LED, turn on or off the blinking alarm feature.

✔ Tips

- Tap the Silent button to turn off all sounds but keep the LED alarm, or tap All Off for complete silent running.

- The Treo's volume settings for System and Game sounds are found in the General preferences. The Sound preferences handle alarm volume and vibration as well as the ability to select different tones for specific actions (such as receiving a call from a known caller) (**Figure 2.44**).

Writing Area

You're no longer bound by your handheld's silkscreened area for textual input or command strokes. With a tweak of the Writing Area preference, you can use the entire screen and see your Graffiti strokes as you write them.

To turn on full-screen input:

1. In Writing Area preferences, tap the On button (**Figure 2.45**).

2. Mark Show pen strokes to see them as you write on the screen (**Figure 2.46**).

✔ Tips

- You'll see a small shaded square in the bottom-right corner of screens that allows for text input, denoting that full-screen input is turned on. To turn it off temporarily, tap the shaded square (which becomes a box outline). Tap it again to return to full-screen input.

- If you're finished writing text (say, within a memo) and want to exit by tapping the Done button, your handheld will interpret a quick, single tap as a period. To avoid this, tap and hold a button until it becomes highlighted, then lift your stylus off the screen to activate that button's action. You can also temporarily turn off full-screen input by tapping the shaded square.

  Alternatively, when coming to the end of a sentence, start writing Graffiti text within the silkscreened area (yes, it's still active), then tap the button. This way, there's no delay in activating a button.

Figure 2.45 The Writing Area's Show pen strokes option can be helpful in improving your Graffiti writing.

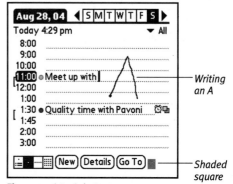

Figure 2.46 As Cole Porter once wrote, "Don't fence me in." With the Writing Area preference turned on, the whole screen is your tablet.

WRITING AREA

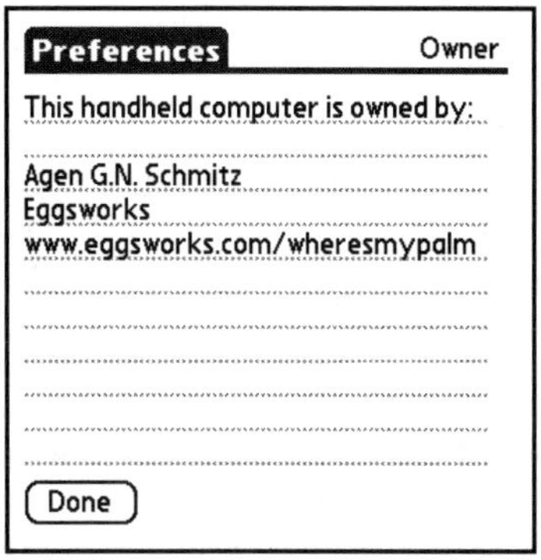

Figure 2.47 The Owner screen can be filled with whatever text you like, though most people enter contact information.

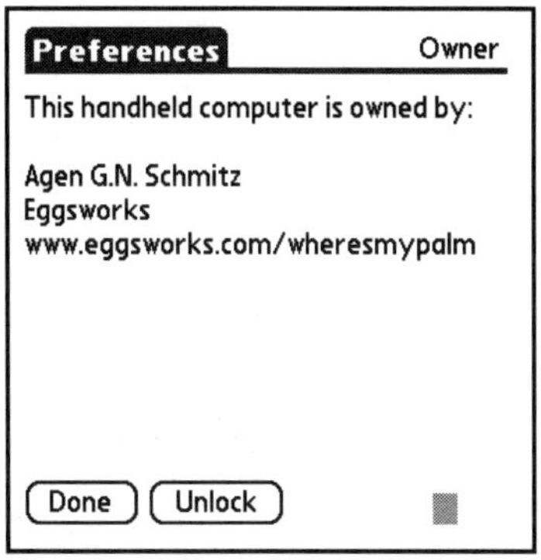

Figure 2.48 If your locked handheld becomes lost, the Owner screen can still be viewed.

Owner Screen

Since you'll likely become attached to your handheld, you should go ahead and put your name in it (thereby resolving any potential playground ownership disputes by asserting that yes, your name *is* on it!).

To set up the Owner screen:

◆ Write your contact information (or other text) on the lines provided. If you should misplace your Palm device someday, the honorable person finding it can learn where to ship it (**Figure 2.47**).

✔ Tip

■ If you assign a password, the Owner screen displays its contents but it is locked. To make it editable, tap the Unlock button and enter your password (**Figure 2.48**).

OWNER SCREEN

Buttons

Although the application buttons on the case and the silkscreened icons near the Graffiti area are handy for directly launching the built-in applications, there are times when you might want to specify different programs, such as Super Names (www.standalone.com) instead of the Contacts application (**Figure 2.49**).

To customize buttons:

1. Select the button or silkscreened icon you wish to replace, and tap the popup menu to the right of its icon.

2. Choose an application from the popup list. To return to the Palm OS factory settings, tap the Default button.

✔ Tips

- The number of items you can modify will differ from device to device. The Zire 72 has five options, while the Zire 31 has only three (two case buttons and one silkscreened icon).

- Only the four buttons found on the Treo's case can be modified (since there are no silkscreened icons), but you can configure four additional actions by pressing the Option key with one of the buttons (**Figure 2.50**).

- You can configure not only the buttons on your handheld's case and the silkscreened icons, but also the one-stroke pen drag. In the Buttons screen, tap More, then tap the popup menu in the center (**Figure 2.51**). Choose to adjust the screen's display, activate the onscreen keyboard, display Graffiti help (the default), turn off and lock the device, or beam data.

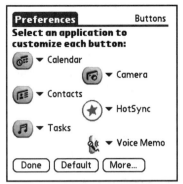

Figure 2.49 Launch other programs from the physical application buttons (or one of the silkscreened icons).

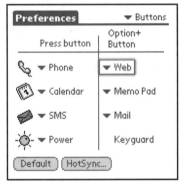

Figure 2.50 The Treo enables you to add the Option button for a total of eight launching shortcuts.

Figure 2.51 Specify an action for the bottom-to-top screen stroke shortcut.

Figure 2.52 Depending on your device, you can also assign shortcuts to the HotSync buttons found on a cradle or modem.

Figure 2.53 Do a makeover of your screen colors with Color Theme or via the Colors popup menu on the Treo.

- Depending on your device, you can also configure the actions associated with the HotSync buttons found on a cradle or modem (Zire 72 used in **Figure 2.52**). On the Treo, tap the HotSync button at the bottom of the Buttons preferences to customize the HotSync cable's button.

- If you want even more flexibility, download Hard Button eXtender (HBX) (www.ranosoft.net/hbx), which enables you to configure a myriad of actions for the hardware and five-way navigator buttons and one silkscreened icon.

Color Theme

If blue isn't your color, change the screen's colors by choosing a different theme.

To modify screen colors:

- ◆ In the Color Theme preferences, tap a theme name to preview what colors are displayed on the screen (top, **Figure 2.53**). When you've made your final decision, tap Done.

✔ Tips

- On the Treo, these settings can be accessed through the Colors popup menu on the General preferences (bottom, **Figure 2.53**).

- A photo background selected for either the Applications screen or the Calendar's Agenda view will override the chosen theme's background color. For more on configuring a photo background, see "Background Image" later in this chapter, and "Agenda View" in Chapter 4.

BUTTONS, COLOR THEME

ShortCuts

Graffiti is an efficient way to input data, but you'll soon get tired of entering commonly used words and phrases letter by letter. Instead, set up ShortCuts that substitute full texts when you enter an abbreviation.

To create and edit ShortCuts:

1. Tap New to create a ShortCut, or Edit to change an existing one (**Figure 2.54**). The Palm OS includes seven built-in ShortCuts.

2. In the ShortCut Entry window, write the abbreviation under ShortCut Name. The shorter the abbreviation, the fewer letters you'll have to write to activate it, but you're not limited to just two or three (**Figure 2.55**).

3. Write the full text that will replace the abbreviation when you activate the ShortCut. Tap OK when you're done.

To use a ShortCut:

1. In any text field, write the ShortCut Graffiti character (⅄); you will see it appear in your text.

2. Write the abbreviation for the word or phrase you're going to use. The abbreviation and ShortCut character will be erased and replaced by the full text.

✔ Tip

■ While you can't write the ShortCut Graffiti character on the Treo's screen, you can access ShortCuts by first typing S, then pressing the Alt key (it's also the 0 key). The special character popup appears, with the ShortCut character at the bottom of the list. Select it, then type your ShortCut to have its text appear (**Figure 2.56**).

Figure 2.54 All but one of the predefined ShortCuts are named with two-letter abbreviations, but you're not bound to that limit.

Figure 2.55 ShortCuts make entering frequently used texts much easier.

Figure 2.56 To write the ShortCut character on the Treo, first type S then press the Alt key to open the special character popup.

Figure 2.57 Choose your default helper application for email, text messaging, and Web browsing.

Figure 2.58 Open Display preferences to adjust both brightness and contrast.

Default Apps (Treo)

The Treo includes a preference for setting helper applications for actions performed in email, text messaging, and Web browsing programs. For example, you can configure your email program to launch a specific Web browser when you tap a link within a message.

To select helper applications:

◆ Tap the popup menus for Email, Messaging, and Browser, and choose your applications (**Figure 2.57**).

Display (Treo)

Since the Treo doesn't have a silkscreened area, the brightness and contrast controls are found in the Display preferences.

To adjust brightness and contrast:

◆ Tap and drag the sliders for contrast (top) and brightness (bottom) until the three shapes at the top of the screen look the best to your eye (**Figure 2.58**).

Communication Preferences

Where early Palm handhelds offered a modicum of communication options—synchronizing with a PC via a serial cable and beaming data via the infrared port—today's PalmOne handhelds add network, wireless Bluetooth, and telephony connectivity. Collected under the Communication heading, you'll find Connection and Network; depending on your device, you may also find Bluetooth and Phone.

Connection

The Connection preferences let you hook up to other devices—modems, phones, PCs, and local networks—via cable, infrared, or wireless Bluetooth connectivity. You'll find three default connections: Cradle/Cable (which lets you create a HotSync connect to your PC via USB), PalmModem (a basic modem configuration), and IR to a PC/Handheld (a basic infrared connection).

To create or edit a configuration:

1. Select Connection from the Preferences popup menu (**Figure 2.59**).

2. Tap the New button, or tap a configuration to highlight it, then tap Edit.

3. From the Connect to popup menu, choose the type of connection that fits your purpose: PC, Modem, or Local Network. If you have a Bluetooth-enabled device, you'll also see a choice for Phone (**Figure 2.60**).

4. Next, use the Via menu to choose the route the connection will take: Cradle/Cable, Infrared, or Bluetooth (if available).

Figure 2.59 Preconfigure a variety of methods of moving data to and from your handheld.

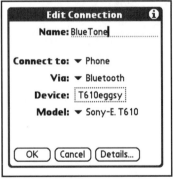

Figure 2.60 Editing a connection type controls how the OS interacts with devices such as modems (top) or Bluetooth-enabled cell phones.

Figure 2.61 Tap the Device field to search for Bluetooth-enabled devices.

Details

Speed: ▼ 57,600 bps

Country: ▼ United States

Flow Ctl: ▼ Automatic

Init String:

AT&FX4 ....
....
....

(OK) (Cancel)

Figure 2.62 Changing the speed or editing the initialization screen can sometimes improve a poor connection.

Edit Connection

Name: BlueTone

Connect to: ▼ Phone

Confirmation

Would you like this to be the default connection for your phone applications?

(Yes) (No)

Figure 2.63 After discovering a Bluetooth cell phone, you can add it as your default phone for future use.

5. Depending on your choice of connection, you'll have a few more choices to configure:

   ▲ If connecting to a modem, choose TouchTone™ or Rotary from the Dialing popup menu, and specify the loudness from the Volume popup menu.

   ▲ If connecting to a cell phone via Infrared or Cradle/Cable, choose the model from the popup menu.

   ▲ If using Bluetooth, the Device field appears; tap its dotted box to find your phone. The Discovery Results screen opens; when your phone is located, select it and tap OK (**Figure 2.61**). Confirm its model back in the Edit Connection dialog.

   ▲ There are no other available options if connecting to a PC or network.

6. Tap the Details button (**Figure 2.62**).

7. Select a data speed from the Speed popup menu. If you're running into HotSync problems under a USB connection, reducing the data speed may help.

8. If you're setting up a modem or phone, the Init String options will be available. Enter an initialization string if you need one, or keep the default that appears.

9. For all but phone connections, set the flow control on the Flow Ctl popup menu. Flow control regulates the rate of incoming information. Leaving this set to Automatic should be fine in most cases.

✔ Tips

■ Setting up a Bluetooth connection, you'll be asked if you want to use the discovered phone as your default connection for phone applications (**Figure 2.63**).

■ If you're having trouble connecting to your Bluetooth phone, make sure Bluetooth is turned on (see "Bluetooth Networking," later in this chapter).

COMMUNICATION PREFERENCES

Network

Attaching a modem to your handheld—or using your cell phone as a modem via a wireless Bluetooth connection—enables you to connect directly to an Internet Service Provider (ISP) (**Figure 2.64**).

To set up Network preferences:

1. Select Network from the Preferences popup menu.

2. Choose the name of your ISP under the Service popup menu. If yours is not listed, select New from the Service menu, or write ╱-N.

3. Write the name you use to connect in the User Name field.

4. Tap the dotted box next to Password to write your login password. If you leave this blank, you will be prompted for your password each time you connect.

5. Choose a connection mode from the Connection popup menu (this setting comes from the Connection screen; see the previous section).

✔ Tip

■ The Palm OS keeps a log of network connections; select View Log from the Options menu (**Figure 2.65**).

Figure 2.64 The Network preferences screen allows you to connect directly to an Internet Service Provider.

Network Log

IPCP<-CfgAck
IPCP<-CfgReq
IPCP Up
IPCP->CfgAck
IPCP->TrmReq
IPCP Timeout
LCP->TrmReq
LCP<-TrmAck

Not Connected

Done

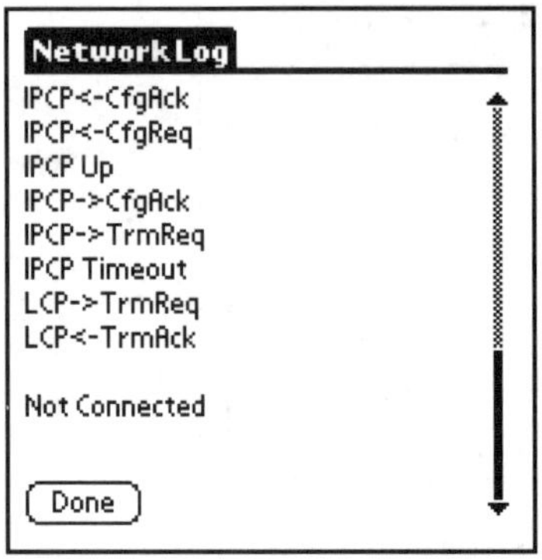

Figure 2.65 Secret code? Not if you know how to read modem commands. Use the Network Log to troubleshoot your connections.

Figure 2.66 Tapping the Phone field in the Network preferences screen displays several dialing options.

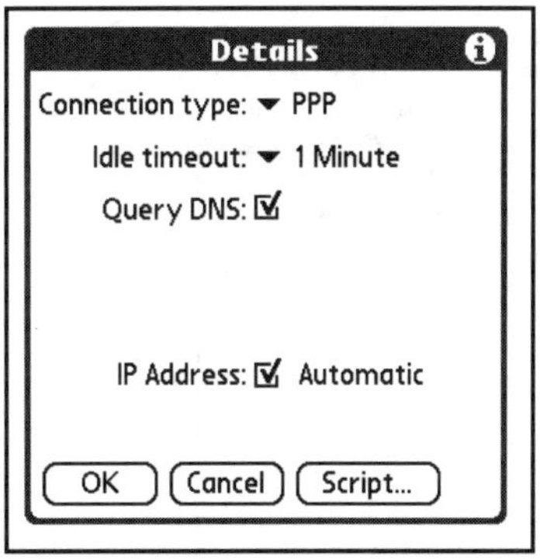

Figure 2.67 Choose the type of Internet connection, along with the action to take if the connection is idle.

To configure Network phone settings:

1. Tap the dotted box next to Phone to configure dialing options (**Figure 2.66**). In addition to the phone number required to dial, you can specify that a calling card be used, that a prefix be dialed (for example, dialing 9 to reach an outside line), or that call-waiting be disabled (if your phone package includes this; the signal tone generated by call-waiting services often breaks existing Net connections). Tap OK.

2. Tap the Details button to continue with the setup (**Figure 2.67**). Depending on the service you use to connect to the Internet, choose PPP, SLIP, or CSLIP from the Connection type popup menu.

3. Use Idle timeout to specify when the network connection should be terminated if there is no activity. The default Power Off setting ensures that an active connection continues until the unit shuts off—even if you switch between applications.

4. Use Query DNS (Domain Name System) to instruct your Internet application (such as an email client or Web browser) to ask your ISP's server to resolve domain names (addresses) on the Internet. If you uncheck this box, you will need to enter your primary and secondary DNS server addresses.

5. Check IP Address: Automatic to grab a random IP (Internet Protocol) address from your ISP, which identifies your machine on the Internet. If you have a fixed IP address, uncheck the box and enter it into the blanks that appear.

6. Finally, tap the Script button to create a customized login script to facilitate connecting to your ISP's server. If you don't require one, leave the first line so that it reads "End."

COMMUNICATION PREFERENCES

Phone

Palm OS 5.2 handhelds with Bluetooth connectivity include the Phone preference for setting a default connection to your Bluetooth cellular phone.

To set Phone preferences:

1. Choose Phone from the Preferences popup menu.

2. Select a connection from the Connection popup menu (**Figure 2.68**). If your phone doesn't appear in the list, you can choose Edit Connections from the popup menu to set up a profile.

3. Tap the Test button to make sure the handheld and phone are communicating (**Figure 2.69**).

Figure 2.68 You can connect to a cellular phone by selecting a profile on the Phone screen.

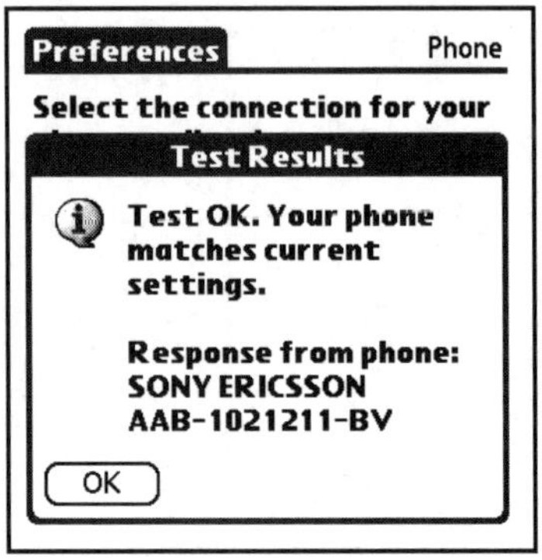

Figure 2.69 Use the Test feature to make sure your handheld and phone are communicating clearly.

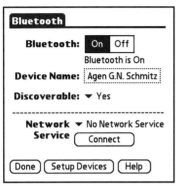

Figure 2.70 Set up Bluetooth network connections in Bluetooth preferences.

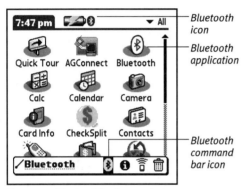

Figure 2.71 Bluetooth's all around, no need to fake it; you're gonna make a connection after all.

Bluetooth Networking

If you've spent years fighting cords and cables, you'll love Bluetooth. This wireless networking technology is built into some Palm OS handhelds as well as an increasing number of computers and cellular phones. It works within a relatively short range (up to 30 feet), which makes it ideal for communicating between, say, two handhelds or a handheld and a cellular phone.

Bluetooth works by setting up pairs of trusted devices—essentially a one-to-one relationship with another Bluetooth device. Once you've established a pair, you can send messages or files, browse directories, or use one device to act as a gateway for another (such as getting online).

To set up your device for Bluetooth:

1. Go to Bluetooth in the Prefs application (**Figure 2.70**). You can also tap the Bluetooth icon in the Applications screen or in the command bar (**Figure 2.71**).

2. Tap the On button.

3. Optionally, configure these other settings:

   ▲ **Device Name:** Your HotSync user name appears here by default. If you want a different name, tap the field and enter a new name.

   ▲ **Discoverable:** This lets other Bluetooth devices locate your handheld.

4. Tap Done to exit Preferences.

✔ Tip

■ When Bluetooth is turned on, an icon appears to the right of the battery level icon in the Applications screen.

To configure advanced settings:

1. Open the Options menu by tapping the silkscreened menu icon or tapping the top-left corner of the screen (**Figure 2.72**).

2. Choosing to Enable device name cache stores the names of previously discovered devices.

3. Choosing to Allow wakeup enables a trusted device to connect to your handheld even when it's turned off.

✔ Tip

■ Allowing the wakeup feature can eat away at your battery even when it's turned off, so you might not want to turn it on when you're running low on juice.

To pair with a trusted device:

1. In Bluetooth, tap the Setup Devices button, then tap the Trusted Devices button.

2. Tap the Add Device button to begin searching for other signals within range. The Discovery Results screen displays which devices responded (**Figure 2.73**).

   If you don't see the one you expected, tap the Find More button to initiate another search. Make sure the other device has Bluetooth active and is discoverable.

3. Select a device by tapping its name, then tap OK.

4. When prompted, enter a passkey for that device. This is a password or series of numbers that you and the other device's owner have agreed to use (**Figure 2.74**). Tap OK.

   The other person then needs to enter the same passkey. He or she also has the option to add your device to their trusted list.

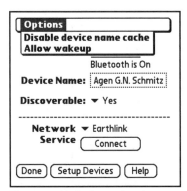

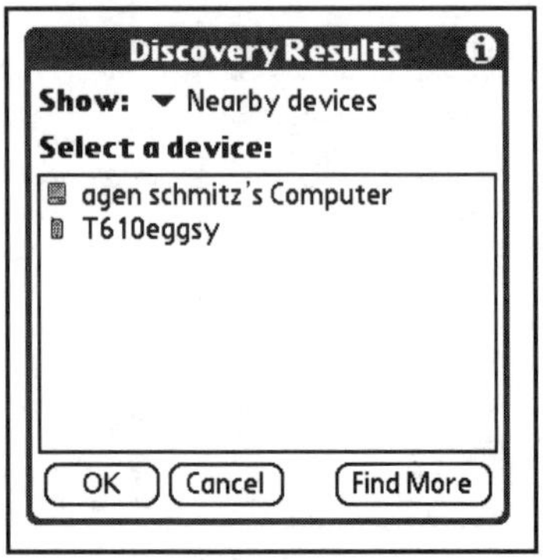

Figure 2.72 Find advanced settings under the Options menu.

Figure 2.73 Filter your Discovery Results by selecting Nearby devices in the Show popup menu.

Figure 2.74 Passkeys ensure that no one can connect to your device clandestinely.

Figure 2.75 Use the various guided tours in Setup Devices to configure wireless connections to your phone, PC, or LAN.

Figure 2.76 Transfer applications using Bluetooth networking.

Figure 2.77 You have the power to just say no...to a sent application.

5. Tap Done, or Add Device if you want to pair with another one.

✔ Tips

- You can thin the list of devices displayed in Discovery Results by tapping the Show popup menu and choosing only nearby devices or previously paired trusted devices. If the device name cache option is turned on, you'll see a list of previously identified devices.

- From the Setup Devices screen, you can also choose to follow a guided setup process for three flavors of connections: a phone, a PC (for performing a wireless HotSync), or a local area network (LAN) (**Figure 2.75**).

To transfer applications via Bluetooth:

1. Once a Bluetooth pair is made, switch to the Applications screen.

2. Choose Send from the App menu.

3. Select the file you wish to send and tap the Send button.

4. In the Send With dialog box, select Bluetooth and tap OK (**Figure 2.76**). Your handheld then searches for other devices.

5. Tap the name of a trusted device and tap OK.

✔ Tip

- If you're sending to another PalmOne handheld, a dialog appears on the recipient's screen asking if he or she wants to accept the application. Tapping No cancels the transfer (**Figure 2.77**).

BLUETOOTH NETWORKING

To transfer records via Bluetooth:

1. Open an application such as Calendar.

2. From the Record menu, select Send Event (**Figure 2.78**). (Or, if in Tasks, choose Send Task, etc.)

3. In the Send With dialog box, select Bluetooth and tap OK. The Palm then searches for other devices.

4. Tap the name of a trusted device and tap OK.

✔ Tips

■ Again, a PalmOne recipient has the opportunity to say Yes or No to the sent record, but he or she can also choose to file it in a previously created category within the target application (**Figure 2.79**).

■ By default, a sent record will be received as unfiled. Categories from your handheld aren't transferred to another person's device, either via sending by Bluetooth or beaming via infrared.

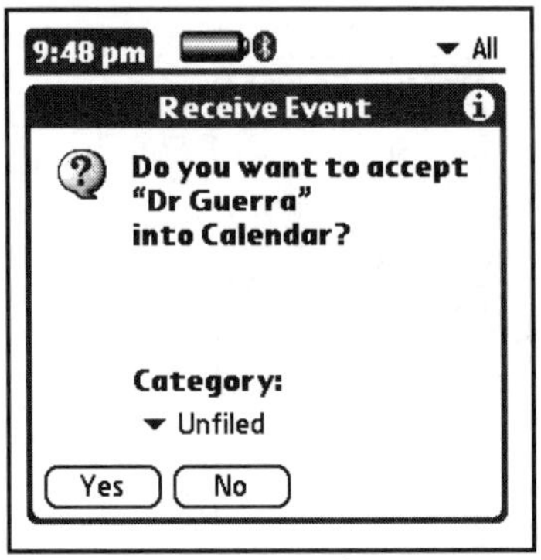

To connect to a network service:

1. From the main Bluetooth screen, select a previously created connection from the Network Service popup menu. Or, choose the clunkily abbreviated Edit Network Servi... option to edit an existing or configure a new connection. (See "Network," earlier in this chapter.)

2. Tap the Connect button to initiate.

Figure 2.78 You can also send important events to another Bluetooth-enabled PalmOne handheld.

Figure 2.79 When you receive a sent record, it is categorized as unfiled by default.

Figure 2.80 Salling Clicker lets you control your Mac with your PalmOne handheld.

✔ Tips

■ Once connected to a phone, you can get onto the Internet. See Chapters 9 and 10.

■ See Chapter 3 for more about performing a Bluetooth HotSync.

■ If, after several attempts, your cell phone won't appear in Discovery Results, try the Phone Link Updater software from the Software Essentials CD-ROM or download it (www.palmone.com/us/support/downloads/phonelink.html). After running it, add it to the Install Tool (Windows) or Install Handheld Files (Mac) dialog, then perform a HotSync. (See "Installing Applications," later in this chapter.)

■ If you use a USB Bluetooth adapter on your PC and find that you have trouble connecting, try re-establishing the trusted pairing between your handheld and the computer.

■ If you use a Bluetooth-capable Macintosh along with a Bluetooth PalmOne handheld, we highly recommend installing Salling Clicker (www.salling.com). With it you can control your Mac from the Palm to do numerous things: control PowerPoint or Keynote presentations remotely; play music using iTunes; search for and display digital photos using iPhoto; and just about anything else that can be scripted on the Mac using AppleScript (**Figure 2.80**). Clicker also has a proximity sensor, so you can set up actions that trigger when you enter the room, such as playing your favorite song or even firing up a Web browser and loading your favorite sites.

Wi-Fi Networking

A friend recently moved into a new house where the previous owner had spent a great deal of time wiring every room with Ethernet for easy networking. A great idea, to be sure, but it might be a couple of years too late. Wi-Fi networking (also known by its technical moniker, 802.11b networking) enables you to connect multiple computers in your house or office without running a meter of wire, as well as go to several coffeeshops and other businesses with a Wi-Fi-enabled laptop—or a Palm OS handheld (like the Tungsten C).

The easiest method for connecting to a Wi-Fi network is to use Palm's Wi-Fi Setup application, if present on your device. However, we're going to cover the settings found in the Preferences application, so you can tweak them later if necessary.

To connect to a Wi-Fi network:

1. Open the Wi-Fi preferences and select On from the Wi-Fi popup menu. The device will start scanning for a nearby Wi-Fi network (**Figure 2.81**).

2. Tap the Network popup menu to view a list of networks, then choose the one you wish to use.

3. Some Wi-Fi networks require a WEP (Wireless Equivalent Password) key to access them. If this is the case, enter the WEP key in the dialog that appears; you need to get this information from the network's administrator (**Figure 2.82**).

4. Once you're connected, tap Done to exit the Wi-Fi preferences.

Figure 2.81 Opening the Wi-Fi preferences initiates a network scan.

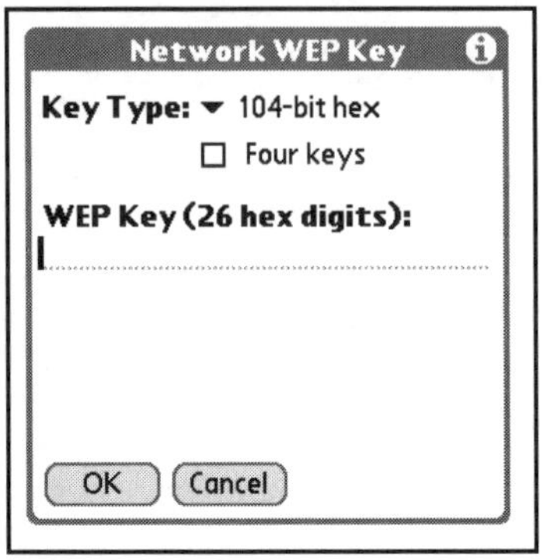

Figure 2.82 Encrypted networks require a WEP key to access.

Figure 2.83 You need to supply the name and password to connect to a closed network.

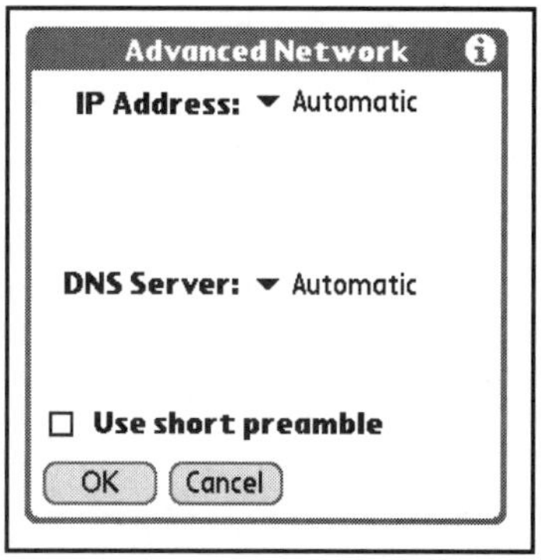

Figure 2.84 If the Wi-Fi network isn't doling out IP addresses, you need to manually specify the information here.

To connect to a closed Wi-Fi network:

1. If you do not see the network you're expecting in the Wi-Fi preferences' Network popup menu, it could be closed, accessible only to those who know of its existence. In this case, choose Edit Networks from the same popup menu.

2. Tap the Add button.

3. Enter the name of the network in the Network Name (SSID) field (**Figure 2.83**). If access is password-protected, mark the WEP Encryption checkbox and enter the WEP key (as before, you need to get this information from the network's administrator).

4. Tap OK if you're finished connecting to the network.

To manually assign IP numbers:

1. Many Wi-Fi networks assign an IP (Internet Protocol) address to computers when they connect; this information routes Internet traffic to your device. By default, this automatic setting is in place. But if you need to manually specify an IP address, tap the Details button instead of OK at step number 4, above.

2. Tap the Advanced button (**Figure 2.84**).

3. Change the IP Address popup menu to Manual. You can then enter the appropriate information.

4. If necessary, enter addresses for DNS (Domain Name Service) servers, which translate understandable Web addresses, such as www.jeffcarlson.com, into the correct IP address numbers.

✔ Tip

■ For much more about Wi-Fi networking, go get the *Wireless Networking Starter Kit*, by Glenn Fleishman and Adam Engst.

WI-FI NETWORKING

Launching Applications

Finally, it's time to start using applications. (You've probably been using applications from the beginning, but we felt it was important to cover some preferences early.)

Unlike nearly all personal computers, a Palm device has no hard drive or floppy disk to store its data—everything is held in RAM (random access memory), including third-party applications and their data (the built-in applications and the core Palm OS files are stored in separate read-only memory, or ROM). As a result, you never have to open or quit programs, technically. All the applications are running concurrently, paused at the state where you last left them. Although we may refer to "launching" or "opening" applications throughout this book, Palm OS is actually only switching between them. (But "launching" sounds more exciting.)

To open an application:

1. Bring up the Applications screen by tapping the silkscreened Applications icon.

2. Tap a program's name or icon to launch it (**Figure 2.85**).

✔ Tips

■ If you have more programs than will fit onto a single screen, write the first letter of the program you want in the Graffiti area to make it visible.

■ Repeatedly tapping Applications switches between application categories (see "Categorizing Applications" later in this chapter).

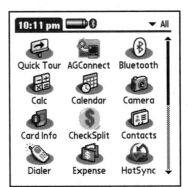

Figure 2.85 Each program has its own icon, listed alphabetically on the Applications screen.

LAUNCHING APPLICATIONS

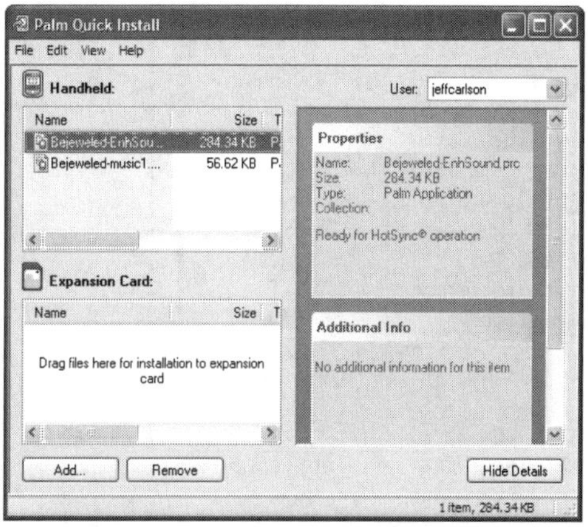

Figure 2.86 Under Windows, click the Add button to prepare programs to be installed. Alternately, you can drag the files to the Palm Quick Install window.

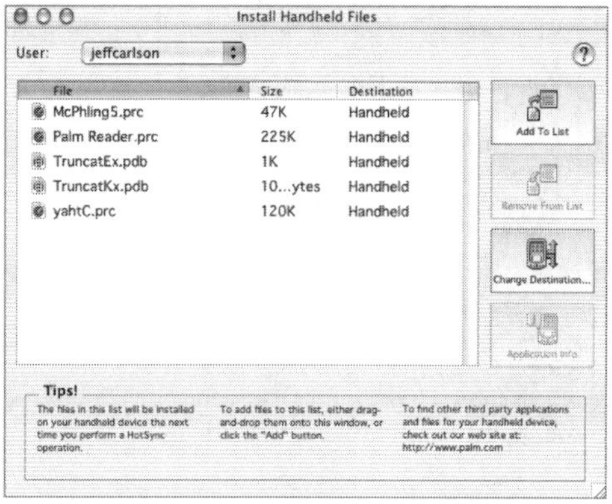

Figure 2.87 The Macintosh installer looks different than its Windows cousin, but works much the same. Clicking the Application Info button displays attributes of the selected file, such as creation date and version number.

Installing Applications

Many handheld owners get by just fine using the built-in applications. However, thousands of third-party programs and utilities are available to install. In most cases, you can download the software from the Web on your desktop computer, then install it onto your Palm organizer.

To install applications using Quick Install (Windows):

1. Launch the Palm Quick Install either from the Windows Start menu, or by clicking the Quick Install button from within Palm Desktop.

2. Click Add to select the programs to install. Palm OS applications end with the extension .prc (whether you use a PC or a Mac). You can also drag the program files from the Windows desktop to the Palm Quick Install window to add them to the list (**Figure 2.86**).

3. When you've added the programs you want to install, perform a HotSync to transfer the programs into the handheld's memory.

To install applications using the HotSync Manager (Macintosh):

1. Launch HotSync Manager or Palm Desktop.

2. From the HotSync menu, choose Install Handheld Files (or press Command-I in HotSync Manager).

3. Click the Add To List button to locate the .prc file you want to add. You can also drag the files to the installation window from the Finder (**Figure 2.87**), or even just drag them to the Finder's HotSync Manager icon.

4. Perform a HotSync operation.

INSTALLING APPLICATIONS

Categorizing Applications

Grouping all of your applications onto the same screen isn't always helpful. That's why the Palm OS lets you set up categories to help organize your programs.

To switch between views:

1. In Applications, choose Display from the Options menu, or write /-R.

2. Choose either Icon or List from the View By popup menu (**Figure 2.88**).

To categorize applications:

1. In Applications, choose Category from the App menu, or write /-Y.

2. You'll see a list of all installed applications. Tap a category name from the popup menu to the right of a program.

3. If you don't see the category you want, select Edit Categories from the popup list to create a new category or edit an existing one (**Figure 2.89**).

To remember the last category:

1. All categories are shown if you switch to the Applications screen from another program. To keep the same category visible, choose Display Options from the Options menu, or write /-R.

2. Mark the Remember Last Category box (**Figure 2.90**).

✔ Tip

■ Tapping the Applications silkscreened button repeatedly scrolls through the categories, but you won't see everything: Unfiled programs don't appear. So, to take advantage of this switching view, be sure to file your unfiled programs.

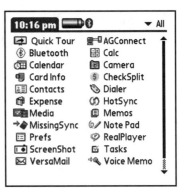

Figure 2.88 See more applications in a single screen when you view by List.

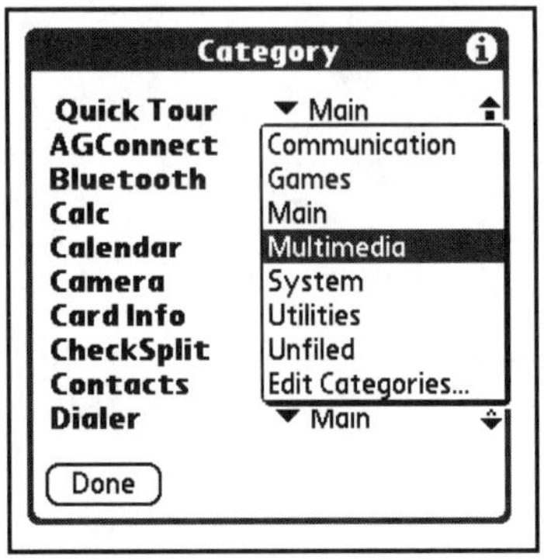

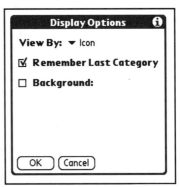

Figure 2.89 Tap the popup menus at right to specify a program's category. New applications are set to Unfiled.

Figure 2.90 Selecting Remember Last Category returns you to your favorite category (or at least the last viewed).

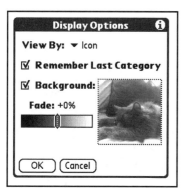

Figure 2.91 The Applications screen Display Options lets you set a background image.

Figure 2.92 Select from images stored either on your handheld or on a memory card.

Figure 2.93 Use the Fader slider to make sure your applications don't get lost in the background photo.

Background Image

In addition to viewing and sorting options, Palm OS 5.2 adds the ability to use a photo in the background to liven up your Applications screen.

To set display preferences:

1. In the Applications screen, choose Display Options from the Options menu, or write ╱-R.

2. Mark the Background checkbox (**Figure 2.91**).

3. Tap the photo box to select an image file from either your handheld's memory or an inserted memory card (**Figure 2.92**).

✔ Tips

- Play with the Fader slider to modify the brightness of your image so that it doesn't overpower the Applications screen (**Figure 2.93**).

- You must have either the PalmOne Photos or Media application installed on your handheld in order to customize the background. The Treo 600 does not include this capability.

Memory Management

Palm data is teeny compared to data on a typical PC, but you can still get carried away and load your memory to maximum capacity.

To view the amount of free memory:

1. From the Applications screen, choose Info from the App menu, or write ╱-I. You can also tap the Info icon (**ⓘ**) on the command bar.

2. The Size button displays memory usage in kilobytes (**Figure 2.94**); tap the Records button to view how many records are stored in each application; tap the Version button to see each program's version number (**Figure 2.95**).

3. Tap Done when finished.

Deleting Applications

At some point a program will no longer hold your attention, or maybe it's time to free up some memory to add more applications. Deleting the ones you don't want is painless.

To delete applications:

1. From within Applications, choose Delete from the App menu, or write ╱-D. You can also tap the Delete icon (🗑) on the command bar.

2. Choose the application you wish to remove, then tap the Delete button and confirm your choice (**Figure 2.96**).

✔ Tips

■ You cannot delete the Palm OS's built-in applications; they are stored in ROM.

■ When you delete an application, any data files associated with it are deleted as well.

■ To quickly jump down to the program you want to delete, write the first letter of its name in the Graffiti area.

Figure 2.94 View your memory usage from within Applications by choosing Info from the App menu.

Figure 2.95 The Info dialog box is also where you can see the version numbers of the Palm OS and installed software.

Figure 2.96 Keep your handheld in fighting trim by deleting little-used applications or deserted files.

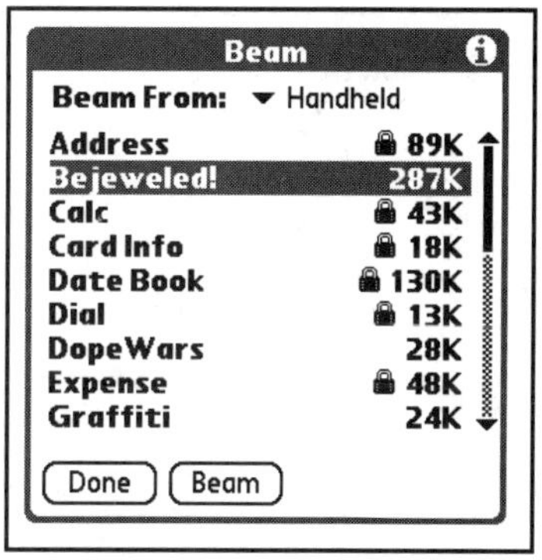

Figure 2.97 Beam programs from the Applications screen.

Figure 2.98 Choose whether or not to accept a beamed application.

Beaming under Tight Memory

If you don't have much free memory on your organizer, you may have trouble beaming applications or records to another handheld: The Palm OS needs enough free memory to store a temporary copy of what you're beaming. So if you're trying to beam a large app and getting an out of memory error, you need to delete some files first. The good news is that if the recipient's handheld has plenty of free space on it, you can temporarily beam smaller files to her, delete them from your device, then get them back after you've transferred the larger file.

Beaming Applications

All but the first Palm devices possess the ability to send data between similar devices equipped with infrared hardware. In addition to sending records (such as addresses), you can transfer full applications.

To beam applications:

1. From the Applications screen, choose Beam from the App menu, or write ╱-B. Under Palm OS 3.5 and later, you can also tap the Beam icon (📡) from the command bar.

2. Select an application from the list that appears (**Figure 2.97**). Programs marked with a padlock symbol beside them cannot be beamed.

3. Aim your infrared port at the recipient's handheld and tap the Beam button.

To receive beamed applications:

1. Go to the Preferences application and make sure that Beam Receive is set to On in the General preferences screen.

2. Aim your infrared port at the sender's handheld and wait for her to initiate the transfer.

3. When the application has been beamed, choose to accept or deny the program (**Figure 2.98**).

✔ Tips

■ Palm asserts that infrared transfers can be achieved from a maximum distance of one meter (39.37 inches).

■ Write the ShortCut ℓ . I (shortcut stroke, period, I) in any text field, which activates Beam Receive in the General preferences for a single instance.

Using Expansion Cards

Expansion cards provide extra memory to store more data; but how do you access the data and copy it to and from the cards?

To access files:

◆ Insert an expansion card into the slot on the Palm device. The Applications screen will display a new category containing the programs stored on the card. The category name includes an icon indicating that you're looking at the card's contents (**Figure 2.99**).

To transfer files:

1. Go to the Applications screen.

2. Choose Copy from the App menu, or write /-C. The Copy dialog box appears.

3. Set the To popup menu to the file's destination (**Figure 2.100**). The Copy From popup menu changes automatically.

4. Highlight a file and tap the Copy button.

5. Tap Done.

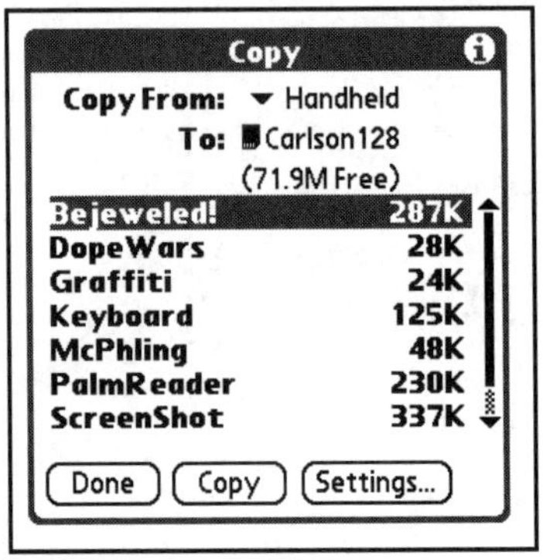

Figure 2.99 Expansion card files show up in the Applications screen as if they belong to another category.

Figure 2.100 You don't need a special application to transfer data files under Palm OS 4.0 and higher.

Replacing the Applications Application

The Applications screen does its job moderately well, but people with more than a handful of programs soon grow weary of scrolling. It wasn't long before an enterprising programmer built a way out of the old Applications box.

The result was Eric Kenslow's LaunchPad, one of those programs that makes you want to say, "Why didn't they think of that sooner?" A few variations of LaunchPad have appeared, but the current favorite seems to be Launcher X (www.launcherx.com).

Instead of one long scrolling field, Launcher X provides a configurable tabbed interface, visual and numeric battery level display, and time and date display (**Figure 2.101**). It also hooks into many features of the Palm OS such as Show/Hide Records, backlighting, Lock & Turn Off, and dragging programs to a trash icon to delete them.

Perhaps the best improvement is the ability to categorize applications simply by dragging their icons to a tab. Forget the endless popup menus in Applications' Category screen.

✔ Tips

- Launcher X makes it easy to work with files stored on an expansion card. Tap the Card Tools icon (it looks like a SD card) to move, copy, and delete files between your Palm's built-in memory and the card.

- Launcher X includes an extra feature that allows you to hide individual tabs, so you can keep some programs and their data under at least one level of security (**Figure 2.102**).

Figure 2.101 A familiar tabbed interface greets users of Launcher X, a replacement application launcher based on Eric Kenslow's LaunchPad utility.

Figure 2.102 Launcher X provides many more options for working with, and viewing, your applications.

HOTSYNC

The underlying approach to functionality in the Palm OS is almost more philosophical than practical: The handheld is not a computer in itself, but an extension of one's computing environment. It recognizes that people aren't going to abandon PCs in favor of PDAs, but rather use both tools to accomplish the greater task of organizing and managing one's information. For it is this goal, grasshopper, that leads to greater productivity, plus the justification to purchase yet another cool electronic gadget.

The key that unlocks this data convergence is the HotSync feature, the ability to synchronize data between the handheld and the PC—not just copy it from one box to the other. This is an important distinction, because it means both platforms will always have the most current information at your disposal.

In this chapter, we also cover alternatives to using HotSync Manager on the Mac as well as how road warriors can synchronize their important contacts and schedules to the Web.

HotSync Overview

Performing a HotSync operation is essentially a one-step procedure: Push a button and it happens. You can do this when connected directly to your PC, or over a modem or network. However, knowing more about what's going on in the background will help you deal with potential problems in the future.

How HotSync works

In normal copy operations, such as when you copy a file from a CD-ROM to your hard drive, the PC's operating system checks to see if a similarly named file exists in the location you're copying to. If a match is found, it checks the modification dates of each file to determine which is newer, then throws up a dialog box requesting confirmation to continue (under some operating systems, this feature can be disabled). If the user clicks OK, the old file is overwritten. The problem here exists when both files have been separately modified; if so, the older data is wiped out (**Figure 3.1**).

In contrast, the Palm OS (by way of the Hot-Sync Manager on the PC) compares every record within a file like the Contacts database. If you make a change to different records on the handheld and the desktop, the changes appear on both platforms following a HotSync. If you make separate changes to the same record on each platform, both versions are retained, and you are notified of the duplication (**Figure 3.2**).

Standard file date comparison

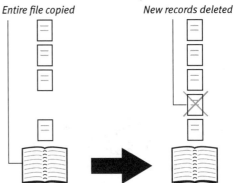

Entire file copied   New records deleted

Figure 3.1 Most files on your PC are "synchronized" by comparing their modification dates and overwriting the older file—big trouble if both files have changed.

HotSync synchronization

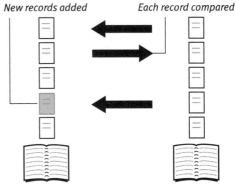

New records added   Each record compared

Figure 3.2 HotSync synchronization compares each record within Palm database files, ensuring that you have up-to-date information on your handheld and on your PC.

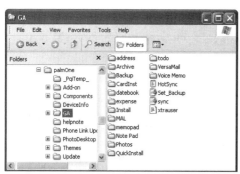

Figure 3.3 Your data is stored on your PC's hard drive, in the user folder matching your Palm user name (though it may be rather truncated).

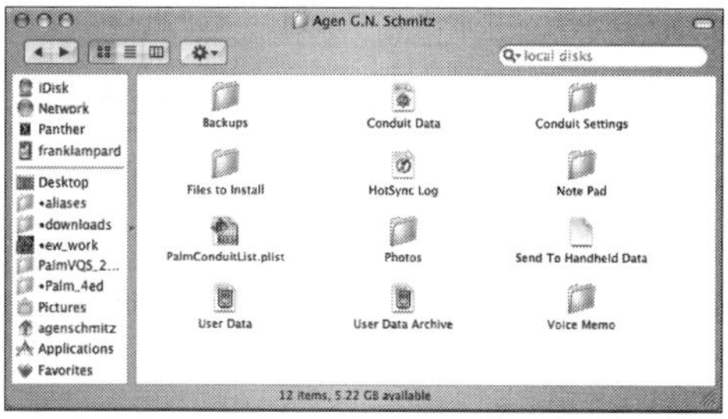

Figure 3.4 The user folder on the Macintosh matches your entire Palm user name.

Table 3.1

User Folder Contents (Windows)	
FOLDER	CONTENTS
address	Contacts data
Backup	Nearly everything except data for the built-in applications. This includes program files, related database files, Doc text files, some preferences files, etc.
datebook	Calendar data
expense	Expense data
Install	Program files to be installed at the next HotSync. See the Tip on this page for important information about this folder.
memopad	Memos data
Note Pad	Note Pad data
QuickInstall	Files to be installed on the handheld or on expansion media
Photos	Still images converted to Palm Database (.pdb) files
todo	Tasks data

Where HotSync stores your data

A HotSync operation copies data from the handheld to the PC and vice-versa, which means that information has to live on your hard drive—but where?

When you install the Palm Desktop software, enter your name (or whatever name you wish to use) at the Create User Account screen. This name becomes the name of the device.

You'll find a new folder on your hard drive named "Palm" (unless you specified a different location and folder name during setup). Within that folder is a folder that closely matches your User Name. For example, on this PC, Agen's files are located in the folder "GA" (**Figure 3.3**), though on his Mac it comes up as "Agen G.N. Schmitz" (**Figure 3.4**). The information in **Table 3.1** and **Table 3.2** (next page) details the folder structure on each platform.

✔ Tips

- When you run the Palm Quick Install utility on Windows, the programs you choose are stored in the Install folder within your user folder. However, under Windows you can't just toss .prc files there and expect them to be transferred at the next HotSync. The HotSync Manager needs to be told that the Install folder is "active" before it will copy the files located within. Running the Install program once toggles this setting—so, after you install one program using the Palm Install Tool, switch to the Windows desktop to copy new program files to the folder in bulk.

- Even though the built-in applications were renamed in Palm OS 5.2.1 (such as Date Book becoming Calendar), the Windows folder structure reflects the older naming convention.

✔ Tips

■ The Mac is a bit more user friendly, enabling you to place Palm-friendly files (with a .prc extension) directly in the Files to Install folder without first adding them to the Send to Handheld droplet.

■ You can't, however, place multimedia files (like JPEGs or MP3s) directly into the Mac Files to Install folder. The Send to Handheld droplet needs to be used to determine mapping to either a handheld or a memory card. If the file is an image or video, it's converted into a .pdb file, which is stored in another Palm user folder within your Documents folder.

■ The Backup(s) folder stores all programs you've installed on your handheld—even ones you've deleted from the handheld. So, if the folder size seems impossibly large, don't be alarmed.

■ It's a good—no, great—idea to regularly make backups of your user folder.

Table 3.2

User Folder Contents (Macintosh)	
FOLDER	CONTENTS
user name	No funky truncation of the user name on the Mac—the folder is titled "Agen G.N. Schmitz." The file within, User Data, contains all of the built-in databases' data.
Conduit Settings	Preferences for each conduit
Files to Install	Files to be transferred at the next HotSync
Note Pad	Note Pad data
Photos	All installed images, converted to .pdb format
Voice Memo	Voice Memo data, with individual memos stored in the Sounds folder
Backups	Everything else

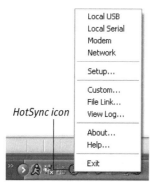

HotSync icon

Figure 3.5 The HotSync icon on the Windows Taskbar offers a quick way to configure HotSync settings.

Figure 3.6 When you add the Mac Palm Desktop icon to the Mac OS X Dock, you can access HotSync Manager commands from the contextual menu.

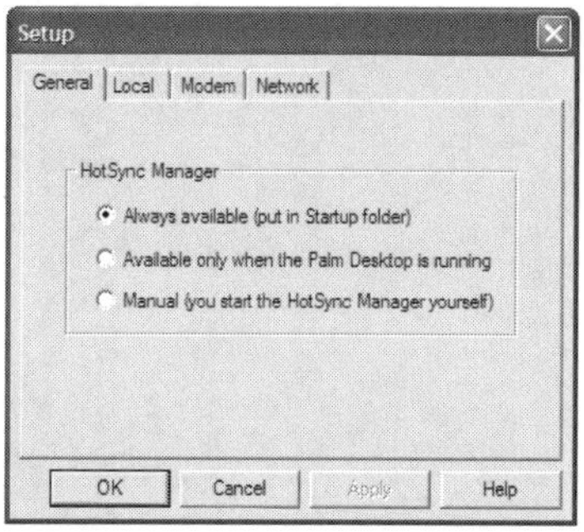

Figure 3.7 Choose when HotSync Manager will be active to avoid port conflicts with other devices.

Configuring HotSync Manager

The HotSync Manager isn't often seen, but it does quite a bit of work behind the scenes to ensure that your data is transferring properly. Its primary task is to monitor the port reserved for the HotSync cradle so it can act when the handheld signals a sync operation.

To access the HotSync Manager under Windows:

◆ From within Palm Desktop, choose Setup from the HotSync menu. You can also click the HotSync icon on the Taskbar, then select Setup from the popup menu (**Figure 3.5**).

To access the HotSync Manager under Mac OS:

◆ Launch HotSync Manager from the Palm folder on your hard disk, or choose Setup from the HotSync (*active user name*) submenu of the Instant Palm Desktop menu (from the Dock in Mac OS X; **Figure 3.6**).

To enable HotSync port monitoring:

Make sure the cable attached to your HotSync cradle is connected to one of your PC's USB or serial ports.

◆ Access the HotSync Manager as described above and go to the Setup screen. Under Windows, you have three options for enabling port monitoring (**Figure 3.7**):

Always available. Activates HotSync Manager when you start your computer.

Available only when Palm Desktop is running. Enables and disables port monitoring when you use Palm Desktop.

Manual. Starts port monitoring at your discretion, freeing up the port for other uses when you're not using HotSync.

Under the Mac OS, you can leave HotSync running all the time by selecting Enable HotSync software at system startup under HotSync Options, or you can choose the Enabled or Disabled radio button at the top of the screen (**Figure 3.8**).

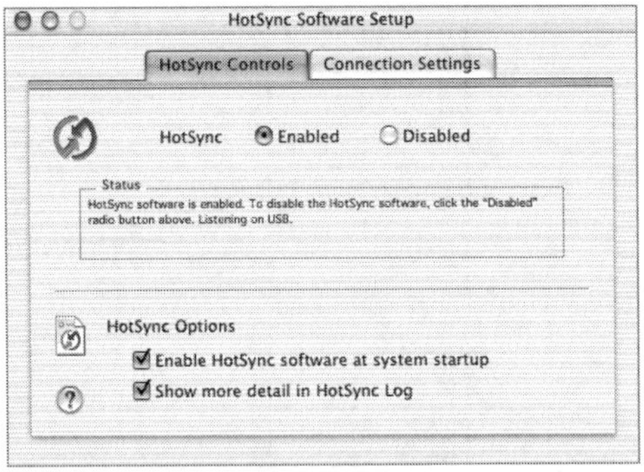

✔ Tips

■ Do you find yourself forgetting to HotSync during the course of your busy day? Let the handheld do the work for you: AutoSync (`www.rgps.com`) can automatically HotSync your handheld according to one or two schedules. Be sure to have your computer running and the handheld in its cradle, then let it go to work (**Figure 3.9**).

■ There never seem to be enough ports on a computer. If you don't want to switch cables each time you need to print or perform a HotSync, consider buying an inexpensive hub that connects multiple devices.

■ If you use an older Macintosh with a serial port (as opposed to newer machines with USB), make sure that AppleTalk is disabled before attempting to perform a HotSync: In the Chooser, select the AppleTalk Inactive radio button. AppleTalk can hog the serial port and not allow other applications, like HotSync Manager, to use it. The same is often true of fax software.

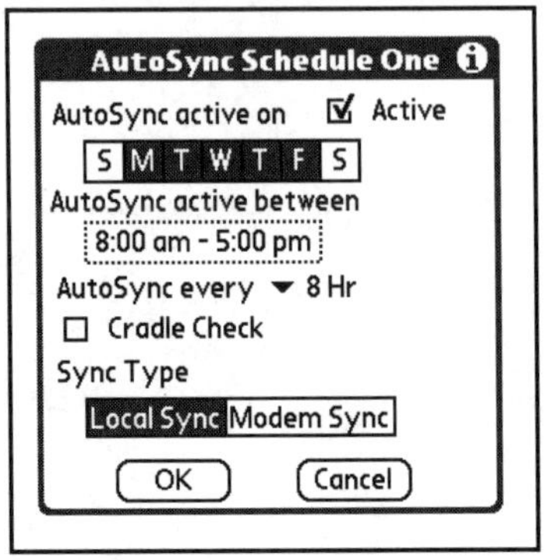

Figure 3.8 Enable HotSync port monitoring from the HotSync Controls tab on the Macintosh.

Figure 3.9 Schedule your HotSync operations at a more convenient hour with AutoSync.

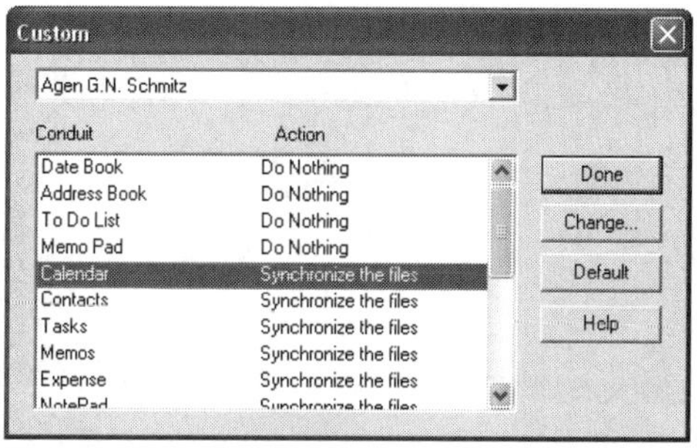

Figure 3.10 Conduits control the way each program's data is handled during a HotSync.

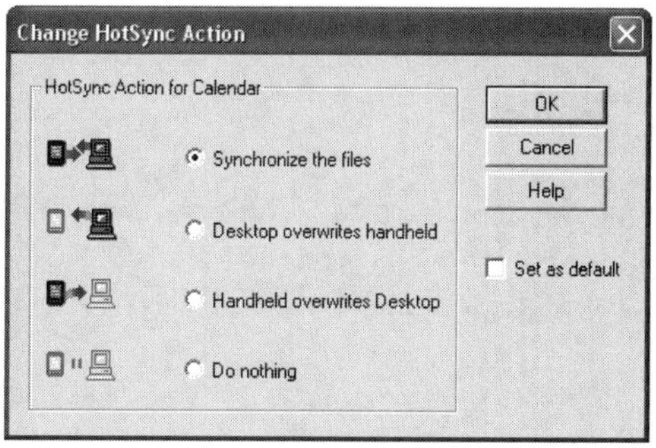

Figure 3.11 Multiple HotSync actions let you override the default synchronization settings.

Table 3.3

HotSync Conduit Actions

SETTING	ACTION
Synchronize the files	All records are compared individually; newer records overwrite older records.
Desktop overwrites handheld	Individual records are not compared; entire desktop file replaces handheld file.
Handheld overwrites desktop	Individual records are not compared; entire handheld file replaces desktop file.
Do nothing	Records are skipped; no action is taken.

Setting Up Conduits

Each of the built-in applications, as well as the Palm OS and the program installer, has its own conduit, a software translator that specifies how records should be compared and copied between platforms. Additionally, many third-party applications, such as AvantGo, include their own conduits for manipulating their specific data.

To configure conduits:

1. Choose Custom from the HotSync menu in Windows. Under the Mac OS, launch the HotSync Manager and choose Conduit Settings from the HotSync menu, or press Command-J.

2. Highlight the conduit you wish to edit, then click the Change (Windows) or Conduit Settings (Mac) button. Double-clicking a conduit also lets you modify its settings (**Figure 3.10**).

3. Choose an action for that conduit (**Figure 3.11** and **Table 3.3**). Click the Set as default checkbox (Windows) or the Make Default button (Mac) to make the new setting permanent each time you do a HotSync. Click OK.

Under Windows, clicking the Default button in the Custom dialog box restores the conduit settings to the last default state.

✔ Tip

- Many people use PIMs such as Microsoft Outlook and Symantec's ACT! instead of Palm Desktop. In addition to the Outlook conduits included with the Palm software, a variety of third-party applications, like PocketMirror (www.chapura.com), replace the built-in conduits with ones that synchronize data with your favorite desktop PIM.

Local HotSync

Most of your HotSync actions fall into the category of Local HotSync, in which the handheld and PC are connected directly by either a serial cable or cradle, or via infrared.

To set up a Local HotSync:

1. Launch Palm Desktop or the HotSync Manager and choose Setup from the HotSync menu.

2. Click the Local tab (Windows, **Figure 3.12**) or the Connection Settings tab (Mac).

3. Windows: From the Serial port popup menu, specify the COM port to which your HotSync cable or cradle is connected.

4. Specify the speed of the connection from the Speed popup menu. Click OK, or close the window.

5. From the Windows Taskbar popup menu, specify that Local HotSync monitoring should be activated by clicking the name; a checkmark appears. On the Macintosh, this information is available in the Connection Settings window.

✔ Tip

■ If you're having trouble maintaining a connection, reduce the speed setting in the Setup dialog box.

To perform a Local HotSync:

1. Place your device in the cradle.

2. Push the HotSync button on the front, or press the button in the HotSync application on the handheld. A short series of tones indicates a successful connection.

3. A window appears on the desktop indicating the HotSync progression. A similar screen also appears on the handheld (**Figure 3.13**). Another set of tones indicates when the synchronization is done.

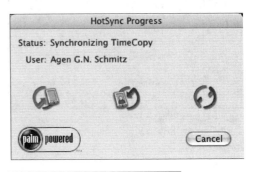

Figure 3.12 Use the Local tab to specify which port your HotSync cradle is connected to.

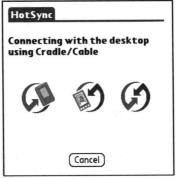

Figure 3.13 Tapping the HotSync button on the silkscreen area (or on a cradle) activates the HotSync; the progression is visible on both the PC (above) and the handheld (below).

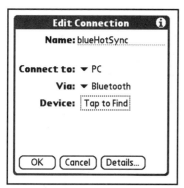

Figure 3.14 On Bluetooth-enabled devices, "Bluetooth" appears as a connection type in the Via popup menu.

Figure 3.15 Locate your device through the Discovery Results screen. If it's not yet listed as a trusted device, you'll be given that option.

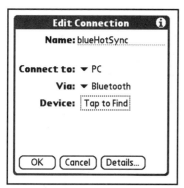

Figure 3.16 Already paired devices will appear in the HotSync popup menu.

Bluetooth PC HotSync

Forget the cradle or a USB cable—if your handheld and PC support Bluetooth, you can synchronize wirelessly. It takes a small amount of setup the first time, but connecting wirelessly is worth it (see "Bluetooth Networking" in Chapter 2 for more on configuring a connection).

To set up a Bluetooth connection (handheld):

1. Launch the HotSync application on your handheld.

2. Choose Connection Setup from the Options menu (or write ╱-S).

3. Tap New, then give the connection a name, like "Bluetooth" (**Figure 3.14**).

4. Select PC from the Connect to popup menu.

5. Change the Via popup menu selection to Bluetooth.

6. Tap the Device field to locate your Bluetooth-enabled PC.

7. Choose your PC from the results list (**Figure 3.15**).

8. Tap OK to return to HotSync.

✔ Tips

■ If you haven't created a pairing between your handheld and PC yet, you'll be asked if you want to add your computer to the trusted device list. Tap Yes, then go through the pairing process (again, refer to Chapter 2 for these steps).

■ If you've previously created a Bluetooth pairing, you'll find the connection names listed in the popup menu (**Figure 3.16**).

BLUETOOTH PC HOTSYNC

To set up a Bluetooth connection (Windows):

1. Click the HotSync icon on the Taskbar, then select Local Serial.

2. Click the Taskbar HotSync icon again and select Setup.

3. Click the Local tab, then select the COM port used by your PC's Bluetooth software.

4. Click OK.

To set up a Bluetooth connection (Mac):

1. Open the HotSync Manager, and make sure that Enabled is selected.

2. Click the Connection Settings tab, then mark the bluetooth-pda-sync-port check-box (**Figure 3.17**).

3. Exit out of HotSync Manager.

To perform a HotSync via Bluetooth:

1. Launch HotSync on your handheld.

2. Make sure the Local button is high-lighted.

3. Choose the previously configured Bluetooth connection name from the popup menu located under the main HotSync button (**Figure 3.18**).

4. Tap the HotSync button in the HotSync application to synchronize.

✔ Tips

- If you leave the Bluetooth connection selected in HotSync's popup menu, this transmission method will become the default when tapping the silkscreened HotSync icon.

- If you're having trouble connecting to a removable Bluetooth module, try reestablishing it as a trusted device.

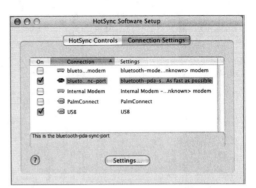

Figure 3.17 Before performing a HotSync with a Mac, check the bluetooth-pda-sync-port option in HotSync's Connection Settings tab.

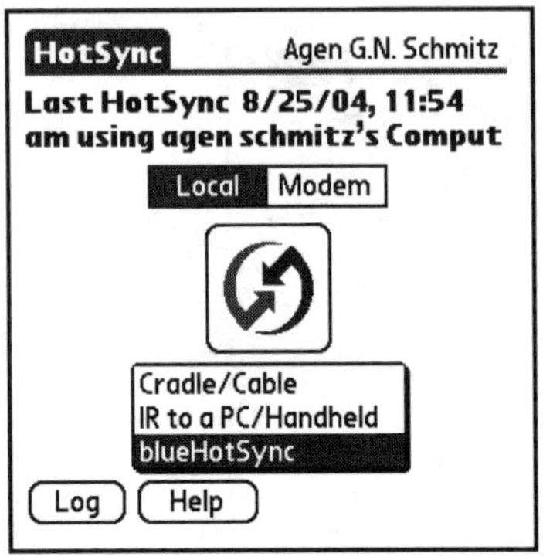

Figure 3.18 With your Bluetooth connection set up, simply select it from the popup menu below the HotSync button before synchronizing.

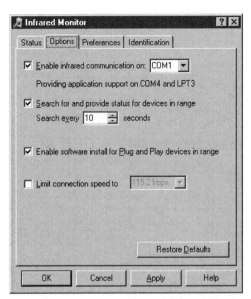

Figure 3.19 If your laptop or desktop PC is equipped with an infrared port, you can set your preferences to recognize the handheld and perform a HotSync.

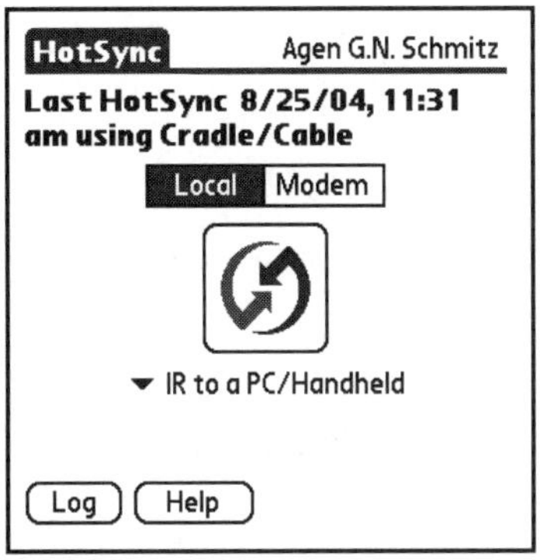

Figure 3.20 Use the HotSync application on the Palm to initiate an infrared HotSync operation.

Infrared HotSync

Knowing a good opportunity when it zaps them in the head, the engineers at Palm incorporated infrared HotSync capabilities into the Palm OS. The system's IR communication is built upon the IrCOMM protocol.

To set up infrared HotSync (Mac):

1. Open the HotSync Manager and switch to the Serial Port Settings tab.

2. Choose Infrared from the Port popup menu under Local Setup.

To set up infrared HotSync (Win):

1. Open the Infrared Monitor from the Settings folder and click the Options tab.

2. Check the box labeled Enable infrared communication on, and choose the COM port (usually COM4 or COM5) used by the infrared port (**Figure 3.19**).

3. In the HotSync Manager, choose the COM port as the Local source.

To perform an infrared HotSync:

1. Launch the HotSync application on the Palm device, and make sure that IR to a PC/Handheld is selected from the Connection popup menu.

2. Tap the large HotSync button to begin (**Figure 3.20**).

Modem HotSync

Make sure you have disabled any programs on your PC (such as fax software) that may cause HotSync headaches.

To set up a Modem HotSync on your computer:

1. Choose Setup from the HotSync menu to bring up the Setup dialog box.

2. Click the Modem tab (Windows, **Figure 3.21**) or the Connection Settings tab (Mac; skip to step 5).

3. From the Serial port popup menu, specify the COM or serial port to which your modem is connected.

4. Specify the speed of the connection from the Speed popup menu. Click OK, or close the window.

5. From the Taskbar popup menu, specify that Modem HotSync monitoring should be activated by clicking the name; a checkmark appears. On the Mac, click the checkbox next to Internal Modem (**Figure 3.22**).

To set up a Modem HotSync on your handheld:

1. Launch the HotSync application.

2. Choose Conduit Setup from the Options menu, or write ∕-D.

3. Choose which conduits should be run by marking the checkboxes to the left of each program's name (**Figure 3.23**). Tap OK.

4. If you haven't set up your Modem preferences, choose Connection Setup from the Options menu (and see Chapter 2).

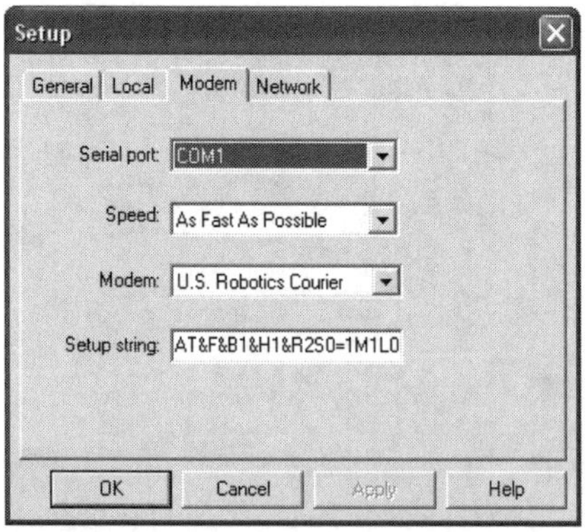

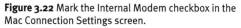

Figure 3.21 As with a Local HotSync, specify your modem's COM port and speed, as well as the model.

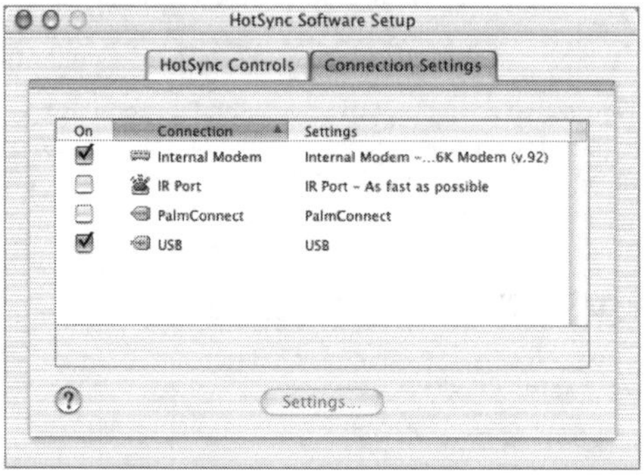

Figure 3.22 Mark the Internal Modem checkbox in the Mac Connection Settings screen.

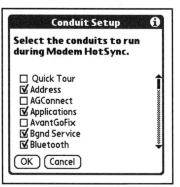

Figure 3.23 To save some connection time, mark only the conduits you want to have synchronized.

sidebar
MODEM HOTSYNC

Figure 3.24 Add the modem number you're dialing to the Phone Setup screen, and specify settings such as a dialing prefix or use of a calling card.

Figure 3.25 With everything configured, simply tap the HotSync button.

To perform a Modem HotSync:

1. Go to the main HotSync screen and tap the Modem button.

2. Tap the dotted Enter Phone # box (under the Connection popup menu) to specify a phone number. This opens the Phone Setup screen, where you'll add the phone number and other connection details (**Figure 3.24**). Tap OK when finished.

3. Attach a compatible modem (connected to a phone line, of course) to your handheld.

4. If you're using a modem with a HotSync button on the case, push it to initiate the HotSync (and skip the next step). If not, launch the HotSync application on the handheld.

5. Tap the main HotSync button (**Figure 3.25**). You should hear the startup tones.

6. When the HotSync is complete, you'll hear the tones signaling the end, and the connection will terminate.

✔ Tip

■ By default, PalmModem shows up as the selection when you tap the Modem button, but this is an outdated add-on.

Bluetooth Modem HotSync

If you've got a Bluetooth-enabled device, you can connect via a compatible cell phone without the hassle of fiddling with wires.

To set up a Bluetooth cell phone:

1. Go to the main HotSync screen.

2. Choose Connection Setup from the Options menu, or write ╱-S. This opens the Connection preferences.

3. Tap New, then give the connection a unique name.

4. Select Phone from the Connect to popup menu.

5. Change the Via popup menu selection to Bluetooth.

6. Tap the Device field to locate your Bluetooth-enabled phone via the Discovery Results screen.

7. Choose which model of compatible phone you'll be connecting with in the Model popup menu (**Figure 3.26**).

8. Tap OK to return to HotSync.

To perform a Bluetooth Modem HotSync:

1. In the main HotSync screen, tap the Modem button.

2. Select the connection name from the popup menu, and specify a phone number in the Enter Phone # box if it hasn't already been set up.

3. Tap the HotSync button and begin the connection to your cell phone (which, of course, is turned on and within 30 feet of your handheld) (**Figure 3.27**).

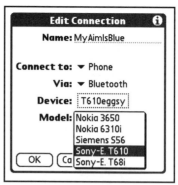

Figure 3.26 Despite having already discovered your phone, Bluetooth requires that you confirm it with the Model popup menu.

Figure 3.27 Tapping the HotSync button initiates a call on your cell phone.

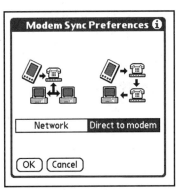

Figure 3.28 The Modem Sync Preferences dialog box lets you choose between a direct dial-up connection or a dial-up network connection.

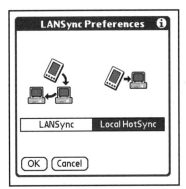

Figure 3.29 By choosing LANSync or Local HotSync, you dictate the action of the main screen's HotSync button.

LANSync/Network HotSync

Network HotSync extends your range and flexibility by providing a method to synchronize your data from any computer on your PC network—whether it's using someone else's HotSync cradle down the hall or several states away. (Network HotSync isn't available for Macintosh computers.) If your network has dial-in remote access, you can also connect using a compatible modem.

To set up a Network HotSync:

1. Launch the HotSync application.

2. Depending on which mode you're in, pressing the HotSync icon will attempt to connect directly to the PC attached to the current HotSync cradle, or to your PC out on the network. If you're dialing in to a modem that acts as the gateway for a network, choose Modem Sync Prefs from the Options menu, or write ∕-O. Tap either the Network or Direct to modem button to specify the Modem Sync action (**Figure 3.28**).

If you're connected directly to the network, choose LANSync Prefs from the Options menu, or write ∕-L. Choose between LANSync and Local HotSync (**Figure 3.29**).

3. Choose Primary PC Setup from the Options menu, or write ∕-P. In most cases, you shouldn't have to change this information, since it's downloaded from your PC when you perform a HotSync.

4. On your PC, bring up the HotSync settings by choosing Setup from either the HotSync menu within Palm Desktop or the popup menu on the Taskbar.

continued on next page

5. Tap the Network tab, then place a check-mark next to the users who will have access to your machine (**Figure 3.30**).

6. If you need to adjust the TCP/IP configuration, click the TCP/IP Settings button. Otherwise, click OK.

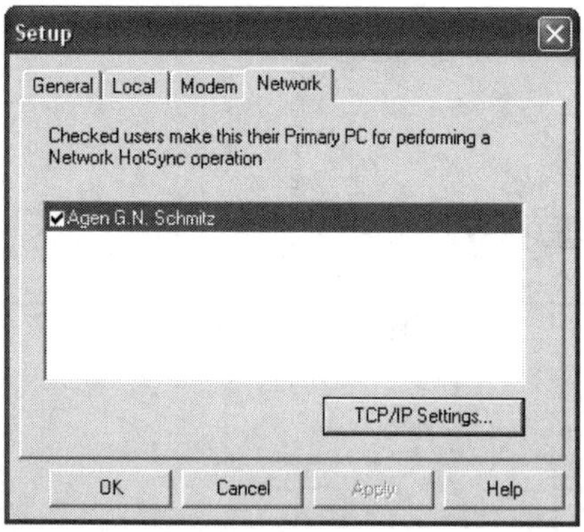

To perform a Network HotSync:

◆ If the computer you're connecting from is on the same local area network (LAN) or wide area network (WAN), and you've set the LANSync preferences to LANSync, tap the Local button, then tap the Hot-Sync icon to connect.

◆ If you need to dial in via modem to connect to your network, and you've set the Modem Sync preferences to Network, tap the Modem button, then tap the single HotSync button. Once connected, the HotSync operation should proceed normally.

✔ Tip

■ Wi-Fi-enabled devices such as the Palm Tungsten C don't really need a cradle to HotSync. Set up a Network HotSync to your PC and synchronize using the faster 802.11b wireless network if you have one.

Figure 3.30 The Network tab in the HotSync Setup screen sets up your PC for LAN synchronization.

```
HotSync 3.2 started 8/25/04 4:11:14 PM

Local Synchronization

OK Install

OK Voice Memo

To Do List did nothing

TimeCopy: host 2004/08/25 16:11:15, palm
2004/08/25 16:10:39, diff: 36s

OK TimeCopy

OK Tasks

OK SplashShopper

OK SplashPhoto with 1 message(s)

OK SplashID

OK Media
```

Figure 3.31 A typical HotSync Log looks like this, with plain-English comments to indicate the steps taken.

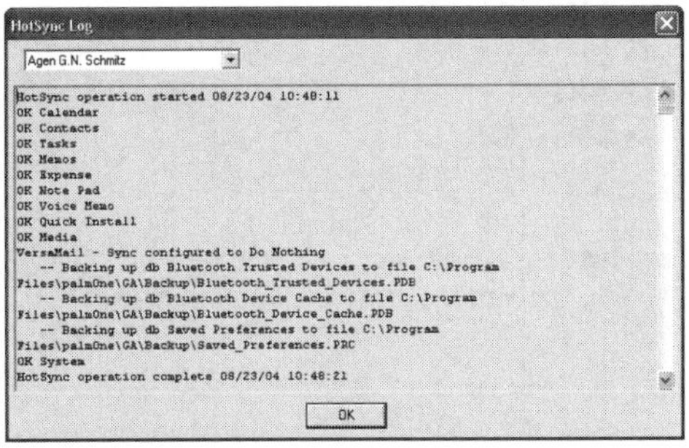

Figure 3.32 The HotSync Log can be viewed from within Palm Desktop (Windows version shown here), or you can use a word processor or text editor to read the file from your hard drive.

Viewing the HotSync Log

The details of each of the last 10 HotSyncs are stored in a text file on your computer. Although the information usually isn't important, the HotSync Log is the first place to turn if you're having HotSync problems (fortunately, most error messages are written in understandable English; **Figure 3.31**).

To view the HotSync Log:

◆ **Windows:** Choose View Log from the HotSync menu within Palm Desktop or from the HotSync popup menu located on the Taskbar (**Figure 3.32**).

◆ **Mac OS:** Choose View Log from the HotSync menu within the HotSync Manager.

◆ **Palm OS:** Tap the Log button on the main HotSync screen. However, don't get angry with us for suggesting it, since the Palm HotSync Log gives only the most basic of information (like the scintillating "OK Calendar").

◆ Alternately, open the log file itself with a word processor or text editor. You'll find the log in your user folder.

✔ Tip

■ To record a detailed log on the Macintosh (instead of the minimal log that's stored on the handheld), mark the Show more detail in HotSync Log checkbox at the bottom of the HotSync Controls screen.

Multiple HotSync Options

The majority of owners use their handhelds on an individual basis: one organizer, one PC. However, there are some cases where you may want to synchronize one device with multiple machines, or several organizers on the same machine.

Since HotSync *synchronizes* your data, not overwrites it, the information on each machine should remain updated without any special work on your part. Simply HotSync as you normally would; the desktop software keeps track of multiple users.

However, if you should happen to lose your handheld's data (for example, due to a hard reset), customize your first HotSync as described here.

To set up a first HotSync on an empty Palm device:

1. On your PC, choose Custom from the HotSync popup menu on the Taskbar, or from the HotSync menu in the Palm Desktop application.

2. Specify Desktop overwrites handheld for all of the conduits (**Figure 3.33**). Click Done.

3. Perform a HotSync. Your data on the handheld should be in the state it was before it was lost.

4. Before you HotSync again, change the conduit settings back to Synchronize.

To set up a new user:

1. In Palm Desktop, select Users from the Tools menu (Windows), or select Edit Users from the User submenu of the HotSync menu (Mac).

2. Click the New (Windows) or New User (Mac) button (**Figure 3.34**) and type a name, then click OK; a new user appears.

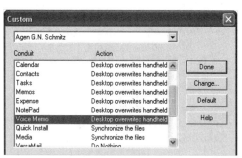

Figure 3.33 In the event of a hard reset, your first HotSync should be set so that the desktop information overwrites the handheld's data.

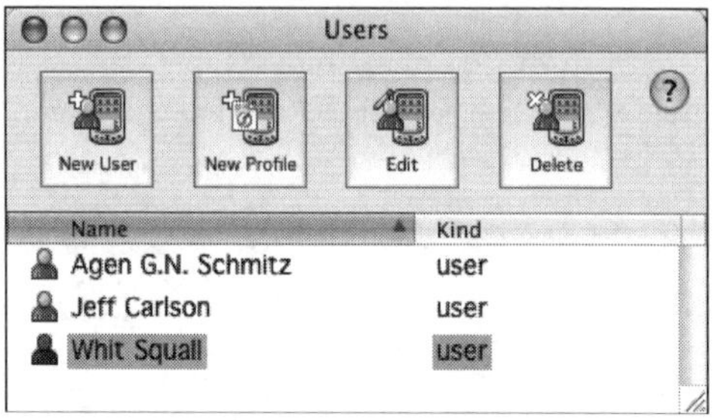

Figure 3.34 Sharing one computer with multiple Palm devices entails creating a new user account for each person. The Macintosh screen is shown here.

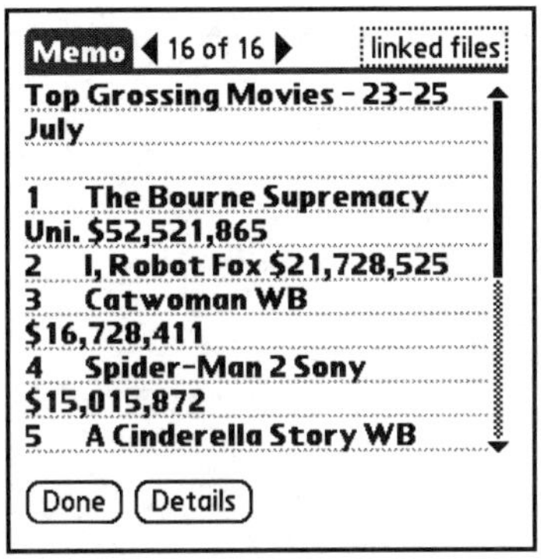

Figure 3.35 Set up a File Link that points to a file filled with important information that changes often.

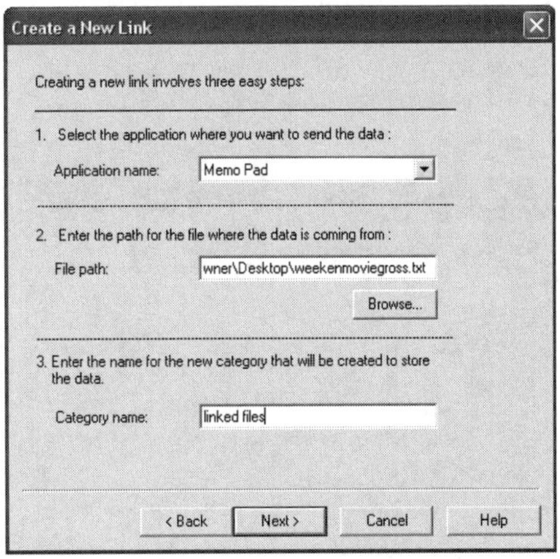

Figure 3.36 Choose the application, file path, and specify a category name to set up a File Link.

File Link

Frequently updating memos or addresses is made simple for Windows users. Using the File Link feature, you can create a Windows file that is in plain text (.txt), comma separated (.csv), or Palm archive format that gets transferred to the handheld according to scheduled intervals (**Figure 3.35**).

To create a File Link:

1. Prepare the file you wish to link. For example, let's say everyone who accesses your PC needs each week's movie box office listing. Save it as either straight text, comma-separated, or as a Memos archive (see later in this chapter for details). If you're saving a list of addresses (say, the month's new clients), save the file as either comma-separated or as an Contacts archive.

2. Choose File Link from the HotSync menu in Palm Desktop, or the HotSync popup menu on the Taskbar.

3. Select a user name, make sure the Create a new link radio button is activated, and click the Next button.

4. Choose either Memos or Contacts from the Application name popup menu.

5. If you know the path to your file, type it into the File path field. Otherwise, click the Browse button to locate it.

6. Linked file data is stored in its own category to avoid conflicts with your other data. Enter a name in the Category name field (**Figure 3.36**), and click Next.

7. A dialog box confirming your link settings appears. By default, the file will be queued for HotSync whenever it changes. If this is okay, click the Done button.

FILE LINK

To schedule a File Link update:

1. If you want to specify other options (such as daily, weekly, or monthly updates), click the Update Frequency button on the Confirm your Link Settings dialog.

2. Specify the interval for how often the category should be updated (**Figure 3.37**).

   If you know the file isn't going to change for a while, mark the checkbox next to Disable the link temporarily but maintain the settings.

3. Click OK to exit the Update Frequency dialog box, then click the Done button.

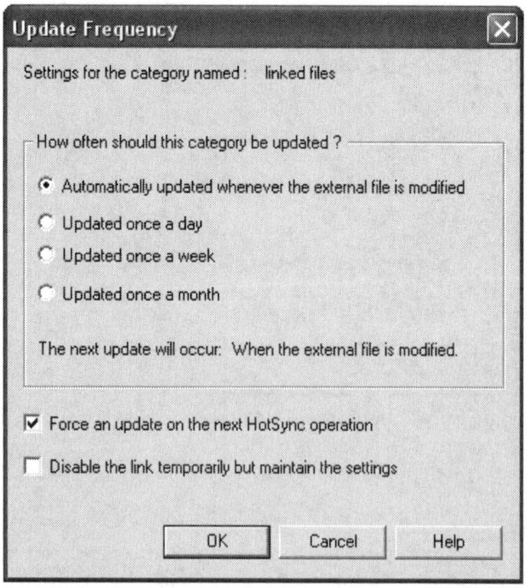

To remove a File Link:

1. Choose File Link from the HotSync menu in Palm Desktop, or the HotSync popup menu on the Taskbar.

2. Choose a user name, and select the option marked Modify or remove an existing link. Click the Next button.

3. Highlight the link you wish to delete and click the Remove button. The Remove Link dialog box appears.

4. Choose how you'd like to handle your existing linked data (**Figure 3.38**).

5. Click OK.

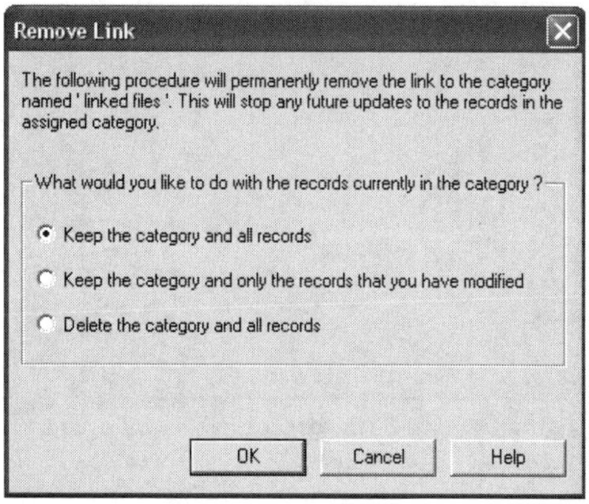

✔ Tips

- Although it may look like something's gone wrong, don't be surprised if, after you've set up a link, the category you set up appears to be empty. The linked data won't get copied to Palm Desktop until you perform a HotSync.

- Unfortunately, File Link is not available on the Macintosh.

Figure 3.37 You can set the frequency at which the linked file is transferred to the handheld.

Figure 3.38 If you want to put your File Link into hibernation for a while, choose to keep the category and records, or just the category, for later.

Figure 3.39 You may have seen this dialog dozens of times...but do you know where the data actually goes? If you mark the checkbox, you can retrieve deleted records from your PC's hard drive at any time.

Figure 3.40 Archives are named according to the deleted records' categories.

— *Archive indicators*

Figure 3.41 Opening an archive file is straightforward, but the records are displayed in the main window, which can be confusing if you're not paying attention. Look to the title bar or an indicator in the lower-right to signal that an archive is currently active.

Working with Archived Records

When you delete a record from the handheld or the Palm Desktop, you're given the option to save it on your PC by marking the Archive deleted *program* item(s) at next HotSync operation checkbox (**Figure 3.39**). This is a great feature if you've accidentally deleted something, or if you need to free up some memory on your handheld, but don't want to lose the information permanently. But where does it go? And how do you get it back?

Each of the built-in applications creates an archive file (such as a Calendar archive, which uses the old Date Book name (datebook.bak)) for each category that contains deleted records. Those files are stored in each application's folder, although recently deleted items won't show up until you perform a HotSync (**Figure 3.40**).

To restore archived records:

1. In Palm Desktop, go to the Palm application module you want to restore records from (such as Memos). Choose Open Archive from the File menu.

2. In the Open Archive dialog box, highlight the archive file named after the category you're looking for (such as "Personal.mpa"), and click the Open button.

   Your deleted records are now visible in the main window. You'll see the name of the file, followed by "(Archive)" in the window's title bar (**Figure 3.41**).

3. Highlight the records you want to restore, and choose Copy from the Edit menu (or press Control/Command-C).

4. Switch back to your active Palm records by choosing Open Current from the File menu.

continued on next page

5. Choose Paste from the Edit menu, or press Control/Command-V to paste the restored records.

6. Perform a HotSync to restore the data to your handheld.

You can also use the archive format to create customized archives, rather than just files containing deleted records. This can be useful if you need to email a batch of addresses to another Palm device owner, for example.

To export archive files in Palm Desktop:

1. Go to the Palm application module you wish to export. If you want to export only certain records, highlight them.

2. Choose Export from the File menu. In the Export As dialog box, choose Currently selected records if you're not exporting the entire contents of the application. Give the file a unique file name, then click the Export button (**Figure 3.42**).

Note that if you have private records hidden, you will need to choose Show private records from the View menu before exporting them.

To import archive files in Palm Desktop:

1. Go to the Palm application module you wish to import.

2. Choose Import from the File menu. In the Import dialog box, highlight a file and click OK (**Figure 3.43**).

✔ Tips

■ You can also import records in text-only and comma-delimited file formats.

■ Change the category for many records at once: Export them, switch to the new category, then import them back in.

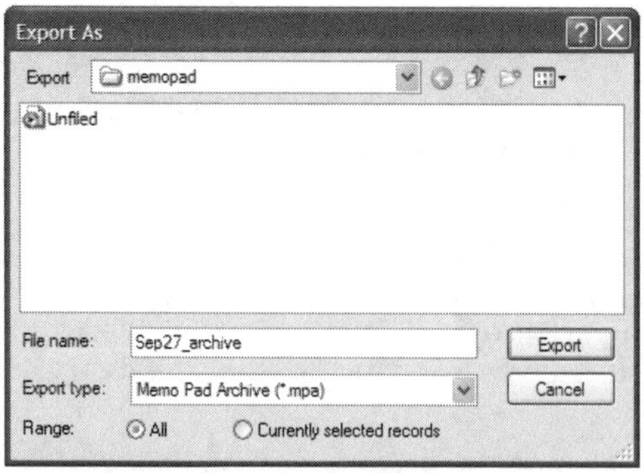

Figure 3.42 You don't have to limit yourself to using archives for resurrecting deleted data. Export selected records, or your entire set of addresses, tasks, and memos into archive format.

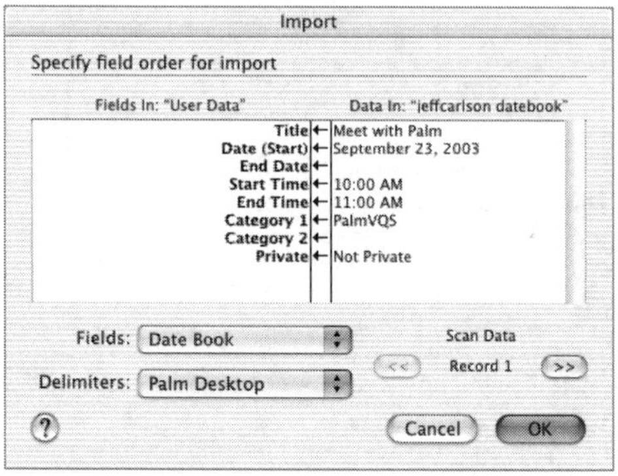

Figure 3.43 Records can be imported from tab- and comma-delimited files, in addition to Palm's archive formats.

WORKING WITH ARCHIVED RECORDS

Figure 3.44 In the Profiles screen, you can toggle between the Users and the Profiles lists.

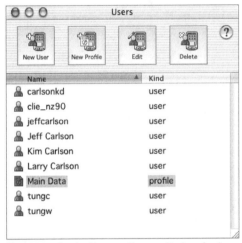

Figure 3.45 On the Mac, profiles are displayed using a separate icon. Click the Edit button to rename them.

Creating HotSync Profiles

Profiles allow you to set up a group of master records that can be transferred to new Palm devices. For example, you can set up a profile containing your company's important meetings to be copied to each person's handheld. However, the profile erases any existing data, so you can only copy a profile to a brand new or empty device.

To create a HotSync profile:

1. Windows: In Palm Desktop, select Users from the Tools menu.

   Macintosh: In Palm Desktop, go to the HotSync menu and select Edit Users from the User submenu.

2. Windows: In the Users dialog box that appears, click the Profiles button to view a list of profiles. Click the New button (**Figure 3.44**).

   Macintosh: Profiles are marked in the Users window with a different icon (**Figure 3.45**). Click New Profile.

3. Windows: Highlight the name of your new profile and click OK.

   Macintosh: After your profile is created, click the close box in the upper-left corner, or press Command-W.

4. Stock your profile with the information that you want to appear on every Palm device you copy it to. Enter the data by hand, or switch between the profile and a user account to copy and paste records.

✔ Tip

■ To preserve your existing categories when copying records to the profile, first set up the category names in your new profile. Then, in your user account, view by category and copy the records you want. Switch to the profile, view the similarly named category, and paste the records.

Synchronizing with Apple's iSync

You also have the option to synchronize your handheld with Apple's Mac OS X iCal and Address Book applications using iSync. Though not without its drawbacks (see Tips), this enables you to synchronize data to your .Mac Internet account as well as publish Calendar events to a Web page (www.mac. com; requires a $99 annual subscription). Before you start, download and install the iSync Palm Conduit (www.apple.com/isync/ devices.html), then be sure to perform a final HotSync as Palm Desktop's contacts, calendar, and tasks conduits will be deactivated.

To synchronize with iSync:

1. After downloading and installing the iSync Palm Conduit, open HotSync Manager.

2. Choose the handheld user name you want this applied to.

3. Open the iSync Conduit settings and mark Enable iSync for this Palm device checkbox (**Figure 3.46**). Click OK.

   If any of the Address Book/Contacts, Date Book/Calendar, or To-Do/Tasks conduits are still found in Conduit Settings, configure their HotSync action as "Do Nothing" and click the Make Default button.

4. Open iSync, where you'll now find a handheld icon. Click it to open its preferences, making sure to mark the Contacts and Calendars checkboxes (**Figure 3.47**).

5. Perform a HotSync (**Figure 3.48**). (You'll still need to initiate this from your handheld.)

Figure 3.46 After installing the iSync Palm Conduit, open it within HotSync Manager and enable it.

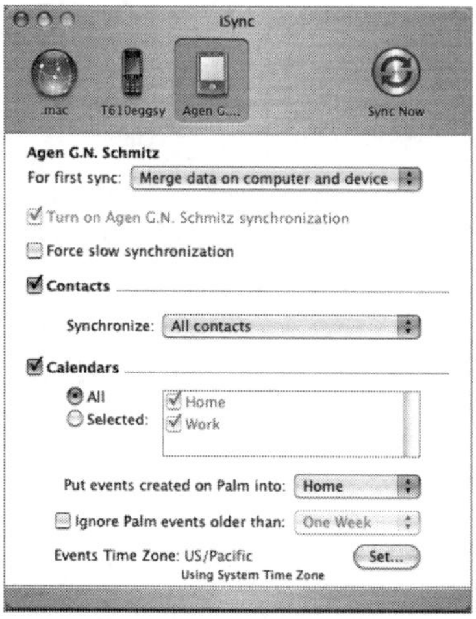

Figure 3.47 Open iSync, select your handheld, and mark the Contacts and Calendars checkboxes.

Figure 3.48 The iSync application works in conjunction with HotSync Manager to provide a visual progression of your synchronization.

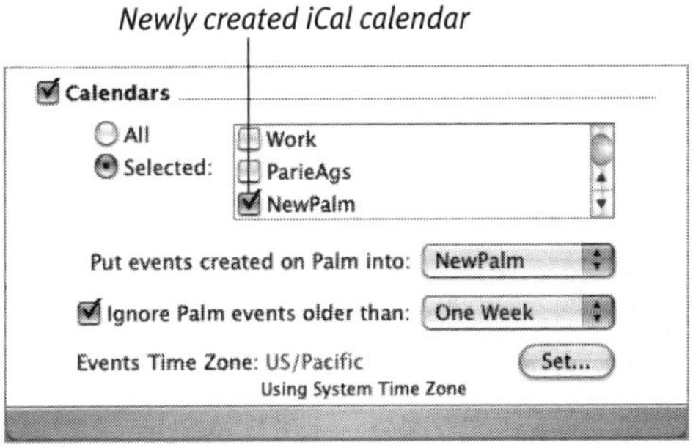

Newly created iCal calendar

Figure 3.49 If you want to synchronize your handheld's events to a new iCal calendar, create a new one first in iCal, then choose it in your device's settings in iSync.

Figure 3.50 Apple's iCal combines the data from your handheld's Calendar and Tasks applications.

Returning to Palm Desktop

If you decide you want to go back to using Palm Desktop as your primary repository of data, you'll have to do a little mining first. Go to Home > Library > Application Support > Palm HotSync > Conduits. Drag the Apple conduit to the Trash; you'll need to verify your administrator's password as this folder has a read-only permission setting. If you want to archive the conduit, drag it from the Trash to a Disabled Conduits folder in the same directory.

✔ Tips

■ In iCal, you can have multiple calendars, such as one for yourself, one for your wife, one for the kids, etc. Before you synchronize for the first time, you need to choose to which iCal calendar that events created in your device's Calendar will be mapped. If you want to merge your handheld's data with an existing calendar, choose that. But if you want to keep things separate, create a new calendar in iCal, then go to iSync and select that checkbox as well as choose it from the Put events created on Palm into a popup menu (**Figure 3.49**).

■ The Tasks application is synchronized with iCal. To view tasks, click the pushpin button in the lower-right corner to open iCal's To Do list (**Figure 3.50**).

■ Select an event or task in iCal, then click the information button (next to the push-pin) to open the editing drawer.

■ Synchronizing to Apple's tools has its benefits. In addition to synchronizing with your .Mac account, your Contacts and Calendar information will also be synchronized with other devices included in iSync, such as a Bluetooth-enabled cell phone. Also, iCal lets you see several calendars at once, making it easier to identify scheduling conflicts with other iCal users.

■ The downside to using iSync, iCal, and Address Book is that you'll be giving up a number of Palm OS features. For one, categories from either Contacts or Calendar aren't exported to Address Book or iCal. This is disappointing in light of Calendar's new color-coded categories—all events take on the color of your selected iCal calendar. You'll also have to utilize Palm Desktop to view items from the Memos application.

The Missing Sync for Palm OS

When PalmSource announced details for Palm OS Cobalt, they also revealed that it would stop supporting the Macintosh. Luckily, long-time Mac developer Mark/Space announced that it was working on software that would be able to replace PalmSource's HotSync technology for new handhelds using Cobalt with The Missing Sync for Palm OS 4.0 (www.markspace. com). (We'll just refer to it as Missing Sync for brevity.) It offers a number of improvements over PalmSource's HotSync software, as well as a few features that go beyond data synchronization: You can also synchronize with iPhoto images and AvantGo Web content. And it offers a direct Internet connection for downloading email.

The slight downside is that (at the moment) it's not free—it costs $40 new, or $20 if upgrading from a previous version. But we feel that the extra features, plus a vote of support for improving the HotSync architecture for the Mac, is well worth it. (PalmOne may include Missing Sync with Cobalt handhelds, but this has not been verified at this writing.)

Missing Sync features:

◆ Under HotSync Manager, if you wanted to prevent one or more conduits from operating during a HotSync operation, you'd have to set each excluded conduit's actions to "Do Nothing" in a separate dialog. In Missing Sync, you can disable a conduit by simply unchecking a checkbox (**Figure 3.51**).

◆ Most existing conduits work just as they do when using HotSync Manager. Double-clicking a conduit brings up the same controls (such as "Macintosh Overwrites Handheld") that are found in HotSync Manager (**Figure 3.52**).

Figure 3.51 Missing Sync's checkbox interface makes it easy to turn on and off specific conduits.

Figure 3.52 You can still access all the synchronization behavior options by double-clicking a conduit.

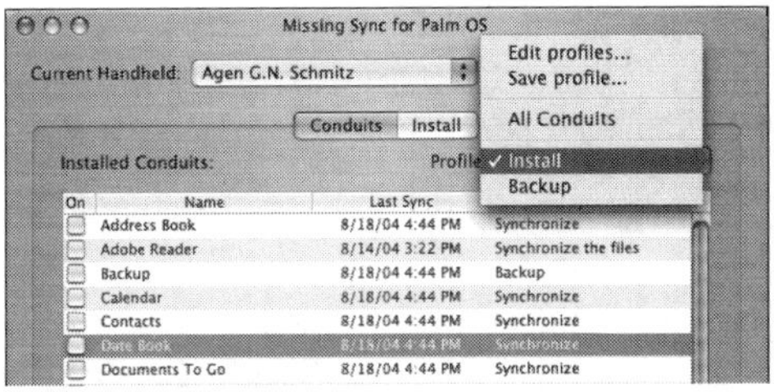

Figure 3.53 Create profiles for common synchronization routines (such as when you want to just install files or only back up the built-in applications).

Figure 3.54 Like HotSync Manager, Missing Sync provides a progress window.

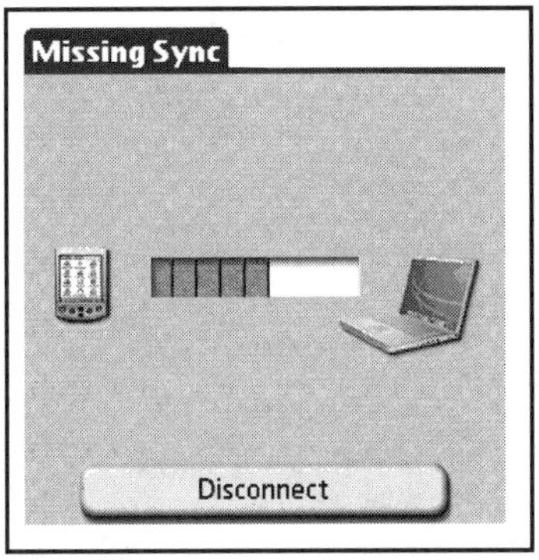

Figure 3.55 The minimalist Missing Sync Palm OS application is used to show connection to your Mac when mounting a memory card, not HotSync progression (the HotSync app does that).

◆ You can create profiles out of saved sets of active conduits. Missing Sync includes two preset profiles: Install, which only installs software during a HotSync operation, and Backup, which skips the other conduits and only backs up the handheld's data (**Figure 3.53**).

To install Missing Sync:

1. Follow the program's installation instructions from the mounted disk image.

2. After restarting your Mac, open Missing Sync and enter your handheld's name.

3. Connect your handheld and perform a HotSync (**Figure 3.54**). The Missing Sync .prc file will automatically be installed.

✔ Tips

■ The Missing Sync Palm OS application is used to mount your handheld's memory card like a disk in the Mac Finder, enabling you to drag and drop files directly to the card (**Figure 3.55**). This feature also enables you to view the memory card in iTunes, so you can transfer files directly from your MP3 library (see Chapter 11 for more on working with digital audio files).

■ If you've been missing your list of AvantGo Web sites on your handheld (due to no Mac OS X synchronization software), be sure to install the AvantGoFixer.prc file. See Chapter 10 for more about configuring Missing Sync and Avant Go.

■ If you do decide to uninstall Missing Sync and return to the original HotSync Manager, you'll have to reinstall the HotSync software from the CD-ROM that came with your handheld.

THE MISSING SYNC FOR PALM OS

To install files to your handheld:

1. In Missing Sync, click the Synchronization button, then the Install tab.

2. Drag files from the Finder to the Handheld or Secure Digital Card areas (**Figure 3.56**). Or, click the plus button and browse for files; click Open to add them.

3. Perform a HotSync.

✔ Tips

- If you decide to switch the location of a file, just drag it from one pane to the other. Select a file and click the minus button to delete it from the list.

- JPEG files can only be installed onto a memory card.

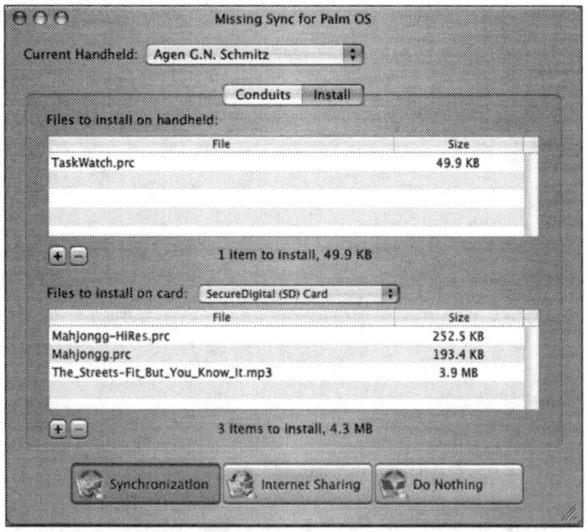

To set preferences:

1. Select Preferences from the Missing Sync menu, or press Command-, (**Figure 3.57**).

2. Mark the checkboxes for the types of HotSync connections you'll be making.

3. Turn on Enable synchronization/sharing at login, otherwise you must manually open Missing Sync to synchronize.

4. If you want to see the synchronization operation in action, mark the Show progress dialog during sync checkbox.

5. Set a reminder to synchronize your handheld by setting an alert and specifying how many days without a HotSync before it appears (**Figure 3.58**).

✔ Tip

- You can set up the same synchronization scheme with Apple's iCal and Address Book (as noted in the previous section). Missing Sync comes with a Memos standalone program, eliminating the need to open Palm Desktop.

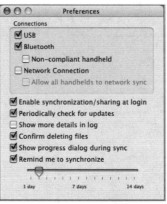

Figure 3.56 Drag files into the handheld or memory card panes to install them to your handheld.

Figure 3.57 Configure your Missing Sync preferences, including enabling synchronization without first having to manually open the program.

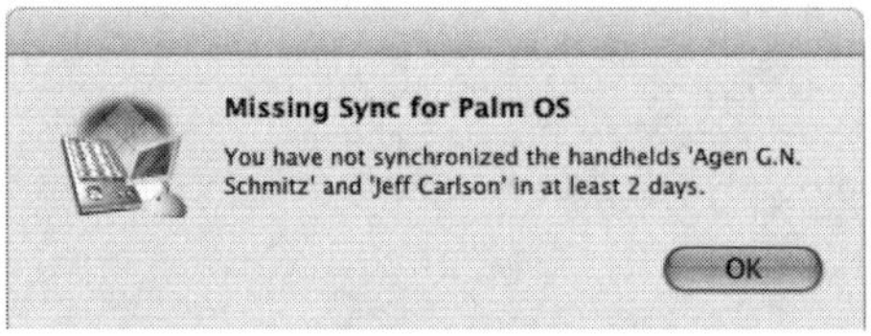

Figure 3.58 Now you won't have to set a reminder for yourself to keep your handheld synchronized— Missing Sync will do it for you.

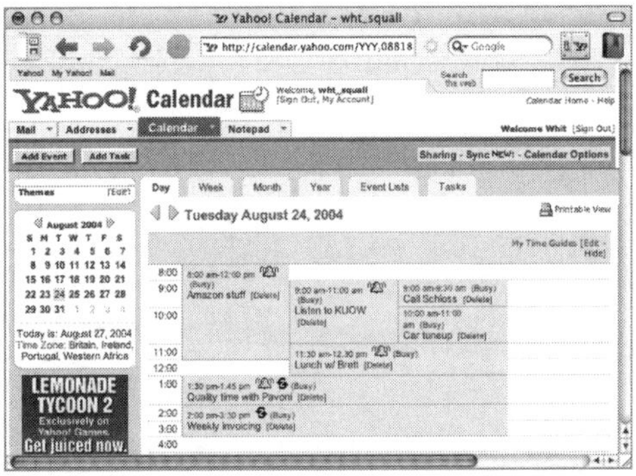

Figure 3.59 Intellisync for Yahoo! synchronizes your handheld data with both Palm Desktop (or other PIM of your choice) and Yahoo's Web-based calendar.

The Really Expensive Calculator

It may seem odd to use the Web to track your schedule, since that's what your handheld is for. Isn't this a step backward?

Rather, it's more like having the option to step to the side when needed. Jeff once took a trip to Britain and brought only one technology item: his PalmPilot. Like any good geek, he'd prepared and stored trip notes, emergency phone numbers, and a host of other important information. Unfortunately, while replacing the batteries at the train station in Chepstowe, things went all pear-shaped (as they say in the U.K.), and he lost his data! Normally, this would be no big deal, but his laptop was thousands of miles away.

If Jeff had put his data online, he could have connected the handheld to a PC at an Internet café later in Windermere (with the HotSync cable he inexplicably brought along), then restored his handheld's data. Instead, he carried around a very swanky calculator for two weeks.

Synchronizing with Web-Based Organizers

A handheld organizer is intended to be an extension of your personal data. But you can extend it even further by storing your calendar and contacts online, enabling you to check (or reload) your most important data from any place with a Web connection.

The original Palm-based service—MyPalm (www.palm.net)—was taken off the shelves as of September 1, 2004. However, there are other options, such as publishing an iCal calendar to your Apple .Mac account or the free Yahoo! Calendar (calendar.yahoo.com), which includes Intellisync software for Windows.

To set up a Yahoo! Web calendar:

1. If you don't already have a personal account set up, go to calendar.yahoo.com to set one up. It takes only a few minutes to get started.

2. Make sure you have a backup of your Palm data for safekeeping, then download and install the Intellisync for Yahoo! software.

3. Open the application and click the Setup button.

4. Select Palm handheld from the Choose Application dialog.

5. Select which conduits—Calendar, Contacts, Tasks, and/or Memos—to synchronize.

   If desired, double-click a conduit to specify advanced settings (such as resolving record conflicts or not synchronizing private data).

6. HotSync the device (**Figure 3.59**).

CALENDAR

Here's a hypothetical scenario that might sound familiar. Your mother (or other close relative or good friend) calls one night, and after updating her on current events, you inquire about what's new in her world. "Not much," she says. "We just finished my birthday cake." This, unfortunately, wasn't hypothetical for Jeff once.

Oops. So, some of our brains aren't hard-wired for dates and holidays. But, that doesn't mean you have to forever miss important events and appointments. That's where Calendar (formerly Date Book) comes in, helping you keep track of all your meetings, social occasions, holidays, *and* birthdays and anniversaries.

Plus, unlike the calendar that hangs in the kitchen, Calendar can remind you of events before they happen, not after. Our moms should be proud.

Setting Preferences and Display Options

The 160 by 160-pixel screen on many Palm devices can display 25,600 pixels, which sounds like a lot until you consider that the minimum PC screen resolution today is 640 by 480 pixels (or a total of 307,200 pixels). It's easy to see why every effort has been made to keep the Palm's small screen uncluttered yet understandable. Even on high-resolution displays, simplicity is key. Calendar displays time in daily, weekly, and monthly views. The amped up Agenda view displays a day's events with due (and overdue) tasks and even your VersaMail inbox (**Figure 4.1**).

Changing some of the display options allows you to specify how dense or sparse your calendar will appear.

To set Calendar preferences:

1. Select Preferences from the Options menu.

2. If you've ever wished you could set your own hours, here's your chance. Select the Start Time and End Time by tapping the arrows to the right of the time boxes (**Figure 4.2**).

3. The Preferences dialog also contains settings for Calendar's alarm. Checking Alarm Preset specifies that each new event includes an alarm, which will go off according to the number of minutes you specify.

4. You can also specify which sound the alarm will use, how often it plays when the alarm goes off, and at what interval it will play until you dismiss it.

5. Tap OK to return to the Calendar views.

Figure 4.1 Calendar displays your time (from top) in daily, weekly, and monthly views. The Agenda view (bottom) shows tasks as well.

Figure 4.2 Most people choose regular business hours. Checking the Alarm Preset box adds an alarm to each new event you create.

Figure 4.3 Select Show Category List (found when editing display preferences for Day or Month) to filter by category in the Day, Week, and Month views.

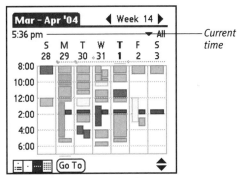

Current time

Figure 4.4 By turning on the Show Category List option, you'll also see the current time in the Day, Week, and Month views.

Display options

Display Options is split into three different screens with a mix of global and individual controls for Agenda, Day, and Month views. The biggest global addition to Calendar is the inclusion of categories and a popup menu that can filter Day and Month views. (We'll cover individual settings within each view section over the next few pages.)

To set global display preferences:

1. Choose Display Options from the Options menu or write ∕ -Y.

2. Tap the Default View popup to choose which Calendar screen will be your default: Agenda, Day, Week, or Month.

3. To add functionality to sort based on categories within the Day, Week, and Month views, mark the Show Category List option—found only when viewing options for Day or Month (**Figure 4.3**).

4. Tap OK to return to the Calendar views.

✔ Tips

- The Show Category List option provides a small bonus—a display of the current time on the Week and Month views (**Figure 4.4**). The current date joins the time display when today's date is selected in Day view.

- For those times when manipulating the stylus is inconvenient, or just to save time, press the Calendar button on the case to switch between views.

SETTING PREFERENCES AND DISPLAY OPTIONS

Agenda View

Recognizing that what you do is often tied to when you do it, the Agenda view brings together your day's events as well as tasks that are coming due (**Figure 4.5**). If you download email to your handheld (either via HotSync or a direct connection), you can choose to display the VersaMail email program's inbox. Tap the first box in the bottom-left corner to bring up Agenda view.

To view events from Agenda view:

◆ Tap an appointment to switch to the Day view, where it will be actively selected.

To manage tasks from Agenda view:

◆ Tap a task to switch to the Date view in the Tasks application, a new addition in Palm OS 5.2.1 and later that displays only those tasks due on a specific date (see Chapter 6).

◆ Tap the checkbox at the left to mark the task completed, and it disappears from the Agenda view (even when you have Show Completed Tasks selected in the Tasks application).

To view email from Agenda view:

◆ Tap a message to switch to the VersaMail inbox.

✔ Tips

■ Yes, though this book isn't in color, those are colored dots next to the events. Palm OS 5.2 introduces color-coded categories, which we cover later in this chapter.

■ Up to three tasks are displayed. If you have more tasks due (or overdue), you'll see the two tasks displayed with checkboxes and a note as to the number of past due tasks.

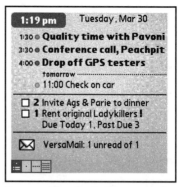

Figure 4.5 View the day's events, tasks, and email in the Agenda view. With Tasks displayed, you'll see the two most current tasks as well as a summary of the number due—or overdue.

Figure 4.6 Set Agenda view display options, including the ability to add a background image.

3:04 pm	Tuesday, Mar 30
3:30 ● **Conference call, Peachpit**	
4:00 ● **Drop off GPS testers**	
tomorrow	
● 11:00 Check on car	
● 1:00 Coffee	
● 4:00 Doc appn	
thursday	
● 11:00 Bank	
● 2:00 Help files – finalize	
● 4:00 Pick up Kim	

Figure 4.7 Focus just on upcoming Calendar appointments by deselecting display for Tasks and Messages.

To set Agenda view display options:

1. Choose Display Options from the Options menu or write ∕ -Y. Tap the Agenda tab to access preferences for this view.

2. Disable Show Due Tasks or Show Messages to eliminate their listings from the Agenda view.

3. Tap the image box to select an image file stored either on your device or an expansion card. Use the Fade slider to adjust the opacity so it's not too dark, thus rendering the Agenda unreadable (**Figure 4.6**).

   Or, disable Background Image to display a blank white background in Agenda view.

4. Tap OK to return to the Calendar views.

✔ Tips

- If you own a camera-equipped Zire 72, you can use a stored image as your background. For non-camera Palms, the Windows AgendaVU shareware application (www.cushysoft.com) enables you to create your own background themes.

- It's best to choose a background image saved to your handheld's internal memory—without the memory card, you'll have a blank background.

- By deselecting the display for Tasks and Messages, you'll be able to view more upcoming appointments, including those occurring during the next day or two (**Figure 4.7**).

- The ability to sort tasks by category from Date Book's Agenda view was not ported over to this new version. Also, Tasks are not color-coded—only Calendar items include the colored dot.

AGENDA VIEW

Day View

The Day view is where you'll enter and edit events, and generally manage your schedule (**Figure 4.8**). Access it from the other Calendar views by tapping the second box (containing one dot) in the lower-left corner of the screen.

Day view features

◆ Events of the day appear on the dotted lines beside their allotted times, which adjust to conform to your schedule (a meeting ending at 10:15, for example, is marked as such, instead of displaying somewhere before 11:00). If there isn't enough space on the screen to view all your events, the Calendar removes any unused lines. To disable this feature, deselect Compress Day View in the Display Options dialog box (**Figure 4.9**).

◆ If you want to display the colored category dots—which really don't take up much room—mark the Show Category Column option.

◆ If you select Show Time Bars in the Display Options dialog box, the black brackets at left will indicate an event's time span—a handy way to see if you've scheduled overlapping events.

◆ Tap the days of the week buttons at the top of the screen to switch days. Tapping the arrows on either side of the buttons moves you forward or backward in weekly increments.

◆ The icons at right signify that an event contains a note (🗋), an alarm (🔔), or that it is a repeating event (🗐). Tapping either the alarm or repeating icon opens up the Event Details screen; tapping the note icon opens the note.

Figure 4.8 Calendar's Day view makes the best of its limited screen real estate, displaying elements such as time bars, icons, and colored category dots while hiding unused time lines.

Figure 4.9 The Day view Display Options add the ability to show the category column.

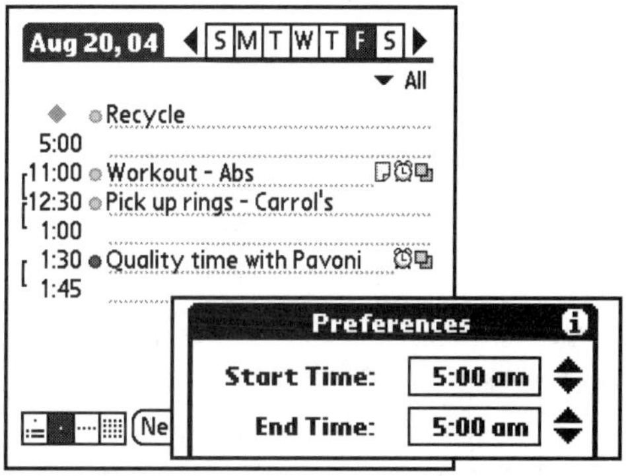

Figure 4.10 Setting the Start Time and End Time to the same hour displays only the lines that contain events. Because the starting time will appear if a day's schedule isn't completely full of items, be sure to select a start time that best works for your schedule.

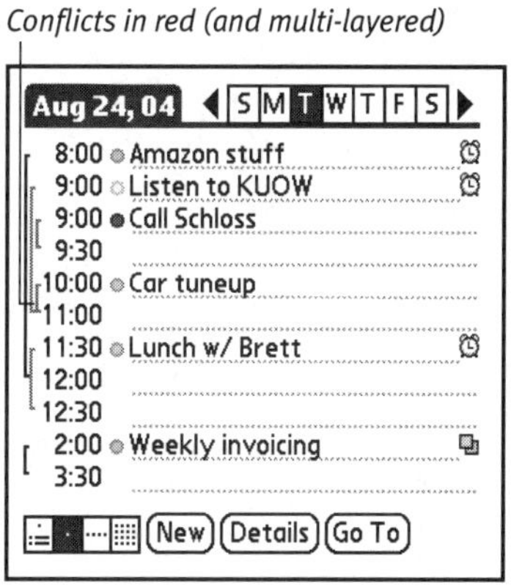

Conflicts in red (and multi-layered)

Figure 4.11 A subtle but helpful touch on color devices is the red time bar indicating conflicting appointments.

✔ Tips

- Tap a time to open the Set Time screen and start creating a new Calendar event. Or, if you need to adjust the time of a previously created event, tap its beginning time and make your adjustments in Set Time.

- With no event selected, press the up and down buttons to scroll to the top or bottom of the Day view screen (helpful if you have a lot of events scheduled on a particular day). Press the center button to select the top-most displayed event on the screen (the text cursor appears at the end of the event title), then use the up/down buttons to move from event to event. The left and right buttons move you from day to day, whether an event is selected or not.

- If you press the center button while in a selected event with a note, the note's contents screen opens. Press the center button again to return to Day view.

- If you're the type of person who can't stand any clutter on your desktop, and are bothered by all the extra dotted lines of non-event-filled time, there is a way to tidy things up. Set the Start Time and End Time to the same hour to display only existing events (**Figure 4.10**). Note, however, that the starting time will appear on days when scheduled items are light.

- On color devices, red time bars indicate time conflicts between appointments (**Figure 4.11**).

DAY VIEW

Week View

Viewing an entire day's schedule is helpful, but we often want to know what's coming up during the week without having to switch between multiple Day views. To get an idea of your schedule's density, display the Week view by tapping the third box (containing a line of four dots) in the lower-left corner.

Week view features

◆ Events in the Week view are represented by colored bars that span vertically across the displayed hours. If the appointments overlap, the blocks become narrower and sit side-by-side on the week's grid. If you have several items happening at once, subsequent events are displayed with a diagonal pattern (**Figure 4.12**).

◆ To see what a particular block indicates, tap it once to bring up a floating window at the top of the screen containing the description you entered in the Day view, its specific time span, location, and category (**Figure 4.13**). Double-tapping a bar opens the Day view to that event.

◆ Tapping the arrows in the upper-right corner of the screen moves you forward or backward one week, indicating the week's number in the year. Pressing the up or down button on the device case also shifts between weeks.

◆ Tapping the weekday abbreviations at the top of the screen switches to the Day view for that day. The current day is bold.

◆ A small diamond to the immediate left of a day's date (beneath the weekday abbreviation) indicates an untimed event. It will appear as the color of its assigned category.

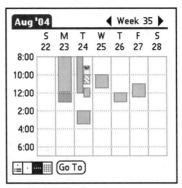

Figure 4.12 The Week view isn't necessarily a weak view: Time blocks show how busy your week is, with overlapping events shown as thin bars. If you have several items occurring at the same time, you'll see a diagonal pattern.

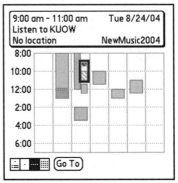

Figure 4.13 Deciphering the identity of a time block is easy—tapping one brings up its description at the top. If you tap on a multiple event cluster, only the first event is displayed.

First repeating event

Untimed event

Second repeating event

Earlier event

End of second repeating event

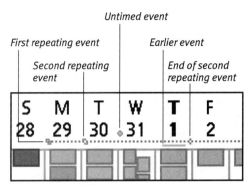

Figure 4.14 The top of the Week view displays a lot of tiny details denoting untimed and repeating events as well as appointments that come before or after the currently displayed time grid.

◆ Unlike the Day view, the week grid does not compress to fit all events onto one screen. Items appearing before or after the visible 11-hour period are indicated by a solid horizontal line appearing above or below the day's column. You can scroll to these events by tapping the arrows in the lower-right corner.

◆ Between the date and the top of the week grid you'll find repeating events. A solid, light blue repeating event icon denotes its beginning; it's followed by a dotted line until it finishes with another icon. If a second repeating event begins within the duration of the first, a gray icon appears within the dotted line (**Figure 4.14**).

✔ Tips

■ The Week view does not have settings of its own in Display Options—just the global Show Category List.

■ The five-way navigator becomes very helpful with the Week view. Press the left and right buttons to move from week to week; if you have events residing outside the default grid, press the up and down buttons to view them. If you're viewing the current week, pressing the center button selects the first event for today's date (if in another week, it selects the first event of that week). With an event selected, the up/down and left/right buttons move from event block to event block (displaying the details at the top). Press the center button again to open an event in the Day view.

■ The biggest disappointment in the move from Date Book to Calendar is the Week view—which has definitely become weaker. In addition to not being able to tap and drag event blocks to another point within the same week, you can't even tap an empty time to create a new event.

WEEK VIEW

113

Month View

So, you're the type of person who likes to see the big picture? The Month view is your viewfinder, although at first glance you may think you've stumbled upon Morse code: Who added all those dots? Tap the fourth box in the lower-left corner (containing a grid of 16 dots) to switch to the Month view.

Month view features

◆ This screen displays the entire month in a typical calendar format, with the days of the week running along the top of each column. Today's date, if you're viewing the current month, shows up as white text within a black square (**Figure 4.15**).

◆ To move forward and backward among months, tap the arrows at the top-right corner of the screen, or press the left and right buttons on the five-way navigator.

◆ Thanks to the new color-coded categories, event blocks are indicated by colored blocks on the day in which they occur. Due to a lack of space, events are noted by the period of the day they occur: morning, midday, and evening. Similar to the Week view, this gives you an idea of the density of your schedule (**Figure 4.16**). Note that a day in Month view will only display one bar for that part of the day, even if you have multiple appointments. However, if the events have different categories assigned to them, the block will actually display all the colors (though at such a tiny size, it may be hard to discern what's what).

◆ If the Daily Repeating Events setting is checked in Display Options (**Figure 4.17**), repeating events show up as a line of dots running along the bottom of the days they occupy. This option, the equivalent of "banners" in most desktop calendar programs, is off by default.

Figure 4.15 Your entire schedule is displayed using a minimum of space.

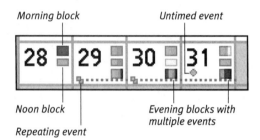

Figure 4.16 Realizing the limitations of their screen, Palm's designers opted for a "less is more" approach to Calendar's Month view. A closer look reveals the Month view's event blocks divided into multiple colors (up to three—see the 31st) when multiple category events occur during the same period of the day.

Figure 4.17 Mark Daily Repeating Events to display the dotted line running along the bottom of a day in Month view.

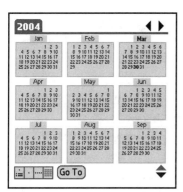

Figure 4.18 Use the Year view to see a global vista of the year to come or jump quickly to another month.

◆ An untimed event (if selected to be shown in Display Options) appears as a small diamond icon in the color of its category, immediately beneath a day's date.

✔ Tips

■ If you want to see just untimed and repeating events, leave them checked, then unmark Timed Events in Display Options.

■ Press the navigator's right and left buttons to move from month to month. Press the center button to select today's day if you're viewing the current month; for other months, you'll select the first of the month. With a day selected, you can use the up/down and left/right buttons to navigate through the calendar day by day. Press the center button again to open that date's events in the Day view.

Year View

Calendar adds the Year view—found previously in Handspring's Date Book+—which displays six months per screen. It's not terribly functional, but it does provide you with a global view of the calendar as well as an easy way to jump from month to month (**Figure 4.18**).

✔ Tips

■ Access the Year view by tapping the Year button at the bottom of the Month view, or selecting it from the Options menu while in the Agenda, Day, or Week view.

■ Pressing the center navigator button selects the current month (if it resides in the displayed half of the year) or the first month that's displayed. Use the directional buttons to move from month to month, then press the center button again to open its Month view.

Changing the Display Font

You can specify which font is used to display event text in the Day view to help make things more readable.

To change the display font:

1. Select Font from the Options menu (or write ✏-F).

2. Tap one of the font styles in the Select Font window (**Figure 4.19**). Tap OK.

✔ Tips

■ PalmOne devices with Palm OS 5.2 feature four text sizes, while most older models (save early high-resolution Tungsten models) include three sizes.

■ Choosing a font size presents a bit of give-and-take on your part. Choosing one of the two large fonts will definitely make the text jump out at you, but you'll need to scroll up and down the screen more. However, if a bold font is more readable, choosing the second smallest font is a good choice. The smaller two fonts are essentially the same size—one being plain Roman, the other bold—and thus present the same amount of information on the screen.

Figure 4.19 The largest font makes events more readable, but you'll need to scroll more to see all your events.

Go To Date

◀ **2004** ▶

Jan	Feb	Mar	Apr	May	Jun
Jul	Aug	Sep	Oct	Nov	Dec

S	M	T	W	T	F	S
					1	2
3	4	5	6	7	8	9
10	11	12	13	14	15	**16**
17	18	19	20	21	22	23
24	25	26	27	28	29	30
31						

(Cancel)   (Today)

Go To Date

◀ **2004** ▶

Jan	Feb	Mar	Apr	May	Jun
Jul	Aug	Sep	Oct	Nov	Dec

S	M	T	W	T	F	S
					1	2
3	4	5	6	7	8	9
10	11	12	13	14	15	16
17	18	19	20	21	22	23
24	25	26	27	28	29	30
31						

(Cancel)   (This Week)

Go To Date

◀ **2004** ▶

Jan	Feb	Mar	Apr	May	Jun
Jul	Aug	Sep	Oct	Nov	Dec

S	M	T	W	T	F	S
					1	2
3	4	5	6	7	8	9
10	11	12	13	14	15	16
17	18	19	20	21	22	23
24	25	26	27	28	29	30
31						

(Cancel)   (This Month)

Figure 4.20 Tapping the Go To button brings up the day (top), week (middle), and month (bottom) navigation screens, depending on your previous view.

Calendar Navigation: Jumping Through Time

We've become so dependent upon our handhelds for scheduling that if an event isn't in Calendar, then it isn't happening. (This approach has prevented many event conflicts!) As a result, we find ourselves frequently looking ahead to specific dates, a process the Palm designers have streamlined pretty well.

To jump to specific dates:

1. From any Calendar view, tap the Go To button. The Go To Date dialog is context sensitive, based on your previous view. So, the Day view gives you the option to jump to a specific day, the Week view jumps to weeks, and the Month view jumps to months (**Figure 4.20**).

2. Select a year using the arrows at the top of the page.

3. Select a month and a date or week. (If you came from the Month view, selecting the month will take you there immediately.)

   If you've been time-traveling and want to get back to the present, tap the Today, This Week, or This Month button.

✔ Tips

- The Year view also features a Go To button, but it duplicates the Day view's Go To Date dialog.

- Only the up/down navigator buttons work in the Go To Date dialog, moving you from month to month.

- A faster method of jumping to today's date is to press the Calendar button on the handheld's case—the first press will return you to today's Agenda view (if marked as the default view in Display Options) from anywhere in the Calendar.

Entering and Deleting Calendar Events

Calendar allows you to enter legible events quickly, using a variety of methods—and delete them just as easily without the mess of strikethroughs and scribbles that you've become accustomed to in your old-time paper organizer.

To enter an event using the New button:

1. In the Day view, tap the New button to bring up the Set Time dialog box. You can also choose New Event from the Record menu, or write ∕ - N in Graffiti.

2. Specify a starting time. If you tap the Start Time box, the day's beginning time (from Calendar's Preferences) is entered by default. The time in the End Time box automatically sets to one hour after the Start Time. Tap on an hour and minute (the first and second vertical columns) to change the Start Time (**Figure 4.21**). The All Day button enters the time span you set up in the preferences.

   You can also elect to create an untimed event by tapping OK before specifying Start and End Times, or by tapping the No Time button if those fields are already filled. Anniversaries and other holidays work best as untimed events.

3. Change the End Time, if desired, and tap OK.

4. Write a descriptive title (**Figure 4.22**).

✔ Tip

■ A slightly faster way to enter an event is to tap directly on one of the times running down the left side of the display.

Figure 4.21 Splitting the time into two vertical bars may appear odd at first, but this approach puts the controls in a smooth path for your stylus.

Figure 4.22 After exiting the Set Time screen, go ahead and give your event a descriptive title.

Figure 4.23 Tap directly on the time you wish to create an event for, and bypass the Set Time dialog.

To enter an event by naming it on the appropriate line:

1. The quickest method for creating a new record is to tap the line belonging to the time you wish to use. Calendar creates a one-hour event and positions the text cursor on the line for you to name the record: No dialog boxes or OK buttons are involved (**Figure 4.23**).

2. Enter the text of your new event by writing in the Graffiti area or opening the Keyboard from the Edit menu. To modify the event's time, tap either the time itself or the Details button.

✔ Tips

- As noted previously, you can't create new events while in Week view—you must return to the Day view.

- If you're feeling like a hunter-gatherer while poking at all of these buttons and locations, consider using a more expressive method to enter Calendar events. In the Day view, begin writing your event's Start Time using Graffiti's number-entry area (the right portion). A new record will be created at that time.

- A similar approach is to just start writing the title of a new appointment in Graffiti. An untimed event appears; use the Details button or tap the time to schedule it.

- Tired of pecking at the vertical hour and minute columns in the Set Time dialog box? Write Graffiti numerals that will show up in the Start Time box (and also in the End Time box after selecting it).

- Create an event with the same start and end time to avoid overlapping other events, such as for task-oriented events (like weekly recycling). See Chapter 6 for more on scheduling task reminders.

"Pencil-in" Events

One capability missing from paper-based organizers is the ability to "pencil in" an event, which you can then confirm later. In Calendar, temporary and confirmed appointments show up the same. What we'd really like to see is the ability to write an event in gray, but until that day comes, here's a simple workaround using the Palm OS's ShortCut feature (**Figures 4.24a**, **4.24b**, and **4.24c**).

To add a "pencil-in" event:

1. From the Applications screen, launch the Prefs utility and select ShortCuts from the popup menu in the upper-right corner.

2. Tap New and name your ShortCut something like "pn".

3. Figure out how you'd like penciled items to display—we've always liked the curly brackets, so we enter both characters under ShortCut Text.

4. Tap OK and return to Calendar.

5. When you want to create a penciled-in event, preface its title with the ShortCut you just created. In this case, the brackets appear and we double-tap "text" to select it and begin writing to replace it.

6. When the event is confirmed, remember to remove the "pencil-in" notation.

✔ Tip

■ While the Palm OS's color support doesn't let you create events in gray, DateBk5 (www.pimlicosoftware.com) does: Create an event, tap the Details button, then tap the Font field to set the color. You can also set up a template to create new penciled-in events.

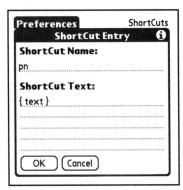

Figure 4.24a Set up your "pencil-in" notation by creating a ShortCut in the Palm OS Preferences application.

Figure 4.24b Write the Graffiti characters you set up as a ShortCut, then enter the event's title.

Figure 4.24c Your event is now easily recognizable as a temporary date/time. After confirming the specifics, remove the "pencil-in" notation.

"PENCIL-IN" EVENTS

Figure 4.25 You can easily change the date and time of any event by accessing the Event Details window.

Figure 4.26 If you don't want an event taking up valuable memory in your handheld, you can keep a copy of it on your PC's hard drive.

Editing and Deleting Existing Events

Once created, events aren't set in stone. The ways to change their attributes are as varied as creating new appointments.

To change an event's time and/or date (the long way):

1. In the Day view, tap a record to select it, then tap the Details button.

2. In the Event Details screen, tap the Time field or the Date field (**Figure 4.25**).

3. Adjust the time in the Set Time window, and the date in the Set Date window.

To change an event's time (the short way):

1. In the Day view, tap on the time to the left of the event you wish to edit.

2. Adjust the time in the Set Time window.

To delete an event:

1. In the Day view, tap the event to select it and then tap the Details button.

2. In the Event Details screen, tap Delete, choose Delete Event from the Record menu, or write ╱-D .

3. If you want the record to be saved on your PC the next time you perform a HotSync, be sure to mark the Save archive copy on PC option; uncheck the box to banish it forever (**Figure 4.26**).

✔ Tip

■ You can simply delete the text from an event to erase it from your Palm and Palm Desktop (on your next HotSync). But this doesn't work with items with notes or repeating events—you just get a blank event with the attached icons.

EDITING AND DELETING EVENTS

Setting Alarms

Remember the days of carrying a travel alarm clock? They're long gone, friend.

To set an alarm:

1. After you've created an event, tap Details and mark the Alarm checkbox.

2. Choose the amount of time before the event that the alarm should go off. Minutes is the default, but you can also select Hours or Days (**Figure 4.27**).

To respond to an alarm:

♦ Tap OK to dismiss the Reminder screen when the alarm activates (**Figure 4.28**).

♦ Tap the Snooze button to give yourself a few extra minutes before the alarm goes off again. A small indicator at the upper-left corner of the screen indicates the impending alarm.

♦ Tap the Go To button to display the event in Calendar.

To change alarm options:

1. Go to the Calendar Preferences dialog box (choose Preferences from the Options menu, or write ╱-R).

2. Choose your favorite Alarm Sound.

3. Choose the "snooze" options: Remind Me specifies how often the alarm will go off before you dismiss it. Play Every sets the time between reminders (**Figure 4.29**).

✔ Tip

■ You can delete an event by simply selecting its text and deleting it—it magically disappears from Palm Desktop on your next HotSync. But if it's a repeating event or has a note attached, you'll have a blank record.

Figure 4.27 Traffic likely to be bad? Specify a longer time period for the alarm to go off before an event.

Figure 4.28 The alarm's Reminder screen appears before an event, accompanied by a cheerful chime.

Figure 4.29 Calendar gives you several options for alarms, including repeating reminders and seven different sounds.

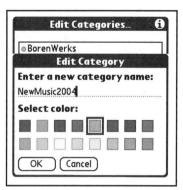

Figure 4.30 Create a new category and assign a groovy color to it.

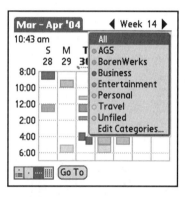

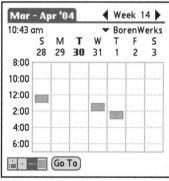

Figure 4.31 Filter only the events you need to see. The top screen shows all events from all categories, while the bottom screen displays only items from the BorenWerks category.

Color-Coded Categories

Like the old Chicago song, Calendar can color your world with color-coded categories, which helps you quickly scan your appointments to see what your day will be like. Category colors show up as small dots in a variety of places: to the left of the time in the Agenda view; in a column between the time and event in the Day view; and as colored blocks in the Week and Month views. These colors manifest themselves automatically, save for Day view (which requires you to select the preference in Display Options).

To create a custom, color-coded category:

1. Tap an event, then tap the Details button at the bottom of the screen.

2. Tap the category popup menu and select Edit Categories.

3. Select a current category from the list and tap the Edit button, or tap the New button.

4. Modify or write a new entry, then tap one of the 16 color boxes to select it as the category color (**Figure 4.30**).

5. Tap OK to accept the changes, then OK again to return to the Event Details.

To filter categories:

1. With Show Category List enabled, tap the category filter popup menu in the upper-right corner of either the Day, Week, or Month view.

2. Tap the category you wish to filter, or tap All to see a complete view of entries (**Figure 4.31**).

✔ Tips

- With Show Category Column turned on, tap the category dot in Day view to display a category popup menu, from which you can modify the event's grouping (**Figure 4.32**). You can't, however, perform this same maneuver in the Agenda view. Also, you'll still need to return to the category popup in Event Details to create new or modify existing categories.

- Colored categories are limited to Calendar, and are not applied to Contacts or Tasks (though we wish they were).

- Category colors are mandatory (no clear categories are allowed), and you can choose from just the 16 colors on hand.

Location

Ye olde Date Book, Calendar's predecessor, always provided the ability to remind yourself of where a meeting was to take place: Just attach a note. But Calendar has added the new Location field, which is more easily accessible than fishing for a note by tapping.

In the Event Details screen, simply write your meeting spot in the Location field (**Figure 4.33**). You'll see it appear at the end of the event's text in Day view, and in the floating window when you tap on an event block in Week view (**Figure 4.34**).

✔ Tips

- Funnily enough, tapping on an event that's displaying a location in the Day view makes the location's text disappear.

- Calendar remembers the locations you enter. Start writing a location you've used before, and the closest match appears highlighted in the field. Keep writing to narrow it down.

Figure 4.32 Change an event's category by tapping the category dot on the Day view.

Figure 4.33 With the Location field, you won't need to create a note to remind yourself where a meeting will take place.

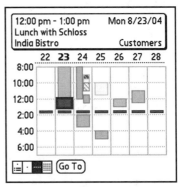

Figure 4.34 Tap a block in Week view to see a floating display of the event with the location in the bottom-left corner.

Change Repeat ℹ

None | Day | Week | Month | Year

Every: ....1 **Week(s)**

End on: ▼ Sat 10/16/04

Repeat on: S M T W T F S

Every week on Tuesday

(OK) (Cancel)

Figure 4.35 Why manually add the same events over and over? Repeating events allow you to specify multiple days of the week, among other options.

Change Repeat ℹ

None | Day | Week | Month | Year

Every: ....1 **Month(s)**

End on: ▼ No End Date

Repeat by: Day | Date

The last Tuesday of every month

(OK) (Cancel)

Figure 4.36 Calendar is smart enough to base the repeated event upon the date that's selected.

Day view

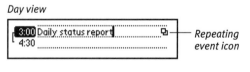

— *Repeating event icon*

Month view

Figure 4.37 Repeated events are shown with an icon in the Day view, and a dotted line in the Month view.

Creating Repeating Events

Scheduling one-off appointments and reminders is a great use for Calendar, but the best reason to own a Palm OS device is to easily keep track of recurring events.

To create a repeating event:

1. Select an event and tap the Details button.

2. Tap the Repeat popup menu and choose whether the event is a daily, weekly, bi-weekly, monthly, or yearly. Or, tap Other to manually modify the repetition via the Change Repeat dialog (**Figure 4.35**).

3. In the Change Repeat dialog, specify if the event is a daily, weekly, monthly, or yearly event by tapping one of the boxes at the top of the screen.

4. Write the numerical frequency of the event in the Every field.

5. If the event stops repeating on a certain date, select Choose Date from the End on popup menu; otherwise, leave it set to No End Date.

6. Depending on your selection in step 3, you can specify additional event criteria.

   Weekly events can be set to repeat on one day or multiple days by tapping in the appropriate Repeat on boxes.

   Monthly events can be repeated by day ("The 1st Wednesday of every month") or by date ("The 5th of every month") (**Figure 4.36**).

   Yearly events, by default, are set to repeat according to the date of the first event.

7. Tap OK to exit the dialog; you'll see the repeating event icon appear to the right of your record in the Day view, and a dotted line in the Week and Month views (the latter if Daily Repeating Events is selected in Display Options) (**Figure 4.37**).

To change a repeating event:

1. Tap any occurrence (you don't have to edit the first record you create) to select it, then tap the Details button.

2. Make any changes you like, including time, date, or attached notes, then tap OK.

3. Choose whether you wish to apply the change to the Current record, All occurrences of the event, or if you'd rather Cancel (**Figure 4.38**).

   The Future option leaves past occurrences intact and applies the changes only to the current and future repetitions.

   If you only change the title of the event, the change is automatically applied to all occurrences without displaying the Repeating Event dialog box.

✔ Tips

■ Tap the repeating event icon in Day view to open an event.

■ What about those events, like Thanksgiving, that occur yearly but are based on a particular day of the week? Since the yearly repeat option only specifies the event's date, you have to out-think Calendar. Set up a monthly repeat that occurs every 12 months, and choose Repeat by Day (**Figure 4.39**).

■ Where scheduling an important recurring event such as a birthday once required a bit of a workaround, Palm OS 5.2 makes it easy peasy. The Contacts application now includes a Birthday field with an alarm that lets you set how far ahead you want to be reminded of the special day.

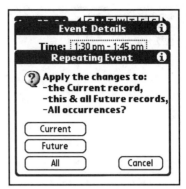

Figure 4.38 If you change an existing repeating event, you're asked how you prefer to implement the changes.

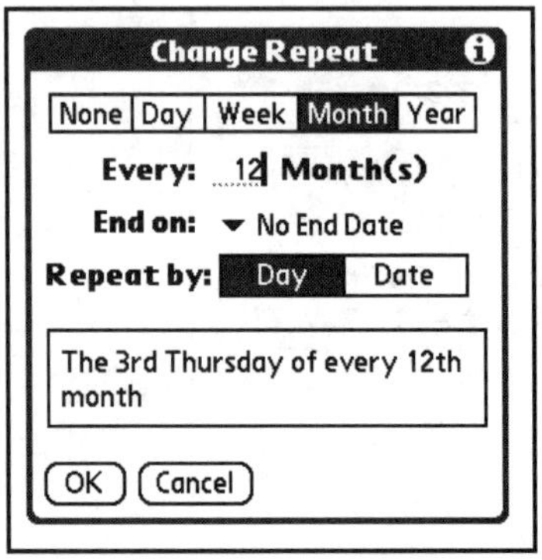

Figure 4.39 Yearly occasions that fall on a particular day of the week, such as Thanksgiving or Labor Day, can be set up as monthly, not yearly, repeating events.

Event Details
Time: 11:30 am - 12:30 pm
Date: Tue 8/24/04
Alarm: 5 Minutes
Location: In Karma
Category: Personal
Repeat: None
Private:
OK
Cancel
Delete...

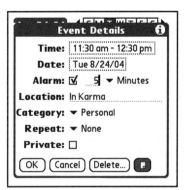

Figure 4.40 Tap the Note button in the Event Details window to attach more text to an event.

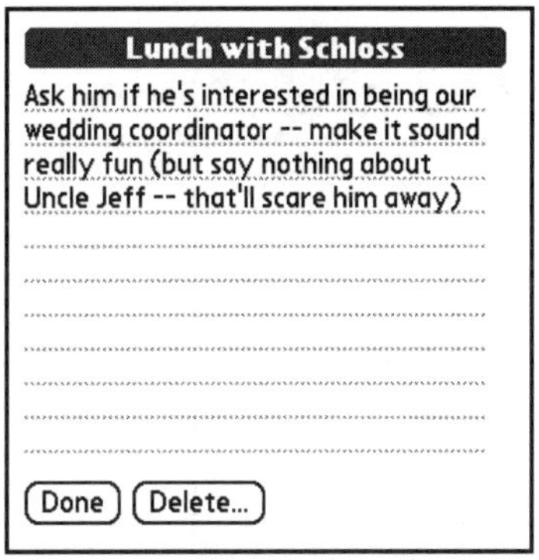

Lunch with Schloss
Ask him if he's interested in being our wedding coordinator -- make it sound really fun (but say nothing about Uncle Jeff -- that'll scare him away)
Done
Delete...

Figure 4.41 A new note presents you with a slightly limited version of the Memos application.

Lunch with Schloss
Ask him if he's interested in being our wedding coordinator -- make it sound really fun (but say nothing about Uncle Jeff -- that'll scare him away)
Delete Note
Delete current note?
Yes
No

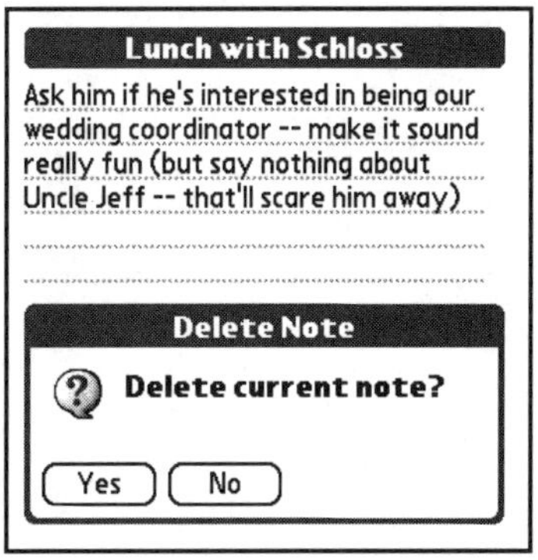

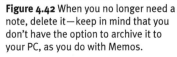

Figure 4.42 When you no longer need a note, delete it—keep in mind that you don't have the option to archive it to your PC, as you do with Memos.

Attaching and Deleting Notes

Initially, the ability to attach notes to an event seemed a superfluous add-on. But they've not only become very helpful to us for jotting random thoughts in context, they're also indispensable for storing information that will be needed at a specific time. Oh, and they're good for recording snide (er, *constructive*) comments during a meeting.

To attach a note to an event:

1. Tap an event to select it.
2. Tap the Details button, then tap Note.

   Alternately, choose Attach Note from the Record menu, or write /-A.
3. Compose your note using Graffiti or the onscreen keyboard (**Figures 4.40** and **4.41**).
4. When you are finished, tap Done.

To delete a note:

1. In the Day view, choose Delete Note from the Record menu, or write /-O.

   Or, if you're on the note editing screen, tap the Delete button. The Delete Note dialog box appears.
2. Click Yes or No to confirm if you really want to delete the note (**Figure 4.42**).

✔ Tips

- To edit the attached note later, follow the steps above to access the note. If you want a quicker method, however, go to the Day view and tap the note icon (▢) to the right of the event's name.
- Attached notes in Calendar behave much like Memos. See Chapter 6 for more on navigating notes.

Performing a Phone Lookup

Luckily for those of us who value good data, the built-in applications don't live independently of each other. One of the handier features employed in the Palm OS is the ability to perform phone number lookups from Contacts while in a Calendar item.

To perform a phone lookup:

1. If you know the name of the person you're scheduling an event with (such as "Coffee with Pedro Finn"), write his or her name into a field in the Day view.

   If you don't know the person's name, just leave that part blank (i.e., "Coffee with").

2. Choose Phone Lookup from the Options menu, or write ∕-L.

3. If a name in Contacts matches the name you wrote, the phone number will be added to your event's description. If not, or if you didn't specify a name, scroll through the list of names and highlight the one you want (**Figure 4.43**).

4. Tap Add to include the phone number in the Calendar record (**Figure 4.44**).

✔ Tips

- The Palm OS searches for last names when performing a lookup, so you can write a person's last name and, if theirs is the only instance of that name, the phone number will appear without making a trip to the Contacts screen.

- Remember, this function searches for last names—even a unique first name (we can't think of any at this time) won't show up if selected for a Phone Lookup.

Figure 4.43 Finally, contact information that's convenient to contact. Performing a phone lookup lists the names in your Contacts with phone numbers.

Figure 4.44 The looked-up number automatically gets added to the time line you created.

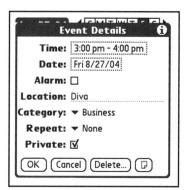

Figure 4.45a Tap the Private checkbox to keep an event safe from curious onlookers.

Event Details
Private Records

You have marked this record Private. Go to the Security application or the Security menu item and choose Mask Records or Hide Records to mask or hide all Private records.

OK

Figure 4.45b If the Current Privacy setting in the Security application is set to Show Records, you are reminded that the event is not yet hidden.

Aug 27, 04 S M T W T F S All
8:00
9:00
10:00
11:00
Change Security
Current
Privacy: Show Records
          Mask Records
          Hide Records
OK Can...

Figure 4.46 Under Palm OS 3.5 and later, changing the security setting alters it in every application.

Marking Events Private

In this era of identity theft, it's even more important to keep sensitive information (even a friend's phone number from a Phone Lookup) close to the vest. (It's also useful for events such as "Buy diamond ring.")

When you mark Calendar events as private, their appearance depends on the state of the Current Privacy option in the Palm OS's Security application. If you've specified an alarm for a hidden private record, a Reminder screen will still appear when scheduled.

To mark events private:

1. Select an event and tap the Details button.

2. In the Event Details dialog box, mark the Private checkbox (**Figure 4.45a**). If the Show/Hide Private Records setting is switched to Show, you will receive a warning dialog about how to hide private records after you tap OK (**Figure 4.45b**).

To change the security setting:

1. Choose Security from the Options menu, write ╱-H, or tap the lock icon from the command bar. The Change Security dialog box appears.

2. From the Current Privacy popup menu, choose Show Records, Mask Records, or Hide Records (**Figure 4.46**). This changes the security setting in all applications on your handheld.

✔ Tip

■ To easily read a masked record, tap it and enter your password. When finished, it becomes masked again.

Beaming and Sending Events

In the movies, conspirators are always synchronizing their watches to make sure everyone's on the same schedule. In the real world, we use the Palm OS to beam appointments to colleagues and family members, and thereby avoid having anyone say, "Why didn't you tell me there's a meeting today?"

Newer PalmOne handhelds such as the Zire 72 and Tungsten T3 include Bluetooth wireless connectivity, which enables you to send records to another Bluetooth-enabled device or to a compatible cell phone. You can also use the Send function to attach a record to an outgoing email message.

To beam an event:

1. Tap an event to select it.

2. Choose Beam Event from the Record menu, write ╱-B, or tap the Beam Event icon (📡) from the command bar (**Figure 4.47**).

   If the recipient's Beam Receive preference is set to On and the IR ports are aimed at each other, the record will be transferred (**Figure 4.48**).

To receive a beamed event:

1. Make sure your Beam Receive preference is set to On. Aim your IR port at the other person's Palm device.

2. After you've received the beamed record, you will be asked if you wish to add it to the Calendar. Tap Yes or No.

✔ Tip

■ Though beamed records are automatically set as unfiled, the recipient can choose to shuffle them to a category of their own or create a new one.

Figure 4.47 Palm devices equipped with infrared capabilities can beam records to one another easily.

Figure 4.48 Be sure your Palm device is pointed at the recipient, and within seconds the record is transferred.

Figure 4.49 Choosing Send Event gives you the option of transmitting wirelessly via Bluetooth (select a device from the Discovery Results, shown above) or sending as an attachment in VersaMail.

Figure 4.50 Choose your category from the Beam Category dialog's popup menu.

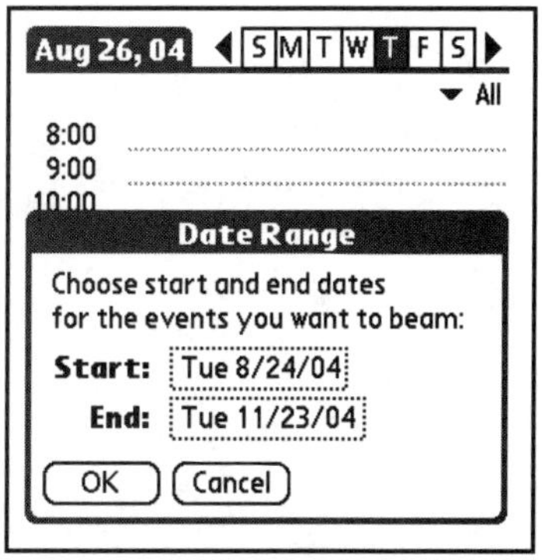

Figure 4.51 Select a specific date range of records to transmit.

To send an event:

1. After selecting a record, choose Send Event from the Record menu.

2. Choose how you want to transmit the record from the Send With dialog and tap OK. Bluetooth opens the Discovery Results screen from which you can select a device (**Figure 4.49**). VersaMail opens a new message with a .vcs file attached.

To receive a sent event via Bluetooth:

1. Make sure the Bluetooth preference is set to On and Discoverable.

2. After you've received the beamed record, you will be asked if you wish to add it to the Calendar. Tap Yes or No.

To beam or send a category:

1. Select Beam or Send Category from the Record menu.

2. Select which category is to be sent from the category popup menu.

3. Tap the Beam/Send events for popup menu and select Next 7 Days, Next 30 Days, or All Future Events (**Figure 4.50**).

   Or, select Date Range and select start and end points from the Date Range dialog (**Figure 4.51**).

4. Tap the Beam or Send button and proceed as above.

BEAMING AND SENDING EVENTS

Purging Old Events

Although the Palm OS has been written to accommodate very small file sizes, there comes a point at which the volume of past events begins to eat into your available memory. Will you have to shoulder the weight of the past forever? Luckily, you don't have to.

Calendar gives you the option to permanently delete older records from your device, while still maintaining an archive of the past on your PC.

To purge old events:

1. From the Day view, choose Purge from the Record menu, or write ╱-E in the Graffiti area (**Figure 4.52**). The Purge dialog box appears.

2. Choose the time frame of records that will be purged by selecting an item on the Delete events older than popup menu. You can select 1 Week, 2 Weeks, 3 Weeks, or 1 Month (**Figure 4.53**).

3. If you want to maintain a copy of the purged records on your PC, be sure the checkbox next to Save archive copy on PC is marked; otherwise, uncheck the box. Tap OK.

Figure 4.52 Some people choose to leave their past behind them—select Purge to wipe away old events.

Figure 4.53 We know people who have saved every event for as long as they've been able. Others wipe the old information and store it on their PCs.

Figure 4.54 Treo's Calendar looks familiar, but includes more views, activated at lower left. Also note the appearance of to do items from the To Do List at the top of the screen.

Figure 4.55 Choose how much of the To Do List to display in Treo's Calendar via the To Do Preferences.

Treo's Calendar

The one thing to remember about the Treo is that it started off under Handspring ownership before finally landing in PalmOne's stable. While it always ran a version of the Palm OS, Handspring made tweaks to several of the built-in applications, including the Calendar application (which was originally called Date Book+).

Treo's Calendar has many of the same features as the Calendar application we've explored so far in this chapter. But it also includes a few different views as well as some special features—floating events, journal entries, etc. We'll cover some of the highlights.

Day View

The Day view presents the familiar list format, overlapping events noted by brackets along the left side of the screen, etc. But it does offer the twist of displaying a range of tasks from the Treo's To Do application at the top of the screen (**Figure 4.54**). Tap the first button in the lower-left corner.

To configure task preferences:

1. Open To Do preferences from the Options menu (**Figure 4.55**).

2. Mark the categories that you want to display. (Note that marking all categories could overpower the Day view.)

3. Select which priorities to show from the Priorities Displayed popup menu.

4. Mark whether you want to display a task's priority as well as show any undated and/or completed items.

5. If you want a heads up on an upcoming task, mark the Show Dated Items checkbox, then choose how many days ahead you want to be reminded of the task.

Treo's Week View with Text View

The standard Week view can be helpful, but its assortment of dots and dashes is often too cryptic. The Week view with Text view displays as many events and to do titles as can fit (**Figure 4.56**). Tap the third button from the left to access this view.

Features of the Week view with Text view

◆ Tap any day area to switch to the Day view.

◆ Tap the numbered box at the top of the screen to switch between viewing one week or two weeks (**Figure 4.57**).

◆ If you have a mix of morning and afternoon appointments, tap the arrow button next to the Go button to display those portions of the day.

Treo's Year View

The Year view offers a similar big picture of your schedule, but doesn't pull out many details (**Figure 4.58**). Tap the fifth button in the lower-left corner.

Features of the Year view

◆ Tap a box on the calendar to view that day's date and the first appointment.

◆ The selected date and the first event of that day are displayed at the top of the screen.

◆ The scroll arrows at the top of the screen advance or go back one year per tap; the scroll arrows at the lower-right corner move one day at a time. Pressing the scroll buttons does the same thing.

Figure 4.56 The awkwardly named Week view with Text view offers a better idea of your schedule.

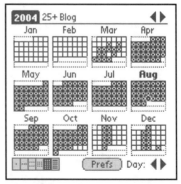

Figure 4.57 View two weeks on the same screen, though it's not as readable.

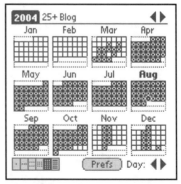

Figure 4.58 The Year view is handy for getting a sense of how crowded your schedule is.

Figure 4.59 Calendar doesn't need to get fancy displaying calendars when a list will do just as well.

Figure 4.60 Tap the up arrow in the List view to choose a range of time to jump back through.

Figure 4.61 Tap the Prefs button to adjust display settings for the List view.

Treo's List View

Sometimes you just want to see a list of what's coming up. Tap the right-most box at the lower-left corner of the screen to activate the List view (**Figure 4.59**).

Features of the List view

◆ Tap an event to display its start and end times in the title bar.

◆ Double-tap an event to view it in the Day view.

◆ If you've used the Go button to view a different day, tap the List view button to return to the current day.

◆ Tap the up arrow at the top-right corner of the screen to specify which increment (day, week, month) to move up the list, or pick a date in the past (**Figure 4.60**). The down arrow advances a full screen.

◆ Tap the Prefs button to specify which records appear in the list (**Figure 4.61**).

✔ Tip

■ From the List Preferences screen, you can filter the list by entering text in the Find field under Filter by Text.

Treo's Calendar Preferences

With more features come more preferences, and Treo's Calendar is loaded with options. These settings define global behavior (**Figure 4.62**).

Important Calendar Preferences

◆ By default, new events appear with a one-hour duration. In Calendar, specify any time span from zero to 23 hours and 55 minutes by tapping the Event Duration field and setting the duration.

◆ Use the Initial View preference to set the view displayed when you enter the application. The Day view is the default.

◆ Pressing the Calendar button on the Treo's case shuttles you through the different Calendar views. Deselect views you don't want to scroll through by tapping them in the Button Views preference.

◆ Gone are the days of the standardized workweek. If you want your weeks to begin on a certain day, like Tuesday, choose it from the Week Start popup menu. Every calendar view is affected (**Figure 4.63**).

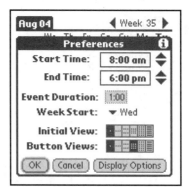

Figure 4.62 Choose the options you wish to use in Treo's Calendar.

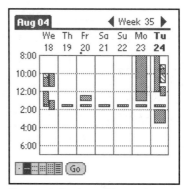

Figure 4.63 Setting a different day to begin the week changes the calendar layout throughout Calendar.

Figure 4.64 The easy way to create new records in Treo's Calendar is to select from the menu that appears when you tap the New button.

Entering Treo Calendar Events

Since Treo's Calendar can display more than just appointments, it adds an easy method of entering new records. Yes, you can choose their commands from the Record menu, write their Graffiti shortcut strokes, or start typing on the keypad, but there's a much easier way.

To enter a new event (the easy way):

1. With no records selected, tap the New button; a popup menu appears, listing the types of records available (**Figure 4.64**).

2. Choose Appointment, Floating Event, To Do, Daily Journal, or Template. A new untimed record appears (or in the case of the journal, a new note screen appears with a time stamp).

3. Fill in the record's title and other pertinent information as you normally would.

To duplicate an event:

1. Select an existing record in the Day view.

2. Choose Duplicate Item from the Record menu, or press Menu-Y.

3. Change the new item's settings in the Details screen, then tap OK to return to the Day view.

Treo Calendar Floating Events

There are times when you need to make sure to do something at a certain time. Floating events can be scheduled like any event, but carry over until the next day if they're not marked completed.

To work with floating events:

1. Create a new floating event from the New popup menu, or by choosing New Floating Event from the Record menu, or by pressing Menu-I. Assign it a title and time. It will be identified by a circle to the left or right of the name, depending on whether it's scheduled or not (**Figure 4.65**).

2. Tap the circle to indicate that the task is completed, or tap Details and select the Done option under Type. If left alone, it will display the following day.

Journal Entries

For an easy method of keeping track of thoughts and ideas, use the Daily Journal.

To create a journal entry:

1. Choose Daily Journal from the New button's popup menu, or New Journal Entry from the Record menu, or press Menu-J. A new note screen appears with the current time entered (**Figure 4.66**).

2. Insert pithy thought, wry observation, erudite comment, or overheard joke.

3. Tap Done to return to the Day view. Journal records appear as untimed records at the top of the screen (**Figure 4.67**).

4. If, at the end of your scribblings, you decide to delete what you've written (or if you wrote over a previous record), tap the Restore button to revert to the state at which you first entered the journal.

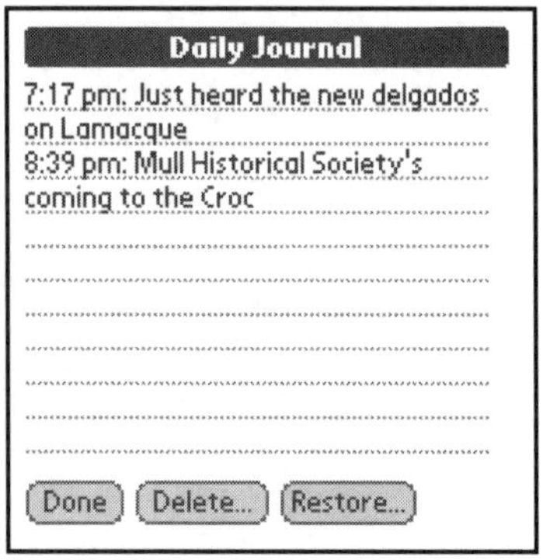

Figure 4.65 Floating events are really just scheduled to-do items.

Figure 4.66 A time stamp is automatically added to the bottom of the day's journal record.

Figure 4.67 The Daily Journal is really just an untimed record with an attached note, but it's a quick method of jotting down ideas and snippets of information.

Figure 4.68 Templates store all the data about a selected event.

Figure 4.69 Set up templates for frequently used events to avoid having to enter the same info time and again.

Treo's Templates

The template feature in the Treo Calendar exemplifies yet another aspect of the Palm philosophy of saving time and avoiding repetition. When you make a template from an existing record, it retains all of the event's settings like alarm, privacy, and attached note.

To create a template:

1. Create a record that you want to use as a template.

2. Select the record and choose Create Template from the Record menu, or press Menu-V (**Figure 4.68**).

To use a template:

1. Tap the New button and choose Template from the popup menu.

2. Select a template from the Appointment Templates screen, then tap OK to place the event (**Figure 4.69**).

To edit a template:

1. Tap the New button and choose Template from the popup menu.

2. Select a template and tap the Details or Edit button to change its properties.

3. Tap OK to return to the Day view.

Windows Palm Desktop Special Features

For the most part, you'll find that working within Palm Desktop's Calendar is similar to using the Palm OS Calendar: Click New Event to create new events; Edit Event to change them; and view them using the Day, Week, Month, and Year views. However, the desktop software also includes several features that make it easier to create and modify appointment times, and add events based on phone lookups. And because it operates on your PC, you can print your calendar.

To add events in the Day view:

1. Select the day you need in the two-month mini calendar view at the right.

2. Click on the time that you'd like to schedule your event. You can click either the time numerals in the left column, or click an empty area in the right column.

3. Type your event's description, then press Enter.

4. To add an alarm or a note, right-click on the event to bring up a contextual menu. You can also delete the record here, as well as access the main Edit dialog box.

5. To quickly move the event to another date, drag it to the calendar in the pane at right. It retains the same time.

To edit events in the Week view:

◆ Click on an empty time slot, or click the time numerals, to create a new event.

◆ As in the Day view, drag events to new times and dates using the event handle, or reschedule lengths using the duration handle (**Figures 4.70, 4.71,** and **4.72**).

◆ Right-click on any event to bring up the editing contextual menu.

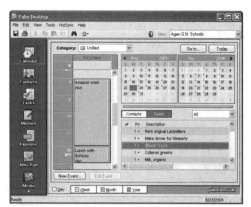

Figure 4.70 Click and drag an appointment's bottom handle to change its time span; click and drag the right-side event handle to reschedule its time or date.

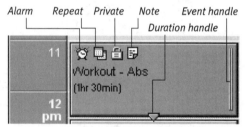

Figure 4.71 Events are more configurable in the desktop Day view than in the Palm OS Day view.

Click here to create a new untimed event.

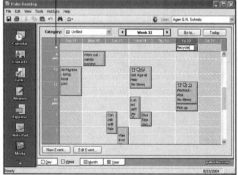

Figure 4.72 Untimed events appear in the upper field marked by a diamond. The field expands to accommodate the number of untimed events.

Figure 4.73 Quickly create an appointment with a phone lookup by dragging a name from the Contacts pane at lower right to the time of the event.

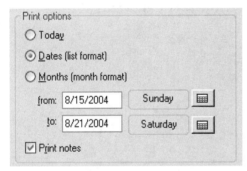

Figure 4.74 Choose how you want your schedule printed. Clicking on the tiny calendar buttons gives you a popup calendar to specify the date ranges.

To perform a phone lookup in Palm Desktop:

1. Switch to the Day view, and select the date on which you wish to create an event.

2. Click Contacts in the lower-right pane to display your Contacts entries.

3. Locate the contact either by scrolling through the names, or typing in the Look up field.

4. Drag the contact's name to the time of the appointment (**Figure 4.73**).

✔ Tips

■ For whatever reason, Palm Desktop 4.1 doesn't include the phone number in the title of an event that's been created by dragging a contact.

■ You can also drag a Tasks item from the lower-right pane onto your day to schedule a task. Although the records aren't linked (changing the date on one won't affect the other), this capability is good for setting aside blocks of time to complete your tasks.

To print your appointments:

1. In any Calendar view, select Print from the File menu, or press Control-P. (This assumes you have a printer connected to and already set up on your PC.) The Print options dialog box appears.

2. Choose a print option: Today's appointments, a list of Dates, or a time span in Months format (**Figure 4.74**).

3. If printing in month format, you can use the small calendar icons to specify which days you want to print.

Color-Coded Categories in Palm Desktop

The colors that you select for Calendar's categories on your handheld are transferred to Palm Desktop, coloring the event blocks in the Day and Week views as well as adding a tiny colored square to the left of an event's title in Month view. Colored categories are on by default, but you can change this setting in Preferences (**Figure 4.75**).

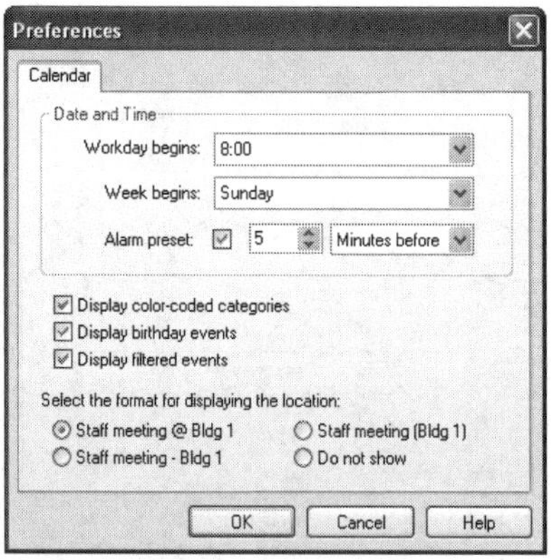

To change Palm Desktop settings:

1. Select Preferences from the Tools menu.

2. Select the time you want the Day and Month views to begin with in the Workday begins popup. You may choose a time earlier than the traditional start of the workday if you set early gym appointments.

3. Choose which day to start your week with the Week begins popup.

4. If you want to create an alarm for every event, mark Alarm preset, then choose a reminder time.

5. Mark or unmark the options for displaying color-coded categories, birthdays, and filtered events.

6. Select your location display format, or choose not to show it at all. Click OK.

Figure 4.75 Keep your category colors displayed in Palm Desktop by marking the Display color-coded categories checkbox. With Display filtered events turned on, you'll see events from other categories when you use the category filter popup menu, but you won't be able to click on them.

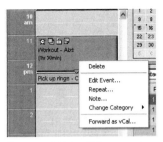

Figure 4.76 Right-click an event to open the contextual menu and access Edit Event features more quickly.

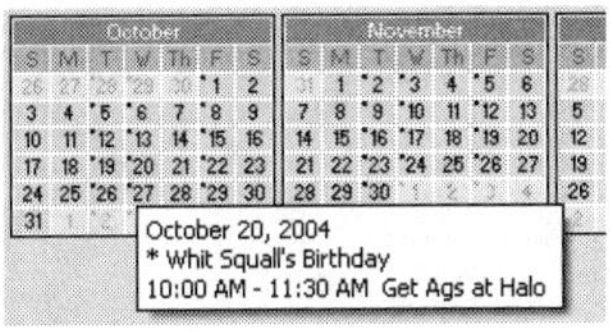

Figure 4.77 Mouse over a date in Year view to see a list of all the events for that day.

✔ Tips

■ With Display filtered events turned on, you'll see the active, colored event blocks for a category you select from the filter popup menu at the top of the Day, Week, or Month view. Other events assigned to categories will display with a lightened shade, but they don't display any text and they can't even be clicked and selected. If you place your cursor on the same line as an event from a non-selected category, you'll start to create a new event within the currently selected category.

If you unmark Display filtered events, only the category you select from the popup menu can be seen—the others disappear until you reselect All.

■ Don't forget to use your mouse's contextual menu. From the Day and Month views, you can right-click on an event and open right to the Repeat and Note tabs of the Edit Event dialog or change the event's category (**Figure 4.76**). If you're in Month view, you can right-click on a date and select to go to either the Day or Week view, or create a new event.

■ In the Year view, mouse over a date to view its event contents in a floating box (**Figure 4.77**).

WINDOWS PALM DESKTOP SPECIAL FEATURES

Macintosh Palm Desktop Special Features

Most cross-platform applications share the same interface and features, but that's not the case with the Macintosh Palm Desktop software. Because it's built on top of Claris Organizer (see Chapter 1), you'll find many features that don't exist in the Windows version of Palm Desktop.

Navigating Palm Desktop for Macintosh

One of the first things you'll notice is the presence of a toolbar at the upper-left corner of the screen (**Figure 4.78**). Clicking on the buttons offers a quick alternative to common actions, such as:

- ◆ **Create New Event** (or press Command-Option-E). This opens the Event dialog box, allowing you to enter the schedule information without finding the time and date on the calendar first (useful when you're entering several events at different times). Click Add Another to stay in the dialog box and enter multiple events instead of switching back to the calendar view (**Figure 4.79**).

- ◆ **Create Untimed Event** (or press Command-Option-U). See the next page for details.

- ◆ **Go To Date** (or press Command-R). This jumps to a specific date (**Figure 4.80**).

- ◆ **Go To Today** (or press Command-T). Jump to the current date. *Carpe diem*, etc.

- ◆ **Show Date Book** (or press Command-Shift-B). If you're viewing tasks or contacts, clicking this button takes you to the last calendar view you were using. (Note that this button uses the old vernacular of Date Book rather than Calendar.)

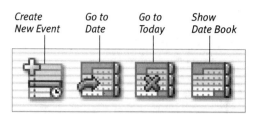

Figure 4.78 A floating toolbar features buttons to access actions within the Calendar module (named Date Book in Palm Desktop for Macintosh).

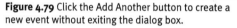

Figure 4.79 Click the Add Another button to create a new event without exiting the dialog box.

Figure 4.80 Go To Date switches your current calendar view to the date you specify. This small window is also handy when you're viewing the Day or Week view, giving you a monthly calendar without switching to the Month view.

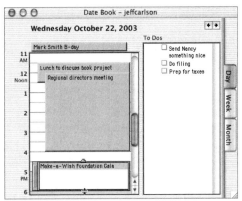

Figure 4.81 Click and drag within the Day or Week view to create a new event.

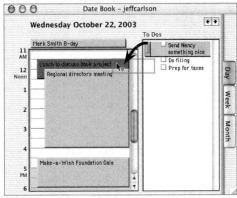

Figure 4.82 Attach tasks in the To Dos pane to events in the Day and Week views by dragging-and-dropping them. Existing links can be viewed by clicking the folder icon that is created after linking.

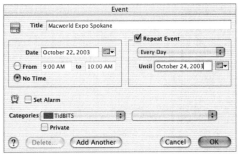

Figure 4.83 If you create an untimed repeating event, it will appear as a banner across the top of the dates within the assigned interval.

To create and edit events:

◆ Double-click in one of the calendar views to bring up the Event dialog box.

◆ Click and drag on the event's time. Unlike the Windows version of Palm Desktop, the Mac software allows you to create an event with one click that spans its full duration (**Figure 4.81**).

◆ Choose Event from the Create menu, or press Command-Option-E.

To edit an existing event, double-click it in any calendar view, or single-click it and select Edit Event from the Edit menu.

You can also attach related records to other records (such as tasks attached to events, or contacts attached to events—the Mac equivalent of phone lookups).

To attach records to events:

◆ If both records are visible, drag and drop one on to the other. A link is created in both records (**Figure 4.82**).

◆ Click the folder icon (🗂▼) and choose Attach To from the popup menu.

To create a repeating event:

1. Choose Untimed Event from the Create menu, or press Command-Option-U. The Event dialog box appears.

2. Set the starting date in the Date field (or use the popup calendar to the right).

3. Click the Repeat Event checkbox (**Figure 4.83**).

4. Specify a time interval from the Repeat Event popup menu, and optionally set an end date in the Until field. Click OK when you're finished.

Attaching Notes in Mac Palm Desktop

The one truly bizarre thing about the Macintosh Palm Desktop software is the roundabout manner of attaching notes to records. Although you can attach records to events (see previous page), that's not the same as adding a note to a record (as discussed at the beginning of this chapter). Fortunately, there is a way to attach notes to events so they show up properly on the handheld device.

To attach notes in Mac Palm Desktop:

1. Attached notes are considered memos just as if you had written them into Memos. So, create a new memo and write your text.

2. In the Title field, type "Handheld Note: Calendar" exactly (**Figure 4.84**).

3. Locate the calendar entry to which you want to add your note. Drag the note's title bar icon to the calendar entry (**Figure 4.85**).

✔ Tips

- There's a faster way of making attachments that will appear on the handheld. With a blank note visible, write "Handheld Note: Calendar" in the Title field as you did above. Now, choose New Template from the Create menu, and enter a name; if you want, choose a Command-key number from the ⌘ popup menu. From now on, choose one of the templates from the Create menu or press the Command-key to display a new formatted note window (**Figure 4.86**).

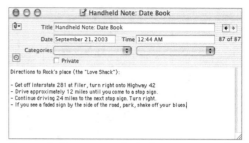

Figure 4.84 To create an attached note, you must first create the note separately (unlike in the Palm OS).

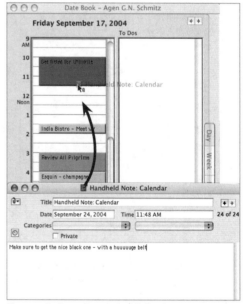

Figure 4.85 Drag the note's title bar icon to an event to attach the note.

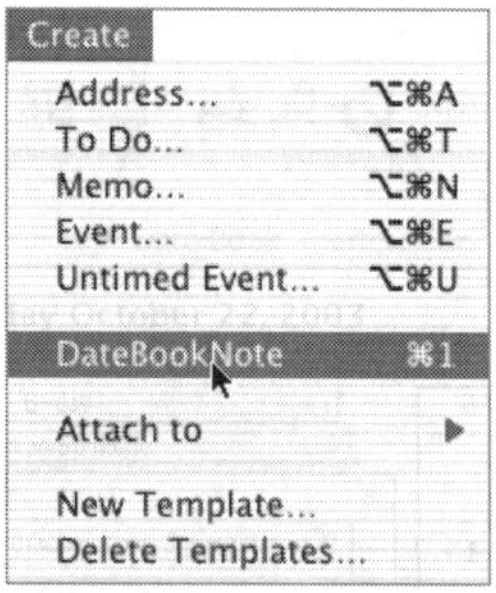

Figure 4.86 Create notes easily with templates.

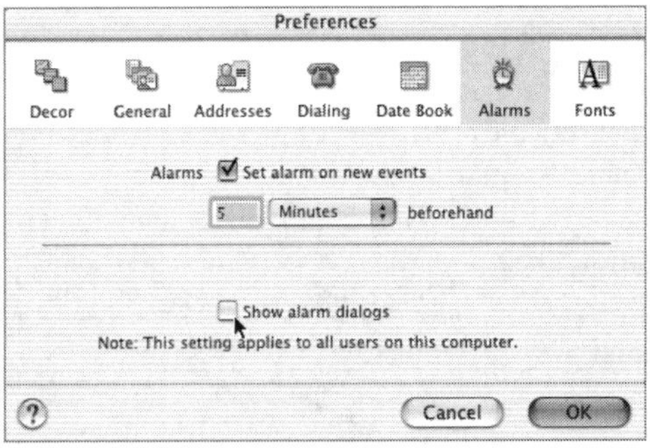

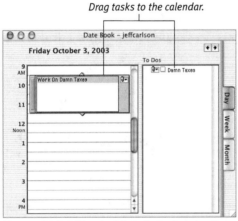

Figure 4.87 Though helpful, turn off the Show alarm dialogs option to avoid interruptions on your Mac.

Drag tasks to the calendar.

Figure 4.88 Quickly schedule tasks by dragging them from the Tasks pane to the calendar.

- In the Palm OS Calendar, performing an address lookup puts a person's name and phone number in the title of an event. On the Mac, however, dragging a contact to an event only creates a link between the two on the desktop. You'll have to manually cut and paste the person's phone information for it to appear in the title.

- In the calendar's Day view, double-click the date to bring up the Go To dialog.

- The Day view also displays the day's active tasks in the right-hand pane; click the word "Tasks" to send completed tasks to the bottom of the list.

- In the Day and Week views, pressing Command and the right or left arrow key advances or goes back one day. Hold down Option or Shift to move in one-week increments.

- In the Month view, you can choose to display Appointments, Tasks, or both (or none). Go to the View menu, then choose the options under the Calendar submenu.

- Palm Desktop for Macintosh includes a feature for displaying an alarm onscreen (**Figure 4.87**).

- You can create scheduled tasks easily in the Day and Week views. Simply drag a task from the Tasks pane to a time in the calendar. The item's title becomes the appointment's title, and any attached notes are copied over as well. The text "Work On" appears in the title, and an attachment link is created between the task and the new calendar item (**Figure 4.88**).

ATTACHING NOTES IN MAC PALM DESKTOP

DateBk5: The Supercharged Calendar

The Palm OS's built-in applications haven't changed much over the past few years, in accordance with Palm's mandate to keep its handhelds simple and useful. As long as appointments are scheduled, tasks recorded, and phone numbers easily looked up, most users don't require more than the basics. But we don't all qualify as "most users." For the most full-featured calendar application on the Palm OS, look to Pimlico Software's DateBk5 (www.pimlicosoftware.com).

DateBk5 essentially adds all the features that you've wanted (or didn't know you've wanted) in Calendar. DateBk5 sports six calendar views, displays tasks as well as events, and features a daily journal, floating events, and templates. In addition, DateBk5 adds categories, icons, time zone support, color, and the ability to set font styles for any record, not just the entire application (**Figure 4.89**).

Figure 4.89 DateBk5 adds more features to the built-in Calendar database than any three programs combined.

But that's not all. You can split the Day view screen and choose the contents for the new window pane. Tasks are usually listed, but you can also view your Calendar records, or memos, and then filter the lists based on any text you specify. Color device owners have good reason to install DateBk5. Like the latest Calendar application, this program enables you to color-code categories; but you can also color-code individual records (**Figure 4.90**). And if that's not enough, you can also link records between the built-in applications (though you have to view them within DateBk5).

What's the dark side to this miracle application? The only serious criticism is its size: around 830K, which is huge by Palm OS standards. For users who don't have that much free space available, Pimlico continues to offer a previous version, DateBk3, which weighs in at 247K. Of all the applications we've installed on Palm devices, DateBk5 remains a permanent fixture.

Figure 4.90 This is the reason to buy a color handheld: Events can be categorized and displayed in different colors for easy recognition—a capability missing from the initial color implementation from Palm.

DateBk5 costs $24.95 (all of which goes to the developer's organization, Gorilla Haven, a non-profit preserve that provides a secure temporary holding facility for gorillas awaiting permanent zoo housing, and helps ensure the welfare and genetic diversity of the species).

CONTACTS

Personal Information Manager (PIM) programs have become more and more robust over the years. Agen left the Palm OS fold for a time, believing that all he needed was Microsoft Outlook on his computer to keep track of all the vendors he communicated with while working at Amazon. But more and more, he found himself printing pages of contacts to keep with him on business trips while stacking a horde of business cards by the side of his computer that he never had time to enter into Outlook. He soon came to realize the error of his ways.

PalmOne's built-in Contacts application (formerly Address Book) offers immediate access to your most up-to-date list of business associates, friends and family, and just plain cool people you want to remember for later. And you can store more than just names and addresses: office and home phone numbers, email and instant messaging addresses, driving directions, birthdays, and much more.

Viewing Contacts

The Contacts application is another example of how Palm OS devices can store and present a great deal of information without cluttering up the limited screen—select it from the Applications screen or press the Contacts button on your handheld.

If you're a veteran of previous Palm OS iterations, you'll notice that the Contact view in Palm OS 5.2 features a refined layout. The contact's name appears in a large, bold font at the top, followed by title and company name. Several sets of divider lines help to group chunks of data, with phone and email information in one, IM and Web site in the next, and physical addresses in the next.

Contacts list and Contact view

◆ Contacts are listed alphabetically either by last name or by company name down the left side of the screen (**Figure 5.1**).

◆ The right-hand column lists each person's primary contact information. If a phone number is displayed, the letter at the end of each line indicates which type of number it is. For example, W equals Work, H equals Home, P equals Pager, F equals Fax, and (confusingly) M equals either Mobile or Main.

◆ A note icon (▯) at the far right indicates that the record includes an attached note.

◆ The triangular arrows in the lower-right corner scroll up and down the Contacts list. You can also use the scroll buttons on the handheld case or jog dial (on some models), which move through the list one screen at a time.

◆ When you tap a record to view it, the Contact view shows you that contact's details (**Figure 5.2**). Tap the arrows to scroll up or down to view the information.

Figure 5.1 The Contacts list displays names and preferred phone numbers—you may not even have to tap a name to get the number you need.

Figure 5.2 Tapping a name brings up the Contact view. All fields that have content are displayed, enabling you to scroll down several screens if a contact is packed with information.

Figure 5.3 Two options are available for sorting the Contacts list, depending on whether you're looking for companies or people's names.

Figure 5.4 Sorting by Company, Last Name reorders the list alphabetically by company, and truncates longer names to show more information.

✔ Tips

- Your eyes did not deceive you in **Figure 5.2**: You can add an image to a Contacts record. See "Add a Contact Photo," later in this chapter.

- If you have a device with only scroll up or down buttons, you can navigate the Contacts list screen by screen. Or, press the scroll up and down buttons when you're at the beginning or the end of the current record in the Contact view to jump to the next (or previous) one.

- These same actions can be used on handhelds with a five-way navigator. But if you're in the Contacts list, pressing the center button selects the top-most record on the viewed screen, enabling you to move from record to record with the up/down buttons. Press the center button again to open the Contact view, or press the left button to deselect any contact. See "Looking Up Contacts," later in this chapter, to see what pressing the right button brings you.

Changing the Sort Order

Since there isn't much space on the screen, you can't tell if, for example, Pedro Finn was the guy you met at last month's conference, or if he's your genius financial adviser. Fortunately, you can choose how you want the records listed.

To change the sort order:

1. Select Preferences from the Options menu.

2. Choose either Last Name, First Name or Company, Last Name from the List By box, then tap OK (**Figures 5.3** and **5.4**).

Specifying a Preferred Number

Suppose you want to view someone's home number instead of their work phone in the Contacts list. Contacts provides a way to do it, although it's slightly buried.

To specify a preferred number:

1. Tap the record you wish to change. This takes you to the Contact view.

2. Tap the Edit button, or tap anywhere within the Contact view to go into the Contact Edit screen.

3. Tap Details.

4. Choose the field you want to appear in the main list by tapping the Show in List popup menu (**Figure 5.5**). Tap OK to return to the edit screen, then tap Done.

✔ Tips

- If you know ahead of time which field you want to appear in the Contacts list, write that number first when you're entering the address. By default, the contact information shown in the Contacts list is the first contact field entered.

- While it takes one more tap, you can automatically connect to phone numbers listed in the Contact view with a Bluetooth- or wireless-enabled PalmOne handheld. With the Enable Tap-to-Connect checkbox marked in Preferences (**Figure 5.6**), just tap on a number or address to connect via your wireless connection or a paired Bluetooth cell phone (**Figure 5.7**). Tapping on an email address will open a new message in VersaMail, PalmOne's email program. However, with this preference enabled, you must tap the Edit button to open the Contact Edit screen (not just tap the record).

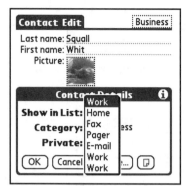

Figure 5.5 Specify a preferred number by using the Show in List popup menu.

Figure 5.6 With a wireless or Bluetooth-compatible device, marking Enable Tap-to-Connect in Preferences...

Figure 5.7 ...allows you to tap a phone number to automatically dial it.

Figure 5.8 Choose from four display font sizes. The larger fonts are more readable, but show less data.

Figure 5.9 Adjust font sizes for each of Contacts' three screens of data.

Figure 5.10 The Treo's Contacts list shows phone numbers on separate lines, which works better in a larger font size.

Changing the Display Font

Contacts provides you with three options for changing fonts in three different screens.

To change the display font:

1. Select Font from the Options menu.

2. Tap one of the font styles in the Select Font window (**Figure 5.8**). Tap OK.

✔ Tips

- As noted above, Contacts allows you to have three font settings—one for the Contacts list, one for the Contact view, and a third for the Contact Edit screen (**Figure 5.9**). We prefer to use a small font for the Contacts list to fit in as many lines as possible, a slightly larger font for the Contact view, and then back to a smaller font for Contact Edit.

- The Treo display includes a contact's phone number on a separate line, which makes it easier to tap for dialing. We prefer to set the list display to the largest font size when using a Treo (**Figure 5.10**). See "Contacts in Treo," later in this chapter as well as Chapter 8 for more information about using the Treo.

Looking Up Contacts

There's a better way to find the person you're looking for than scrolling through the list.

To search using Look Up:

1. In the Look Up field, write the first letter of the last name (or company name, depending on the sort order) you're looking for; the first match will be highlighted (**Figure 5.11**).

2. If the first letter doesn't match the intended name, keep writing letters until you get a match. If you know you're close, use the arrows in the lower-right corner to scroll through the list by individual record, or the scroll buttons (or jog dial) on the case to scroll by screen.

To perform a find:

1. If you're looking for a word located within a record or a record's attached note, tap the silkscreened Find icon.

2. Enter the text you're searching for, then tap OK. The results (including matches in other programs) appear in a new window. Tap the match you want (**Figure 5.12**).

✔ Tips

- Find will begin its search within the application you're currently running.

- To quickly clear the Look Up field, press either the up or down scroll button.

- If you have a phone with Caller ID and an unfamiliar number pops up, do a quick Find for part of the number to see if it matches someone in Contacts.

- On devices with five-way navigators, press the right navigation button to display a name selector. Scroll up or down to select letters, then press right again to go to the next letter (**Figure 5.13**).

Figure 5.11 Begin writing the last name of your contact in the Look Up field to jump to the closest match.

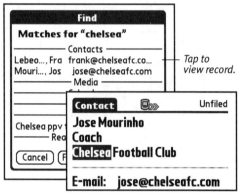

Figure 5.12 The Find function can be helpful when searching for text located within a record.

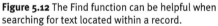

Figure 5.13 Use the navigator to look up contacts one-handed.

Figure 5.14 After tapping New, write the contact's information in the fields.

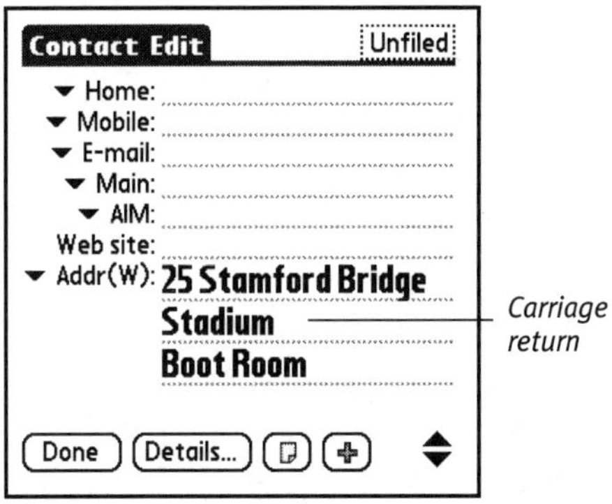

Carriage return

Figure 5.15 Don't worry if there aren't enough fields (such as a second address field); simply write a carriage return to make a new line.

Entering and Deleting Contacts

Graffiti is a great method for entering text into a handheld, but we won't pretend it's always the best option. If you need to create lots of new records, you're better off typing them into Palm Desktop on your PC. But for one or two, here's how to enter them quickly.

To create a new record:

1. From the Contacts list or the Contact view, tap the New button.

2. Fill in the fields using Graffiti or the built-in keypad (if you're using a Treo) (**Figure 5.14**). Tap Done.

✔ Tips

■ Write the tab Graffiti character (⌐) to go to the next field without moving the stylus from the Graffiti area. Or, on devices with keypads, press the Tab key.

■ You can enter more than one line of text into each field. Write a carriage return (∕) and add another line of information; it stays in the same field (**Figure 5.15**).

■ Tap the address field (Addr) popup menu to choose its location (H for Home, W for Work, O for Other).

Adding Fields

Contacts in Palm OS 5.2 lets you add more fields for phone numbers, addresses, and nicknames for instant messaging (IM) applications. You can add up to two addresses (for a total of three), two IM addresses, and a combination of up to seven phone/pager/fax/mobile numbers or email addresses.

To add Contact fields:

1. Select a contact from the Contacts list, then tap the Edit button on the Contact view.

2. At the bottom of the Contact Edit screen, tap the Add (✛) button.

3. Select either Phone/Email, IM, Address, or a custom category from the popup.

4. Tap Done when you're finished.

✔ Tips

■ Fields you add in Contacts will be added to Palm Desktop the next time you perform a HotSync.

■ If you add an IM field, tap its popup menu and select one of the application options (AIM, MSN, Yahoo, AOL ICQ, or IM) (**Figure 5.16**).

■ By default, only the first four custom fields are displayed at the bottom of the Contact Edit screen (out of a total of up to nine). If you have created more than four custom fields, you'll have to add them manually using the Add button (**Figure 5.17**).

■ In the past, we always used one of the custom fields to store birthdays. But Palm OS 5.2 has added a Birthday field. Tap its box to set the date, then set a number of days ahead of the date to be reminded in the Birthday dialog (**Figure 5.18**).

Figure 5.16 After adding an IM field, tap its popup to choose which IM application the nickname is associated with.

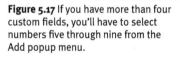

Figure 5.17 If you have more than four custom fields, you'll have to select numbers five through nine from the Add popup menu.

Figure 5.18 Now you have no excuse for forgetting a birthday.

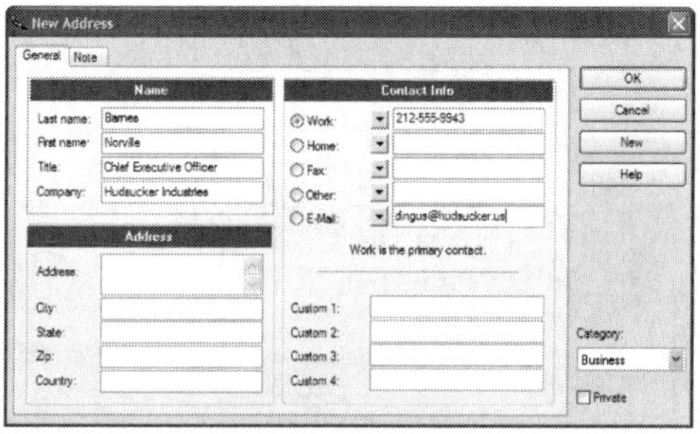

Figure 5.19 The New Address dialog includes all contact info on one screen. Press Ctrl-Tab to easily switch to the Note tab if you want to add more information.

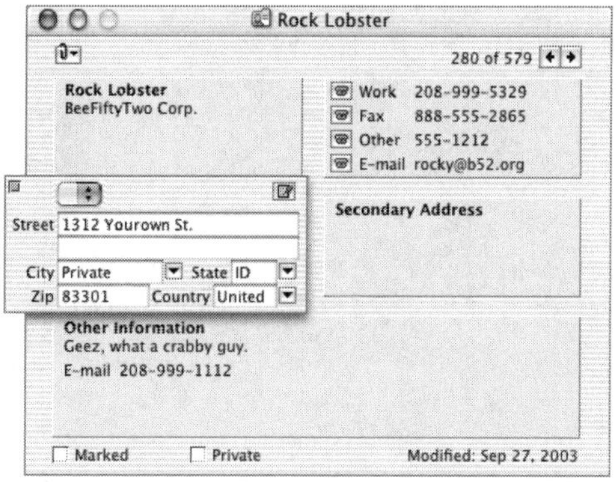

Figure 5.20 The Macintosh Palm Desktop features information areas that pop up entry fields when you click on them.

Palm Desktop Entry

Satisfy your need for data entry speed by adding Contacts entries in your PC's Palm Desktop application, then perform a HotSync.

To create a new record using Palm Desktop (Windows):

1. Click the Contacts button to view the Contacts application.

2. Click the New Contact button, select New Contact from the Edit menu, or press Control-N.

3. Enter the text in the appropriate fields, then click OK (**Figure 5.19**).

✔ Tip

■ To create another contact without leaving the New Contact dialog, click the New button.

To create a new record using Palm Desktop (Macintosh):

1. Click the Addresses button from the toolbar, choose Contacts list from the View menu, or press Command-Shift-A.

2. Click the New Address button, select Address from the Create menu, or press Command-Option-A (the keyboard shortcut works anywhere in the program, not just with the Contacts list viewed).

3. Click on an information area to access the entry fields (**Figure 5.20**). When you're finished, close the window or press Command-W.

Chapter 5

✔ Tips

- You can jump between the information fields by pressing the Tab key.

- If you're typing something that's been entered before, such as a city name, Palm Desktop automatically completes the word for you.

- Two areas are provided for entering an email address: the E-mail field in the Other Information area, or as a popup item in the Phones fields. Choose one, or use them to list more than one email address.

- Because PalmOne has not offered a significant update to Palm Desktop for Mac, the extra phone, IM, and custom fields that can be added to Contacts in Palm OS 5.2 won't be synchronized. Instead of adding an extra phone number field, you might consider dedicating one custom field for Pager or Fax, thus leaving room for other numbers.

To delete a contact (handheld):

1. Tap the contact to select it.

2. Select Delete Address from the Record menu, or write ╱-D.

You can also tap Edit, then Details, then the Delete button—but who has that kind of time?

3. If you want to store the record in the PC's Palm archive files, be sure to check Save archive copy on PC. Click OK to delete (**Figure 5.21**).

Figure 5.21 Sometimes we lose track of people who were once dear to us. Check Save archive copy on PC to save deleted records at the next HotSync.

Figure 5.22 Use the Select Image/ Media screen to find a photo stored on either your handheld or memory card.

Contact Edit

Figure 5.23 If you have a Zire 72, you can choose to snap a photo of your new contacts.

Figure 5.24 The Camera application automatically uses a square format. To zoom, tap the x2 button.

Adding a Contact Photo

Palm OS 5.2 provides the ability to associate a photo with a Contacts record (except for the Treo 600), either from your handheld's internal memory or a photo shot with the camera-enabled Zire 72.

To add an image to a contact:

1. Tap an item to open the Contact view, then tap the record or the Edit button to open the Contact Edit screen.

2. Tap the blank image icon, then tap one of the available photos from the Select Image screen (**Figure 5.22**).

   If you have a Zire 72, choose Camera or Photos (which opens the Select Media screen) from the popup (**Figure 5.23**).

3. If you elect to shoot your own, the Camera application opens. Snap the pic by tapping the Shutter button, or tap Cancel (**Figure 5.24**).

4. Save the photo by tapping the floppy disk icon, or delete it by tapping the trash can.

5. Once chosen from Select Image/Media or saved from the camera, the image appears in the contact you were editing.

✔ Tips

- Delete an image by tapping the photo box in Contact Edit and selecting Remove from the popup. Or, choose Camera or Photos to start over.

- Don't worry about choosing a photo from your memory card—the image is reprocessed into a smaller format and saved to the device's memory.

- The Camera application automatically uses a square format for your shot rather than the typical rectangular format.

Duplicating Records

Contacts' ability to duplicate existing records is especially helpful, for example, when you're adding several people who work at the same company.

To duplicate an existing record:

1. Select a contact from the Contacts list or tap it to open the Contact view.

2. Select Duplicate Contact from the Record menu, or write ╱-T (**Figure 5.25**). The new record adds the word "Copy"at the end of the text in the First name field (**Figure 5.26**).

✔ Tip

■ If you've accidentally made more duplicates than you intended, or if for some reason your records have been duplicated during a bad HotSync, Palm Desktop for Windows offers a solution. From the Tools menu, choose Delete Duplicates from the Addins submenu. Or, click the Delete Duplicates button on the toolbar (to the left of the user field). The Delete Duplicates dialog appears, which you can use to search for and remove any duplicate records (it also searches Calendar, Tasks, and Memos).

Figure 5.25 Duplicate records: don't re-enter the same information.

Denotes copy

Figure 5.26 When a record is duplicated, Contacts adds the text "Copy" to the First name field.

Figure 5.27 If your device supports Quick Connect, an icon appears at the top of the Contacts list window.

Figure 5.28 Tap a phone number to dial it, or an email address to create a new message in supported email software.

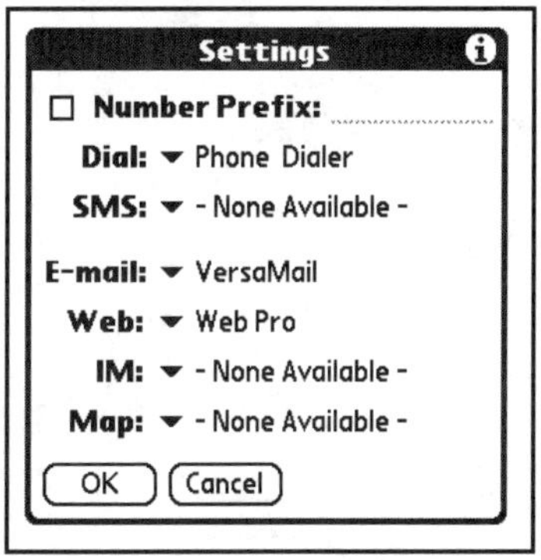

Figure 5.29 Choose which programs handle which Quick Connect tasks.

Using Quick Connect

Palm handhelds no longer exist alone—they can communicate with the outside world with the help of Quick Connect. Depending on the capabilities of your device, you can dial a phone number; send an email, fax, or instant message; or locate an address on a GPS-assisted map.

To use Quick Connect:

1. Tap a Contacts record.

2. Choose Connect from the Record menu, write ∕-I, or tap the Quick Connect icon at the top of the screen (**Figure 5.27**).

3. Tap a number in the Quick Connect list to activate it (**Figure 5.28**). Only supported actions appear (for example, an email address won't show up if you have no compatible email software installed).

To configure Quick Connect settings:

1. At the Quick Connect list (see step 3 above), tap the Settings button.

2. Tap a popup menu next to the type of action you want to define. For example, if you have multiple compatible email programs installed, choose one from the Email popup list (**Figure 5.29**).

3. If a phone number requires a dialing prefix (such as dialing an international number), tap the Number Prefix box and enter the prefix in the field provided.

✔ Tip

■ To dial a number without going to the Quick Connect list, turn on Tap-to-Connect mode. In the Contacts preferences, mark the Enable Tap-to-Connect checkbox. This disables the capability to edit a record by tapping anywhere on the screen, but you can still tap the Edit button to make changes.

USING QUICK CONNECT

161

Changing and Editing Phone Field Labels

Although there are five fields for contact numbers such as work and home phones, many of us have more access numbers than that. Contacts includes eight labels accessible via popup menus.

To change phone field labels:

1. Tap on a record to view it, then tap the Edit button (**Figure 5.30**).

2. Tap the popup menu next to the number you want to change. With the menu active, choose from Work, Home, Fax, Other, E-mail, Main, Pager, or Mobile.

3. Tap Done to exit the Contact Edit screen.

To edit phone field labels in Palm Desktop (Windows):

1. Highlight a name and click Edit Contact, or double-click the name.

2. In the Contact Info area (**Figure 5.31**), click the field name next to the number you want to change, and choose the desired label from the popup menu.

3. Click the radio button to the left of the popup menu for the number you wish to appear in the Contacts list.

To set default phone field options in Palm Desktop (Windows):

1. Choose Preferences from the Tools menu.

2. Change the labels in the Default Labels area as described above (**Figure 5.32**).

3. Click OK.

Figure 5.30 The popup phone label options provide for more than just work and home numbers.

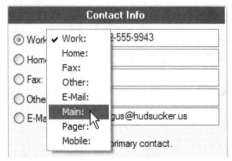

Figure 5.31 Changing the phone field names in Palm Desktop for Windows works the same as in the Palm OS.

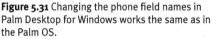

Figure 5.32 The Contacts tab in the Preferences dialog sets the default labels for all new contacts.

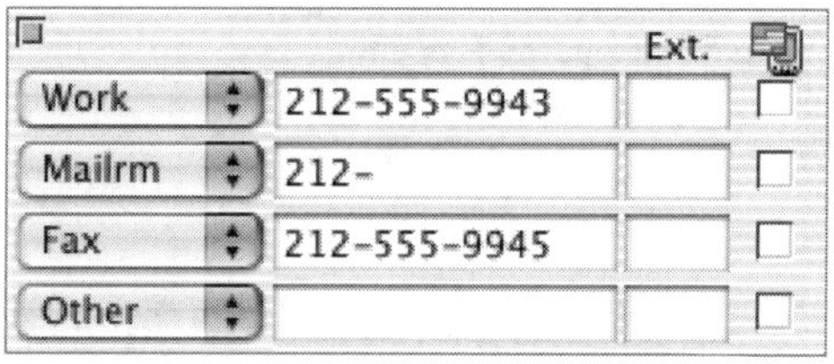

Figure 5.33 The Phones box in Palm Desktop for Macintosh features popup menus to label the fields, plus an option for adding numbers to the Instant Palm Desktop menu.

Figure 5.34 A phone field in Palm Desktop for Macintosh can have any name, though it appears as Other on the device if it's not one of the existing labels.

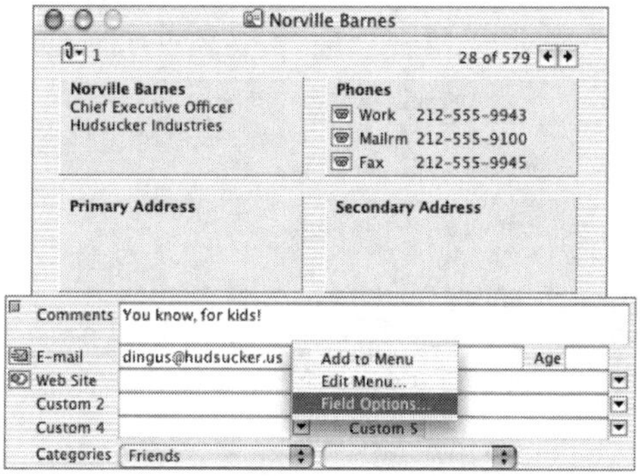

Figure 5.35 Email shows up in the Other Information area instead of in Phones like on the Palm OS and under Windows.

To edit phone field labels in Palm Desktop (Macintosh):

1. Click the Phones box within a Contact window to edit the phone fields (**Figure 5.33**).

2. Choose a label from the popup windows to the left of each field.

3. If you want that contact's name and a number to appear in the Instant Palm Desktop menu (see the end of this chapter for more information), mark the box to the far right of the desired number.

To customize phone field labels in Palm Desktop (Macintosh):

1. Choose Other from the popup menu to create a custom field name.

2. To permanently add a custom label to the menu, choose Edit Menu (**Figure 5.34**).

3. Enter a new name and click OK.

✔ Tips

- If you enter an extension into the Ext. field, it appears on the same line as the number in the Palm OS.

- Only a maximum of four fields appear in a contact's Phones section, but there are five on the handheld. The fifth field is the E-mail field, found in the Other Information area (**Figure 5.35**). An E-mail option appears on the Phone field popup menu as well, giving you a way to record multiple email addresses for contacts.

- You can use any name to describe a phone field, but keep in mind that anything not matching the predefined labels will appear as Other on the handheld.

CHANGING AND EDITING PHONE FIELD LABELS

163

Renaming the Custom Field Labels

In addition to standard fields such as Address and City, nine custom fields are available for text input. Since "Custom 1" and "Custom 2" are boring labels, you can change field names to anything else.

To rename custom field labels:

1. Choose Rename Custom Fields from the Options menu to display the Rename Custom Fields dialog box (**Figure 5.36**).

   In Palm Desktop for Windows, select Preferences under the Tools menu (**Figure 5.37**).

   If you're using Palm Desktop for Macintosh, getting there is a little more tricky: Open a contact by double-clicking on it, then click in the Other Information area. Choose the field you want to edit, click the popup menu to the right, and select Field Options; or, just double-click the name of the field (**Figure 5.38**).

2. Type the words or phrases you'd like to use. I find that Birthdate, Web, and Anniversary are essential labels; other possibilities include Spouse, Children (remember, you can type more than one item in the fields by writing a return character in the edit screen), or even Known Allergies.

3. Tap OK to exit.

✔ Tip

■ Remember that if you beam a contact to another Palm device, your custom label names won't transfer with the record. So, any data in these fields might confuse someone who uses different labels.

Figure 5.36 Name the custom fields according to the information that's most important to you.

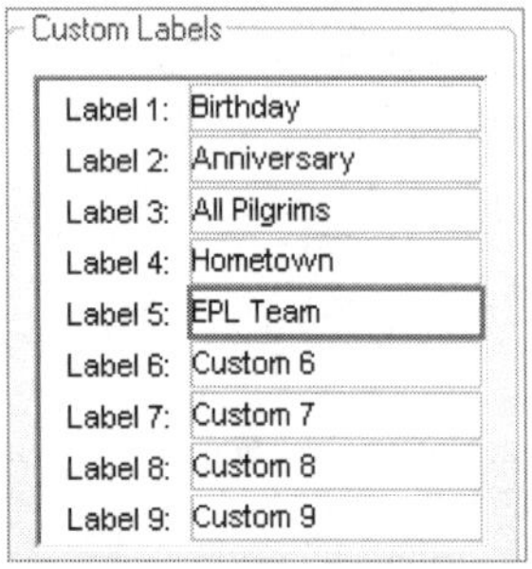

Figure 5.37 Changing these labels applies them to every record in Contacts.

Figure 5.38 Change the field names from within an active record by selecting Field Options from a field's popup menu.

Figure 5.39 From the Contact Edit screen, attach a note by tapping the Note button.

Figure 5.40 An attached note appears in the record as if it was a regular field. Use the scroll arrows to read more.

Attaching and Deleting Notes

The Palm OS's notes feature gives you a blank slate to add all sorts of information about a person or company, from a favorite movie to invaluable driving directions.

To attach a note to a contact:

1. Tap a contact to select it.

2. Tap the Edit button to bring up the Contact Edit screen, then tap the Note button (**Figure 5.39**). Or, select Attach Note from the Record menu, or write ╱-A.

3. Compose your note using Graffiti or the onscreen keyboard.

4. When you are finished, tap Done.

✔ Tips

■ To edit the attached note later, follow the steps above to access the note. If you want a quicker method, however, tap the note icon (☐) to the right of the contact's preferred phone number.

■ You don't have to open the note separately to view it. The text appears at the bottom of the contact's Contact view, and can be read using the scroll arrows (**Figure 5.40**).

■ A quick way to scroll, though harder to navigate, is to "select-scroll" through long notes. Position your cursor somewhere in the text and, without lifting the stylus, drag down the screen.

To delete a note:

1. In the Contact view or Contact Edit screen, select Delete Note from the Record menu, or write /-O.

2. If you're on the note editing screen, tap the Delete button.

3. You will be asked to confirm your choice. Tap Yes or No (**Figure 5.41**).

To attach a note (Windows):

1. Double-click a contact or click the Edit button to view the Edit Contact screen.

2. Click the Note tab, or press Control-Tab to switch to it.

3. Type the text of your note, then click OK.

To attach a note (Macintosh):

1. Create a new note by clicking the New Memo button, or pressing Command-Option-N.

2. Write "Handheld Note: Contacts" in the Title field.

3. Type the text of your note.

4. Link the new Memos record to the desired contact by dragging the memo icon in the window's title bar to the Address List window (**Figure 5.42**). (See later in this chapter for information on linking records.)

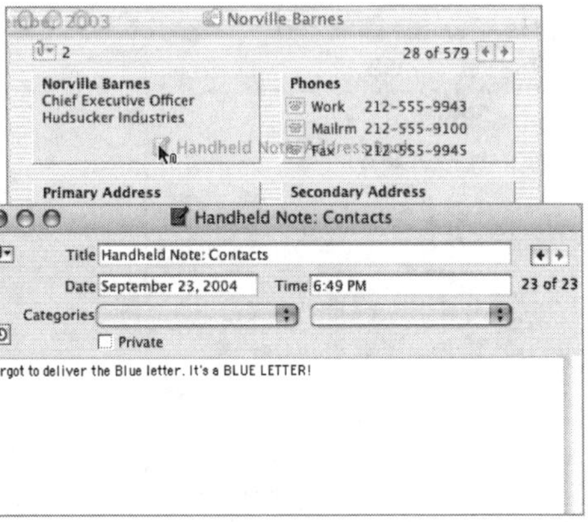

✔ Tips

- The memo icon in the title bar is hard to handle (not to mention awkward). Click and hold on the icon before you start dragging it.

- We'll never be lost again! We used to keep a tattered libraries of paper scraps in our cars containing driving directions. Now, we store directions in notes attached to people's addresses (**Figure 5.43**).

Figure 5.41 When you delete a note, you're asked to verify your action.

Figure 5.42 On the Mac, create a new attached note by dragging the memo icon to the intended contact.

Boren, Herman

1: Start out going North on 25TH AVE SW toward SW HUDSON ST.
2: Turn RIGHT onto SW HUDSON ST.
3: Turn LEFT onto DELRIDGE WAY SW.
4: Take the ramp toward I-5/WA-99 N.
5: Merge onto W SEATTLE BRIDGE.
6: Merge onto I-5 N via the ramp- on the left- toward VANCOUVER BC.
7: Take the N 85TH ST exit- exit number 172- toward AURORA AVE N.

Done   Delete...

Figure 5.43 Attach driving directions to contacts and impress your relatives.

Figure 5.44 The option to edit your categories is strategically placed at the bottom of the popup category list.

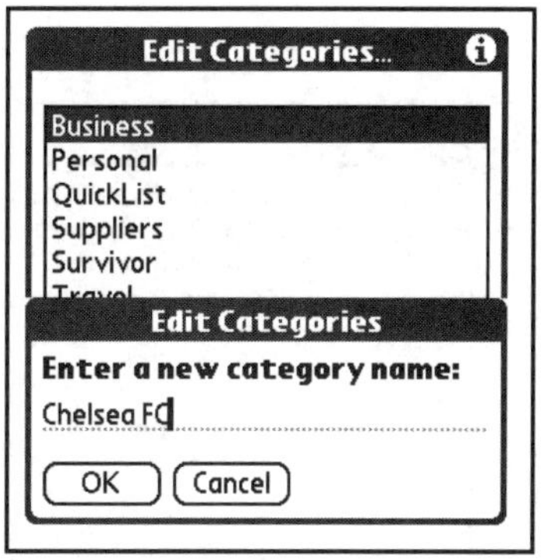

Figure 5.45 Create or rename categories using up to 15 characters.

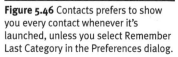

Figure 5.46 Contacts prefers to show you every contact whenever it's launched, unless you select Remember Last Category in the Preferences dialog.

Setting Up Custom Categories

The categories that are preset in the Palm OS barely hint at the value of organizing records by category. In addition to preventing data confusion, it makes it easier to view your data in comprehensible chunks, rather than one big list.

To create a custom category:

1. Select Edit Categories from the category popup menu in the upper-right corner of the screen (**Figure 5.44**).

2. Tap New and give your category a name (**Figure 5.45**).

3. Tap OK to return to the list.

To specify the last category viewed:

1. Select Preferences from the Options menu, or write ╱-R.

2. Mark the Remember Last Category box, then tap OK (**Figure 5.46**).

✔ Tips

- To quickly switch to the next category, press the Contacts button on the handheld's case. If you've created a category that currently has no records assigned to it, Contacts skips to the next category containing records. Highly annoying, however, is that the Unfiled category is skipped using this method.

- Create several records that share the same category by displaying that category and tapping New from the Contacts list; each new record will remain assigned to the current category.

- Palm Desktop for Macintosh doesn't store categories for each built-in application, so you can only have a total of 15 categories shared among those programs.

Marking Contacts as Private

It's fun to show off your handheld some-times, but you don't want everyone to have unlimited access to your private information. It's easy to hide records from wandering eyes.

To mark contacts as private (handheld):

1. Tap the record you wish to mark as private, then tap the Edit button.

2. Tap the Details button.

3. Mark the Private checkbox, then tap OK (**Figure 5.47**).

4. Tap Done when finished (**Figure 5.48**).

To mark contacts as private (Windows and Macintosh):

1. Select a record in the Contacts list, then double-click it to display the contact's information window.

2. Mark the Private checkbox (**Figure 5.49**).

3. Click OK (Windows) or close the infor-mation window (Macintosh).

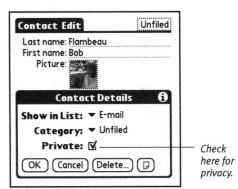

Check here for privacy.

Figure 5.47 It takes a few taps to get to the Contact Details dialog, but it's worth it if you want to ensure that your private records are hidden or masked.

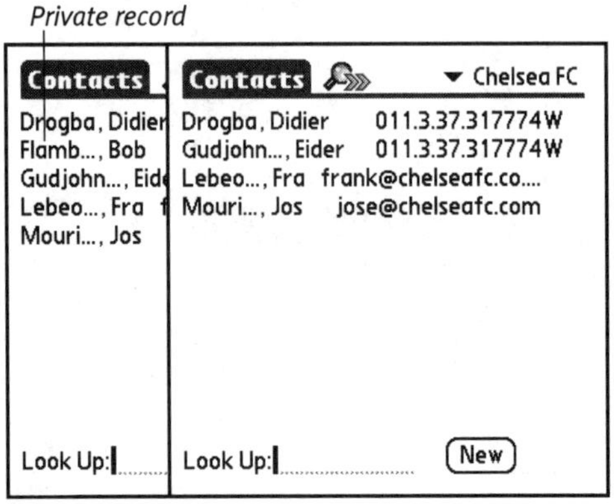

Private record

Figure 5.48 When you set the Security application's settings to Hide Records, private records disappear in the Contacts list.

Figure 5.49 A checkbox appears in Palm Desktop to mark private records.

Figure 5.50 Change the security setting from within any application.

Figure 5.51 Palm Desktop for Macintosh can only show or hide private records.

Changing the Security Setting

Private records can be either hidden entirely or masked. Although the procedure below changes the display option throughout the system, you can change the security setting from within any of the built-in applications.

To change the security setting (handheld):

1. Select Security from the Options menu, write ╱-H, or tap the Security icon in the command toolbar.

2. Select an option from the Current Privacy popup menu: Show Records, Mask Records, or Hide Records (**Figure 5.50**).

3. Tap OK.

To change the security setting (Windows):

◆ In Palm Desktop for Windows, choose a setting from the View menu, or click the small Lock icon on the toolbar to choose a setting: Show Private Records, Mask Private Records, or Hide Private Records.

To change the security setting (Macintosh):

1. Choose Preferences from the Palm Desktop menu (Mac OS X) or from the Edit menu (Mac OS 9).

2. In the Preferences dialog box, switch to the General preferences.

3. Click the Private records popup menu and choose either Show or Hide (**Figure 5.51**). Palm Desktop for Macintosh does not support masked records.

Beaming and Sending Contacts

Every Palm device includes an infrared (IR) port for beaming data from one device to another. Most folks use IR to swap electronic business cards directly into other people's Contacts. If you've ever returned from a conference or trade show with a stack of business cards (and then lost them), you'll appreciate how useful beaming can be. And, if you own a Bluetooth-enabled handheld, you can choose to send to another wireless device.

To specify your business card:

1. Find yourself (in the Contacts list—we can talk more about philosophy later). Tap the record to select it.

2. Choose Select Business Card from the Record menu (**Figure 5.52**).

3. If you're sure, tap Yes in the confirmation dialog. A special icon appears next to the Contact view and Contact Edit tabs (**Figure 5.53**).

To beam your business card:

◆ Choose Beam Business Card from the Record menu, or just press and hold the Contacts button on the handheld's case.

To beam a contact:

1. Tap the record you wish to beam.

2. Choose Beam Contact from the Record menu, or write ╱-B. Private records become public when beamed individually.

Figure 5.52 Choose the record you want for your business card (preferably the one with your name on it), then activate it from the Record menu.

Beaming file card icon

Figure 5.53 The record designated as your business card displays a "beaming file card" icon next to the Contact tab. The best way to zap it to another IR-equipped Palm device is to just hold down the Contacts button on the front of the handheld.

Figure 5.54 Choosing Send Contact gives you the option of transmitting wirelessly via Bluetooth (choose a device from the Discovery Results screen, above) or sending as an attachment in VersaMail.

To send a contact:

1. After selecting a record, choose Send Contact from the Record menu.

2. Choose how you want to transmit the record from the Send With dialog and tap OK. Bluetooth opens the Discovery Results screen from which you can select a device (**Figure 5.54**). VersaMail opens a new message with a .vcs file attached.

To beam or send a category:

1. Make your chosen category visible in the Contacts list.

2. Choose Beam Category from the Record menu. All records in that category, except private records, will be transferred.

   If you select Send Category, choose your transmission method from the Send With dialog.

✔ Tips

- To beam or send all records in a category, choose All from the category popup menu.

- A business card can only be beamed—the Send feature will only work if you have selected your business card record.

- Though beamed records are automatically set as unfiled, the recipient can choose to shuffle them to a category of his or her own or create a new one.

BEAMING AND SENDING CONTACTS

BEAMING AND SENDING CONTACTS

✔ Tips

- You don't have to view a record before beaming it. Use the Look Up field to find a record, which highlights the match in the Contacts list (**Figure 5.55**). Write the command stroke (╱) to view the command toolbar, then tap the Beam Contact icon (☎).

- Some people prefer to leave the Beam Receive option off in the Preferences application to conserve battery life (see Chapter 2). If you fall into that camp, but need to receive beamed business cards from other Palm users, there is a way to activate Beam Receive without making a side trip to the Preferences application (**Figure 5.56**). Press and hold the Contacts button on the handheld's case as if you were going to beam your business card—your handheld will then receive the sender's beamed record (which you can tap OK to accept). Your Beam Receive setting will remain on until you otherwise change it.

- It's possible to "spread-beam" records to multiple handhelds at once. This is great if you're in a small group of Palm users and exchanging business cards; as long as the recipients are in range of the IR beam, they will all receive your business card even if you send it only once.

Figure 5.55 Find a record and beam it from the Contacts list using the Beam Contact icon on the command bar.

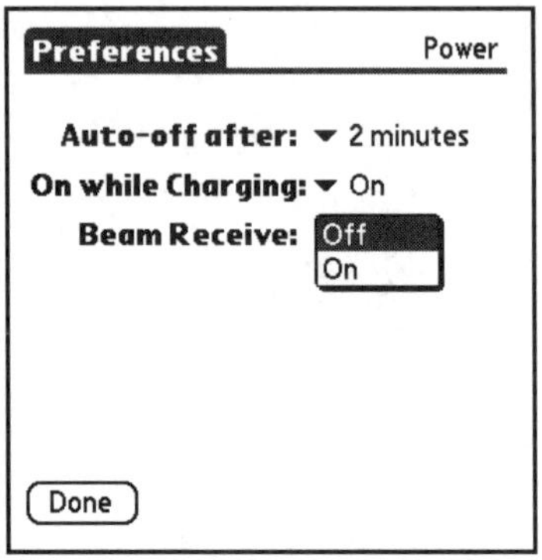

Figure 5.56 You can choose to keep the Beam Receive option turned off, knowing that there's a shortcut for turning it on without coming back to Preferences.

Contacts in Treo

At first glance of your Treo's Applications screen, you might think that PalmOne forgot something: Contacts. But don't worry, it's just hidden. In a somewhat confusing move, the only way to access Contacts is via the Phone application. (Nope, we checked; it can't even be added as one of the physical application buttons in the Preferences application.)

To open Contacts on the Treo:

1. Tap the Phone icon from the Applications screen, or press the Phone button on the Treo's case.

2. Press the down button on the five-way navigator, select Contacts from the Views menu, or press Menu-J on the keypad to open Contacts. (ShortCuts aren't written on the Treo; you use the Menu button to start the shortcut.)

To set preferences for accessing Contacts:

1. Open Display Preferences from the Options menu, or press Menu-Q (**Figure 5.57**).

2. Select which navigator button to associate with the Contacts application.

3. If you want a reminder of which buttons activate which applications, mark the Show button settings checkbox (**Figure 5.58**).

4. Tap OK.

✔ Tip

■ The Contacts list displays a record's name on one line (aligned to the left side of the screen), with phone numbers below (aligned to the right). Tap a number (or select it via the five-way navigator) to begin dialing. (There's no Enable Tap-to-Connect setting to select from Preferences—it's a default action.) Or, tap the name to get to the Contact view (where you'll see the rest of the record's data, from email and physical addresses to custom fields).

Figure 5.57 Choose the five-way navigator's button layout in Display Preferences.

Figure 5.58 Mark the Show button settings checkbox in Display Preferences for a reminder of the layout while in the Phone application.

Importing Contacts into Palm Desktop

There's a good chance that you already have a stash of contact information stored in a desktop PIM program, or maybe even a customized database or Excel spreadsheet. If so, you should be able to transfer your records into Palm Desktop with a minimum of fuss.

To import contacts from a PIM:

1. In your existing PIM, select the export function—most programs include something like Export under the File menu.

2. Export the file as a tab-delimited text file; if you are presented with the option to include field names (such as "Last Name" or "City"), go ahead and include them.

3. In Palm Desktop, choose Import from the File menu.

4. Click and drag the field labels in the left pane of the Specify Import Fields (Windows) or Import (Macintosh) dialog box to match the data in the right pane (**Figures 5.59** and **5.60**).

5. When the data looks right to you, click OK to begin the import process. After a few seconds, the records will be available to use.

✔ Tip

■ If you select a category from the Contact List's category popup menu before you import, the new records will belong to that category after being imported.

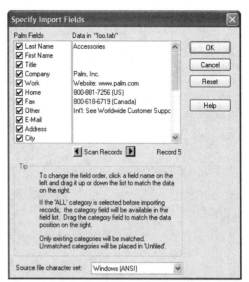

Figure 5.59 In Windows Palm Desktop, drag the field labels to match the record's field-mapping order.

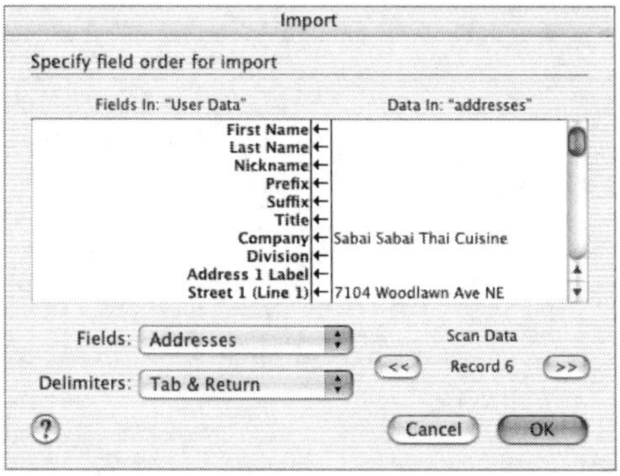

Figure 5.60 The Mac Palm Desktop takes a similar approach to Windows. This step can be slightly monotonous, but you'll appreciate it later on.

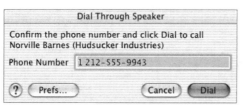

Figure 5.61 Let the computer do the work for you—never memorize a phone number again!

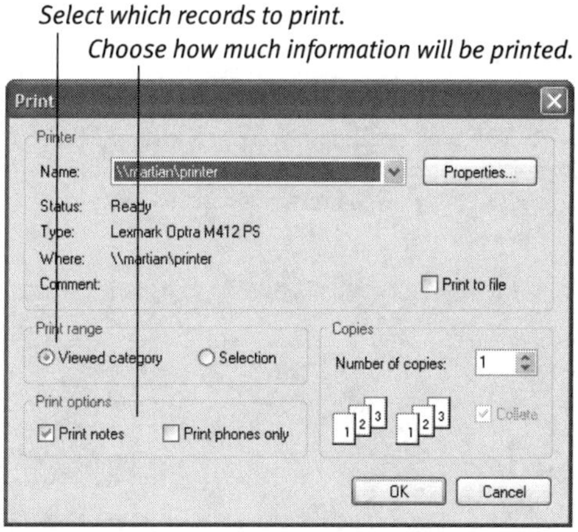

Select which records to print.
Choose how much information will be printed.

Figure 5.62 Printing Contacts records requires only two specialized fields in the standard Print dialog.

Palm Desktop Special Features

In general, the desktop software mirrors the Palm OS in functionality. However, a few features of Palm Desktop also add functionality, such as dialing phone numbers (if your PC is connected to the phone line you use for making calls), printing records, and sharing data with other applications.

To dial phone numbers:

1. In the Contacts list, click the contact you wish to call.

2. In Windows, choose Dial from the Edit menu, or right-click the contact and select Dial from the popup menu that appears. In Palm Desktop for Macintosh, open the contact's information and click the Dial button (**Figure 5.61**). (In Mac OS X, you can dial only through the computer's speaker, however.)

3. Pick up the phone after the number begins dialing, and press the Talk button (Windows) or the Release button (Mac OS 9 version).

To print records:

1. Choose which records you want to print. If you want only a few, select them by Control/Command-clicking their names. To print an entire category, select it from the category popup menu. To print all records, select the All category.

2. Choose Print from the File menu, or press Control/Command-P. The Print dialog box appears (**Figure 5.62**).

3. Set the print range to either Viewed category or Selection, and specify full records or just phone numbers to be printed. You can also choose to print notes or just phone numbers.

To create vCards:

◆ If you use an email program that supports vCards (a method of attaching contact information to an email message), select a contact and choose Forward as vCard from the Edit menu. A new message is created with the vCard information attached.

You can also create a standalone vCard file (.vcf) by choosing Export vCard from the File menu.

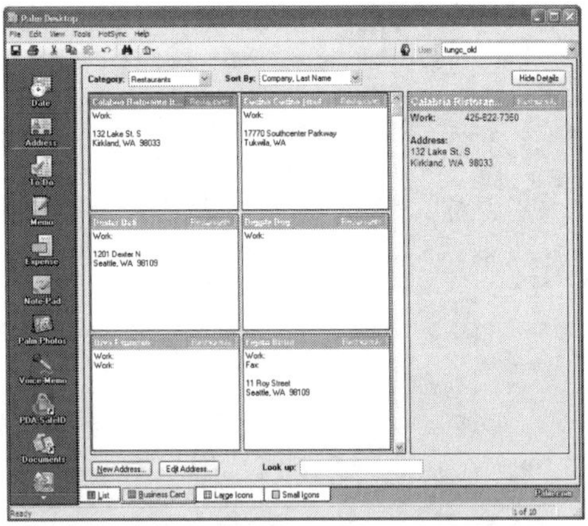

To change the Contacts view:

◆ With the Contacts application visible, click the tabs at the bottom of the screen. The default view is the List view, but you can also arrange your contacts in the easier-to-read Business Card view (**Figure 5.63**) or the Large Icons and Small Icons views (**Figure 5.64**).

The Hide Details button allows you to display more contacts by removing the details pane, and becomes the Show Details button when the pane is hidden.

Figure 5.63 Some people find it easier to use the Business Card view to browse contact information.

Figure 5.64 Using the Large Icons (shown here) and Small Icons views means you never have to feel left out of the crowd.

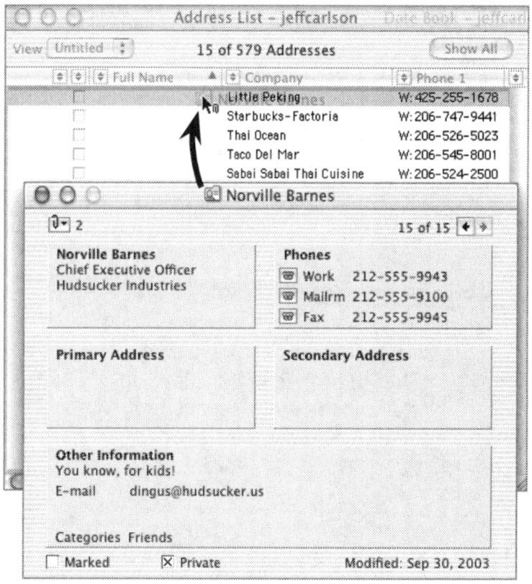

Figure 5.65 Create relational links between records by dragging them onto one another.

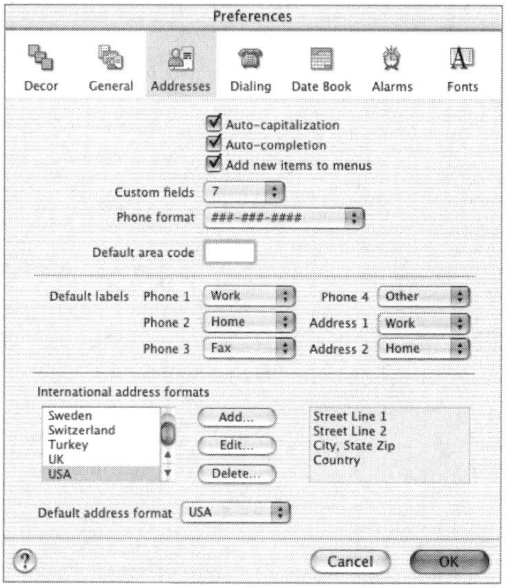

Figure 5.66 Palm Desktop offers several options for working with Contacts data.

Macintosh Palm Desktop Special Features

Palm Desktop for Macintosh includes several features not found in the Windows software. For example, it offers the ability to attach not only notes to records, but also to create links between related records. Unfortunately, the links don't transfer over to the handheld. Note that Contacts is referred to as Addresses.

To link records:

1. Open an Address record by selecting it and pressing Return, or double-clicking it.

2. Grab the title bar icon (📇) in the upper-left corner and drag it to the contact you wish to link. You can drag contacts onto events, to do items, and memos as well (**Figure 5.65**). You can also just drag one record in the Contacts list onto another without viewing the details of either.

   Alternately, click the attachment popup menu (📎▾) and choose an item from the Attach To submenu.

To set Addresses preferences:

1. Choose Preferences from the Palm Desktop menu (Mac OS X) or the Edit menu (Mac OS 9). The Preferences dialog box appears (**Figure 5.66**).

2. Click the Addresses button. Notable preferences here include:

   ▲ **Phone popup menu.** No matter how you type the number, it will be formatted according to this selection.

   ▲ **Auto-capitalization.** Similar to the Palm OS, Palm Desktop capitalizes information within Addresses fields.

   ▲ **Auto-completion.** Palm Desktop stores lists of field contents; when you're entering information, it searches for a match and displays the likely result as you type.

To find contacts:

1. Choose Find from the Locate menu, or press Command-F to display the Find dialog box (**Figure 5.67**).

2. Begin typing the name you're searching for. If you're looking for text within a contact, but it isn't a name or company name, click Display Results in list window.

3. Click Display when it's found.

To sort records:

◆ To sort each list according to a column's contents, click the column's title (it will become underlined to indicate it's the active method) or choose Sort from each title's popup menu (**Figure 5.68**).

◆ You can also edit the columns to customize your display. Click and drag a column's right border to change its width. To rearrange the columns' order, click and hold in the area next to a column name, then drag left or right to position it (**Figure 5.69**). To choose which columns are displayed, select Columns from the View menu and mark the ones you want.

✔ Tips

■ Palm Desktop has the added ability to sort using secondary criteria as well. For example, if you want to sort a list of people within a specific company, click the Company column title, then Shift-click the Full Name column title.

■ The Mark checkbox (**Figure 5.70**) enables you to mark records from multiple categories, then quickly view them without creating a filter by choosing Marked from the popup menu in the column head. When printing, you can opt to print only the marked records without first locating them in the Contacts list.

Figure 5.67 The Find command displays matches containing the entire text in the Starts With field. Type more letters to narrow the search if several items appear.

Click name to sort...   ...or choose popup menu item.

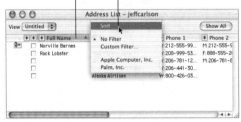

Figure 5.68 Sort the list by any column's contents by either clicking on the column's name, or choosing Sort from the popup menus.

Click and hold here.

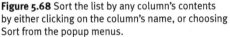

Figure 5.69 Click in the title area and drag to change the order of the visible columns.

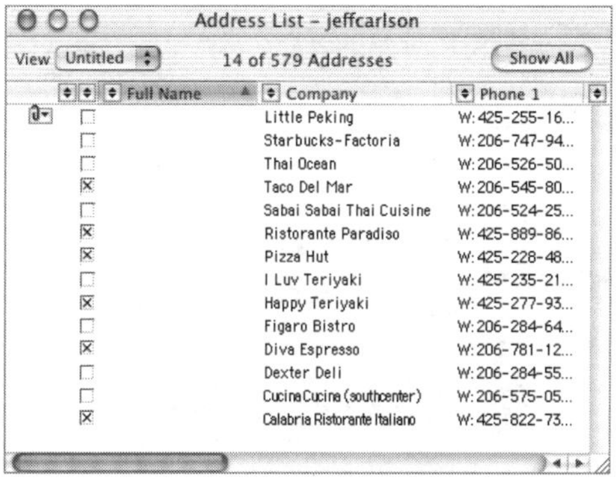

Figure 5.70 Mark records that you use frequently to view and print them quickly, without creating a filter.

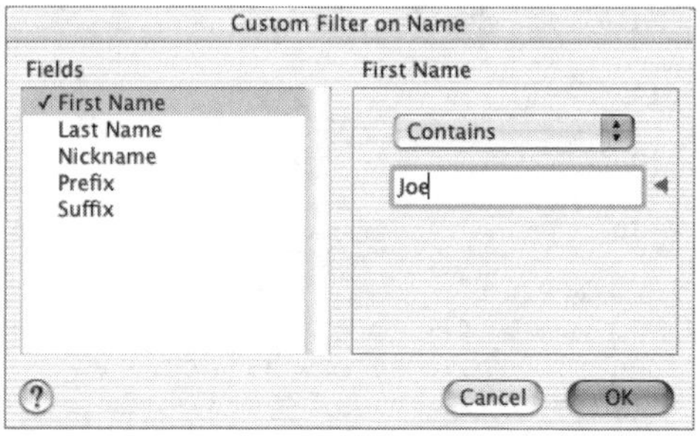

Figure 5.71 Create custom filters to display only the contacts matching specified criteria.

Figure 5.72 The custom fields can be customized even further. Here, the E-mail field is set to create a pre-addressed message in Eudora Pro.

To filter specific data:

◆ You can also configure the sorting method by choosing Custom Filter from the popup menus, which displays only the items that meet the filter's criteria (**Figure 5.71**).

To save memorized views:

◆ When you've set up a sort order and specific filters, choose Memorize View from the View popup menu to save them. This way, you can see related tasks and notes without repeating the sorting steps above. To see the full list again, click the Show All button.

To create a pre-addressed email message:

1. In a record's Address window, click the Other Information area.

2. Click the email button beside the E-mail field in the Other Information section. A blank email message is created in your email program with the contact's email address in the To field.

✔ Tip

■ You can change the email client that's tied into the E-mail field's button. Choose Field Options from the field's popup menu, then choose your email client from the Script File popup menu (**Figure 5.72**).

Using the Instant Palm Desktop Menu

The Instant Palm Desktop menu appears in the Dock icon for Palm Desktop in Mac OS X (**Figure 5.73**), or next to the Mac OS's Applications menu in Mac OS 9. It allows you to access addresses and other records quickly.

To access contact information using the Instant Palm Desktop:

◆ Click the menu and highlight a contact to view or edit its details; or, choose Open Palm Desktop to launch the program.

◆ Search for an address by selecting Find Address (**Figure 5.74**). To make a contact appear permanently on the menu, click the Add to Menu button. You can also dial phone numbers directly from the contact detail window (**Figure 5.75**).

◆ Create new addresses, events, tasks, memos, and event banners from the Create submenu.

To add contacts to the Instant Palm Desktop:

◆ In a record's Instant Palm Desktop contact view, or the Address window within Palm Desktop, check the box to the right of the phone number you want to appear in the Instant Palm Desktop menu.

To remove contacts from the Instant Palm Desktop:

◆ In the Address window, uncheck the box to the right of the phone number.

✔ Tip

■ If you find yourself writing your address frequently in letters or email, put yourself in the Instant Palm Desktop menu, then click the Copy All button to get the info.

Figure 5.73 Under Mac OS X, the Instant Palm Desktop is accessible from the Dock.

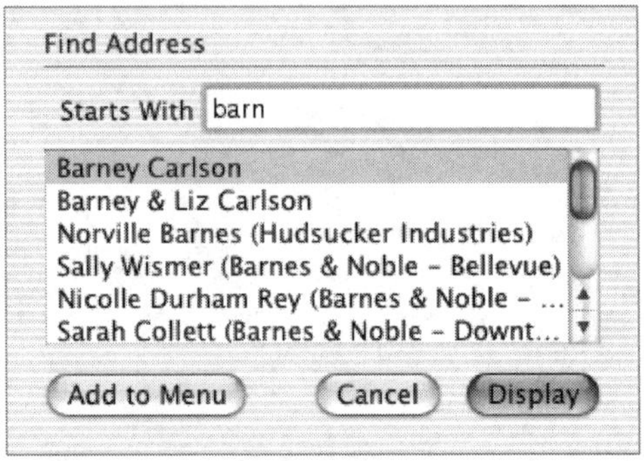

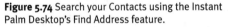

Figure 5.74 Search your Contacts using the Instant Palm Desktop's Find Address feature.

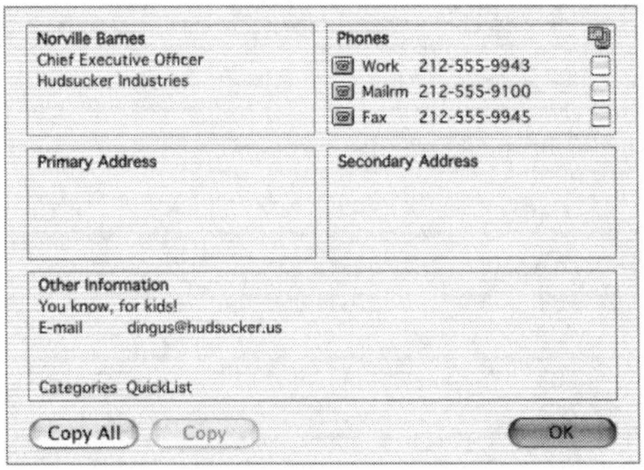

Figure 5.75 All of Palm Desktop's information is available when you select a record from the Instant Palm Desktop menu.

Alternative to Using Contacts

Contacts offers a lot of power in a svelte package, but what if you want to supercharge your address book? Although there are plenty of alternatives, we're most impressed with Super Names (www.standalone.com). It uses Contacts' database as its data source, which means your contacts are still synchronized with your PC.

Super Names

We were dubious of Super Names at first, mostly because we respond strongly to interfaces. A quick look at the Super Names main screen shows how crowded it can be (**Figure 5.76**). But notice what's there: categories appear as tabs across the top of the screen; an alphabet running beneath the tabs lets you tap a letter to jump to that range of contacts; an optional panel below the Contacts list previews the highlighted name, with icons to specify which info appears.

In addition to cramming a lot of useful information on one screen, Super Names lets you link contacts to other contacts, or even to records from Calendar, Tasks, or Memos (**Figure 5.77**). Linked records can be displayed by tapping a paper clip icon at the top of the screen.

Figure 5.76 Once you get the hang of the Super Names interface, you'll like how easy it is to view contact info.

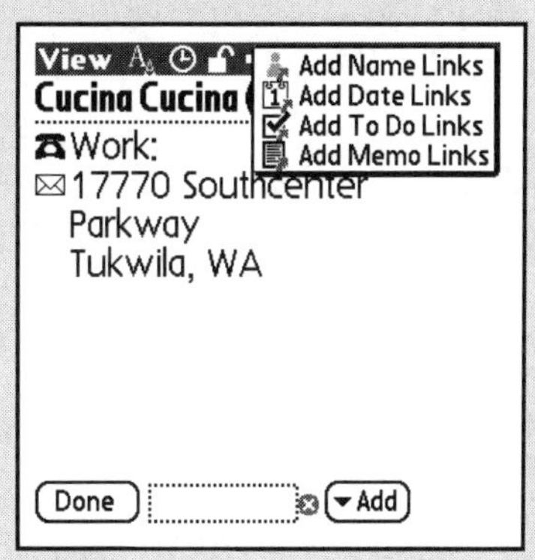

Figure 5.77 Link contacts or other records to view them quickly next time.

Tasks,
Memos, and Notes

When folks first hear about Palm handhelds, most seem to get excited about Contacts and Calendar, two applications that can greatly decrease the amount of paper they carry. But when Jeff was first considering whether to buy a handheld, it was the To Do List—now called Tasks—that thrilled him. He needed to *see* tasks that had to be accomplished, or else he risked forgetting about them until it was too late. A digital to do list that keeps reminding you of tasks not yet finished sounded irresistible.

Memos, formerly Memo Pad, didn't seem quite as thrilling. Sure, it's a necessary element (what's the point of having a palmtop device if you can't jot down quick notes?), but light bulbs are also necessary elements, and you don't see anyone drooling over the latest 100-watt GE soft-white bulb.

Now, Jeff considers both applications to be essential—especially with the new tabbed Tasks layout in Palm OS 5.2. And as PalmOne devices have evolved their multimedia capabilities, now you can jot short notes or doodle during a meeting with Note Pad and leave an audible reminder to yourself with Voice Memo (featured on select devices like the Zire 72 and Tungsten T3).

Tabbed Views in Tasks

The To Do application gets a welcome revamp to the multi-tabbed Tasks in Palm OS 5.2. It also adds the ability to create repeating tasks, as well as assign alarms to signal your attention at a specific time during the day (not just at the beginning).

All view

This view is much like the To Do of old, with your entire library of tasks presented in one screen, and with the ability to show priority, due date, and category (**Figure 6.1**).

Date view

Tapping the Date tab filters tasks via the popup menu to see those that are due today, during the last seven days, during the next seven days, and those that are past due (**Figure 6.2**). The numbers in the menus indicate the number of records that apply to each option.

Category view

To see specifically themed tasks, tap the Category tab and choose a category name from the popup menu that appears (**Figure 6.3**).

✔ Tip

- Although you've always been able to add notes to To Do items, the new Tasks Note button (to the right of the Details button) is a faster way to access the note editing screen. Simply select a task from the list and tap the Note button to add more context to the task at hand.

Figure 6.1 The new Tasks application is now divided into three sections: All, Date, and Category.

Figure 6.2 Use the popup menu in Date view to filter those tasks due today, during the last/next seven days, and those that are overdue.

Figure 6.3 With the Category view's popup menu, you can filter to see only those tasks assigned to a category.

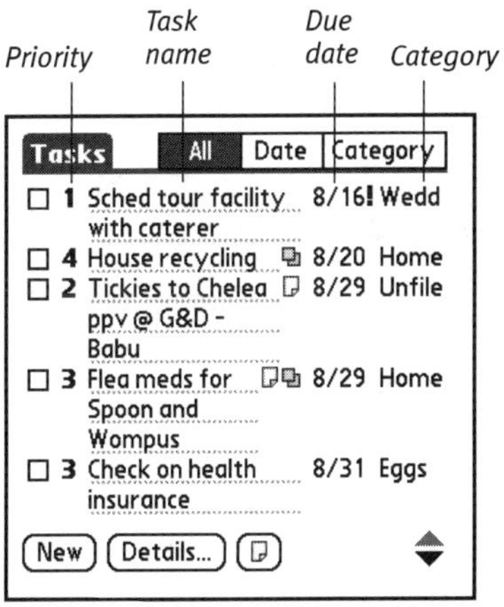

Priority   Task name   Due date   Category

Figure 6.4 The Tasks application, with all aspects visible, includes each task, plus its priority, due date, and category.

Figure 6.5 Depending on your tolerance for visual clutter, you may want more options visible.

Viewing Options

Tasks can be as sparse or as detailed as you want. Select Preferences from the Options menu (✐-R) to access the Preferences window, which provides the following options (**Figure 6.4**).

◆ If you prefer to see the items you've accomplished, mark the Show Completed Tasks checkbox.

If you uncheck this option to hide completed items, the records are still held in the device's memory until you manually purge them (see "Purging Records," later in this chapter).

◆ Marking Record Completion Date changes an task's due date to the date it was checked off when finished.

◆ Show Due Dates, when marked, adds a date column to the right of the task names; items with no due date specified are represented by dashes.

◆ Marking Show Priorities displays a column of numbers, representing the importance of each task (1 is highest, 5 is lowest), between the checkboxes and item names.

◆ As with Contacts and Memos, Tasks records can be assigned to categories. Show Categories adds a category column to the right side of the screen.

◆ Tap the Alarm sound popup menu to choose a specific alarm sound for task reminders that will be different from other audio alerts (**Figure 6.5**).

Changing Security View

Private records can be displayed, masked (grayed out), or hidden from within Tasks.

To change the Security view:

1. Select Security from the Options menu (✓-H).

2. Tap the Current Privacy popup menu to choose one of three methods: Show Records, Mask Records, or Hide Records (**Figure 6.6**).

3. Tap OK to exit.

Figure 6.6 Choose how your private records are displayed.

Setting the Sort Order

Once you've decided which elements will be visible, you need to figure out how to sort Tasks' records. Feel free to experiment with each setting for a few days to get a sense of what works best for you.

To set the sort order:

1. Tap Show to bring up the Preferences window (**Figure 6.7**).

2. Tap the Sort by popup menu to choose one of four methods: Priority, Due Date; Due Date, Priority; Category, Priority; or Category, Due Date (**Figure 6.8**).

3. Tap OK to exit.

✔ Tip

■ We can't stress how much we love to check off a task and have it *disappear*. It's understandable that people like to see what they've accomplished, but to us it's all just clutter. Show Completed Tasks is therefore never marked on either of our handhelds.

Figure 6.7 The Sort by popup menu organizes tasks to fit your preferences.

Figure 6.8 Sorting by Category, Due Date can do funky things with dates: The task for "Catch up..." is set for December 25, 2004, over four months after "Sched tour..." due to their different categories and the category alphabetizing.

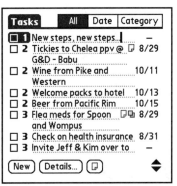

Figure 6.9 Tapping the New button creates a blank record for you to name.

Completed task   Overdue

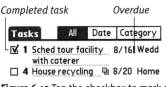

Figure 6.10 Tap the checkbox to mark a task completed. Feels good, doesn't it?

Figure 6.11 Automatically assign new tasks to a category by creating them in the Category view.

Entering Tasks

Creating new tasks takes more than just having someone say "Do this!" over your shoulder. But not much more.

To create a new task:

1. Tap the New button. A flashing cursor appears on a blank line.

2. Write the name of your task—feel free to use multiple lines (**Figure 6.9**). Tap anywhere in a "null" area of the screen (such as the lower-right corner) to deselect your new task.

To mark a task completed:

◆ The moment of ultimate satisfaction—tap the checkbox at left to mark the task completed (**Figure 6.10**). If your device has a five-way navigator, press the center button to mark a record completed.

✔ Tips

■ You don't have to tap the New button to create a new task. With nothing selected, start writing in the Graffiti area; a new record will be created automatically.

■ The default settings for new tasks are Unfiled, no date, with a priority of 1. If you want a new task to share attributes of an existing item, you can maintain category, priority, and/or due date by highlighting an existing record and then tapping New.

■ If a task is created while you are in the Category view, any new records are assigned to the category that's displayed in the popup menu (**Figure 6.11**).

■ The Tasks application indicates a missed deadline by displaying an exclamation point (!) in the due date column (see "Sched tour facility..." in **Figure 6.10**).

Editing Tasks

Depending on which options you've chosen to show, almost every aspect of a task can be changed from the main Tasks screen (except for privacy and repeat frequency). However, if you prefer a cleaner window, the options are no more than two taps away (**Figure 6.12**).

To prioritize a task:

1. If visible, tap the priority column to the left of the task name and choose a different priority level. Or, tap the task, then tap the Details button.

2. Choose a priority from the buttons at the top of the Task Details window. Tap OK to make the change.

To change a task's category:

1. If visible, tap the category column at the far right of the screen and choose a new category. Or, tap the task, then tap the Details button.

2. Tap the category popup menu and select a new category (**Figure 6.13**). To add or edit categories, see "Categorizing Tasks, Memos, and Notes" later in this chapter. Tap OK.

To make a task private:

1. Tap the task, then tap the Details button.

2. Mark the Private checkbox (**Figure 6.14**). If you've chosen Hide Records or Mask Records from the Security application, the record's text will not be visible when you tap OK. (See Chapter 2 for information on hiding and showing private records.)

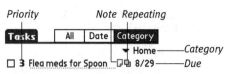

Figure 6.12 You can edit most aspects of a task without leaving the main Tasks screen by tapping these areas.

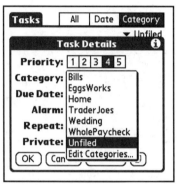

Figure 6.13 Tap the Details button to bring up a dialog box where you can change any aspect of a task.

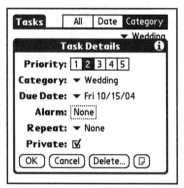

Figure 6.14 The only aspects of a task you can't edit from the main list are its privacy state and alarm.

EDITING TASKS

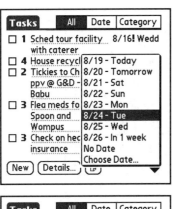

Figure 6.15 Select a due date by tapping either the due date column in one of the three tabbed views (above) or the Due Date popup menu in Task Details (below).

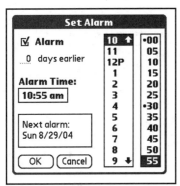

Figure 6.16 Set an alarm for "*0*" days earlier to have it alert you on the day of the task.

Setting Due Date and Alarm

The Tasks application replicates the former To Do's due date functionality, which reminds you of the task at the beginning of the day. But Tasks amps up the reminder power with the Alarm feature, enabling you to set a time of day to be reminded.

To set a task's due date:

1. If it is visible, tap the due date column and choose a new date (**Figure 6.15**). Otherwise, tap the task, then tap the Details button.

2. Tap the Due Date popup menu. The list of dates for the next seven days makes it easy to reschedule tasks.

3. If you need to switch to a specific date, tap Choose Date and select a new day. Tap OK.

To set a task's alarm:

1. Select a task and tap the Details button.

2. If you haven't already, tap the Due Date popup menu to select a date.

3. Tap the Alarm box to display the Set Alarm screen.

4. Tap the Alarm checkbox to enable the feature, then set how far ahead of the task's due date you want the alarm to sound, and at what time during the day (**Figure 6.16**).

5. Tap OK to return to the Task Details screen, then tap OK again.

✔ Tip

■ Set a task's alarm for "0" days earlier for the alarm to sound on the due date.

Repeating a Task

Do you need to complete a project each Wednesday at 3:00 p.m.? Tasks can now repeat, just like events in Calendar do.

To create a repeating task:

1. Select a task and tap the Details button.

2. Tap the Repeat popup menu and choose from the list of common repeating schedules, or tap Other (**Figure 6.17**).

3. If you choose Other, tap Day, Week, Month, or Year in the Change Repeat screen to configure the repetition elements (**Figure 6.18**). Tap OK.

4. Tap OK again to return to the Tasks main view.

✔ Tip

■ Choosing Other enables you to select from two types of repetition: Fixed Schedule or After Completed. You're probably most familiar with the Fixed Schedule concept, which will repeat a task, say, every other day or every first Monday of the month. With the After Completed option, you can schedule a repeated task for a period of time after completing a task, useful for following up on a phone call or setting a regular appointment. For example, you could create a repeating task for changing your car's oil three months after you mark the original task completed (**Figure 6.19**).

Figure 6.17 Five common repeating options are included in the popup menu.

Figure 6.18 If you need to be more precise, choose Other and then configure your preferences.

Figure 6.19 Set a repeating task for a date after you initially completed it (helpful for setting up recurring appointments like oil changes or dentist visits).

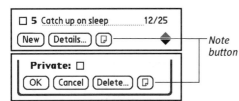

5 Catch up on sleep 12/25
New
Details...
Note
button
Private:
OK
Cancel
Delete...

Figure 6.20 Tap the Note button on either one of the tabbed views (top) or in the Task Details dialog (bottom) to add important information to a task.

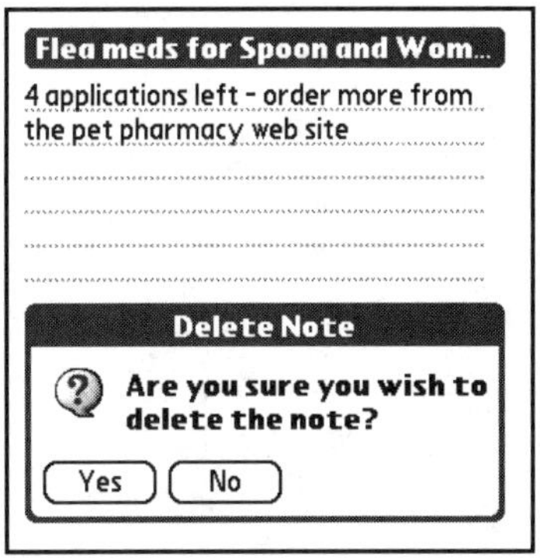

Flea meds for Spoon and Wom...
4 applications left - order more from the pet pharmacy web site
Delete Note
Are you sure you wish to delete the note?
Yes
No

Figure 6.21 To delete a note attached to a task, tap the Delete button, then confirm the deletion.

Adding and Deleting Notes to Tasks

Embellis your tasks with descriptive information stored in attached notes.

To attach a note to a task:

1. Tap an item to select it.
2. Tap the Note button (**Figure 6.20**).

   Alternately, tap the Details button and tap the Note button from the Task Details dialog, or select Attach Note from the Record menu, or write ⁄-A.
3. Compose your note using Graffiti or the onscreen keyboard. Tap Done when you are finished.

✔ Tip

- To edit the attached note later, follow the steps above to access the note. If you want a quicker method, tap the note icon (▢) to the right of the task's name.

To navigate a note:

- Use the scroll bar on the right side of the screen, the physical scroll buttons, or the up/down buttons to move through the text.

To delete a note (from main list):

1. Tap the task to select it.
2. Select Delete Note from the Record menu, or write ⁄-O. Confirm its deletion by tapping Yes or No.

To delete a note (standard method):

1. Tap the Note button, or tap Details and then the Note button.
2. Tap Delete in the Note window. Confirm whether you want to delete it by tapping Yes or No (**Figure 6.21**).

Purging Records

It may bring you a measure of satisfaction to know there are dozens, maybe hundreds, of completed tasks in your handheld. But that means they're also taking up RAM. Free up some memory by purging them (**Figure 6.22**).

To purge old records:

1. From the main Tasks screen, select Purge from the Records menu, or write ╱-E.

2. If you want to remove items from your handheld, but keep them stored on your PC's hard drive, mark the Save archive copy on PC option (**Figure 6.23**). They will be transferred at the next HotSync operation, and removed from your handheld.

3. Tap OK.

Navigating Records

If you have a long list of tasks, the onscreen up and down arrows appear in the bottom-right corner. Tap them to move between screens. But you can do everything single-handedly with the five-way navigator.

To use the navigator buttons:

◆ With no record selected, press the up and down buttons to move a screen at a time.

◆ Pressing the center button selects the top-most record in a screen and places your cursor at the end of its text. The up and down buttons now move from task to task. Press the center button again to mark a task completed. Or, press the left button to deselect any record.

◆ With no task selected, press the left and right buttons to move from one category (or tab) to the next. If you're in the All view, pressing the right button takes you to the Date view; pressing it again moves to the next date range, and so on.

Figure 6.22 You can see how much space your completed and pending tasks are filling by going to the Applications screen and selecting Info from the App menu. Here, the amount of free memory has increased dramatically following a purge.

Figure 6.23 The urge to keep all those successfully completed tasks can be overpowering, but at some point you'll need to free up some memory on your handheld. Mark Save archive copy on PC to ensure that the tasks aren't lost forever.

Memos
▼ All

1. Farsape ep. list
2. Books to read
3. Wedding - Dance song list
4. Million-dollar ideas
5. Good Nick Hornby quotes
6. Good Shakespeare quotes
7. Movies to rent
8. People to thank
9. Web sites to visit
10. Fave brekkie spots
11. Garden planning

New

Figure 6.24 Memos lets you store all those random scraps of information.

Memo ◀ 3 of 12 ▶ Wedding

Wedding - Dance song list
••Banned:
Celebration - Kool & Gang
Electric Slide, Dancing Queen

••Watch List:
Chicken Dance

••Definite:
I'd Rather Dance - Kings of Convenience

Done   Details

Figure 6.25 The text on the first line of your memo becomes its title. From there, write your memo, or paste the text in from the clipboard.

Creating and Editing Memos

Memos is straightforward, yet surprisingly useful. Imagine all of your Post-it notes—plus the crumpled papers discovered in last week's laundry—stored in one location (**Figure 6.24**). The power here is not in the number of features that Memos offers, but in its overall utility.

To create a new memo:

1. Tap the New button, or start writing in the Graffiti area.

2. Start writing. The first line of your memo will become its title, so don't write something generic like "Note" (**Figure 6.25**).

3. Tap Done when you're, well, done.

To edit a memo:

1. Tap once on the title of a memo.

2. To change the memo's category, select one from the category field in the upper-right corner. Or, tap the Details button.

3. Tap Done.

To make a memo private:

1. After tapping the memo you want, tap the Details button to display the Memo Details dialog box.

2. Mark the Private checkbox. If the Security preferences are set to hide private records, the memo will not appear in any of the Memos category lists.

3. Tap Done.

Sorting Memos

Information, unlike dark socks, begs to be sorted. Some prefer alphabetical listings, while others are quite content with chaos. Although Memos doesn't claim to be the storehouse of the world's information, its sorting capabilities—though limited—can appeal to both extremes.

To sort memos:

1. Select Preferences from the Options menu, or write ⁄-R, to display the Memo Preferences dialog box (**Figure 6.26**).

2. Choose a sorting method from the Sort by popup menu. Alphabetic lists items based on their first letters; Manual gives you the power to list items randomly, or by your own secret sorting code. Tap OK.

Note that you must first select Manual sorting before you can begin moving items within the Memos list. If you've been manually sorting and want to switch back to Alphabetic, you will lose your sort order. Unfortunately, the sorting method you choose applies to all memos, so you can't have some categories sorted manually and others sorted alphabetically.

✔ Tip

■ If you want to type on the road, consider the Palm Portable Keyboard (`store.palmone.com`). See Chapter 1 for more keyboards.

Figure 6.26 Memos gives you two options for sorting the Memos list.

Navigating Memos

Moving around in memos isn't much different than navigating notes (see "To navigate a note" earlier in this chapter), but a few aspects do stand out.

To navigate memos:

◆ Use the scroll bar at right (if the memo extends past one screen length) to move up and down the text.

◆ With the Zire 21, press the physical up and down buttons to move a screen at a time.

◆ If your device has a five-way navigator, select an item from the Memos list by pressing the center button. Press up and down to navigate within the memo, or press the left and right buttons to move between memos. Press the center button again to return to the main list.

✔ Tips

■ The Treo's five-way navigator seems to have a bit of a hitch. Pressing the down button brings you to the bottom line of a memo, even though its scroll bar still shows you at the top of the memo. Pressing down again highlights the Done button. However, by pressing the up button, you can then move line by line back to the top—not an optimal navigation solution.

■ Although the old-school Go to Top of Page and Go to Bottom of Page commands were removed in Palm OS 3.5, there's still an easy workaround to zap through your text: Tap and drag up or down to select the text and quickly go to the top or bottom. It may not be the most elegant solution, but it's easy and it works.

Is Memos Good Enough for Taking Notes?

You'd think that having a palm-sized device to write with would make people want to ditch paper forever. Although some people use their handhelds as note-taking machines, we've found that writing longer texts takes more effort and headache than regular ink and wood pulp.

The advantage of writing longhand is that you can write several letters with one stroke (depending on your handwriting style, of course), whereas Graffiti requires that each character be a separate entity. Plus, extended Graffiti writing tends to aggravate the hands and wrists, which can lead to repetitive strain injuries (RSIs) (**Figure 6.27**). We prefer to use Memos as a great place to store information, not necessarily create it.

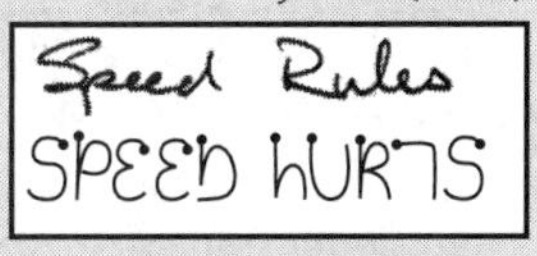

Figure 6.27 Longhand text is a little easier on the hands and wrists than Graffiti.

Using Note Pad

Memos is good for taking extensive notes or accumulating thoughts over a period of time. But if you need to jot down a quick reminder in a Post-it note fashion or doodle during a meeting, Note Pad is for you. Unlike Memos, the records in Note Pad are simple drawings; a separate Note Pad application displays the pictures on your Mac or Windows PC.

To create a new note:

1. Launch Note Pad from the Applications screen. A new blank record is created and named according to the date and time.

2. Write on the screen. Tap the pencil icon in the lower-right corner to change the thickness of the line, or select the eraser icon to remove what you've drawn (**Figure 6.28**).

3. If you want a more descriptive title than the timestamp, highlight the title field and write a title using Graffiti.

4. Tap Done when you're finished. Tap New to immediately create a new note. Or, of course, you can destroy your masterpiece by tapping Delete.

   When you HotSync your device, you can view or copy your notes using the Note Pad application on your computer (**Figure 6.29**).

To set Note Pad alarms:

1. With a Note Pad record open, choose Alarm from the Options menu, or write ╱-A. The Set Alarm dialog appears.

2. Select a day and time. Unlike the Calendar, where you specify a lead time before an event, the time chosen here is the actual time the alarm will sound.

3. When the alarm goes off, the note is displayed; tap OK (**Figure 6.30**).

Figure 6.28 Select a line weight and then draw words or pictures.

Figure 6.29 View your notes on the computer using the basic Note Pad application. Palm Desktop for Windows offers a built-in application, while the Macintosh version uses a separate program (shown above).

Figure 6.30 Note Pad is a quick and easy method of creating simple alarms.

Figure 6.31 Tap the Pause button to take a break from recording, or tap Stop to end the session.

Figure 6.32 The Palm Desktop Voice Memo application lets you review your audio notes (Windows shown above).

Figure 6.33 Categorize your voice memos, or mark them as private.

Using Voice Memo

Some recent PalmOne models, such as the Tungsten T3 and Zire 72, include a digital voice recorder. Once activated, the Voice Memo application opens; a separate Voice Memo application on your Mac or Windows PC also plays back the audio.

To create a new voice memo:

1. Press the Voice Memo button on the side of the handheld, or launch Voice Memo from the Applications screen.

2. Tap the New button.

3. Tap the red Record button to begin recording. Tap the Pause button to take a break, or tap the Stop button to end the session (**Figure 6.31**).

4. After stopping, you can review your voice memo by tapping the Play button.

5. If it's not up to snuff, tap Delete. Tap the New button to add another thought. Or, tap Done to save it.

   When you HotSync your device, you can review your memos using Palm Desktop's Voice Memo application (**Figure 6.32**).

✔ Tips

- Press and hold the Voice Memo button on the side of the handheld to record, then release it when you're done.

- By default, the time the memo was recorded is used as the title. Give it a more descriptive title so you can easily return to it.

- To add a voice memo to a category, tap the category popup menu in the upper-right corner. Or, select Details from the Options menu (/-O) to open the V Memo Details dialog, which also includes an option for marking the memo private (**Figure 6.33**).

Categorizing Tasks, Memos, and Notes

The Tasks, Memos, Note Pad, and Voice Memo applications share a standard method of categorizing a record, plus a few individual twists.

To assign a category to a task:

1. With Show Categories selected in Preferences, tap the category column and choose a new category from the popup menu that appears (**Figure 6.34**).

   If categories are not visible—or you're in the Category view—select the record and tap the Details button.

2. Select a name from the category popup menu.

3. Tap OK to return to the list.

To assign a category to a memo or note:

1. Tap a record to open it.

2. Select a category name from the popup menu in the upper-right corner of the screen (**Figure 6.35**).

3. In Memos, you can also tap the Details button and choose an item from the category popup menu.

4. Tap OK to return to the list.

To assign a category to a voice memo:

1. Tap a record to open it.

2. Select Details from the Options menu.

3. Select a name from the category popup menu (**Figure 6.36**).

4. Tap OK to return to the list.

Figure 6.34 Assign categories quickly by tapping the category column in Tasks.

Figure 6.35 Tap the category popup menu in either Memos or Note Pad...

Figure 6.36 ...or select Details from the Options menu to set the category (the only method available for Voice Memo).

Figure 6.37 You can specify up to 15 categories for each of the four built-in applications.

Figure 6.38 Save space on your handheld by moving voice memos to a memory card.

Figure 6.39 Instead of manually reassigning a category to multiple records, merge two existing categories into one.

To set up custom categories:

1. In Memos, Note Pad, or Voice Memo, tap the category popup menu in the upper-right corner. In Tasks, you'll first need to go to the Category view.

2. Select Edit Categories from the bottom of the list to bring up the Edit Categories dialog box.

3. Tap the New or Rename button and write the category name (**Figure 6.37**) or tap a name and Delete to remove a category.

✔ Tips

- From Voice Memo's category popup menu, you also have the choice to move the memo's WAV file to an inserted memory card (**Figure 6.38**). This doesn't copy the memo—the original will be deleted from the handheld's memory after it's been moved. The voice memo will then display a small card icon to the right of the record in the list view. If a voice memo is stored on a memory card, you cannot set an alarm for it. To move it back to the internal memory, simply select one of the categories from the popup menu.

- Remember, you can have a maximum of 15 categories.

- To create multiple records sharing the same category, go to that category's screen, then create your records there.

- You can merge categories without changing each record individually. Simply rename the categories so they share the same name; you will receive a dialog box confirming your action (**Figure 6.39**).

Beaming and Sending Records

Save a friend some writing time and transfer your tasks or memos—or brighten their day with a cartoon or audio message—via infrared. You can also choose to send a task either via email or to a handheld or compatible cell phone via a wireless Bluetooth transmission.

To beam a record:

1. Open a record, then choose Beam Task from the Record menu, write ∕-B, or tap the Beam icon from the command bar (🕿) (**Figure 6.40**).

2. If the recipient's Beam Receive preference is set to On and the IR ports are aimed at each other, the record will be transferred.

To send a record:

1. After selecting a task, choose Send Task from the Record Menu.

2. Choose how you want to transmit the record from the Send With dialog and tap OK. Bluetooth opens the Discovery Results screen from which you can select a device. VersaMail opens a new message with a .vcs file attached (**Figure 6.41**).

To beam or send a category:

1. From the list view of Memos, Note Pad, or Voice Memo, or from the Tasks Category view, select the category you wish to beam from the category popup menu at the top-right corner. To beam all categories, choose All from the popup.

2. Select Beam Category from the Record menu. Note, however, that your categories will appear as Unfiled on the recipient's Palm device. If you select Send Category, choose your transmission method from the Send With dialog.

Figure 6.40 Tap the Beam icon in the command bar.

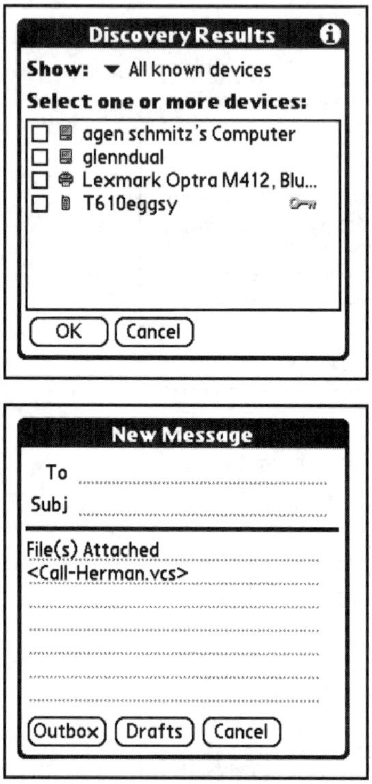

Figure 6.41 Choosing Send gives you the option of transmitting wirelessly via Bluetooth (choose a device from the Discovery Results, above) or sending as an attachment in VersaMail (below).

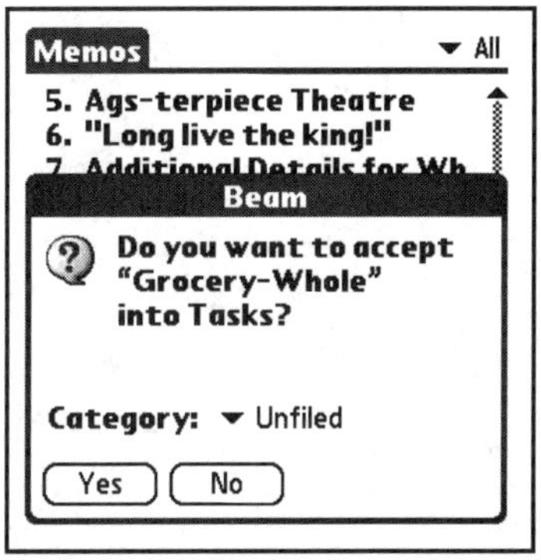

Figure 6.42 A beamed record is automatically set as "Unfiled," but your recipient can get it sorted according to his or her own category scheme.

Figure 6.43 Select a font size for the list view; in Memos, you can also select a different size for the record view.

✔ Tips

- Though beamed records are automatically set as unfiled, the recipient can choose to shuffle them to a category of his or her own or create a new one (**Figure 6.42**).

- In Tasks, what category you beam or send depends upon which Tasks view you are in. If you choose Beam or Send Task while in the All view, you'll send your entire list of tasks. To transmit a single category, tap the Category tab, then choose your method.

- If you want to send several tasks that are more time specific and associated with multiple categories, open the Date view. Select one of the filtering options from the popup menu, then choose your transmission method.

Changing the Font

You can set a different font for list and record views in Tasks, Memos, Note Pad, and Voice Memo.

To change the font:

1. In either the list view or the record view, select Font from the Options menu, or write ╱-F. The Select Font dialog box appears.

2. Choose the font from the boxes provided, and tap OK (**Figure 6.43**).

✔ Tip

- Memos allows you to have two font settings—one for the list view and one for the record view.

Working in Palm Desktop for Windows

Using the Tasks, Memos, Note Pad, and Voice Memo within Palm Desktop is, for the most part, the same as working on the handheld (**Figure 6.44**). There are also a few features that can only be accessed on your PC.

To filter records:

1. Click the category popup menu to filter to a specific category, or choose All.

2. Click the Sort By popup to choose the sorting order. For example, as on your handheld, you can sort Memos alphabetically or by the order you manually placed them.

✔ Tips

- Click the Hide/Show Details button to display a preview of the record. With Voice Memo, the preview window includes a Play button and a slider to help you move forward and backward within the recording.

- The Memos and Note Pad applications include tabs at the bottom of the screen that enable you to switch between list and icon views (**Figure 6.45**).

- Tasks is the only Palm Desktop application that provides additional settings. Select Preferences from the Tools menu to set view options for showing completed tasks, only due tasks, and completion date (**Figure 6.46**).

- Don't forget the contextual menu—right-click with your mouse to access such controls as creating or editing a record, changing the category, or sending to another program.

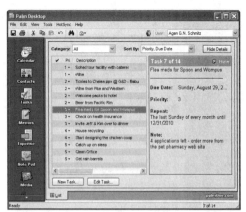

Figure 6.44 The Tasks application within Palm Desktop presents all of your options on one main screen.

Figure 6.45 Choose to view Memos in either list or icon (large or small) format.

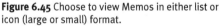

Figure 6.46 Tasks provides options for viewing completed tasks, only due tasks, and completion date.

Figure 6.47 Use the contextual menu to send a record (or selection of records) to another application or forward via an email message.

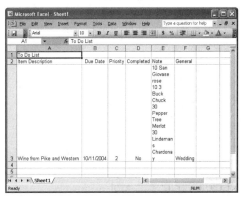

Figure 6.48 Sending a task to Excel doesn't produce a pretty format right off the bat.

To print records:

1. Choose the items you want to print, or choose the category to print.

2. Choose Print from the File menu, or press Control-P.

3. Specify how you want the data to appear in the Print Options box (such as printing the whole category versus just a selection). Click OK to create a printout.

To share records with other applications:

1. Select a record or selection of records to transfer.

2. Go to the Edit menu or right-click to open the contextual menu and choose an option from the Send To submenu (Tasks and Memos), Forward as PNG (Note Pad), or Forward as WAV (Voice Memo) (**Figure 6.47**).

✔ Tips

■ Choosing Send To for Tasks and Memos provides you with options for opening your installed word processing or spreadsheet programs (such as Microsoft Word and Excel). The Forward option will open a new message in your email program.

■ Sending to Word or Excel produces a table of data that definitely will need layout manipulation (**Figure 6.48**).

■ You might be asking, "What does Papua New Guinea have to do with Note Pad?" The PNG (Portable Network Graphics) format is a relatively new image format that's an improvement over GIF, as its compression is lossless (i.e., images won't look out of focus when compressed).

Working in Palm Desktop for Macintosh

Palm Desktop for Macintosh 4.1 provides essentially the same functionality and features as its Windows counterpart, though it looks different and uses different names (To Do List for Tasks, Memo List for Memos).

To view tasks or memos:

◆ Select To Do List or Memo List from the View menu, or press Command-Shift-T or Command-Shift-N.

◆ Click the To Dos or Memos button on the Toolbar (**Figure 6.49**).

To create new tasks and memos:

◆ Double-click an unused portion of the To Do List window or Memo List window (**Figure 6.50**). You can also double-click the To Dos pane of the Day calendar view.

◆ Choose To Do or Memo from the Create menu, or press Command-Option-T (To Do item) or Command-Option-N (memo).

◆ You can also click the New To Do or New Memo button on the Toolbar.

✔ Tips

■ The Day calendar window also displays tasks for that day only. The only time we ever need the full To Do List is if we're looking ahead at future tasks.

■ In the Day calendar window, set aside a block of time to work on a task by dragging it to the day's schedule. Palm Desktop adds "Work On" to the task name—or "Celebrate" if it's a birthday reminder created by Palm Desktop (**Figure 6.51**)!

Figure 6.49 The Toolbar offers quick access to the To Do and Memo controls.

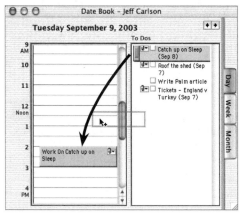

Figure 6.50 Double-clicking in the To Do List brings up a new To Do window.

Figure 6.51 Dragging a task to the Day calendar blocks out time for needed work.

Click name to sort... ...or choose a popup menu item.

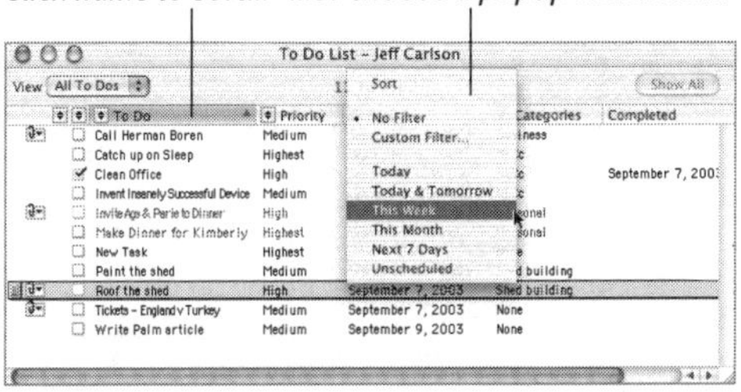

Figure 6.52 Sort the list by any column's contents either by clicking on the column's name, or choosing Sort from the popup menu.

Click and hold here.

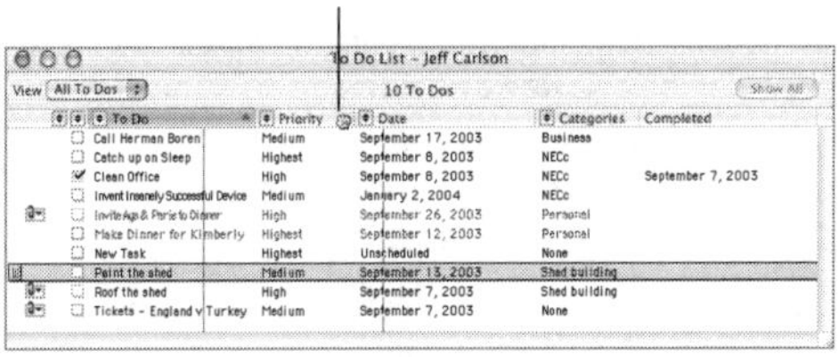

Figure 6.53 Click in the title area and drag to change the order of the visible columns.

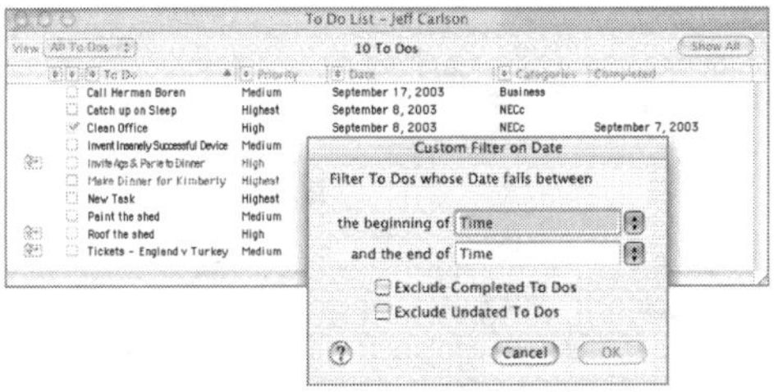

Figure 6.54 Create custom filters to display only the tasks or memos that match specified criteria.

To sort records:

◆ To sort each list according to a column's contents, click the column's title (it will become underlined to indicate it's the active method) or choose Sort from each title's popup menu (**Figure 6.52**).

◆ You can also edit the columns to customize your display. Click and drag a column's right border to change its width. To rearrange column order, click and hold in the area next to a column name, then drag left or right to reposition it (**Figure 6.53**). To choose which columns are displayed, select Columns from the View menu and mark the ones you want.

To filter specific data:

◆ You can also configure the sorting method by choosing Custom Filter from the popup menus, which displays only the items that meet the filter's criteria. For example, if you want to list only the phone calls you need to make, set up a filter that searches for the word "call" or "phone" (**Figure 6.54**).

To memorize views:

◆ When you've set up a sort order and specific filters, choose Memorize View from the View popup menu to save them. This way, you can see related tasks and notes without repeating the sorting steps above. To see the full list again, click the Show All button.

✔ Tips

■ You can sort a list according to multiple criteria. Click a column name to perform the first sort, then Shift-click another column name to then sort the sorted results.

■ In the Day calendar view, sort the day's To Do List according to completion by clicking the phrase "To Dos" above the list.

You can attach related records to other records (such as memos attached to tasks). Although this linkage does not transfer to the handheld, it can be a valuable way of working with your data on the desktop.

To attach records to tasks and memos:

◆ If both records are visible, drag and drop one to the other. A link is created in both records (**Figure 6.55**).

◆ Click the folder icon ( ) and choose Attach To from the popup menu.

The biggest confusion arising from Macintosh Palm Desktop is the way it handles notes belonging to records (such as in Calendar or Contacts). Whereas the Windows Palm Desktop treats attached notes as separate entities, the Mac software uses its Memos feature to handle attached notes.

Each note attached to a To Do item exists as a separate record in the Mac Palm Desktop Memo List, and each is titled, "Handheld Note: Tasks" (using the name of the Palm OS application rather than the Palm Desktop name). It is then linked to its associated record using the Palm Desktop's attachment feature explained above. With that in mind, it becomes relatively easy to attach new notes on the desktop.

To attach notes to tasks:

1. Click the New Memo icon or press Command-Option-N.

2. Type "Handheld Note: Tasks" exactly as shown in the Title field.

3. Write the text of your note.

4. Click and hold the note icon in the title bar, then link the note by dragging it to its associated task (**Figure 6.56**).

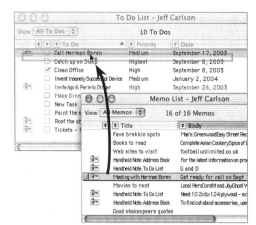

Figure 6.55 Drag and drop records onto each other to create links, indicated by the folder icon that appears to the left of records.

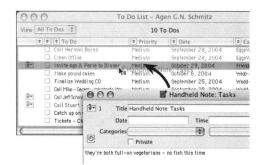

Figure 6.56 Drag the note icon in a memo's title bar to associate it with a task. Be sure to use the title "Handheld Note: Tasks" to ensure that your note will appear as an attached note on your handheld.

To Do List
Memo List
HotSync (Jeff Carlson)
Find Address...
Create
Events
To Dos
Roof the shed
Tickets - England v Turkey
Addresses
Show In Finder
Quit

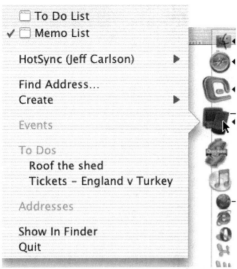

Figure 6.57 You don't even need to open Palm Desktop to access its features; the Instant Palm Desktop menu is a quick method of accessing or creating records.

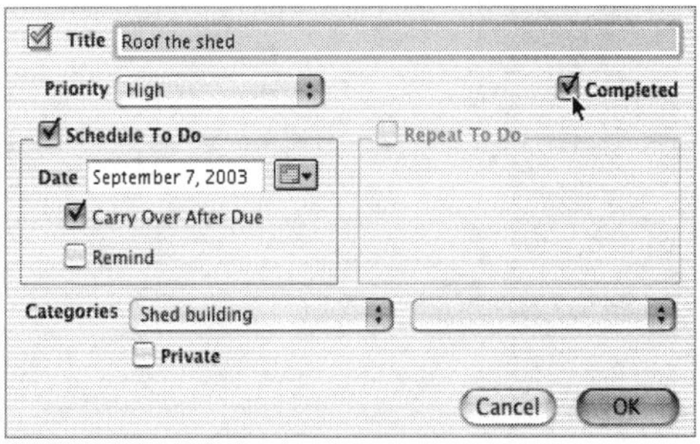

Title
Roof the shed
Priority
High
Completed
Schedule To Do
Repeat To Do
Date
September 7, 2003
Carry Over After Due
Remind
Categories
Shed building
Private
Cancel
OK

Figure 6.58 Experience the joy of completing a task without even launching Palm Desktop to mark it done.

Instant Palm Desktop menu

The day's current tasks are also listed in the Instant Palm Desktop menu, from which you can edit or create tasks without switching to the Palm Desktop application. You can access the menu in Mac OS X by right-clicking the Palm Desktop icon in the Dock (**Figure 6.57**), or in Mac OS 9 via the icon at the right side of the menu bar.

- Highlight an item to view or edit its details, or choose Open Palm Desktop or Switch to Palm Desktop (if it's already running) to launch the program.
- To mark an item as done, highlight it to open the Task dialog box. Click the Completed checkbox and click OK (**Figure 6.58**).
- Create new To Do items by selecting To Do from the Create submenu.

✔ Tip

- In Mac OS 9, you can edit tasks without launching the Palm Desktop. However, with Mac OS X, the application has to be open in order to access Instant Palm Desktop.

CALCULATOR, EXPENSE, AND CLOCK

Remember when having one of those calculator watches was the coolest? Imagine! A whole calculator on your wrist—and if you could just sneak it into math class without anyone suspecting....

The screen is now bigger than the old calculator watches (and the buttons are certainly larger!), but the utility of having a calculator on our handhelds has been helpful for those times when numbers overwhelm our Humanities-educated brains.

The number fun doesn't stop at the calculator, though. If you have to keep track of expenses for work, the included Expense application should save you a headache at month's end when you're trying to explain to your boss where that $100 went in Las Vegas. (If you want to get even more granular with your money and investments, see Chapter 14, *Managing Your Money*, for a bevy of third-party applications such as Pocket Quicken.)

If you're a global day trader, or some else who need to know the time around the world, the World Clock application will keep you current.

Using the Calculator

Admittedly, the Palm OS's built-in calculator isn't what you'd call comprehensive (especially if you're a real number cruncher). It adds, subtracts, multiplies, and divides. It has big buttons so you can use your finger instead of the stylus if you want to. And it reinforces the Palm philosophy that something doesn't have to be complicated and bloated with features in order to be useful.

Still, several things lurk just below the surface of the Calculator application that make it better than a cheapo math machine hiding somewhere in the back of your desk drawer.

To perform calculations:

1. Launch the Calculator application by tapping the silk-screened icon (on devices that include it), or the Calculator icon from within Applications (**Figure 7.1**).

2. Tap the buttons to enter numbers and basic mathematical operations.

3. Tap the percentage button to convert a number to a decimal percentage (for example: **2** **5** **%** = 0.25).

4. Tap the **%** button to make a number either positive or negative.

To clear the results field:

◆ Tapping **C** clears the entire calculation.

◆ Tapping **CE** clears the last number you entered without wiping out everything.

✔ Tip

■ You can operate the calculator by writing in the Graffiti area (**Table 7.1**). We're not sure why exactly you'd want to, but at the very least it's good Graffiti practice!

Figure 7.1 There's no mistaking that this is a calculator, right down to the finger-friendly buttons.

Table 7.1 Yes, it's true! Use the Calculator without tapping buttons by writing numbers and symbols in the Graffiti area.

Graffiti Calculator?			
BUTTON	**GRAFFITI**	**BUTTON**	**GRAFFITI**
1	|	**CE**	Ɛ
2	2	**C**	C
3	3	**MC**	m
4	4²	**MR**	R
5	5	**M+**	p
6	6	**%**	\
7	7	**÷**	/
8	8	**×**	X²
9	9	**−**	—
0	0	**=**	—
.	•	**+**	✝²

Figure 7.2 View the last several steps in an operation by bringing up the Show History screen.

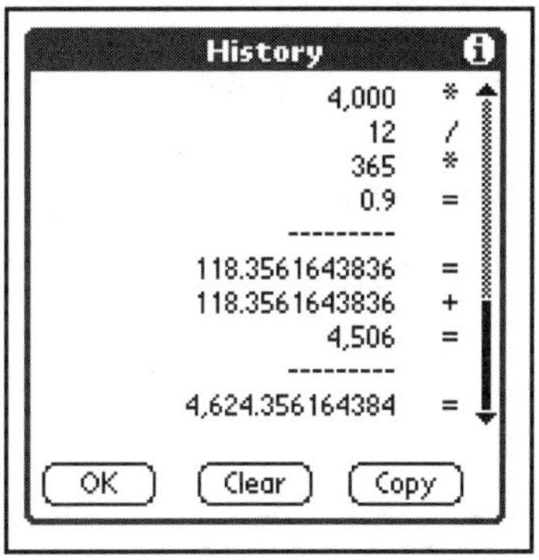

Figure 7.3 The Calculator's "tape" makes it easier to see where mistakes are made.

To memorize calculation results:

1. Tap the [M+] button to store the current result in memory; a small "m" will appear in the number field. If you tap the button again later, the new result is added to the stored number, instead of replacing it.

2. Tap [MR] to display the stored number; you can use it as part of a calculation in progress.

3. Tap [MC] to clear the contents of the stored memory.

To view "the tape":

1. You can access a list of the most recent numbers in a calculation by choosing Show History from the Options menu (**Figure 7.2**).

2. You'll see all the calculations from your current Calculator session in a list running down the right side of the screen (**Figure 7.3**).

✔ Tip

■ In earlier versions of the Palm OS, you could see one screen of recent calculations. But with Palm OS 5.2.8, Calculator was updated so that you could scroll up to see all calculations within a Calculator session.

Copying and Pasting Calculations

Being able to take your calculation results to another application is one of the reasons Calculator is more useful than most calculators. Sure, you can write the numbers on paper, but that's just *so* 1995.

To copy and paste calculations:

◆ On the main Calculator screen, choose Copy Total from the Edit menu (or write ╱-C) to copy the current number to the Palm OS's Clipboard for pasting into other programs. Similarly, you can copy a number from another application and choose Paste (or write ╱-P) to add it to your calculation.

◆ In the Show History screen, tap the Copy button to grab the visible list of calculations for pasting elsewhere or the Clear button to erase the history (**Figure 7.4**). Alternatively, back in the main screen, write ╱-T to copy the calculation history, and write ╱-X to clear it (**Figure 7.5**).

✔ Tips

■ If you make a calculation, then switch to another application, the calculation result is held in memory. However, the last set of operations normally viewed by the Show History screen gets erased! If you're going to need the full transcript of a calculation later, copy it first before exiting the Calculator. You may want to set up a Memos record to paste in your results before moving on to the next task.

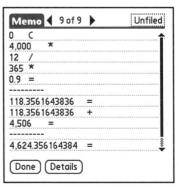

Figure 7.4 Paste calculations or results into other applications, like Memos, shown here.

Figure 7.5 Copy recent calculations from either the History screen (top) or the main screen's Edit menu (bottom).

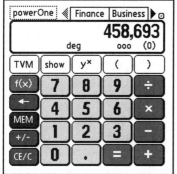

Figure 7.6 Other calculators, such as RPN (top) and PowerOne Finance (middle) take over where the built-in Calculator leaves off. The 2xCalc (bottom) offers a wide variety of built-in conversions, including a weekly update of 160 currencies.

- There are several calculators you can download that should be able to handle whatever you throw at them (**Figure 7.6**). For example, RPN (www.nthlab.com) is an advanced calculator that also accepts plug-ins written by other developers. PowerOne Finance (www.infinitysw.com) specializes in financial calculations. The handy 2xCalc (www.wizu.com) is a calculator full of everyday conversion tools, from length and temperature to area and volume. And when you pay the shareware fee, you're able to download a weekly refresh of 160 currencies—a very useful tool for travelers.

Advanced Calculator Mode (Treo)

One of the holdovers from the Handspring era, the Treo's built-in Calculator retains the advanced mode found in the old Visor models. It features nine built-in views, accessible by tapping the View popup menu: Math, Trig, Finance, Logic, Statistics, Weight/Tmp, Length, Area, and Volume. The top two rows of buttons change depending on the view.

To switch to Advanced mode:

◆ Push the Menu button and use the five-way navigator to choose Toggle Mode from the Options mode. Or, simply press Menu-M.

To change calculator views:

1. Tap the left-most popup menu below the calculator's number field.

2. Select a view name; the calculator's buttons change depending on the view (**Figure 7.7**).

Creating Custom Views in the Advanced Calculator

While we aren't the sharpest slide rules in the mathematician's toolbox, we do know a cool feature when we see one. The Treo's Advanced Calculator comes with nine built-in views, but that's not the limit. You can create a custom view that operates according to your whims, changing the functions of the view-specific buttons.

To create a custom view:

1. First, export an existing view to use as a template. Choose Export from the Program menu, or press Menu-E.

2. Select a view style to export from the popup menu that appears, then tap Export (**Figure 7.8**).

Figure 7.7 The Advanced Calculator mode's View popup menu switches between the different calculators.

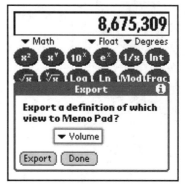

Figure 7.8 To create a new view, you must first export an existing definition.

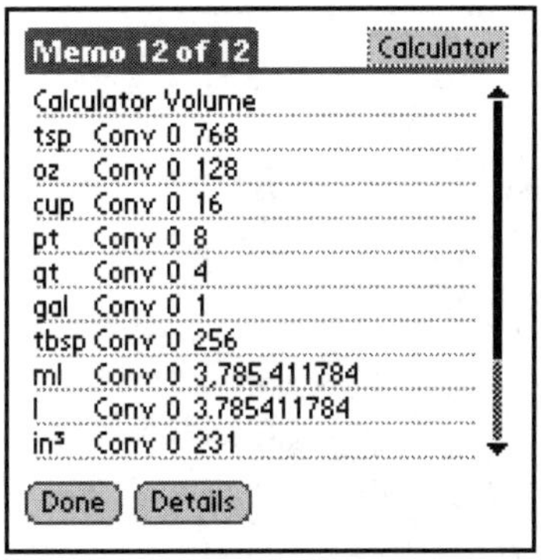

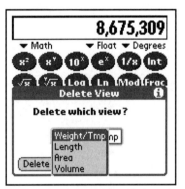

Calculator Volume
tsp Conv 0 768
oz Conv 0 128
cup Conv 0 16
pt Conv 0 8
qt Conv 0 4
gal Conv 0 1
tbsp Conv 0 256
ml Conv 0 3,785.411784
l Conv 0 3.785411784
in³ Conv 0 231

(Done) (Details)

Figure 7.9 Each line represents a different customizable calculator button.

8,675,309

▼ Math   ▼ Float ▼ Degrees

(x²) (xʸ) (10ˣ) (eˣ) (1/x) (Int)

(√x) (ʸ√x) (Loa (Ln (Mod(Frac
Delete View   ❶

Delete which view?

Weight/Tmp np
Length
(Delete) Area
Volume

Figure 7.10 You can delete only four of the built-in calculator modes.

3. Switch to Memos, then choose Calculator from the category popup menu.

4. Tap the record you exported. The first line is the title; each subsequent line corresponds to one of the view-specific buttons (**Figure 7.9**).

5. To change a button's title, write the new title at the beginning of the line. Edit the last number in the line to specify the calculation amount to be applied when the button is pressed. To make the button blank, replace the line with "Unused."

6. Switch back to the Calculator's Advanced mode and choose Import from the Program menu, or press Menu-I.

7. Select the modified view from the Import window's popup menu. If the name already exists, choose to Replace the original, Add to the list (it appears at the bottom of the View popup menu), or Cancel.

8. Select the new view to begin using it for advanced calculations.

To delete a view:

1. Choose Delete View from the Program menu.

2. Select one of four views (Weight/Tmp, Length, Area, or Volume) to erase from the popup menu in the Delete View dialog box (**Figure 7.10**). The other views are off-limits.

3. Tap OK. The view reverts to the previous one in the View popup menu if the deleted view was active.

To restore the default views:

◆ If you've replaced one of the built-in views with a custom view, you can get back to the calculator's defaults. Choose Restore Defaults from the Program menu.

✔ Tips

- Unless you really want to replace an existing view, be sure to give your custom view a unique name. If you don't, and you choose to add it to the view list (instead of replacing an existing view), that view's name will appear twice in the popup menu (**Figure 7.11**).

- You can tweak your custom calculator views in multiple iterations; just export a view you created earlier and give it a new name. This way you can fine-tune your calculations to come to the combination of features you're looking for without rebuilding the view from scratch each time out.

- When you export a view, a new category called Calculator is created in Memos. If you already have 15 categories (the Palm OS's maximum for each application), the exported view text appears in the Unfiled category.

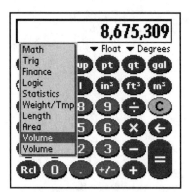

Figure 7.11 You don't have to give your custom view a unique name, but it makes things less complicated.

Figure 7.12 Expense records are shown in a basic list that's easy to read and quick to access.

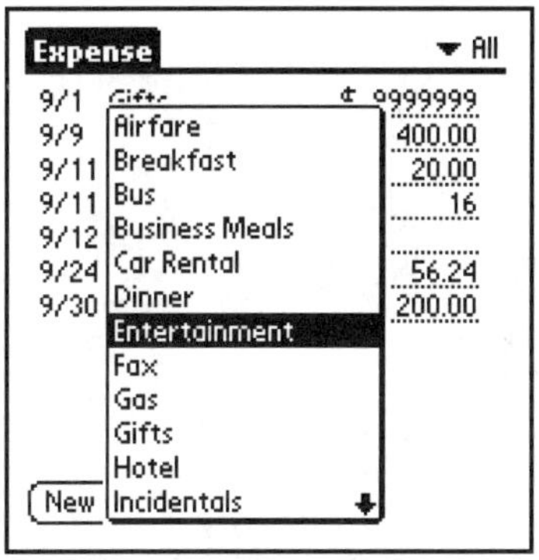

Figure 7.13 Choose from 28 different expense types when creating records.

Using Expense

Business people who are continually on the move have adopted the Palm OS platform in droves. Not only can they retrieve their valuable information quickly, they can manage one of the most dreaded aspects of modern business: expense reporting. Keeping track of charges that will be reimbursed by your company is often no more involved than three or four Graffiti strokes. At the end of the month, the data can be transferred easily to a Microsoft Excel file.

To create new Expense items:

1. Launch Expense from the Applications screen by tapping its icon.

2. Tap the New button (**Figure 7.12**). A new record is created with today's date, the temporary title "-Expense type-", and a field for entering the expense amount.

3. Write the amount in the numbers section of the Graffiti area. Expense will automatically enter ".00" after the number if you don't specify a cent value.

4. Tap a title to access the Type popup menu, then select from a list of 28 expense types (**Figure 7.13**). If none of them match your expense, select Other; unfortunately, you can't edit the Type list.

5. Tap on a blank area of the screen to deselect the record.

✔ Tip

- Don't just leave "-Expense type-" as the type—the record won't be saved!

USING EXPENSE

To edit Expense records:

1. Tap a record to select it; the date will become highlighted to indicate your selection.

2. To modify the date, expense type, or amount, tap those elements and make the change directly (**Figure 7.14**).

3. Tap a blank area of the screen to deselect the record.

To toggle the "automatic fill" feature:

1. Choose Preferences from the Options menu, or write ╱-R. The Preferences window appears.

2. Mark or unmark the Use automatic fill when entering data checkbox, then tap OK (**Figure 7.15**).

✔ Tips

■ Once Expense is launched, you can avoid the New button entirely by writing the expense amount in the Graffiti area. A new record will be created automatically with the numbers in place.

■ Additionally, you can begin writing the name of an expense type in the Graffiti area. If you have the automatic fill feature turned on (see below), the first match will be selected (**Figure 7.16**).

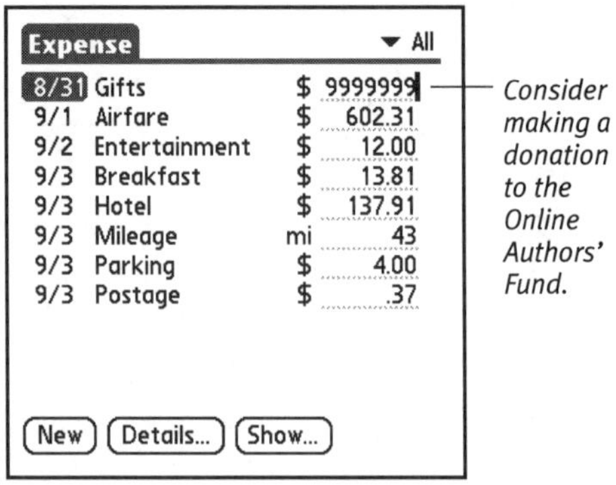

Consider making a donation to the Online Authors' Fund.

Figure 7.14 The amount fields can hold a maximum of seven characters. (And if that's not enough, why do you have to expense it?)

Figure 7.15 The automatic fill feature can dramatically decrease the time it takes to enter an expense record.

Figure 7.16 Create records by writing the first letter of an expense type in Graffiti.

Figure 7.17 The Receipt Details screen is where you find the bulk of your expense information. Taxi rides and plane trips are good times to flesh out your expense information.

Editing Expense Details

The Receipt Details screen lets you specify more information about an expense (**Figure 7.17**)—but don't feel compelled to fill in everything if it doesn't apply (such as the City field, if you never travel).

To edit Expense details:

1. With a record selected, tap the Details button to bring up the Receipt Details window.

2. Select a category from the category popup menu. To set up a new one, choose Edit Categories.

3. If you didn't select an expense type in the main screen, tap the Type popup menu to choose one.

4. Select the method of payment from the Payment popup menu.

5. Select other currencies from the Currency popup menu.

6. Write the name of the payee in the Vendor field. With automatic fill activated, Expense will display previous vendors that match letters alphabetically as you write them (for example, writing D would bring up "Dan's Café," but writing Di would switch to "Diva Espresso").

7. Write the city name in the City field. The automatic fill feature works here, as well.

Recording Attendees and Notes

Expense offers the ability to easily add notes, such as who was present at a lunch.

To record attendees:

1. In the Receipt Details window, tap the dotted box beside Attendees (if no attendees are listed, the box reads Who).

2. Write the names of the people present. If their names are located in your Contacts, tap the Lookup button. Selecting a person copies the name, title, and company information to the Attendees screen (**Figure 7.18**).

To add and delete notes:

1. Tap the Note button on the Receipt Details screen to open a Memos-like window where you can jot down miscellaneous details about the expense (**Figure 7.19**).

   Change the typeface by selecting Font from the Options menu (or writing ╱-F).

2. You can record a person's name and phone number by choosing Phone Lookup from the Options menu (or writing ╱-L).

3. Tap the Delete button to kill the note, or tap Done to complete your edits.

✔ Tips

■ Although you can specify a separate note for each expense record, you can also write notes in the Attendees screen, consolidating some of your information in one place.

Figure 7.18 Use the Lookup button on the Attendees screen to quickly record the participants of a meeting.

Figure 7.19 The Note feature is very much like Attendees, but sticks closer to a Memos record.

Figure 7.20 Sort your list of expenses by Date or Type. If you drive often, note whether you want to use Miles or Kilometers to record your travel.

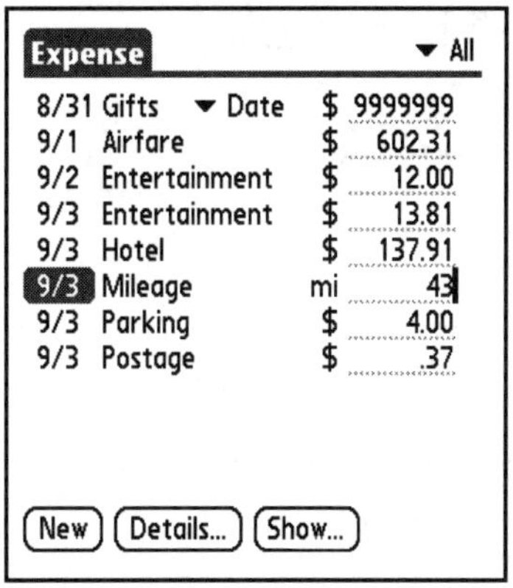

Figure 7.21 Mileage is the only expense type that doesn't show a currency indicator next to the amount.

Viewing Options

One problem with keeping track of expenses is that they all tend to blur together at a certain point (specifically, just before you need to compile them and turn them in). As you're reviewing expenses, choose to view them chronologically or by type, as well as display distance and currency indicators.

To change the sort order:

1. Tap the Show button on the main Expense screen to display the Show Options window (**Figure 7.20**).

2. Tap the Sort by popup menu to sort by Date or Type.

To change the distance measurement:

1. Tap the Show button on the main Expense screen to display the Show Options window.

2. Tap the Distance popup menu and choose either Miles or Kilometers.

3. When you choose Mileage as the type, either mi or km appears instead of a currency symbol, depending on your choice (**Figure 7.21**).

Specifying Currency

The default currency type is set to dollars ($), but Expense also includes English pounds (£), German deutschmarks (DM), and the Euro (€) on its Currency popup menus (you can add others).

To set the default currency:

1. Choose Preferences from the Options menu, or write ╱-R.

2. Tap the Default Currency popup menu to choose a currency type, then tap OK.

To add countries to the Currency popup menus:

1. Choose Edit Currencies from any Currency popup menu (found in the Preferences and Receipt Details windows).

2. Specify countries for up to five currency list items by tapping the popup menus to the right of each currency slot (**Figure 7.22**). Tap OK when finished.

To create custom currencies:

1. Choose Custom Currencies from the Options menu, or write ╱-Y.

2. Tap a dotted box to specify a new country (**Figure 7.23**).

3. In the Currency Properties window that appears, write the name of the country and its symbol (**Figure 7.24**). Tap OK.

4. You can create up to four currencies. Tap OK to return to the main window.

✔ Tip

■ If you use only one type of currency, or you're just tired of seeing that dollar sign on every record, you can opt to hide the currency symbol. Tap the Show button on the main Expense screen and unmark the Show currency checkbox. Tap OK.

Figure 7.22 View up to five countries in the Currency popup menu by specifying them here.

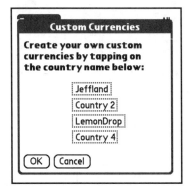

Figure 7.23 Is the currency list missing a few countries? Enter them at the Custom Currencies screen.

Figure 7.24 Be omnipotent! Create countries out of thin air and...assign them currency symbols.

Click here to "launch" Expense.

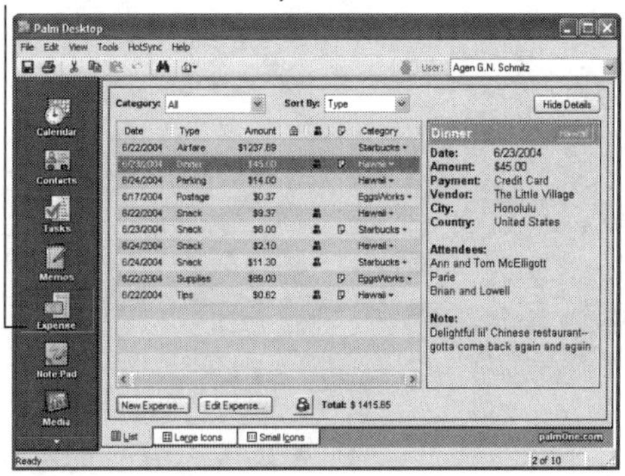

Figure 7.25 Your Expense records are just a simple click away in Palm Desktop for Windows.

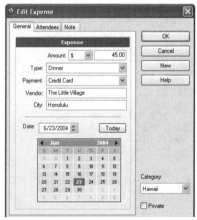

Figure 7.26 If you're a more visual person, use one of the Icon views to sort through your records.

Figure 7.27 Edit all details, including attendee information and additional notes, from the Edit Expense dialog box.

Expense in Palm Desktop

In previous versions, clicking the Expense button in Palm Desktop began a complex tango with Microsoft Excel, where macros formatted the data into a spreadsheet. Happily, Palm Desktop 4.1 provides Expense as its own built-in application, though you can still export to Excel for serious number crunching.

Unfortunately, this still only applies to Palm Desktop for Windows, as there is no built-in support for Expense in Palm Desktop for Macintosh. However, see Chapter 14 for alternatives to Expense, which include some Mac-based solutions.

To open Expense:

◆ In Palm Desktop, choose Expense from the View menu or click the Expense button at left (**Figure 7.25**).

To view Expense records:

◆ Expense offers three different views—List, Large Icons, and Small Icons—found in tabs at the bottom of the window. Each view displays information in the same manner: Select the record to see details in a column at right (**Figure 7.26**).

To edit or create new Expense records:

◆ To edit an existing Expense record, select a record and either double-click it or click the Edit Expense button. Alternatively, double-click the details box (referred to as the Record Pane).

◆ To create a new Expense record, click the New Expense button or an empty area of the Expense application's View Pane.

Either of the actions above will open the Edit Expense dialog box, from which you can edit General information (amount, type, date, etc.), Attendees, and a Note about the expense (**Figure 7.27**).

To export to Excel or Word:

1. Select a record or multiple records within any view of the Palm Desktop Expense application.

2. Go to the Edit menu and choose either MS Excel or MS Word from the Send To submenu. You can also right-click the selection to access the same submenu (**Figure 7.28**).

3. Format the data in your program of choice (**Figure 7.29**).

✔ Tips

- Clicking the New button in the Edit Expense dialog box creates a new expense record with the same category of the viewed record.

- By default, not every piece of information from an expense record shows up in the List view. To add more data (such as city, vendor, or payment), right-click the top row and select Show Columns to see a list of available columns. If you've got too much information, select Remove Columns.

- Like other applications within Palm Desktop for Windows, sorting is limited to the two choices in the Sort By drop-down menu: Date and Type.

- Selecting an individual category from the drop-down menu displays only those records, as well as the expense amount for that category in the Total section at the bottom of the application (**Figure 7.30**).

- If you're looking for a more robust expense tracking program, WalletWare's ExpensePlus for Palm (www.walletware.com) offers more features than Palm's Expense application, plus conduits for both Macintosh and Windows.

Figure 7.28 Exporting to Microsoft Word or Excel is a breeze in Palm Desktop 4.1.4.

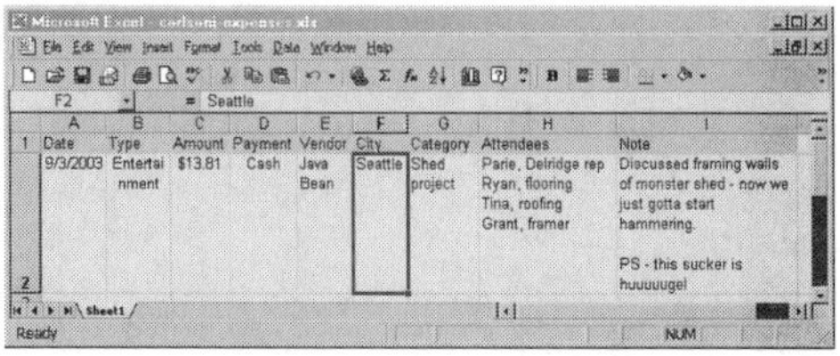

Figure 7.29 Expense can be very useful in Palm Desktop, but you'll be able to ramp up the formatting in Excel for the expense report you turn in.

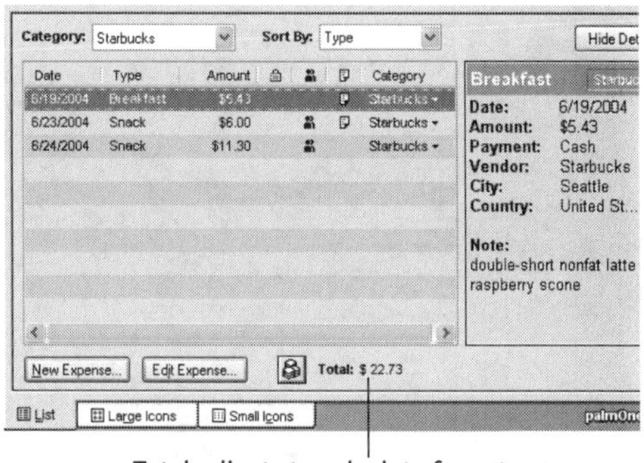

Total adjusts to calculate for category.

Figure 7.30 The Total section at the bottom of the Expense application calculates just the records selected from the Category popup menu.

Figure 7.31 View the current date and time in up to three time zones with World Clock.

Figure 7.32 Add a city to your active list from the Locations screen. Your home town might not be on this list, so choose another city within your time zone.

Figure 7.33 Add notes to city names (or rename them completely).

Using World Clock

Palm OS 5.2 and higher devices include the World Clock application, which provides date and time views for up to three locations. It uses the same procedure as Clock for setting and using alarms.

To view the time with World Clock:

◆ Launch World Clock from the Applications screen or tap the clock icon in the upper-left corner of the silkscreen area (**Figure 7.31**).

◆ On devices with five-way navigator directional buttons, press the center one when the power is turned off.

To set time and date:

◆ On the main World Clock screen, tap the Set Date & Time button to set your location as well as current date and time.

To change and edit locations:

1. Tap any of the displayed cities, and choose a city from the available popup list.

   If a city from your desired time zone isn't in the list, tap Edit List.

2. In the Edit List screen, tap the Add button to place another city into your active list. Select a city from the list in the Locations screen (**Figure 7.32**).

3. To change location details, tap a city in the Edit List screen, then tap the Edit button. In the Edit Location screen, you can modify the city's name as well as daylight saving time details (**Figure 7.33**).

✔ Tip

■ You can only select from the cities World Clock includes in its location list. Thus, while you can't choose Birmingham, England, you can choose a city within the same time zone, such as London.

Using City Time (Treo)

The Treo eschews World Clock for City Time (version 5.2H), which Handspring originally bundled with its Visor handhelds. You can download a more recent version that includes more features, such as a time calculator (www.codecity.net/prodctpalm.html), for all PalmOne handhelds.

The first thing you notice is the graphical display of the day/night areas of the globe, but City Time is more than just a pretty face (**Figure 7.34**).

- The four fields at the bottom of the screen provide popup menus to list favorite cities (two more than World Clock). To change a location, tap one of the popup menus and choose from a very long list of cities.

- Add new cities to the list by choosing Edit Cities from the Options menu, writing ╱-E, or pressing Menu-E on the Treo. Enter the time zone difference from Greenwich Mean Time (such as "-8" for Seattle); the latitude and longitude coordinates if you know them (you can also tap the approximate location on the map); and the dates when Daylight Saving Time is active.

- To quickly check the time in a city from the list, tap the screen directly to view a time label. The newest version (5.5.3 when we went to press) includes a zoom feature that lets you move the map about with your stylus.

- The downloadable version also includes a Time Calculator, which lets you plug in a time and date to see what the times will be in your four selected cities, as well as a Distance/Time calculator—both found under the Utilities menu (**Figure 7.35**).

Figure 7.34 City Time gives you two more time zones to track, a graphical view of where night falls on the globe, and the ability to tap on the map to find the time in a specific city.

Figure 7.35 The new version of City Time includes a Time Calculator (top)—no more counting out time zones on your fingers and toes—and a Distance/Time calculator, which allows you to set your estimated speed (bottom).

Part 2
Communicating

Extending Your Handheld's Reach

Palm OS devices were designed as extensions of the personal computer, not replacements for it. And despite the fact that handhelds are immensely portable, your data is really only being transported from one computing box to a smaller box. Now, with the addition of a modem or network connection, you can have the world's information literally in the palm of your hand using electronic communication hardware and software.

Chapter 8, **Smartphones**, explores an intriguing hybrid: the cellular phone with a Palm organizer built in (or is it the other way around?). We cover the PalmOne Treo in depth.

Chapter 9, **Email**, covers what you need to access your email from Palm OS handhelds.

Chapter 10, **Web Access**, gets you surfing the World Wide Web on a tiny screen—but the screen size is less limiting than you may think.

SMARTPHONES

When you leave the house in the morning, do you wear a Batman-style utility belt of dangling gadgets? Handheld, pager, cellular phone.... Even though our modern organizational tools continue to get smaller and more portable, it's still a problem to juggle them all.

Although you could just get rid of the gadgets entirely and hole up in a cabin (a tempting alternative some days), another solution that once seemed far off has now become reality: the PDA phone, or "smartphone." Not only does a smartphone reduce the number of items you need to carry, it adds something exceptional to the field: a decent cellular phone user interface. If you've spent any time at all trying to look up numbers in a typical cellular phone's address book, or attempted to set up a three-way conference call, you know how frustrating it can be.

Several of these hybrid phone/organizers (or is it organizer/phones?) have emerged over the last few years, including the Kyocera Smartphone and the Palm Tungsten W. But we'll focus on the cream of the crop, PalmOne's Treo 600, which features the Handspring legacy Palm OS 5.2.1H as well as a built-in digital camera (see Chapter 11, *Images and Multimedia*, for more on snapping pictures).

Smartphone Basics

Smartphones come in two flavors of wireless network access: CDMA (Code Division Multiple Access), which covers most of the United States, and GSM (Global System for Mobile communications), which is predominant throughout much of the world and is finally gaining ground in the United States. In addition to making and receiving calls, GSM phones can take advantage of SMS (Short Message Service) text messaging and create data connections like a regular modem.

You can hold one up to your ear like any other phone (**Figures 8.1** and **8.2**); or, better, plug in the included headset to talk hands-free and continue using the device's other applications.

✔ Tips

- If you already own a GSM phone, you can simply pull out its SIM card and put it into a GSM smartphone. Your phone number and billing won't change. However, be aware that buying one of these units without a service plan (such as through T-Mobile or AT&T) is significantly more expensive.

- I highly recommend using the included headset adapter. Not only is it safer, but (to be honest) you won't smudge up the screen with oil from your skin.

Figure 8.1 The PalmOne Treo 600 is a compact organizer that works as a cellular phone.

Figure 8.2 Kyocera's 7135 Smartphone, which runs the older Palm OS 4.1, incorporates a Graffiti silkscreen area above its number keys.

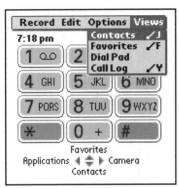

Figure 8.3 The Phone application includes a "virtual" navigator at the bottom of the screen to access other applications; you can also get to them via the Views menu or keyboard shortcuts.

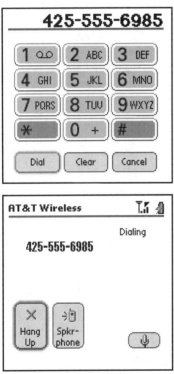

Figure 8.4 Tap the Dial button at the bottom of the Phone application (top), which takes you to the Dial screen (bottom).

Making Calls

Instead of going through the process of setting up the Treo (which is explained in the manual), let's jump to making calls. The Treo has added a new entry point called the Phone application, which provides a basic telephone keypad, but also acts as the gateway to Favorites, Contacts, and the built-in camera (**Figure 8.3**).

To make a phone call:

1. Press the Phone button on the front of the Treo or select the Phone application icon (either using your stylus or the five-way navigator) from the Applications screen.

2. Use the Treo's keypad or onscreen buttons to dial, then tap the Dial button to place the call (**Figure 8.4**). The Dial screen appears and your call is active; you're given options to hang up, go to speakerphone, or mute the sound.

To access other applications and views:

- Use the five-way navigator to switch to Applications, Favorites, Contacts, and Camera.

- Select Contacts or Favorites from the Views menu (as well as the Dial Pad and Call Log).

- Press shortcut keys to reach Contacts (Menu-J) and Favorites (Menu-F).

✔ Tips

- Get used to accessing Contacts via one of these methods, as its icon doesn't appear on the Application screen.

- With the Treo's five-way navigator, onscreen actions can be triggered without ever using a stylus. We'll continue to refer to tapping the screen unless there's a difference in functionality in the two selection methods.

Favorites

You can assign up to 50 buttons for your most-dialed numbers from the Favorites screen. Simply tap or navigate to an assigned button to start dialing its number.

To set up a Favorites number:

1. If a button is empty, tap it to display the Add Favorite screen; or, select Edit Favorites Button from the Edit menu, then tap an empty slot (**Figure 8.5**).

2. Select Speed Dial from the Type popup menu (**Figure 8.6**).

3. Write the button name and number in the appropriate fields. Or, tap the Lookup button to get the name and number from Contacts.

4. If you want even quicker access to a number, assign a Quick Key (such as "L"). When you're in either the Phone or Dial Pad view, just press and hold that key on the front of the Treo.

5. Tap the More button to add extra digits, specify a ringtone for received calls from this person, or add an image (which pops up on the screen when that person calls you) (**Figure 8.7**). Tap OK when finished.

6. Tap OK to return to the Favorites screen.

✔ Tips

- Use the Treo's navigator buttons to page through the five Favorites screens.

- On the Edit Favorites Pages screen (found under the Edit menu), drag buttons to other slots to rearrange them. Dragging one name atop another causes the two to trade positions.

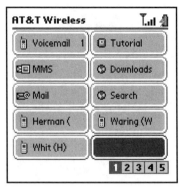

Figure 8.5 Add phone numbers, applications, and Internet addresses to the Favorites screen.

Figure 8.6 Use the Add Favorite dialog to perform a Lookup into Contacts, customize how a name appears, and add a Quick Key.

Figure 8.7 Use the More Options dialog to add extra digits and specify a ringtone and image for an incoming call from this person.

Figure 8.8 Press keys on the Treo's keyboard to narrow the scope of your Contacts list. For cell numbers, the Message button appears.

Figure 8.9 Tap a number to bring up the Dial confirmation dialog. If it's a mobile number, you'll also get the choice to send an SMS text message.

Dialing from Contacts

What's the point of having an organizer/ phone hybrid if you can't use all those numbers stored in the Contacts application?

To dial from Contacts:

1. From the Phone application, press the down button on the five-way navigator, or press Menu-J.

2. Scroll through the list of names and numbers and select the number to dial. You can also press letters or numbers on the Treo's keyboard to narrow your search; the keys that are pressed appear in the top-left corner of the screen (**Figure 8.8**).

3. Highlight the number you wish to dial. Tapping the number onscreen brings up a confirmation dialog; tap the Dial button to make the call (**Figure 8.9**). Selecting the highlighted number with the five-way navigator takes you directly to the Dial screen.

✔ Tips

■ If you select a highlighted name within Contacts, you'll open the Contact View, from which you can then choose to edit that contact.

■ Tapping a cell phone number adds an SMS button to the Dial confirmation dialog so you can send a text message, but you won't get this option if you select the number using the five-way navigator.

■ Due to the presence of the Treo keyboard, Contacts' tried and true Lookup feature is not included.

MAKING CALLS

Multiple calls

When you're in the middle of a call, the Phone application displays the recipient's phone number (and name, if it came from Contacts), the status and time of the call, and buttons for actions you can take depending on the call. In addition to offering obvious commands like Hang Up and Hold, the Treo makes it easy to juggle multiple callers and establish conference calls with up to five participants.

To make a conference call:

1. Call the first party ("Agen," for example), then put him on hold by tapping Hold.

2. Tap the Add Call button that appears, which brings you back to the main Phone application screen. Call the second party ("Frank") by dialing from the keypad, Contacts, or Favorites (**Figure 8.10**).

3. Tap the Conf button to begin the conference (**Figure 8.11**).

During the conference call, use the following options (**Figure 8.12**).

- ◆ Tap Spkr-phone to put the call into speakerphone mode.

- ◆ Tap the Mute button (the microphone icon) to put both parties on hold.

- ◆ Tap the Keypad button to dial in another participant.

- ◆ Tap Hold to put all parties on hold.

- ◆ Tap Hang Up to end the call.

✔ Tip

- ■ You can't put one party on hold and talk to another caller during a conference call—you can only hang up and end the call with the entire group.

Figure 8.10 Adding a second party to the call using Contacts

Figure 8.11 Keep two people on the line either by swapping between them or by enabling a three-way conference call. Note that each call timer remains independent.

Figure 8.12 Once you go to Conference mode, the names of the participants disappear.

Figure 8.13 An incoming call from Agen (who has a saved image associated with his Favorites entry).

Figure 8.14 The Call Back button saves time spent looking up the caller.

Call Log	▼ All
◁ Agen(W)	2:47p
▷ Agen(W)	2:45p
▷ Agen(W)	2:44p
▷ Agen(W)	2:43p
▷ Agen(W)	2:38p
▷ Agen(W)	2:37p
▷ Agen(W)	2:37p
◁ Agen Schmi...(W)	2:35p
◁ Frank(H)	2:23p
◁ Agen(W)	2:22p
◁ Agen Schmi...(W)	2:21p

(Details)

Figure 8.15 See where your talk time is going at a glance.

Receiving Calls

Just as Christmas isn't only about giving, using a cellular phone isn't just about making calls. When your fans start calling, the Treo can help you out. If your cellular service plan includes Caller ID, the phone compares the incoming phone number with Contacts and displays the caller's name if it finds a match.

To answer an incoming call:

◆ Tap the Answer button to speak to the caller (**Figure 8.13**).

◆ Tap the Ignore button to direct the caller to your cellular service's voice mail system.

◆ If you do nothing, the Missed Call screen gives you the option to call the person back or just forget it (**Figure 8.14**).

Call History

The Treo records details of the previous 1,000 incoming or outgoing calls, which are accessible from the Call Log list. Select Call Log from the Views menu, or press Menu-Y (**Figure 8.15**).

The triangle to the left of each item indicates outgoing (◁), incoming (▷), and missed (▷) calls. To dial a number (if present), select an entry and tap the Dial button (or tap Menu-D). Tap the Details button (or press Menu-O) to view information about the call.

✔ Tip

■ If the Call Log becomes too unwieldy, select Purge from the Record menu. You can choose to delete all calls, calls older than 1 week, 1 month, or 2 months, or all calls save for the last 10.

SMS Text Messaging

A good, long conversation is fine now and then, but sometimes you need to keep things short. Using SMS, you can send brief text messages to other GSM-capable phones or to Internet email addresses.

To send an SMS text message:

1. Press the Messaging button or launch the SMS application. It acts much like the built-in Mail program, with mailboxes for received, pending, and sent messages.

2. Tap the New button to create a new message.

3. Enter the recipient's phone number in the To field, tap the popup menu to choose from a list of recent numbers, or perform a Lookup in Contacts and choose a mobile phone number (**Figure 8.16**).

4. Begin writing your message in the Text field, or tap the QuickText button to access a list of frequently used phrases (**Figure 8.17**). Tap the smiley face button to choose from a range of emoticons.

5. Tap the Send button to dispatch the message immediately.

To send an SMS email message:

1. Create a new message just as you would for sending to a phone, but type an email address instead, choose from the list of recently used addresses, or perform a Lookup and choose an email address.

2. In the Text field, enter the text message.

3. Tap Send to zap it on its way.

✔ Tip

■ If you're watching your character count, cut down on the smileys, which can add three or four characters.

Figure 8.16 The SMS application makes it easy to find a recipient—perform a Lookup in Contacts or choose from a list of recent numbers.

Figure 8.17 Use included QuickText entries to quickly write text messages, or create your own.

Figure 8.18 Incoming! An Alert screen appears to inform you of a new SMS message.

Figure 8.19 Create your own QuickText entries and add your own personality.

Figure 8.20 When selecting an SMS destination from Contacts, you'll see all available cell numbers and email addresses.

To receive an SMS message:

◆ If you're in another application or within one of the mailboxes, an SMS Alert screen appears. Tap OK to continue working within that application, Snooze to be reminded of it in five minutes, or Go To to open the message in SMS (**Figure 8.18**).

✔ Tips

■ You can create your own QuickText entries or modify existing ones by selecting Edit QuickText from the popup menu (**Figure 8.19**).

■ Remember, you can also start an SMS message from Contacts or Favorites. When you choose a cell phone number from Contacts, you'll see a Message button at the bottom of the screen; tap it to open the SMS Compose screen. In Favorites, you can create a Message button and a Speed Dial button for the same cell phone number; make the choice from the Type popup menu in the Add Favorite screen.

■ When you perform a Lookup, you'll see all email addresses and cell phone numbers associated with that contact (**Figure 8.20**).

■ Each message can be up to 160 characters (which are counted at the top of the screen). Longer texts are sent as multiple messages.

SMS Chatting

You can also engage in a back-and-forth conversation using SMS, with a string of all your messages and replies collected in one screen.

To chat using SMS:

1. Select a received message from the Inbox.

2. Tap the Respond button and choose Reply from the popup menu. You can also choose Forward or Call Sender (**Figure 8.21**).

3. The Chat screen opens, divided into two halves with the received message in the top and a Text field at the bottom.

4. Type your text and tap the Send button. Once you get confirmation that the message was sent, your reply appears in the top half. As you continue to chat, all messages between the two recipients appear in this list (sans the SMS Alert screen) (**Figure 8.22**).

5. Tap Done when finished with your chat. Return to it by selecting the Inbox item, which is noted with "chat thread."

✔ Tips

■ When you're finished with a chat, you can delete it from the Inbox screen. However, this action deletes all text messages from that thread—there's no way to delete individual threads.

■ Use the stylus to select text from the messages in the top half of the screen, then copy and paste into the Text field of your message.

■ Modify how your name appears on the screen, choose a color, and add a timestamp to the message list through Chat Preferences (found under the Options menu) (**Figure 8.23**).

Figure 8.21 Reply to a message, or go the direct route and call that person.

Figure 8.22 Who needs to talk when you can wear out your thumbs chatting to each other?

Figure 8.23 Modify how your chats look in Chat Preferences.

Figure 8.24 When adding a photo to an MMS, you can only select from the photos stored in the Treo's memory.

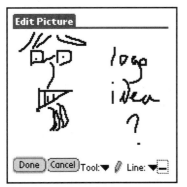

Figure 8.25 Are you the next Manet? Create your own drawings and send them to friends via MMS.

MMS Messaging

With the addition of a camera, the Treo 600 has entered the world of MMS (Multimedia Messaging Service), which enables you to send pictures and ringtones to friends' cell phones and email addresses.

To send an MMS text message:

1. Choose MMS from the Applications screen, then tap the New button.

2. Enter a phone number or email address as you did with the SMS application. Enter a subject in the Subj line.

3. Tap the large Add Picture icon to open a popup menu with two choices. Choose Add Photo to select from the library of images stored on the Treo; select an image from the list and tap OK (**Figure 8.24**). To better illustrate your point, choose Add Drawing and create your own masterpiece from the Edit Picture screen's various shape and pencil tools and choices for line width and color (**Figure 8.25**). Tap Done to return to the message screen.

4. Write a message in the Text field.

5. If you wish to include sound in your MMS message, tap the Sound icon at the bottom of the screen, select a ringtone from the Manage Sound screen, and tap Insert.

6. Tap the Preview icon to view the message (and play any sound, if inserted). Tap OK to finish.

7. Tap the Send button, or press Cancel to either save the message in Drafts, delete the message, or delete the page.

To create an MMS slideshow:

- After completing the first three steps on the previous page, tap the right Page Selector arrow at the top of the screen. On the new message page (labeled "2 of 2"), write more text, or add another photo or drawing.

- Select Page Time from the Compose menu (Menu-T) to configure how long each pane in the slideshow will play.

- Tap the Play icon to preview your message before you send it; tap the Rewind and Forward icons to bypass the set Page Time (**Figure 8.26**).

To receive an MMS message:

- An MMS Alert screen appears. Tap OK to acknowledge receipt but continue working within whatever application you're in. Or, tap Snooze to be reminded later, or tap Go To to open it.

- Sound and moving graphics will begin playing within a second or two; tap the Play icon to replay them (**Figure 8.27**). Tap the Sound icon to play just the sound file or save it to the Treo's memory.

- Tap the Respond button and choose to Reply (via MMS), Reply with SMS, Reply All, or Forward.

Templates

If you find yourself recreating the same message (or portion of a message) again and again, save some time by creating and saving a template to start from (**Figure 8.28**).

To create an MMS template:

- Create a message, but instead of sending it, select Save as Template from the Compose menu (Menu-W).

- Select Templates from the popup menu at the top of the screen, then tap New.

Figure 8.26 Preview your MMS slideshow before you send it; tap the Rewind and Forward icons to review.

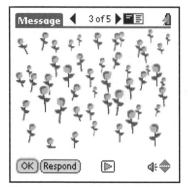

Figure 8.27 Play a rich-media MMS again by tapping the Play icon, or tap the Sound icon to play just the audio.

Figure 8.28 Save frequently used boilerplate messages in the Templates mailbox.

Figure 8.29 Unlike SMS, you won't get instant gratification when you press Send. Watch the square icon in the bottom-right corner while you wait.

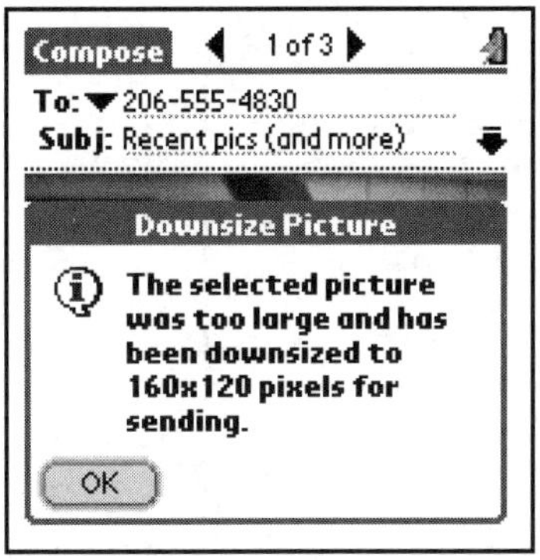

Compose ◀ 1 of 3 ▶

To: ▼ 206-555-4830
Subj: Recent pics (and more)

Downsize Picture

ⓘ **The selected picture was too large and has been downsized to 160x120 pixels for sending.**

OK

Figure 8.30 For once, downsizing that's welcome. Choose Edit Picture to have MMS resize your image for speedy transmission.

✔ Tips

- Due to the larger size of MMS messages (made larger by including a multimedia file), the message is first sent to the Outbox (**Figure 8.29**). You can watch the status icon turn as the message gets sent into the ether.

- Photos can only be added from those saved to the Treo, and not an expansion card. If you snap a picture that you want to send via MMS, make sure to copy it from the card to the Treo's memory.

- You're limited to sending a maximum 64 KB file via MMS, as well as the following multimedia file types: JPEG/GIF (up to 640 by 480 pixels), AMR sound clips (up to 30 seconds), and MIDI/iMelody ringtones.

- If you're not ready to send a message, simply save it in the Drafts mailbox by selecting Save in Drafts from the Compose menu or pressing Menu-V.

- To delete a photo added to a message, tap the image and select Remove Picture from the popup. If you choose Edit Picture, you can add your own artistic flourish with the drawing tools in the Edit Picture screen. Also, if the MMS application deems the image too large, it will automatically resize it (**Figure 8.30**).

- If you reply only by text, you'll be automatically switched to the SMS application.

- If a sender is new to you, remember them for future messaging by choosing Send to Contacts from the Message menu.

- Move messages from the Inbox to the Saved box by selecting Save Message from the Message menu, or pressing Menu-I.

MMS MESSAGING

Selected Preferences

Here are a few options for customizing the Phone application and other applications associated with it, including SMS and MMS. The following preferences are accessed from the Phone application.

To set Phone application preferences:

1. Choose Display Preferences from the Options menu.

2. Select either the Dial Pad or Wallpaper (a saved image) from the Show popup menu (**Figure 8.31**). To change the wallpaper, tap the image to show a list of saved pictures, choose an image, then tap the Select button.

3. From the Typing popup menu, choose what happens when you start typing—dialing a phone number or doing a Lookup in Contacts.

4. Configure the applications associated with the onscreen button settings (triggered by pressing five-way navigator buttons), or choose to not show this virtual navigator.

To set sound preferences:

1. Choose Sound Preferences from the Options menu.

2. Choose an application from the popup menu.

3. Tap Volume and set options for the two settings offered by the Ringer switch on top of the Treo (**Figure 8.32**).

4. Tap Tones to configure different tones for different actions. Within Phone, choose one tone for someone within Contacts and another for an unknown caller; for SMS and MMS, you can only choose the alert tone (**Figure 8.33**).

Figure 8.31 Choose to show the Dial Pad or your favorite image from the Phone application.

Figure 8.32 Sound Preferences manages the sound for Phone, Mail, Calendar, MMS, and SMS.

Figure 8.33 You can select different tones to be played for different callers.

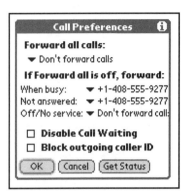

Figure 8.34 These call preferences apply to your cellular service account.

Figure 8.35 If you're out of your home area or want to try for better reception, try changing networks.

To set call preferences:

1. Choose Call Preferences from the Options menu. These settings are read from your cellular service provider.

2. If you know you're going to be out of your calling area, specify a forwarding number in the Forward all calls popup menu.

   You can also disable the call waiting feature of your phone, or prevent your phone number from being broadcast to the recipient when you make a call, by marking the other two checkboxes in this screen (**Figure 8.34**).

To select a different cellular network:

◆ If you're traveling and need to use a cellular service other than your own, choose Select Network from the Options menu. The Treo queries available networks and gives you the opportunity to choose which one to use (**Figure 8.35**).

9

EMAIL

As freelancers, we've learned the value of "flexible portability." We both alternate our working time between office at home, office spaces shared with several colleagues, and an assortment of coffeehouses in the Seattle area. A large part of that portability (both in importance and size) is a laptop, which enables productivity from just about anywhere. However, it can be heavy and awkward to lug around.

The Palm organizer, on the other hand, is easily the most portable device in our arsenal. It fits into a shirt pocket, weighs almost nothing, runs for weeks on the same battery charge, and continues to spark spontaneous conversations from nearby gawkers. Yet despite these advantages, it remained—until recently—a second-class citizen to our laptops because it lacked the ability to connect directly with two of the lifebloods of modern business: email and the World Wide Web.

Now, with several alternatives on the market for expanding the Palm handheld's communications abilities, the laptop can be safely left at home or at the office and we can still be connected to the information we need.

Making the Connection

Before you can retrieve email, you'll need a modem of some sort to connect to the Internet.

Palm cellular organizers

Using the built-in wireless circuitry of PalmOne's Treo (as well as older devices such as the Tungsten W and i705), you can grab email and surf the Web without requiring a single phone line. Someday, every handheld will offer built-in wireless communication, but until then, these few remain the darling devices of people who need their information long before they return to the office.

Cellular phones

A growing number of cellular companies are offering Internet-access services with their phones via infrared, Bluetooth, or cable connections to the Palm device. Using PalmOne handhelds like the Zire 72 or Tungsten T3, you can easily establish a connection with a Bluetooth-enabled phone such as the Sony Ericsson T-610 (**Figure 9.1**).

Palm modems

With the Bluetooth standard becoming more widely adopted by both PalmOne and cell phone manufacturers, the idea of a clunky, clip-on modem is starting to go the way of the dodo. However, older models (including Tungsten C/T/T2, Zire 71, and the m500 series) are compatible with the Palm Modem, which offers connectivity speeds of up to 56Kbps—not particularly fast, but quite acceptable for your largely text-based transmissions (**Figure 9.2**).

Your PC and modem

That's right, your computer is actually the Palm OS method of choice for sending and receiving email.

Figure 9.1 Many of today's cellular phones include infrared or Bluetooth receivers, which you can use to dial your ISP from a Palm handheld, such as the Sony Ericsson T-610.

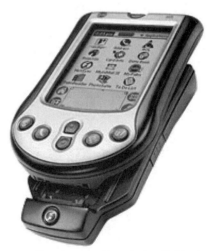

Figure 9.2 If you have an older Palm handheld with a universal connector, such as this m130, you can use the Palm Modem to access a dial-up account.

Matching mail records

Figure 9.3 Palm's VersaMail synchronizes with your Windows email client during each HotSync operation.

Preferences   Network

▾ **Service:** Earthlink

User Name: ELN/m

Password: -Assigned-

Service Connection Progress

🤝   **Signing on**

(Cancel)

Figure 9.4 Direct-dial makes connecting easier, if you have the hardware.

Getting Online: Two Approaches

Connecting via HotSync

In keeping with its philosophy of simplicity, Palm's VersaMail program acts as an extension of your desktop email software.

When you perform a HotSync operation, the data in VersaMail and in your desktop application are synchronized (**Figure 9.3**); the next time you check your email, you send out what was composed on the handheld. A few Web browsing applications, such as AvantGo (see Chapter 10), use HotSync to transfer content to your handheld for later viewing.

Direct connection

The second method, which is probably more familiar, is to establish an active Internet connection directly from the handheld, avoiding the need to HotSync the data before any action can be taken (**Figure 9.4**).

This is quite easy from a Treo, but many recent devices can also make direct connections to your email server or the Internet, either wirelessly (Bluetooth, wi-fi, or infrared) or wired (an external modem). With any of those options, VersaMail (or Mail on the Treo) can get online and grab your latest email without the need of a PC.

✔ Tips

■ If VersaMail isn't already on your handheld, check your installation CD for an installer.

■ Other handheld makers may include different email software; we're using VersaMail as an example, but the basic functionality is similar.

Email via HotSync

If you want to print a record that's on your handheld, you have to transfer that information to your PC and print from there. Using VersaMail works the same way: Any emails you create on the handheld must first pass to your desktop email application to be dispatched out to the Internet.

To set up VersaMail:

1. If VersaMail hasn't been added to your handheld, choose the installer from the installation CD and begin the process. If your PC has multiple HotSync accounts, make sure to choose your profile.

2. Perform a HotSync operation.

3. Open VersaMail on your handheld, which then displays the Account Setup screen.

4. Add a unique account name for your Palm, choose your email provider from the popup list, and select which email protocol you'll be using (POP or IMAP) (**Figure 9.5**). Mark Synchronize Only Account to get and send email when you HotSync. Tap Next.

5. Enter the username for your email account. Tap the box below Password and enter that in the Password Entry dialog. Tap Next.

6. Review settings for your email address and incoming and outgoing mail servers (check the account on your PC's email program) (**Figure 9.6**). Tap Next.

7. At this point, you can tap Done, which brings you to the Inbox. Or, tap Next to further configure VersaMail (see the next page).

Figure 9.5 The account name can be unique, as it's not tied to logging into your account—just for identification on your handheld.

Figure 9.6 Double-check your ISP's incoming and outgoing mail settings.

Mail on the Macintosh

Palm has never supported synchronizing email with the Macintosh, leaving many Mac users with another icon to ignore in the Applications screen. PalmOne's VersaMail Web page says that you can install VersaMail under Mac OS X 10.2 and later, but it won't synchronize email.

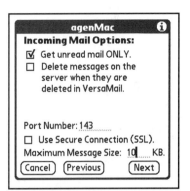

Figure 9.7 Select whether you want to receive just unread email, or everything that's in your inbox.

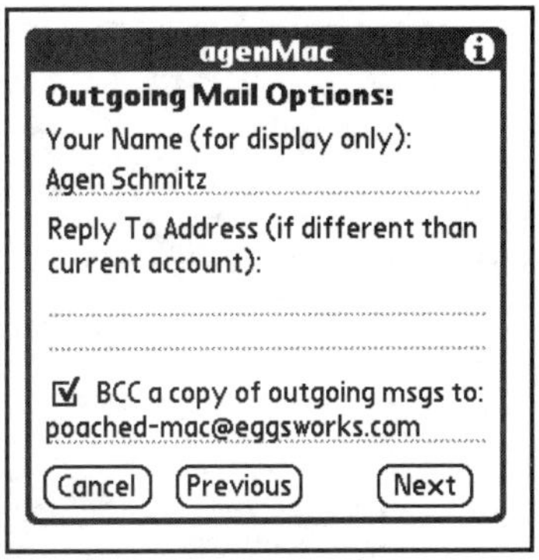

Figure 9.8 Create a BCC email for outgoing VersaMail messages for record-keeping on your PC.

Figure 9.9 Create a unique signature for your VersaMail messages.

✔ **Tip**

■ Don't know if your email account is POP or IMAP? Selecting one of the preset accounts from the Mail Service popup menu automatically adjusts to the correct protocol.

To set up advanced VersaMail settings:

1. After tapping Next from the basic VersaMail settings, manage your incoming mail settings. Choose to receive unread email only or delete mail from the server once it's been deleted on your handheld (**Figure 9.7**).

   But you can also modify the PC port number that's used to check email. Mark Use Secure Connection if you'll be using the SSL protocol, and set the maximum message size. (If a message is larger than, say 5KB, you'll still be able to see it on your PC.) Tap Next.

2. If need be, change the name that recipients will see on outgoing mail or add a different address. You can also BCC a copy of your sent messages to another email address (**Figure 9.8**). Tap Next.

3. Mark Attach signature to messages, then create a signature in the space below (**Figure 9.9**). Tap Next.

4. You have another opportunity to make SSL, PC port, username, and password changes, this time for outgoing mail. Mark the ESMTP (Extended Simple Mail Transfer Protocol) if your server requires it. Tap Done.

EMAIL VIA HOTSYNC

To configure VersaMail on a PC:

1. Choose Custom from the HotSync Manager in the Windows Taskbar.

2. Locate VersaMail in the list and click the Change button (**Figure 9.10**).

3. Make sure Synchronize Active Accounts is selected. If you want information about sending and receiving from your email accounts added to the HotSync log, check Enable Informational Logging.

4. Double-click the account you created on your Palm in the left window to get an overview of your current profile and open other settings in the tree.

5. Click Mail Client Sync Setup and mark the box to synchronize email when you HotSync. Select the email program you use on the PC from the Mail Client popup (**Figure 9.11**). If you don't check your email on that machine, select the Direct IMAP or Direct POP options; the VersaMail conduit will then check email for you and transfer it to your handheld.

6. Choose a name to use from the Mail Profile popup menu, and provide your password in the Mail Password field.

7. Under Advanced Sync Options, adjust how much data gets transferred to the handheld by changing the maximum message size and number of days' worth of synchronized mail (**Figure 9.12**). Choose to receive attachments on your handheld, send mail from VersaMail's outbox, synchronize unread mail, and synchronize your handheld's and your email program's inboxes.

8. Click the Save button (the floppy disc icon).

9. Perform a HotSync.

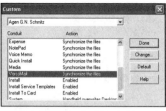

Figure 9.10 Make changes to the VersaMail conduit via the HotSync Custom settings.

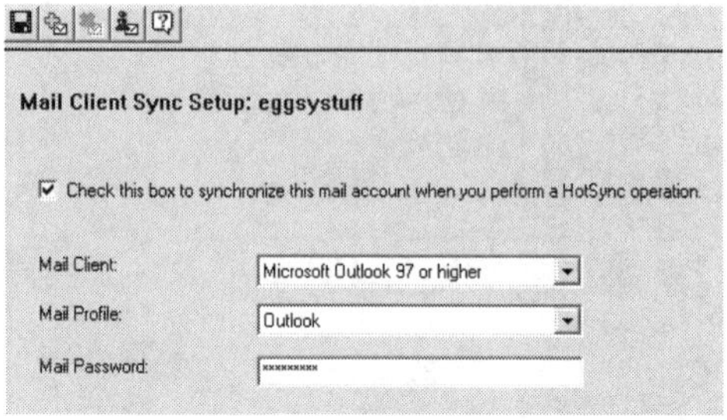

Figure 9.11 If you aren't synchronizing with a mail program such as Outlook, choose Direct IMAP or Direct POP from the Mail Client popup menu.

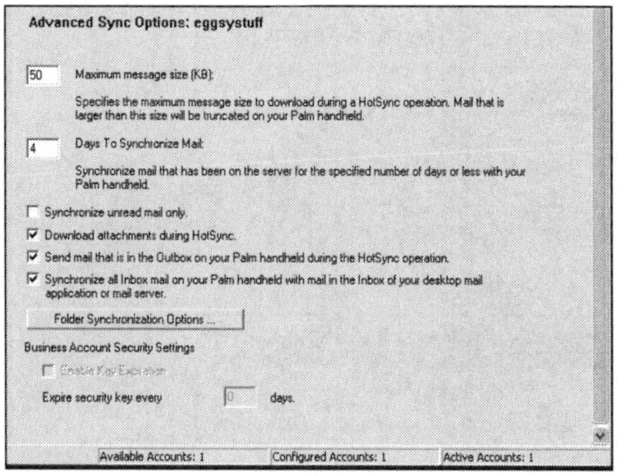

Figure 9.12 Tweak settings such as the maximum message size transferred to your handheld and the number of days' worth of mail to synchronize.

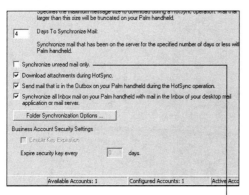

Unread mail option

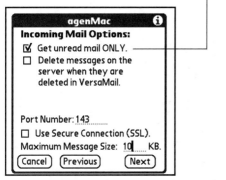

Figure 9.13 Make sure that the setting for unread mail is in sync on both the handheld and desktop preferences.

✔ Tips

- The Handheld Settings essentially sweep up the preferences you set on your handheld, so you don't have to worry about fiddling with them.

- Free email services, such as Hotmail or Yahoo!, won't work with VersaMail unless you sign up for an upgraded package with access to a POP account. As of this writing, you can sign up for Yahoo! Mail Plus for an annual $20 subscription. However, if you sign up for a free AvantGo subscription, you can now download email from all Yahoo! Mail accounts. (See Chapter 10 for more on the AvantGo Web clipping service.)

- The VersaMail application and HotSync VersaMail settings can conflict with one another. For instance, if you check the Get unread mail only from VersaMail's Incoming Mail Options, but leave this preference unchecked in the HotSync Advanced Sync Options, the latter trumps your handheld's settings and you will receive all read and unread messages (**Figure 9.13**).

Using VersaMail

When you open VersaMail, you're presented with the contents of your Inbox in a default two-line view (**Figure 9.14**). VersaMail includes five built-in mailbox folders: Inbox, Outbox, Drafts, Sent, and Trash. Tap the popup menu in the upper-right corner of the screen and select the one you want to view. Note that the Trash folder is functionally equivalent to the other folders until you perform a HotSync, at which point its contents are removed.

The two-line display makes glancing at senders' names and subject lines much easier than the one-line display, which puts the squeeze to the text (but enables you to see more emails in one screen) (**Figure 9.15**). Unread emails are marked in bold type. Use the scrollbar or the navigator buttons to scroll through messages.

By default, messages are listed according to the date they were received.

✔ Tip

■ If your PalmOne device has a five-way navigator, press the up/down buttons to move one screen at a time. Press the center navigator button to select an email and use the up/down buttons to move from one message to the next. Pressing the right button (or tapping the envelope icon) opens a contextual menu with standard email actions like Reply, Mark Read, etc. that can also be manipulated by the five-way navigator (**Figure 9.16**). To revert to the screen movement and deselect the individual email, press the left button.

Figure 9.14 VersaMail collects all your email on your handheld.

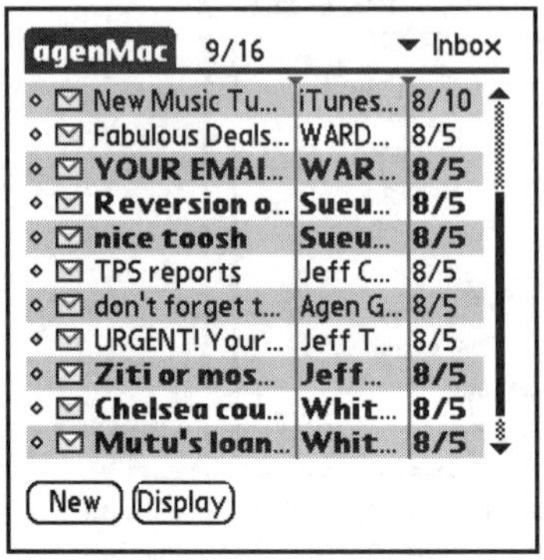

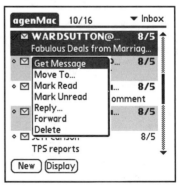

Figure 9.15 The one-line display gets a bit scrunched compared to the two-line display in Figure 9.14.

Figure 9.16 Tap the envelope icon or press the right directional button on the navigator to open the contextual menu.

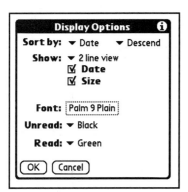

Figure 9.17 Select your sorting scheme and one- or two-line display.

Figure 9.18 Add flair to your email (or important contact information) with a signature that will be added to each message.

To change the display:

1. Tap the Display button, or select Display Options from under the Options menu.

2. Tap the two Sort by popup menus to organize the list by Date, Sender, or Subject, and whether the listing is descending or ascending (**Figure 9.17**). This setting applies to all folders, not just the active one.

3. Choose whether to display the mailboxes with one or two lines. If you want to view other columns, mark the checkbox next to Date or Size (or Subject with the one-line display) in the Show category. When viewing the two-line display, the Date and Size data appear in columns on the same line as the subject.

4. Tap a Font button to change the text size in the list.

5. Choose a color to denote Unread and Read emails. Tap OK.

To specify a signature:

1. Choose Preferences from the Options menu, or write ⁄-R.

2. Tap the Signature button, and write your signature text on the lines provided (**Figure 9.18**). A blank line will automatically be inserted between a message's body text and signature. Tap OK.

To create a new VersaMail message:

1. From any folder view, tap the New button; you can also choose New Message from the Message window, or write ∕-N.

2. Write the email address(es) of the email's recipient(s) in the To field, separated by commas.

   To make entering addresses easier, VersaMail inserts a name from Contacts based on the text you write (**Figure 9.19**). If the matches aren't correct, just keep typing an email address.

3. If you want to CC ("carbon copy") or BCC ("blind carbon copy") other recipients, write their email addresses in the CC or BCC field.

4. Write a descriptive title in the Subj field.

5. In the Body field, write the text of your message (**Figure 9.20**).

✔ Tip

■ Tapping one of the address field titles (To, CC, or BCC) opens the field in a full screen, making it easy to add multiple addresses. The bottom of the screen also includes buttons of commonly used email text (such as "@" and ".com") (**Figure 9.21**). Tap the Lookup button to add addresses from the Contacts application.

To send a message:

◆ When you've written your message and specified its options, tap Send (or Outbox, if you're connecting via HotSync).

   If the message isn't quite ready to be sent, tap the Drafts button or choose Save to Drafts (∕-W) from the Message menu to store it in the Drafts folder.

Figure 9.19 Previously entered email addresses appear in a popup menu when you start writing the first letters.

Figure 9.20 Write your message's text in the Body field.

Figure 9.21 If you need more room to write addresses, tap the name of the field for a full-screen, Memos-like interface (complete with common email text).

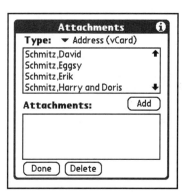

Figure 9.22 Tap the Type popup menu to select what kind of attachment you want to send—vCard, photos, etc.

Figure 9.23 The Select Media dialog opens if you choose photos or videos; tap media items to add a plus icon, then tap Done to add them to the message.

Figure 9.24 Move from email to email in a mailbox using the back and forward buttons at the top of the screen.

To edit a saved outgoing message:

1. Tap the Folder popup menu and choose Outbox or Draft.

2. Tap the message you want to modify.

3. Tap the Edit button.

4. If you've edited a draft message, tap the Outbox button to move it to the Outbox when it's ready to be sent.

To send attachments:

1. Choose Attachments from the Options menu, or write ∕-A (**Figure 9.22**).

2. Tap the Type popup menu to select a particular type of file—from vCards (addresses) and vCals (appointments and tasks) to photos and voice memos.

3. Select a file from the Type field and tap the Add button to move it to the Attachments field. Some file types, such as Photo/Video, open up another dialog from which you select items (**Figure 9.23**).

4. Tap Done.

To read messages:

1. Tap an email's subject or author to read its contents (**Figure 9.24**).

2. Use the scrollbar at right to scan down the full text of the message.

3. The arrows at the top of the screen take you to the previous (left arrow) and next (right arrow) emails in the list, without having to return to the main screen.

Due to the limited screen space, only the sender's name and the subject line are shown at the top of each message you read.

USING VERSAMAIL

To view email header information:

◆ Tap the Complete Header icon (the right-most one) in the upper-right corner. To return to the shorter view, tap the Abbreviated Header icon. The option you choose applies to all messages, not just the current email.

To reply to a message:

1. After you've read a message, tap the Reply button to respond to the author.

2. The Reply Options window will appear (**Figure 9.25**). Choose whether you want to reply to the Sender of the message, or to All recipients who received it (including the sender).

3. Mark the Include Original Text checkbox to send the full message in your reply. The text appears with a greater-than symbol (>) before each line of the existing message to differentiate between the original author and your remarks (**Figure 9.26**).

4. Specify the recipients in the To and CC fields, write your message, then tap Send (or Outbox).

To file a message:

1. To store a message in a different folder, choose Move To from the Options menu, or write ╱-V.

2. If you want to create a new folder for storing mail, tap the Edit Folders button (**Figure 9.27**).

3. In the Edit Folders dialog, tap New to create a folder, or Rename to edit an existing folder, then tap OK.

4. Select the name of a folder and tap OK to move the message.

Figure 9.25 Tapping the Reply button opens the Reply Options dialog.

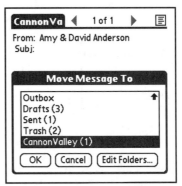

Figure 9.26 Adding text from the original email will help put everything in context.

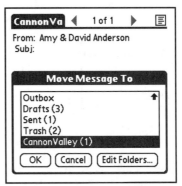

Figure 9.27 Create other folders where you can file your mail (and not clog up your Inbox).

USING VERSAMAIL

Figure 9.28 Tap the space to the left of each message to mark several in a group.

Figure 9.29 Keep your email folders (and your handheld's memory) lean by deleting old messages.

To move or delete multiple messages:

1. In a folder list, tap the small diamond icon to the left of a message to mark it; the diamond becomes a checkmark (**Figure 9.28**).

   You can also select or deselect all messages by choosing Select All (✓-S) or Deselect All (✓-Z) from the Message menu.

2. Choose Delete (✓-D) from the Message menu. The messages are moved to the Trash folder until the next HotSync.

To purge deleted messages:

◆ If you need to free some space on your handheld, select Empty Trash from the Message menu (✓-E). Tap Yes to confirm your action.

To delete older messages:

1. If you just want to cull your Inbox (or any other folder) of old messages, choose Delete Old from the Message menu.

2. Choose a folder from the Folder popup menu.

3. Select a date range from the Older than popup menu (**Figure 9.29**). You can delete mail older than one week, one month, or you can choose a cutoff date.

USING VERSAMAIL

To filter incoming messages:

1. Choose Filters from the Options menu. This feature lets you set certain criteria for transferring emails from your desktop based on message content.

2. Tap New to create a new filter, then give it a name.

3. In the section labeled "If the," tap the first popup menu to choose an email header (To, From, Subject, CC, Date, or Size).

4. Tap the second popup menu to define the state of the email header (Contains, Starts with, or Does NOT Contain).

5. Enter the filter strings that VersaMail will use when analyzing the incoming messages in the text field.

6. Define an action by choosing a folder name under the heading Then get mail and move to (**Figure 9.30**).

7. Tap OK to save the filter, then tap OK to exit the Filters screen.

✔ Tip

■ You can assign different filter settings for when you're using an active connection versus a HotSync connection. A more stringent set of filters for when you're on the road, for example, can save you money if you're paying hotel phone rates or using a calling card to connect to your desktop computer at home. Choose either Connected or Synchronize from the popup menu at the top of the Filters screen (**Figure 9.31**).

Figure 9.30 Filters can help by organizing your mail as you receive it, instead of requiring your time to process it.

Figure 9.31 Choose different filter settings for a HotSync or direct connection.

Direct Connection Email

The Treo has thrown out the notion that sending and receiving email directly from your handheld is difficult and cumbersome—what with having to line up infrared receivers between phone and PDA and configure mind-boggling settings full of technobabble. Just tap into to your cellular provider's Internet connection, and press the Send and Receive button.

But don't worry if you don't own a Treo. The fact is, the advance of technology (especially the adoption of the Bluetooth wireless standard) and the ubiquity of cell phones have combined to make it fairly painless to connect to the important business of your email.

In this section, we'll first cover connecting to email using the Treo's Mail application, then cover some of the basic elements required for setting up direct-dial email connections for other PalmOne handhelds using VersaMail as the sample program. We didn't have room to hit every feature, but once you have a grasp of the basics, you'll be able to pick up the specifics of each program with no problems.

Setting Up a Direct Connection (Treo)

The Treo makes it easy to connect to data services (as the Treo instruction book calls them; you might be old-school and use terms such as email or the Net).

To connect to a wireless data service:

◆ With an active wireless connection (press and hold the Wireless Mode button on the top of the phone), open Mail and tap the Send and Receive button. You'll then be asked if you want to connect to the Internet; tap the Yes button (**Figure 9.32**).

◆ Open the Prefs application and select Network from the popup menu. Make sure your wireless data network is selected from the Service popup menu, then tap the Connect button (**Figure 9.33**).

To set up a wireless data service:

1. Open the Prefs application and select Network from the popup menu. If your Treo is already set up with wireless data service, tap the Modify button to create a copy of the settings from which you can make adjustments (**Figure 9.34**).

2. Type a unique name in the Service field.

3. Choose GPRS from the Connection popup menu.

4. Enter your username and password.

5. Enter the APN (Access Point Name). Contact your wireless provider for the correct setting.

6. Tap the Details button to set a fallback GPRS network (if you've made a copy).

7. Tap OK to return to the main screen, then tap Connect.

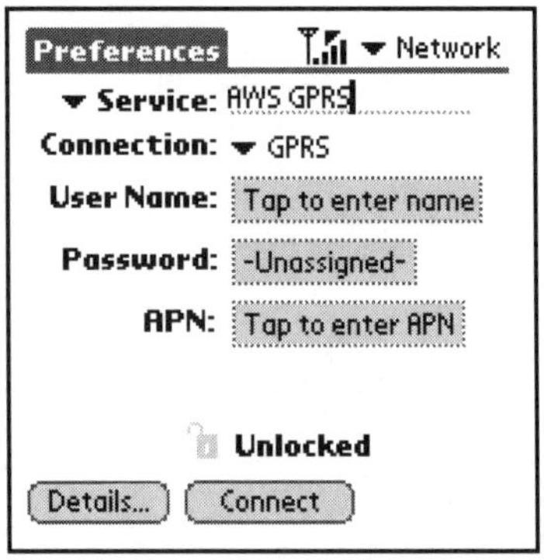

Figure 9.32 If Wireless Mode is on, tap the Send and Receive button, then tap Yes to connect to the Internet.

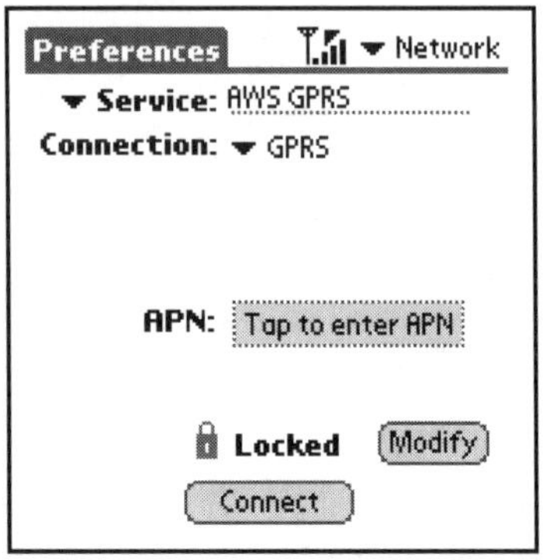

Figure 9.33 In Network preferences, tap the Connect button. When finished with your Internet session, return here and tap the Disconnect button.

Figure 9.34 Set up your GPRS network if it hasn't already been entered by your provider.

Figure 9.35 Open the View menu to select from three sorting schemes.

Figure 9.36 Create an automatic delivery schedule for when you're connected to your Internet service.

Using Mail (Treo)

The Mail application is a close cousin to VersaMail, so we won't exhaust ourselves with rehashing the obvious. But a few differences are worth noting.

Treo Mail feature highlights:

◆ The most obvious difference is the inclusion of the Send and Receive button at the bottom of the screen (though VersaMail includes a Get Mail button when configured to connect directly to an ISP).

◆ From the View menu, you can choose from three sorting methodologies: by date (press Menu-Z), name (Menu-H), or subject (Menu-J) (**Figure 9.35**).

◆ The universally used mailboxes—Inbox, Outbox, Draft, Deleted, and Sent—are included, as is a new one named Filed. Unfortunately, this is the only place you can move mail to save it out of the Inbox. (VersaMail includes the ability to create additional folders for storage; Mail doesn't.) With a message selected or opened, choose File from the Message menu (Menu-I).

◆ Because of the Treo's ability to stay connected to the Internet (or connect when needed), you can set up a schedule to automatically send messages and check for new email. Open Preferences under the Options menu. On the Delivery tab, tap the Get Mail popup menu and select from the preset schedules. You can also choose a time range and when during the week the schedule will be active (**Figure 9.36**).

Setting Up a Direct Connection (VersaMail)

To check email—wirelessly or wired—you need a POP or IMAP server: the machine that you connect to when checking for new incoming email. Check your desktop email application for these settings, or contact your ISP or system administrator.

To send email, you need to access an SMTP (Simple Mail Transport Protocol) server that directs your messages through the complicated paths of the Internet. This server is often the same machine that you specified in the POP or IMAP setup, but not always.

Also, be sure your general modem or network settings are ready to go; see Chapter 2.

To set up mail servers in VersaMail:

1. In VersaMail, choose Mail Servers from the Options menu.

2. If you have multiple accounts set up, select one from the Account popup menu.

3. Select the type of server, either POP or IMAP, from the Protocol popup menu.

4. Enter your username and password in the fields provided (**Figure 9.37**).

5. Mark the Always connect using checkbox, then select a connection method other than Synchronize Only from the Service popup menu.

6. Tap the Details button.

7. Enter your email address as others will see it in the Email Address field.

8. Write the name or IP number of the servers in the Incoming Mail Server and Outgoing Mail Server fields (**Figure 9.38**).

9. Tap OK, then OK again on the Mail Servers screen to exit.

Figure 9.37 POP is the protocol that handles your incoming email. If you don't assign a password, you will be asked to enter it each time you connect.

Figure 9.38 If you don't already know it, get the server information from your system administrator or ISP.

Figure 9.39 The Palm OS's Network preferences panel controls dial-up Internet access.

Figure 9.40 If you're on a speedy connection, consider using Messages to download full messages; otherwise, Subjects Only quickly grabs the address and subject information.

Figure 9.41 These options can reduce the time it takes to receive mail.

Connecting to Your ISP

Dial-up email clients rely on the Network preferences screen to establish an initial connection with your ISP's servers. If you want to open a connection before working in your email program, tap the Connect button (**Figure 9.39**).

If you don't connect manually, the clients will automatically initiate a connection when you send or retrieve mail if you've properly specified the settings.

To retrieve mail headers and/or messages:

1. In VersaMail, tap the Get & Send button to initiate a connection, which displays the Get Mail Options dialog.

2. Tap the Subjects Only button to download only the incoming subject lines. This lets you preview the sender and subject of an email, then decide if it's something you want to download (**Figure 9.40**).

3. Tap the Messages button to download all pending emails without reviewing them first.

4. Tap OK to send and receive your email.

To filter incoming email:

1. Before tapping OK, above, tap the Details button.

2. Mark these options to determine which mail you receive (**Figure 9.41**).

3. Tap OK to return to the Get Mail Options dialog.

✔ Tip

■ If you don't have any messages waiting in your Outbox, the Get & Send button just says Get Mail.

To attach files to outgoing emails:

1. After tapping the New button to create a new message, choose Add Attachment from the Options menu, or write ∕-A. The Attachments dialog appears.

2. Choose a file format from the Type popup menu. You can send text files from Memos, applications, addresses, calendar items, or Palm databases.

3. Tap Done.

To send or save mail:

1. After composing your outgoing mail, tap the Send button to dispatch it immediately (**Figure 9.42**). If a connection is established, that message will be sent; if not, VersaMail will dial your ISP.

2. Tap Outbox if you want to store it in the Outbox for sending later (switch to the Outbox and tap Send when you're ready).

Direct Connection Using a Mac

If you're running The Missing Sync on your Macintosh, you can set up a direct Internet connection between your handheld and your computer, thus getting around the fact that you can't synchronize your email like Windows users can. You won't be able to grab email that's already been downloaded to your Mac's email client (such as Apple Mail or Microsoft Entourage), but it can be handy to grab mail that's waiting for you on your ISP's server before heading out for the day. Depending on your device, you can connect using either a USB cable or wirelessly via Bluetooth.

Figure 9.42 After writing your message, just press Send—it's that simple.

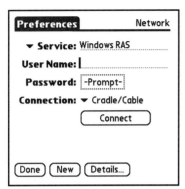

Figure 9.43 Choose Windows RAS from the Network preferences, then select Internet Sharing Assistant from Missing Sync.

Figure 9.44 While you can't download email from a free Yahoo! mail account into VersaMail (because it requires a POP account), you can sign up for a free AvantGo account and use it to download mail.

To set up an Internet connection using Missing Sync:

1. If you have a Bluetooth-enabled device, make sure your Mac and handheld are paired. (For a refresher on pairing Bluetooth devices, see Chapter 2.) Then skip to Step 4.

2. If you will connect via USB, open the Network preferences pane.

3. Tap the Service popup menu and select Windows RAS (**Figure 9.43**). (If you're a hardcore Mac user, this may feel dirty—don't worry, it's just bits and bytes, not your soul.) Tap Done.

4. Choose Internet Sharing Assistant from the desktop Missing Sync program.

5. Back on your handheld, open VersaMail, and get or send mail from your account.

✔ Tip

- This is also how you will set up a connection to your Mac to synchronize with the AvantGo Web clipping service (see the next chapter, *Web Access*). But AvantGo isn't just about Web site content—you can download mail from a Yahoo! account (even a free account) (**Figure 9.44**).

WEB ACCESS

Slowly but surely, the World Wide Web has been making inroads into Palm handhelds, first with the wireless Palm VII (which used small Web-clipping programs called Palm Query Applications, or PQAs, to view selected sites) and now with the Treo, which can make the jump to just about any Web site in mere seconds without much hassle. But you don't need a cellular handheld to surf the Net. You can dial into your ISP using a compatible cell phone via either infrared or Bluetooth.

If you don't have the option of dialing in directly, you can still download Web content during the HotSync process using AvantGo (even if you use a Macintosh, which isn't officially supported). We find ourselves reading articles or news items from a handful of sites on our handhelds while waiting in line, stuck in traffic, or otherwise stalled.

Browse the Web via AvantGo

As with email, there are two approaches to getting Web content on your handheld: Hot-Sync and a direct connection. Using HotSync to connect is great for saving news stories and other longer documents to be viewed later; having a direct connection is helpful when you need to look up information on the spot.

Using AvantGo (www.avantgo.com), you download content from various channels when you perform a HotSync, then view it on your handheld (**Figure 10.1**). AvantGo doesn't provide a desktop synchronization conduit for Mac OS X, but The Missing Sync for Palm OS 4.0 from Mark/Space (www.mark-space.com) offers a workaround.

To set up AvantGo (Windows):

1. Download the AvantGo client software for Windows from the company's Web site, and run the installer.

2. After the desktop software is installed, the AvantGo QuickStart process will open in your default Web browser. Follow the directions to choose the channels you wish to subscribe to; you'll have to perform a HotSync twice before you're finished.

To connect to the Web:

◆ Once you've chosen your channels and installed the software, HotSync the hand-held—that's it. When the AvantGo conduit springs into action, it will connect to the Web and download the most recent news and information (**Figure 10.2**).

Figure 10.1 AvantGo offers news stories from several key content providers.

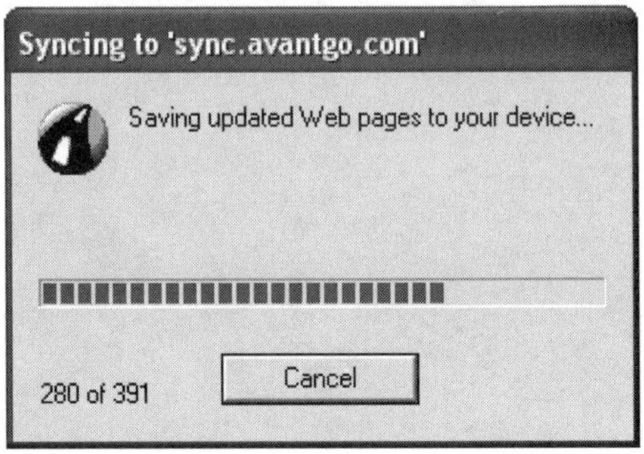

Figure 10.2 When you perform a HotSync, AvantGo downloads the most recent headlines and articles from the channels you specified during setup.

Figure 10.3 When you download just AvantGo's Palm executable files, you end up with these four. Drag them to the Send to Handheld droplet to install.

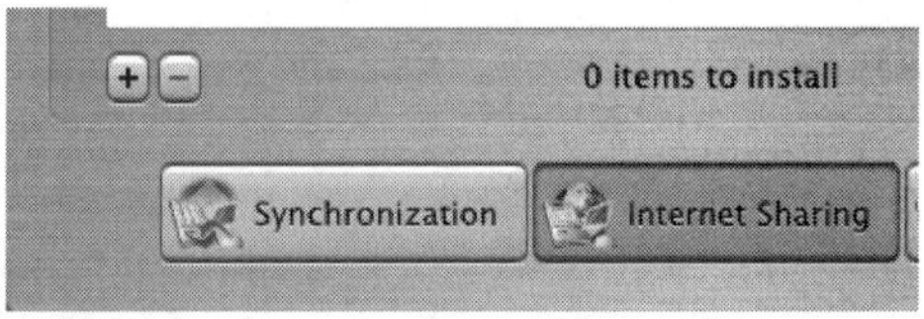

Figure 10.4 Selecting Internet Sharing will create a direct connection to the Web from your handheld.

Figure 10.5 You may have gone through a bit more perspiration than a Windows user, but it was worth it!

To set up AvantGo (Macintosh):

1. Download just the Palm executable files from the AvantGo Web site.

2. Drag the four .prc files to the Send to Handheld droplet, then perform a HotSync (**Figure 10.3**).

3. If you haven't already, choose Internet Sharing Assistant from the desktop Missing Sync program and configure your transmission preference: USB or Bluetooth.

4. Click the Internet Sharing button on Missing Sync's main window (**Figure 10.4**).

5. In the AvantGo handheld application, open Server Preferences from the Options menu, and tap the Settings button.

6. Add "sync.avantgo.com" to the Server Addr field, and enter your AvantGo username and password. Tap OK.

7. Connect the handheld to your Mac with your USB cable/cradle (or ensure that you're connected via Bluetooth).

8. From AvantGo's Channels menu, tap Sync or write ╱-Y, then let the magic begin (**Figure 10.5**).

✔ Tips

- AvantGo won't automatically download content when you perform a HotSync. You'll need to connect to your handheld via Missing Sync's Internet Sharing feature separately.

- If you're still running Mac OS 8 or 9, you can still download the AvantGo Connect for Macintosh software. Also, AvantGo provides Palm executable software for both Palm OS 3.x to 4.x and Palm OS 5.x.

To view AvantGo content on your handheld:

1. Tap the AvantGo program icon to launch AvantGo.

2. Tap a channel from the list on the home screen to view its content (**Figure 10.6**). The home icon () takes you back to the main list, while the arrows beside it move back and forward as in most browsers (**Figure 10.7**).

3. Tap an article title to read its full contents.

To add new channels:

1. On your PC, connect to the AvantGo site (www.avantgo.com).

2. Browse the selection of available channels grouped into several categories (**Figure 10.8**). Click the Add Channel icon to add it to your list of channels.

3. HotSync your device.

✔ Tips

■ The AvantGo application on your handheld also offers a short list of featured channels. Tap the Add button on the home page (at the top right of the My Channels section), make a selection, then perform a HotSync.

■ AvantGo does its best to format a Web page's content to suit the small Palm device screen. For this reason, table cells aren't displayed by default. However, if you want to get a better feel for how a page is laid out (since designers often use tables as page structure), or just want to view tabular data coherently, choose Preferences under the Options menu (or write ╱-R), and mark the Show Tables checkbox. You'll find yourself scrolling horizontally as well as top to bottom, but the contents may be more readable.

Figure 10.6 Tap a channel name to view the contents that were downloaded during the last HotSync.

Figure 10.7 AvantGo acts like the Web browser on your desktop, with Back, Forward, and Home buttons in the upper-right corner of the screen.

Figure 10.8 Edit, add, or delete channels using the AvantGo Web site.

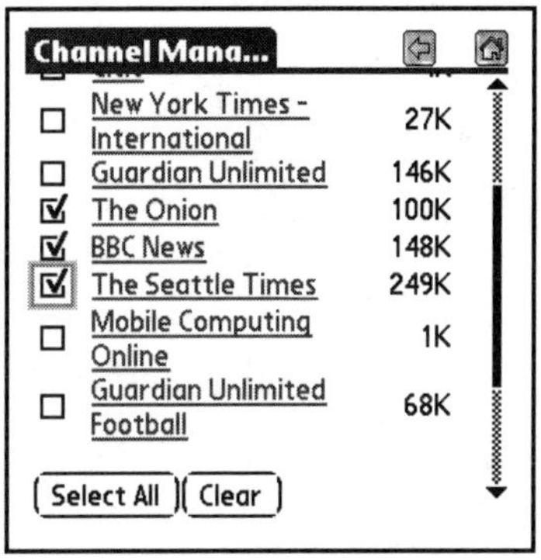

Channel Mana...		
☐ New York Times - International	27K	
☐ Guardian Unlimited	146K	
☑ The Onion	100K	
☑ BBC News	148K	
☑ The Seattle Times	249K	
☐ Mobile Computing Online	1K	
☐ Guardian Unlimited Football	68K	

[Select All] [Clear]

Figure 10.9 Mark the channels you no longer wish to read and they'll be deleted at the next HotSync operation.

To remove channels:

1. In the AvantGo application, choose Channel Manager from the Channels menu (**Figure 10.9**).

2. Check the channels you wish to delete, then tap the Clear button.

3. HotSync your device.

✔ Tips

■ Alternatively, tap the Remove button on the AvantGo home page, where you can *uncheck* any channel you wish to delete.

■ AvantGo supports active loading of Web sites if you have a modem connection. Use the Connect option in the Channels menu to initiate a connection (if you're not already online), then choose Modem Sync from the same menu.

■ Try not to go crazy when adding Avant-Go channels to your profile; having too many can substantially increase your download times, and in a worst-case scenario, cause the HotSync process to time out before completing.

■ You can also remove channels from your account at the AvantGo Web site.

BROWSE THE WEB VIA AVANTGO

Blazer Web Browser (Treo)

First, a warning on the wonders of hand-held Web access: You'll probably be under-whelmed. We've grown accustomed to highly visual Web pages, with multiple graphics and scrolling Java whatsits. You're not going to get the same experience on a 320 by 320-pixel screen. What you will get is extremely portable access to information anywhere in the world—not all of it just text-based, either.

PalmOne's Treo features the built-in Blazer Web Browser—listed simply as Web on the applications screen—which is a holdover from its Handspring origins.

To connect to a Web site:

1. Choose Go to Web Page from the Go menu, press Menu-G, or tap the "www" icon (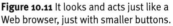). The Go to Web Page dialog appears (**Figure 10.10**).

2. Type the destination address in the field provided. If you previously visited a site, the address is inserted as you write it.

3. Tap the OK button to access the site.

Navigating Blazer Web Browser

◆ Blazer's interface is wonderfully minimal, starting with its toolbar at the bottom of the screen (**Figure 10.11**). Tap the scrollbars at the right edge of the screen to scroll vertically. Better yet, use the five-way navigator's up and down buttons to jump a screen at a time.

◆ Links are marked with underlines in the text, just like desktop Web software. Tap one to jump to its destination URL, or select links with the left/right navigator buttons and push the center button.

Figure 10.10 Enter the Web address, then tap OK.

Figure 10.11 It looks and acts just like a Web browser, just with smaller buttons.

Figure 10.12 Use the Find Text on Page function to jump to the right content.

Figure 10.13 Speed up data transmission by not downloading images.

Figure 10.14 If you find something you need to share, Send Page Address opens the SMS application for sending to email addresses or to a phone.

✔ Tips

- Blazer's default Optimized Mode (under the Page menu, or Menu-O) scrunches the Web page so that it fits within the width of the Treo's screen. Choosing Wide Page Mode (Menu-W) renders the site's layout as you would see it on your PC. The Optimized Mode takes advantage of the Treo's one-handedness—up/down buttons scroll, while left/right buttons select links. While you avoid a compacted layout with Wide Page Mode on, the left/right buttons take on scrolling duties, thus requiring you to tap links with your stylus.

- If you know what you're looking for, you can minimize scrolling. Select Find Text on Page under the Page menu, enter a search term, and tap the Find button (**Figure 10.12**).

- Do you have itchy fingers waiting on Web pages to load? Tap the stop sign icon to cease transmission of the page if it gets to be unbearable. Or, open Preferences under the Options menu and mark Don't show images to reach just the textual meat of the matter (**Figure 10.13**).

- Send URLs to others (or to yourself as a reminder) by selecting Send Page Address from the Page menu (**Figure 10.14**). An SMS Compose screen opens, enabling you to send a message to either another phone or to an email address. When finished, tap the Send button. (You'll need to navigate back to Blazer from the SMS application to continue browsing.)

- Believe it or not, people still design framed sites. If you run across one, tap the magnifying glass icon that appears in the toolbar at the bottom to switch between frames.

BLAZER WEB BROWSER (TREO)

To save a bookmark:

1. To keep a page location in memory for accessing later, choose Bookmark URL (Menu-A) from the Page menu. The New Bookmark dialog appears.

2. Change the name or URL of the bookmark. The site's title will usually be sucked up into the Description field; modify it for your own brevity or clarity. The Preview box shows you what the entry will look like on the Bookmarks screen.

3. Tap OK.

To edit bookmarks:

1. Tap the Bookmark icon to access the Bookmarks screen (**Figure 10.15**). You can edit a bookmark's name and URL by highlighting it and tapping the Edit button. Or, select a bookmark and tap the Go to button to jump to the bookmarked URL.

2. Tapping the Edit button brings you to the Edit Bookmark List dialog, which provides you 10 pages—each filled with 10 bookmark slots (for 100 total) (**Figure 10.16**).

3. Tap an occupied slot to edit its contents, or tap an empty slot to create a new bookmark.

4. Tap OK to exit Edit Bookmarks, then tap OK to exit the Edit Bookmark List.

✔ Tips

- Open Web pages from the Bookmarks screen by either tapping on a slot or scrolling to it and selecting with the five-way navigator. Tap the Go to button to type in a non-bookmarked URL.

- Tap and hold a slot, then drag it to another location in the list to rearrange the bookmarks.

Figure 10.15 Blazer's bookmarks are nicely compartmentalized.

Figure 10.16 You have a total of 100 bookmark slots to fill (10 slots on 10 pages).

BLAZER WEB BROWSER (TREO)

Figure 10.17 History isn't a mystery—it's the story of your Web browsing.

Figure 10.18 Save a Web page, such as your favorite weblog, for offline reading.

Figure 10.19 Saved pages appear in Bookmarks marked with an orange corner.

- Use the 10 available bookmark pages to divide Web sites thematically (one for soccer, another for news, and so on).

- If you're already in the Bookmarks screen, you can add a bookmark manually by pressing Menu or selecting Add Bookmark from the Bookmarks menu.

- Select History from the Page menu to see a list of all accessed Web pages (**Figure 10.17**). Tap an item to open it. Or, select an item, then tap the Bookmark button.

- Rather than break your page-reading flow by grabbing the stylus to tap the Bookmarks icon, press the spacebar on the Treo keyboard to jump from the Web page to all the tool icons at the bottom of the page.

To save pages:

1. You can store Web pages on your device for viewing later. Choose Save Page (Menu-A) from the Page menu (**Figure 10.18**).

2. Adjust the Name and Description on the New Saved Page Bookmark dialog to taste.

3. Tap OK to save.

4. To view the page later, tap the Bookmarks icon and select the bookmark slot marked by an orange corner (**Figure 10.19**).

✔ Tips

- Saving pages can be especially useful for taking a daily snapshot of a lengthy blog for reading when you have an extra minute (such as commuting home on the bus). Sounds like a familiar concept....

- With Documents to Go and/or Adobe Reader for Palm OS installed on your device, you can download word documents and PDFs. They're saved to the handheld memory, but you can move them later to a memory card.

BLAZER WEB BROWSER (TREO)

To adjust settings:

1. Select Preferences from the Options menu.

2. Choose your default home page and which view (Web or Bookmarks) to see first.

3. Tap the Advanced button.

4. Choose how much of your available memory will be used for storing cached Web pages (**Figure 10.20**).

5. Tap the Memory Management button to see what's stored—recently viewed pages saved into the cache, the history list, cookies, and saved pages. (The "B" after a number refers to bytes, "K" to kilobytes, and "M" to megabytes.) Tap the Clear button to flush each individual type (except for Saved Pages, which need to be manually deleted from Bookmarks).

6. If your ISP requires you to get online via a proxy server, tap Set Proxy to enter the name of the server and the port number.

7. Keep the Accept cookies box marked to enable some sites you regularly visit to recognize you when you return.

8. Tap OK.

✔ Tip

■ When you're finished browsing the Net, select Disconnect from the Options menu to conserve power and keep your data charges to a minimum.

Figure 10.20 Determine how much of your memory will be dedicated to Web page cache.

Figure 10.21 Web Browser Pro places its toolbar at the top of the screen.

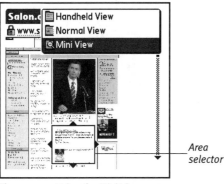

Area selector

Figure 10.22 Using the Mini View, you can get an overview of the Web page's landscape, then choose a specific area to magnify.

Web Browser Pro

PalmOne's non-cellular handhelds come with Web Browser Pro, which you'll need to install from the software CD that came with your device. Once you establish a connection to the Web (such as via a Bluetooth connection to a cell phone), you're off and running (**Figure 10.21**). While it offers many features similar to Blazer, it does have a few tricks up its sleeve.

Mini View

In addition to the two views offered by Blazer—one optimized for your handheld's screen (Handheld View) and one wide view replicating what you'd see on your PC (Normal View)—Web Browser Pro also offers a unique way to scan a Web page's landscape.

To use Mini View:

1. Tap the folder-like icon on the far-right of the toolbar to access views.

2. Select Mini View, which shrinks the page and adds an area selector (**Figure 10.22**).

3. Move the area selector by either dragging it with your stylus or pressing the five-way navigator's directional buttons.

4. Scroll to an interesting area of the page, press the center button to blow up the view to Normal size. Or, drag the area selector with your stylus, then lift it off the screen to magnify.

✔ Tip

■ A fourth view, Full Screen, hides Web Browser Pro's toolbar buttons and URL field. Select Full Screen from the Options menu, or write ╱-O. Select it or write the shortcut again to return the toolbar to its proper place.

Optimize Images

Web Browser Pro offers several steps of image compression to help speed page loading.

To change image compression:

1. Select Display Options from the Options menu, or write ╱-Y.

2. Tap the Graphics popup menu and choose from the four quality settings— Low, Normal, High, or Best—or choose not to load images at all.

3. Tap OK to return to the browser. To test the new compression settings, tap the Refresh button on the toolbar, choose Refresh from the Page menu, or write ╱-Q (**Figure 10.23**).

✔ Tips

- Like Blazer, you can download Word documents and PDFs. But Web Browser Pro offers you the choice of downloading to handheld memory or an installed memory card (**Figure 10.24**).

- If you find a page that needs to be shared with another Web Browser Pro user, choose Send from the Page menu or write ╱-Q to email it or beam it.

- While Bookmarks aren't as neatly compartmentalized as they are in Blazer, you can assign categories to Web Browser Pro bookmarks.

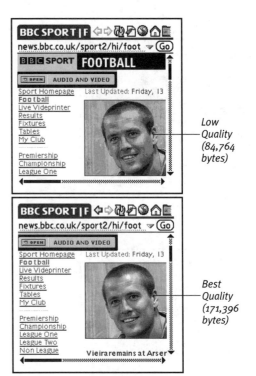

Low Quality (84,764 bytes)

Best Quality (171,396 bytes)

Figure 10.23 Specify the quality level of graphics—Low to improve load performance (top) or Best to see the pretty pictures in all their glory (bottom).

Figure 10.24 Save handheld memory and download files to an installed SD card.

Part 3
Your Handheld, Your Life

Getting Control of
Your Information

We bought our first Palm OS-based devices for the same basic reason most people do: We needed to improve our organizational skills, keep track of people's contact information, and maintain lists of to do items to keep ourselves on task with our freelancing lifestyles. This section deals with the many ways a handheld can not only record your information, but also help improve the way you use it.

Chapter 11, **Images and Multimedia**, displays how you can add images, movies, and digital audio files to the Palm OS's predominantly text-based environment.

Chapter 12, **Long Texts**, breaks the 4,000-character barrier of the Memos application. Read reports, memos, or even a classic novel on the train ride home.

Chapter 13, **Games and Entertainment**, offers a few favorites that can significantly aid your efforts to facilitate a stress-free paradigm amid the ever-changing global business zeitgeist.

Chapter 14, **Managing Your Money**, explores how you can keep your accounts up to date by tracking them on a handheld.

Chapter 15, **Managing Your Time**, points out several techniques for tracking and making the most of your time.

Chapter 16, **Managing Your Data**, covers ways to control the ever-increasing load of information that comes from all directions.

Chapter 17, **Protecting Your Data**, looks at the darker side of being able to share important data—unintentionally sharing it with the wrong people. You'll find information on password protection, encryption, and tips for keeping your handheld's contents secure.

IMAGES AND MULTIMEDIA

For years, Palm handhelds stuck to the mantra of simplicity that Jeff Hawkins envisioned (i.e., a text-based information retrieval system). This meant that Palm was slow to add functionality for imagery and multimedia while third-party developers added such bells and whistles.

But as users clamored for more of these features, PalmOne slowly opened the floodgates to multimedia expansion possibilities. Now, with Palm OS 5-compatible devices (and beyond), you can use your handheld to display a slide show of digital photos, play your favorite MP3s, and view QuickTime and MPEG videos.

There are also other options: Who would have guessed a few years ago you could turn your handheld into a digital video camera? But the Zire 72 comes along and captures both video and sound (both quite decent, if you remember that it's not a high-end digital camcorder).

Importing Photos and Videos into Your Handheld

Soon, having a set of photographs in your wallet will be *so* passé. Starting with Palm OS 5.2, PalmOne devices included the Photos application, which enables you to view your still images as well as organize them into albums. Using Palm OS 5.2.8, the Zire 72 includes the Media application, which adds the ability to view (and record) videos.

Palm Desktop 4.2 for Windows includes a built-in tool called Media that makes transferring images from computer to either the Palm OS Photos or Media as easy as performing a HotSync. On the Macintosh, Palm's Send to Handheld application lets you drag and drop files in the Finder.

To import photos and videos in Windows:

1. In Palm Desktop, select Media from the toolbar.

2. Click the Add Media button at the top of the Media application (or press Ctrl-N) and locate image or video files on your hard drive (**Figure 11.1**). Or, drag and drop image files from Windows Explorer into Media or onto the PalmOne Quick Install icon on your desktop.

3. Perform a HotSync operation.

✔ Tips

■ When you add files to Media, they're not just added to your handheld. They're also copied into a secondary directory within your user folder: [Identity] > Photos > Offline Copy Location (**Figure 11.2**).

■ Media lets you convert a wide variety of formats (**Figure 11.3**). Video files will be reprocessed as Windows Media (.asf).

Figure 11.1 Adding photos using Palm Desktop for Windows. You can also drag and drop files from Windows Explorer into the Palm Photos application.

Figure 11.2 After an image file is added to Palm Desktop's Media, a copy of the image file is added to the Photos folder within your user directory.

Figure 11.3 Palm Desktop's Media can handle a wide variety of image and video formats.

Figure 11.4 Drag and drop images onto the Send to Handheld droplet, located in the Palm folder within Applications in Mac OS X. For easier access, make an alias to it and keep that on the desktop.

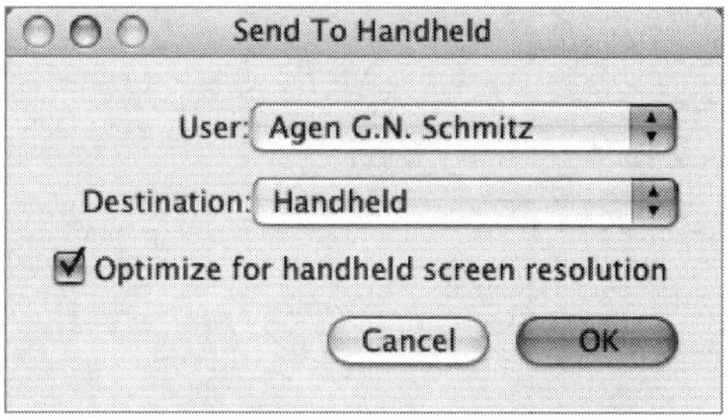

Figure 11.5 After dragging and dropping, you'll be asked to verify the file's destination. If you have an expansion card, choose that option to save memory on your handheld.

To import photos in Macintosh:

1. Locate the Send to Handheld application (also referred to as a "droplet")—it is placed by default in the Palm folder within Applications.

2. Drag and drop image files from your hard drive onto the Send to Handheld droplet (**Figure 11.4**).

3. Confirm the destination of the file (either the handheld's memory or its expansion card) (**Figure 11.5**).

4. Mark Optimize for handheld screen resolution if you wish to have the image automatically downsized to the handheld's resolution.

5. Perform a HotSync operation.

✔ Tips

- In addition to storing multimedia files in the Photos folder within your user directory, Zire 72 users will also find these files copied to one of two folders, entitled "HandHeld" and "Expansion Card," depending upon their destination in your handheld. In Mac OS X, these folders are located in a directory with your HotSync name within Home > [Pictures or Movies] > PalmOne [Photos or Videos].

- Although the Mac is such a multimedia-oriented platform, you can't import video files to a PalmOne handheld from a Mac—just JPEG, GIF, BMP, and uncompressed TIFF image files.

- If you have a handheld with only the Photos app, you'll need another application to view video. Kinoma Player (www.kinoma.com), which comes with some PalmOne models, and TealMovie (www.tealpoint.com) are two options, though the latter is Windows-based.

IMPORTING PHOTOS AND VIDEOS

Using Photos

Once you've imported images from your PC, you can show them off to friends, family, and hijacked partygoers using the Photos application. On a Zire 72, the Media application replaces Photos; however, Photos' features are the basis for Media (covered later in this chapter).

To view images:

1. Launch the Photos app to view thumbnails of imported images (the default view) (**Figure 11.6**). Alternatively, tap the List button at the bottom left of the screen to see the details of your image library (**Figure 11.7**).

2. Tap an image in either view to open it in full-screen mode.

3. Tap the screen again to return to either the List or Thumbnails view.

4. Tap the Slide Show button to review all images in order.

To edit image details:

1. With a selected image (either in full-screen mode or highlighted in either Thumbnails or List view), choose Details from the Photo menu or write ╱-I (**Figure 11.8**).

2. Modify the image's file name. By default, the camera names files starting with "Set," then it adds the session number and the shot number within that session.

3. Assign the image to an album. To create a new album, tap Edit Albums in the pop-up menu, then tap the New button.

4. Add a descriptive message in the Notes section.

5. Tap the Done button. To discard the image, tap Delete or write ╱-D.

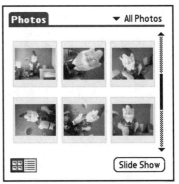

Figure 11.6 View your image library via the Thumbnails view...

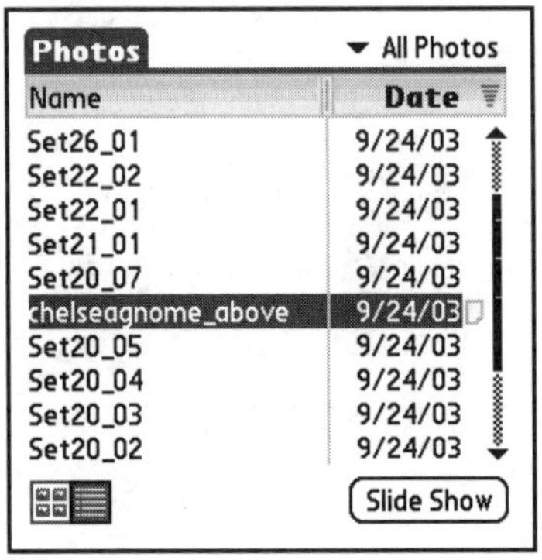

Figure 11.7 ...or view details such as the capture date and file name in the List view.

Figure 11.8 Give your image a more intelligible name, associate it with an album, and add notes in Photo Details.

Figure 11.9 To add several images to an album, select that album, then tap the Organize button to display the Organize dialog.

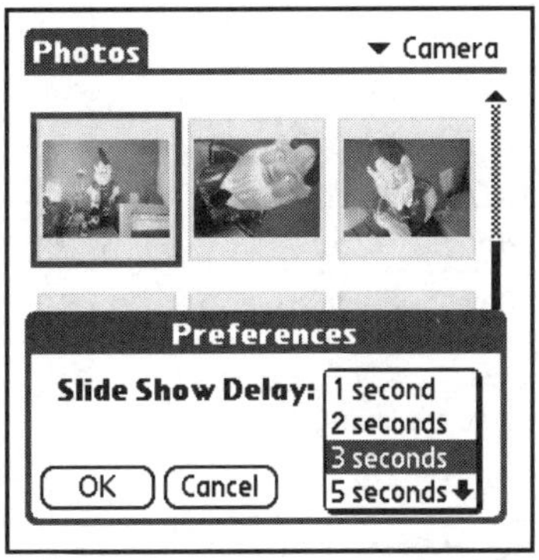

Figure 11.10 Speed up or slow down the delay between images in Slide Show via the Option menu's Preferences.

To move images to an expansion card:

The Zire 72 only has so much memory (OK, 32 MB to be exact), so it's wise to utilize expansion memory cards to store loads of snapped photos.

◆ With an image selected, choose Copy to Card or write ╱-C. You can also beam images to other Palm OS handhelds (choose Beam Photo) or send via email (choose Send Photo).

To add multiple photos to an album:

1. Select a photo album from the popup menu at the top right of the screen.

2. Tap the Organize button.

3. Tap selected images to add them to this album; a green plus sign denotes that it's ready to be added (**Figure 11.9**).

4. Tap Done.

✔ Tips

■ To change the delay between images in Slide Show, choose Preferences from the Options menu and adjust the timing (**Figure 11.10**).

■ There's only one on-board photo editing option: rotating an image. Choose Rotate Photo or write ╱-R. For a more robust application, PhotoBase (www.arcsoft.com/en/products/photobasepalm) adds a bit more image management and editing features.

USING PHOTOS

Capturing Photos

PalmOne offers two Camera applications for their two handhelds with built-in cameras: the Treo and the Zire 72 (which pulls double duty in capturing video and offers an easier-to-use camera).

Still Images (Zire 72)

The Zire 72 bumps up the resolution from PalmOne's original camera handheld to 1.2 megapixels—not enough for an African safari, but good enough to produce 4 by 6-inch prints.

To take a picture:

1. Open the Camera application by selecting it from the Applications screen or pressing the application button on your handheld's case. The screen changes to an active camera view (**Figure 11.11**).

2. Tap the still camera icon (**Figure 11.12**).

3. Tap the category popup menu to save photos to a particular category on your handheld or memory card.

4. Tap the resolution popup menu and choose from four preset options: 1280 by 960, 640 by 480, 320 by 240, or 160 by 120.

5. If you want to zoom in on your subject, tap the x2 button to double the power of the lens.

6. Tap the shutter button on the screen. (If you have the shutter sound turned on, you'll hear a click.)

7. A preview of your shot appears, with the name of the image file and the number of shots remaining in memory. Tap the floppy disk icon to save, or the trash icon to delete (**Figure 11.13**).

Figure 11.11 Line up your shot, then tap the Shutter button with your stylus or finger.

Figure 11.12 The Camera's main screen lets you switch between still image and video capture as well as select a category and still image resolution.

Figure 11.13 Review the captured image—if it's not up to snuff, just tap the trash can icon to delete and try again.

Figure 11.14 Adjust default resolution, white balance, shutter sound, and more from Photo Settings.

Figure 11.15 Change the default auto-naming convention to something more useful or personal.

Figure 11.16 Under Advanced Photo Settings, use the sliders to adjust Contrast, Brightness, Saturation, and Sharpness.

To change image capture options:

1. With the camera active, tap the photo settings icon in the bottom-left corner.

2. Adjust the settings for White balance, Low light, and Effects from the popup menus; you'll be able to see changes take effect in the preview window (**Figure 11.14**).

3. Tap the Resolution popup to select a default resolution.

4. If you don't want to minimize time between shots, select Off from the Review photos popup menu, or choose On, timeout to start a three-second onscreen countdown.

5. Choosing to add a date stamp to your photo adds the current date to the upper-right corner of your image (much like a film camera's quartz date feature).

6. To change the default naming convention for image files, choose Custom from the Auto name format popup menu, then modify the naming prefix (**Figure 11.15**).

7. Select whether you want to enable or disable the digital zoom.

8. For stealthy snapping, keep the Shutter sound selected to Off.

9. For more control over your imagery, tap the Advanced button. Here you'll be able to adjust sliders for Contrast, Brightness, Saturation, and Sharpness, keeping an eye on the preview window to see how adjustments change the image (**Figure 11.16**). Tap the Default button to make these settings stick.

10. Tap Done to return to the main Photo Settings screen, then Done again to return to capturing images.

CAPTURING PHOTOS

✔ Tips

■ The higher the resolution you choose, the larger a file's size will be. A 1280 by 960-pixel image can exceed 300K, so save your handheld's memory by choosing to save photos to a category on a memory card.

■ Should you always shoot at 1280 by 960 pixels? That depends on what you plan to do with the photo. If you're taking vacation photos, you'll want to capture as much image data as you can for possible prints down the road, and a smaller resolution will look grainier. But if you're shooting a head shot of a friend for entering later into Contacts, a lower resolution will be just fine. (See more about shooting directly from the Contacts application in Chapter 5.)

■ Having a zoom feature is nice, but digital zoom (which interpolates an image) really only produces a very jaggy, pixel ated image (**Figure 11.17**). Also, you'll have to keep your hand very still, as the 2x digital zoom is sensitive, leaving your finished shot potentially blurry. We look forward to the day that a PalmOne handheld includes an optical zoom lens.

■ Tap the menu icon on the Zire 72's silkscreen area to open Photo Settings.

■ Press the Camera application button on the front of the Zire 72 once you're in the Camera application to switch to Media.

Figure 11.17 It's nice to have the option of a digital zoom (utilized for the bottom photo), but the camera is more suscep tible to shake-induced blurring and produces a pixelated image.

Figure 11.18 Camera for Treo features a simpler interface for one-handed operation than Camera for the Zire 72.

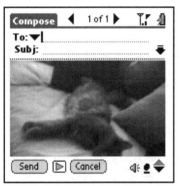

Figure 11.19 Tapping Send from the Camera opens either a new Mail or MMS message (shown above).

Figure 11.20 Keep your image sizes slim by automatically resizing a photo to fit the Treo's screen dimensions.

Still Images (Treo)

The Treo's Camera application is similar—and has a built-in photo application—but offers a few interface variations and additional features (**Figure 11.18**).

Treo Camera feature highlights:

◆ Toggle between Camera and the Pictures list by tapping the two icons in the lower-left corner.

◆ The most obvious difference between the two Camera applications is that you can send images directly from the Treo to others. After taking a shot, tapping the Send button gives you the choice of sending the single photo via the Mail or MMS application (**Figure 11.19**). (If you choose MMS, you can send to a friend's cell phone.) You can also select multiple images from the Pictures list to send via either program (up to 98K for an MMS).

◆ To keep image file size to a minimum—an important consideration if you plan to send images to cell phones—you can automatically trim a photo. Select an image from the Pictures list, then choose Downsize from the Picture menu. You'll get a warning that this procedure cannot be undone, but you can also save a copy of the original image (**Figure 11.20**). The resulting downsized photo weighs in at about 3K.

Videos (Zire 72)

The Zire also takes handheld imaging to the next step—video with sound.

To capture video:

1. Open Camera and tap the movie camera icon.

2. Tap the category popup menu to save the video to a particular category on your memory card. Directly beneath this popup, you'll see how much space (in time) you have left to fill.

3. Tap the resolution popup menu and choose from two preset options: 320 by 240 or 160 by 120.

4. Tap the red Record button to begin shooting; you'll hear a beep and the time begins to count down in red under the category popup (**Figure 11.21**).

5. Tap the Pause button to halt shooting; tap it again to resume recording.

6. Tapping the Stop button brings you to a preview screen. Review your video, save it to the memory card, or delete it (**Figure 11.22**).

✔ Tips

■ To shoot video, you will need a memory card—the Zire 72 will not save video files to the handheld's memory.

■ Video capture settings are the same as those for still images, except for one addition: the ability to turn the microphone on and off.

Figure 11.21 When you start recording, the display shows how much time you've shot and how much space you have left on the memory card.

Figure 11.22 Just as with taking photos, you have the opportunity to review a video before saving or deleting it.

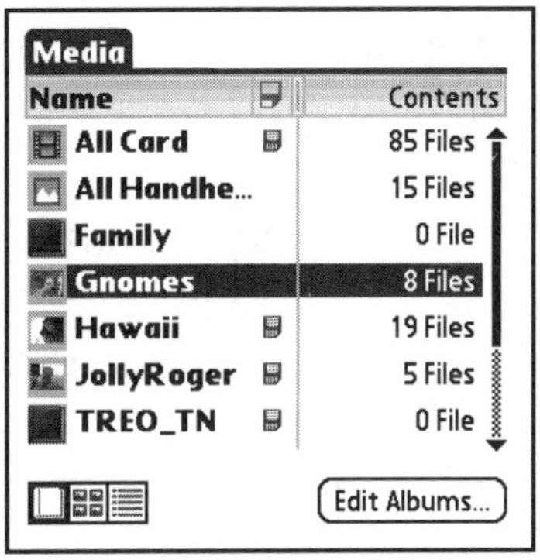

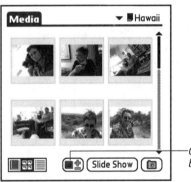

Figure 11.23 Media for the Zire 72 includes the Album view.

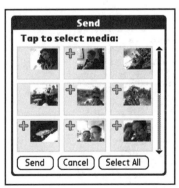

Organize button

Figure 11.24 When in Thumbnails view, tap the Organize button to add more unfiled images to the album.

Figure 11.25 Manually select multiple images to send when no file is selected in either Thumbnails or List view.

Reviewing Photos and Movies

Unlike the Treo's Camera application, the Zire 72 has a companion image and video organization program called Media. It offers the same basic viewing, editing, and organizing features as Photos, but adds a few new twists (including the ability to view videos).

Media feature highlights:

◆ In addition to the List and Thumbnail views, Media adds an Album view, which displays a listing of all albums, where they reside (handheld or memory card), and how many photos or videos the album contains (**Figure 11.23**). Tap an album to view its contents in Thumbnails view.

◆ The Thumbnail view displays an Organize button when viewing an album (**Figure 11.24**). Tap it to add more photos to the album from the source where the album resides (either handheld or memory card).

◆ You can send a photo or video (or an album) to a VersaMail message, or send it wirelessly to another Bluetooth-enabled device (such as a laptop or Palm OS handheld). Select a photo or video in Thumbnails view, then choose Send from the Media menu. With no file selected, this menu option lets you manually mark the photos you want to include (**Figure 11.25**). If you choose VersaMail, a new message opens with the media as an attachment. If you choose Bluetooth, the Discovery Results screen opens, displaying what Bluetooth-enabled devices are available.

To Send an album (up to 13 MB in size), select an album from the Album view, or select one from the category popup menu in the Thumbnails or List view.

✔ Tips

- Use the five-way navigator to select and navigate files. If no file is currently selected (i.e., is not highlighted), the up/down buttons move one screen at a time. Press the center button to select the top-most file on the current screen, then move from file to file with the up/down buttons. Press the right button to view the file's details, or press the left button to deselect any file from the list (helpful if you want to manually select files to send).

- In either Album or List view, tap one of the column headers to sort it. Tap it again for a descending sort.

- Manage album names and create new ones by tapping the Edit Albums button in Album view. Make sure to tap the location (Handheld or Card) where you want the album to reside (**Figure 11.26**).

- Select Album Details from the Album menu to view how many images it contains, the total file size, and the last time it was updated. You can also add a descriptive note or delete the whole album from this screen (**Figure 11.27**).

- In Preferences (under the Options menu), mark Display zoom controls to zoom into a photo. With this option on, you'll see a magnifying glass icon in the bottom-right corner of images larger than 320 by 320 pixels. Tap the icon, then tap and drag the image to move it about (**Figure 11.28**).

- When you choose Slide Show, videos will be included. If you don't want to see them when viewing an album's slide show, open Preferences and unmark Show videos in Slide Show.

Figure 11.26 Add new albums or rename them—either on handheld or card—from Edit Albums.

Figure 11.27 Album Details shows you an album's total number of images and file size.

Figure 11.28 Make sure to mark Display zoom controls in Preferences in order to magnify images larger than 320 by 320 pixels.

Figure 11.29 Media in Palm Desktop for Windows features two collections of albums, one from your handheld's memory and one from a memory card.

Figure 11.30 The Slide Show and Video icons on the toolbar

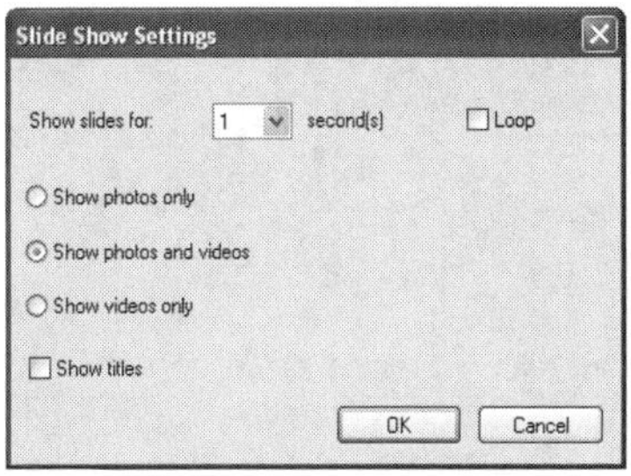

Figure 11.31 Your saved settings will affect both slide shows that you watch from Palm Desktop and videos that you create.

Media in Palm Desktop for Windows

While simple enough, the Media application within Palm Desktop also features some helpful editing and organization tools (**Figure 11.29**). You'll find a main viewing area, and two collections of albums—one from your handheld's memory, the other from the expansion card—in trays below the view area. Switch between different views by clicking the tabs at the bottom of the screen.

Slide Shows

To play a slide show on your PC's screen (or on a TV, if connected), click the Play Slide Show button (**Figure 11.30**). The screen goes to black, and images and videos from the open album begin to play. When the slide show reaches its end—or you want to end a show prematurely—press Esc.

To set slide show preferences:

1. Click the Settings button in the toolbar.

2. Click the Show slides for popup menu to choose the time interval between images (**Figure 11.31**). Check Loop if you want the slide show to begin again when it comes to the end.

3. Choose to show only photos, only videos, or both photos and videos.

4. Checking Show titles displays the title at the bottom of the screen as the slide show plays. Click OK to save.

To create a slide show video:

1. Select an album from either the Handheld or Expansion Card trays. Depending on the Slide Show settings, all images and videos from this album will be aggregated into the video slide show.

2. Click the Make Video button to open the Make Video dialog (**Figure 11.32**).

3. Choose whether to save the video to your hard drive for PC viewing or to Palm Desktop for transferring to your handheld.

4. If you selected the hard drive, choose a directory where you want to save the file. If you selected Palm Desktop, choose an album in the Expansion Card.

5. Type a name for the file and click the Make Video button.

✔ Tips

■ Unfortunately, you can't create a video of a manual selection of images from an album—the entire album gets the video treatment. To be more selective, just create a new album by selecting New Album from either the Tools or contextual menu (right-clicking), then shuffling those specific images into the new album.

■ Double-click a video in Palm Desktop to open it in the Video Editor (**Figure 11.33**).

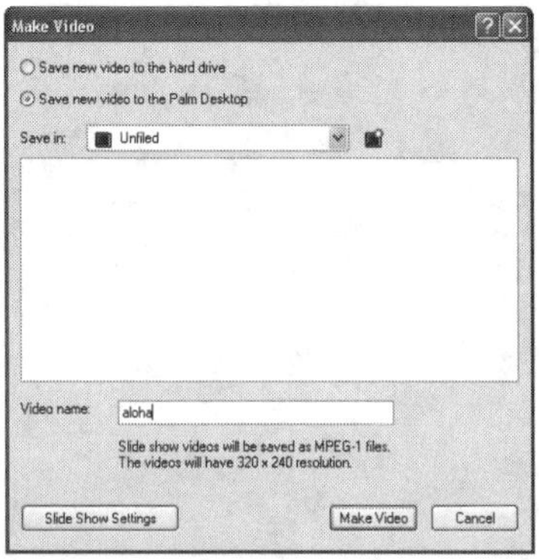

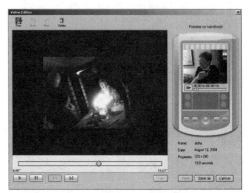

Figure 11.32 Save slide show videos to your PC's hard drive or to Palm Desktop for viewing on your handheld after performing a HotSync.

Figure 11.33 Double-clicking a video within Palm Desktop opens the Video Editor, from which you can play the slide show as well as make edits.

Figure 11.34 Double-click a photo to open the Photo Editor, which provides editing options in the toolbar and a rendering of how the photo will look on your handheld.

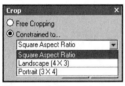

Figure 11.35 Choosing one of the constrained options lets you resize an image proportionally.

Editing Photos

Double-click an image to open it in Photo Editor. Or, select an image from one of the three views (List, Thumbnail, or Details) and click the Edit Media button or choose Edit Media from the File menu (**Figure 11.34**). The Photo Editor offers a number of editing tools, zooming options, and a preview screen that displays how the image will appear on your handheld—even as you edit it.

To crop a photo:

◆ Click the Crop button in the toolbar to automatically reduce the size of the image to a square aspect ratio.

Or

1. Click the popup menu to the right of the button to open the Crop tool, from which you can choose a constrained option or Free Cropping.

2. With Free Cropping selected, drag over the area that you want to save.

   If you choose either Square, Landscape, or Portrait constrained modes, click and hold a selection border and drag to your desired size (**Figure 11.35**). The selection area resizes according to the chosen aspect ratio. You can also click and drag the selection area to another location in the image.

3. Click the Crop button in the toolbar again to apply the change, or click the Crop Photo button at the bottom of the screen.

4. Click the Save button to save the change and return to the View pane.

✔ Tips

- After making a selection with the Crop tool, click and drag that selection rectangle to highlight another area of your image. The photo will render on your handheld in the Preview on Palm Handheld section to the right of the main window (**Figure 11.36**).

- If you want to manipulate an image with any of the editing tools but save its original file, rename the opened file's name in the field below the Preview on Palm Handheld area before making any adjustments.

To resize a photo:

1. Click the Resize button to open the Resize dialog (**Figure 11.37**).

2. Click Match Handheld resolution to automatically reduce the image's pixel dimensions to fit your handheld screen (as well as shave file size).

3. Selecting the Scale uniformly option enables you to type a size in either the width (W) or height (H) field. The value in the inactive field automatically updates to constrain to the aspect ratio.

4. Click the Save button to save the change and return to the View pane.

To rotate a photo:

1. Click the 90° Left or 90° Right button.

2. Continue clicking until you reach your desired rotation.

3. Click the Save button to save the change and return to the View pane.

Figure 11.36 Use the Crop tool to modify a photo's size or to highlight a specific area. Check to see how it renders using the Preview on Palm Handheld option.

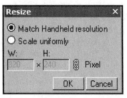

Figure 11.37 Automatically resize to handheld resolution or choose your own pixel dimensions.

Figure 11.38 Choose just the right degree of enhancement with the Select Favorite dialog.

Figure 11.39 Click the arrow to the right of the Red-eye button to adjust the size of the selector brush.

To enhance a photo:

◆ Click the Enhance button to automatically improve the image.

Or

1. Click the popup menu to open the Enhance dialog and choose Manual.

2. The Select Favorite dialog presents you with views of the original and nine options with varying degrees of enhancement (**Figure 11.38**).

3. Click the plus or minus buttons below the original image to adjust the zoom. Click and hold within any one of the squares to move to another area within the image.

4. Click one of the enhanced squares, then click OK to apply the change.

5. Click the Save button to save the change and return to the View pane.

✔ Tip

■ Keep the Preview option checked to see selected options appear in the Preview on Palm Handheld tool.

To reduce red-eye effect:

1. Click the Red-eye button. The cursor changes to an arrow with an eye icon.

2. Click and drag the pointer to add a gray "wash" to a selected area.

Or

1. Click the Red-eye popup to open the Remove Red-eye dialog. Choose your brush size (from Small to Extra Large), then click and draw around your selected area (**Figure 11.39**).

2. Click the Red-eye button to apply the change.

3. Click the Save button.

✔ Tip

■ The resulting brush stroke from the Red-eye tool is hard to pick out. When making adjustments, bump up the viewing size of your image, then use the hand tool to maneuver to the spot that needs help. Then, change the size of the Red-eye selector brush by clicking the arrow to the right of the Red-eye toolbar button and adjusting the size in the popup menu.

To add text to an image:

1. Clicking the Text button opens the Text dialog (**Figure 11.40**).

2. Make adjustments in the format popup menus (including font, size, effect, and color).

3. Type your message in the Note field. A hard return positions text on the next line.

4. Click, hold, and drag the text on the image to move it to your desired spot (**Figure 11.41**).

5. Click Apply on the Text dialog, then click Save on the Photo Editor to save the changes.

✔ Tip

■ The formatting options produce global changes to the note—you can't choose to make one word bold and leave the rest as Roman. But you can make multiple text additions, enabling you to achieve just the right text layout and format.

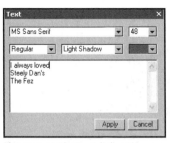

Figure 11.40 The Text dialog gives you control over font formatting, text color, and drop shadow.

Figure 11.41 If you do add hard returns to your text, all lines will be centered.

Figure 11.42 The Draw dialog lets you choose a stroke size and a color.

Figure 11.43 Add flair or a special message to a photo with the Draw tool.

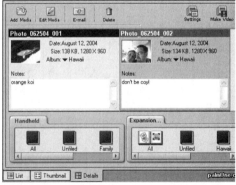

Figure 11.44 The Details view enables you to add a photo to an album as well as type a descriptive note.

To add a drawing to an image:

1. Click the Draw button.

2. With the pen tool, create your drawing with the default color and line size.

Or

1. Click the Draw popup menu to access the Draw dialog (**Figure 11.42**).

2. Choose the pen size (or Eraser) and the color from the popup menus. Click OK to return to the image, where you can create your masterpiece (**Figure 11.43**).

3. Click the Save button to save the change.

To organize albums:

◆ To create a new album, choose New Album from the Tools menu or after right-clicking within the Album bar. Or, select Edit Album to create, delete, or rename.

◆ Drag single or multiple image selections from the View pane and drop them onto a desired album in the Album bar. Photos can reside in multiple albums.

✔ Tips

■ If you don't like how your edits are forming, click the Undo button, or press Ctrl-Z. But do this before you click the Save button, as you can't undo the image's edits after you hit Save. To preserve the original image, click the Save As button and give the edited image file a different name.

■ Toggle between the Undo and Redo for before and after versions of the edit.

■ Change the views within Palm Photos by clicking the tabs at the bottom of the application: Thumbnail displays small images, List shows file information, and Details replicates the file information and adds the ability to file the image into an album and add notes (**Figure 11.44**).

Editing Videos

Viewing and editing videos in Palm Desktop for Windows is very similar to still images—but with fewer tools at your fingertips.

To edit videos:

1. Double-click a video file from Palm Desktop's Media to open it in the Video Editor (**Figure 11.45**).

2. To start a movie, click the Play button, or halt it by clicking the Pause button. Click and drag the slider to another frame position within the video. Click either the Backward or Forward button to view the next video in the list.

3. To modify the length of a video, click the Trim button in the toolbar.

4. Click and drag the "S" slider to a later frame, or click and drag the "F" slider to an earlier frame (**Figure 11.46**).

5. Click the Trim button to accept this edit.

6. Click the Save button to save this file, or Save As to preserve the original and save to a new file. Clicking Cancel will lose the edits you just made.

✔ Tips

- Just as with the Photo Editor, you have the Undo and Redo buttons at your disposal.

- Before hitting the Trim button, remind yourself what you've edited out by replaying the movie in the Preview on Palm Handheld area. Once you click Trim, that footage is deleted.

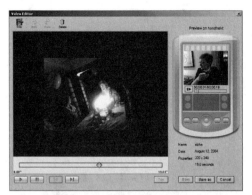

Figure 11.45 The Video Editor doesn't offer as many tools as the Photo Editor, but you can trim the length of your movie.

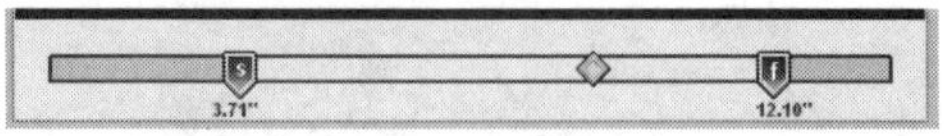

Figure 11.46 Use the Start ("S") and Finish ("F") sliders to modify the beginning and end of a movie.

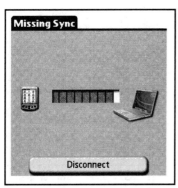

Figure 11.47 Tap the Connect button in Missing Sync, or set the preference to automatically connect whenever you open the program.

Synchronizing Photos for Macintosh

While there isn't a handy-dandy photo editing and organization tool built into Palm Desktop, the Mac does offer its own (sort of) built-in application: iPhoto. But here's where things get tricky. You can export photos from your iPhoto library to your handheld with help from The Missing Sync and its included SplashPhoto application for the Palm OS—but you can't synchronize or import (easily).

You can buy the SplashPhoto desktop application for Mac at a discount after purchasing The Missing Sync (`www.splashdata.com/missingsync`). And, with its HotSync conduit, it is the only way currently to synchronize the image libraries on your Palm and on your Mac without fiddling with a workaround or two.

By the way, SplashPhoto for the Palm OS, on its own, is a very capable image tool that performs many of the same tasks; plus, it uses the same database as Photos or Media.

To export photos from iPhoto to your handheld:

1. Connect your handheld to your Mac via USB cable or cradle, then open The Missing Sync on your handheld. If you haven't set the application to automatically connect at startup, tap the Connect button (**Figure 11.47**).

2. The memory card will mount in the Finder. If you haven't named the card, it will open as a disk entitled "NO NAME." Open it by clicking it in a Finder window, or double-clicking the disk icon on the desktop.

continued on next page

SYNCHRONIZING PHOTOS FOR MACINTOSH

3. In iPhoto, select one or several photos from the Photo Library or an album

4. Select Export from the File menu, or press Command-Shift-E.

5. Click the Missing Sync tab (**Figure 11.48**).

6. Choose to transfer the full-size image, or provide a maximum pixel dimension (a good option if you're trying to save space).

7. Click the Export button.

8. Select the mounted memory card in the Export Photos dialog, then open the DCIM folder (**Figure 11.49**).

9. Click OK, and let the files transfer.

10. When finished transferring, go back to the Finder and eject (unmount) the disk image. (If you were using iPhoto, quit the program before unmounting.)

✔ Tip

■ While you can't use iPhoto's Import function in conjunction with The Missing Sync, you can import images from the folder where photos are placed after a HotSync: Home> Pictures > PalmOne Photos. Select the user, then choose either Handheld or Expansion Card. You'll inevitably run into duplicates, but you can avoid doubling up by checking Applies to all duplicates and clicking No in the Duplicate Photo dialog (**Figure 11.50**).

To synchronize photos using SplashPhoto:

1. Shoot pictures with your Zire 72 or Treo, or add images to the SplashPhoto desktop application.

2. Perform a HotSync. (It's just that easy.)

Figure 11.48 The Missing Sync adds its own tab into iPhoto's Export Photos dialog.

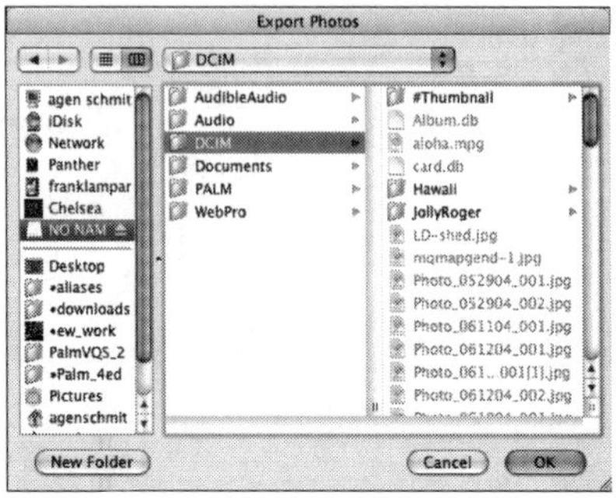

Figure 11.49 Export image files to the DCIM folder on the memory card.

Figure 11.50 If you perform the Import workaround for iPhoto, you'll need to watch out for duplicates.

Synchronizing Photos for Macintosh

Figure 11.51 Take your tunes with you and relax on those long commutes.

Playing Digital Music

Playing digital music from your handheld computer: The notion was probably less than a glimmer in most people's eyes at first, yet today the idea is becoming as natural as storing your addresses. As long as the information is digital, why not? And while the storage capacity is inferior to multi-gigabyte players like the Apple iPod, it's nice not to have to juggle between too many portable devices at once.

For its Palm OS 5 handhelds and beyond, Palm has partnered with Real Networks (www.real.com) to include the RealOne Player for Palm application (**Figure 11.51**).

✔ Tips

- As of this writing, Real Networks released updated PC software—RealPlayer 10.5, which now supports AAC files (the format used by Apple's iTunes Music Store)—as well as a newly renamed RealPlayer for Palm 1.5.1. You can transfer your MP3 files (including those purchased from the Real Music Store), but music purchased (in AAC format) from Apple can't be transferred due to their encoded digital rights management (DRM) that limits the number of computers and portable devices that can play a file.

- A memory card is required to store and play digital audio. Since music files take up a lot of memory, plan on purchasing at least a 128 MB memory card. As of this writing, we found 256 MB SD cards hovering around $50.

- If your audio tastes tend toward the spoken word, you can sign up for a subscription to Audible (www.audible.com) and download audiobooks, radio shows, and even daily editions of newspapers.

Transferring Music (Windows)

The instructions below utilize the latest PC and Palm OS software versions of RealPlayer and do not require a HotSync.

To transfer digital music files to your handheld:

1. Connect your handheld with inserted memory card to your PC via USB cable, and switch to RealPlayer for Palm.

2. In your PC's RealPlayer, click the Burn Transfer tab (**Figure 11.52**).

3. Select Palm Handheld (Card) from the Current Burner/Device menu. RealPlayer divides into two panes: My Library on the left and Palm Handheld (Card) on the right.

4. Search for music in the My Library pane, then drag and drop songs into the memory card pane.

5. Click the Start Transfer button. RealPlayer will initiate contact with your device and begin downloading files.

✔ Tips

■ You must open RealPlayer on your Palm OS handheld while connected to your PC in order to transfer files.

■ Alternatively, right-click a song (or selection of songs) while in the Music & My Library tab, then select Copy To > Palm Handheld from the contextual menu.

■ Create a playlist in My Library, then drag it from the My Library pane in the Burn/Transfer tab to the handheld pane to copy all songs from the playlist.

■ With Palm Handheld selected in Devices, click the Configure button to have RealOne automatically convert files to a lower bit rate (**Figure 11.53**).

Figure 11.52 Song files that are added to the Palm Handheld (Card) pane are noted with "Ready to Transfer" in the Transfer column.

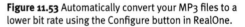

Figure 11.53 Automatically convert your MP3 files to a lower bit rate using the Configure button in RealOne.

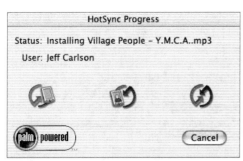

Figure 11.54 It takes a HotSync to transfer Village People MP3 files from your Mac to your handheld (unlike the Windows version, which uses RealOne to transfer files).

Figure 11.55 You'll see the memory card mounted in a Finder window.

Figure 11.56 Drag-and-drop simplicity via your iTunes library.

Transferring Music (Macintosh)

Mac users will need to rely on the old standby Send to Handheld droplet. But if you have The Missing Sync, you can mount your handheld's memory card onto your desktop and transfer music from your iTunes library.

To transfer digital music files to your handheld (droplet):

1. Drag and drop MP3 files onto the Send to Handheld droplet.

2. Select your memory card as the destination for the file(s).

3. Perform a HotSync (**Figure 11.54**).

To transfer digital music files to your handheld (Missing Sync):

1. Connect your handheld to your Mac via USB cable or cradle, then open The Missing Sync on your handheld. If you haven't set the application to automatically connect at startup, tap the Connect button.

2. The memory card will mount in the Finder. If you haven't named the card, it will open as a disk entitled "NO NAME." Open it by clicking it in a Finder window, or double-clicking the disk icon on the desktop (**Figure 11.55**).

3. Drag and drop music files into the Audio folder.

4. Or, open iTunes. Drag and drop MP3 files from your library onto the mounted device titled Missing Sync (**Figure 11.56**).

5. When finished transferring, go back to the Finder and eject (unmount) the disk image. (If you were using iTunes, quit the program before unmounting.)

✔ Tips

- Songs purchased from the iTunes Music Store (iTMS) are encoded using the AAC format. Unfortunately, AAC is not compatible with RealOne Player for Palm (version 1.1), thus you won't be able to play tunes from the iTMS on your handheld.

- The file transfer process leaves iTunes a bit dazed (i.e., you won't be able to click around the application until the transfer is finished). If you plan on downloading a number of files to the memory card, choose several at a time.

Playing Music

To listen to digital music:

1. Launch RealOne Player (**Figure 11.57**).

2. Tap the Songs button to select from the audio files available on your memory card. Alternatively, tap the Playlists button to view song lists either created on your handheld or transferred from the Windows version of RealOne. The audio file begins playing immediately after your selection.

3. Switch between songs by tapping the Forward or Backward button.

4. Tap the Information button to view details about the current track (**Figure 11.58**).

5. Tap the Continuous Play button to move forward through the Songs list or a selected playlist. Tap the Random Play button to mix things up.

6. Tap the Volume button to adjust sound through your headphones or through the handheld's AM-radio-like speaker.

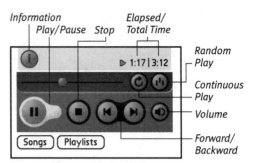

Figure 11.57 The RealOne Player includes controls familiar to anyone who has used a portable audio device or the PC version of RealOne.

Song Details

Title:	I'm On Standby
Artist:	Grandaddy
Album:	Sumday
Genre:	Alternative & Punk
Track #:	
Format:	160k Mp3
Size:	3.6MB
Filename:	I'm On Standby.mp3

(Done)

Figure 11.58 Tap the Information button to see details about the song, including album title, MP3 file encoding, and file size.

Figure 11.59 Mix and match your own music collection. No more carrying around an entire CD just to listen to the one good song on it.

Figure 11.60 Let the music play, even when you switch to other applications, when you select Enable Background Playback.

To create or edit a playlist:

1. Tap the Playlists button, then tap New. Or, select a playlist and tap Edit.

2. Add a title in the Name field.

3. Tap the Add button, and check the songs from your memory card that you want added. Tap Done.

4. Select a song and use the up and down arrows at the lower-right corner of the screen to adjust the position of songs within your list (**Figure 11.59**). Or, select a song and tap Remove to delete it from the list.

5. Tap Done to save the playlist and return to the Playlist library. Tap Done again to return to the Player.

To set preferences:

1. Open the Options menu and select Preferences, or write ╱-R (**Figure 11.60**).

2. Tap the Auto-powersave popup menu and choose how long to wait until the screen dims in Powersave mode. If the player is stopped or paused, Powersave will turn off your handheld.

3. Mark Enable Background Playback to have music continue playing while you work in other Palm OS applications. When the song or playlist is finished, the player will automatically stop.

4. Tap OK.

PLAYING DIGITAL MUSIC

LONG TEXTS

Like the concept of a truly paperless office, the notion of electronic books replacing traditional printed texts has been floating around for years. Instead of carrying around an armful of bound paper, you can store hundreds or thousands of books without felling a single tree or throwing out your back. Reading a lot of text on a small screen isn't an ideal task, but it's not as bad as you might expect. Plus, 400 pages of fiction are a lot lighter to carry when stored in a shirt pocket.

Palm OS device owners have been enjoying ebooks for years and publishers continue to offer more and more book-length works—just take a look at eReader's current best sellers (`www.ereader.com`).

Today's Palm handhelds can also handle a wide variety of electronic documents, from Microsoft Word and Excel files to Adobe's Portable Document Format (PDF). And don't forget the Doc format, an easy way to create and read your own long texts on your Palm handheld.

Reading Ebooks

A few years back, the ebook (aka, electronic book) was supposed to revolutionize the publishing world. We're still waiting. But until the tipping point of a paperless publishing universe arrives, your Palm is a ready-made ebook reader.

Many recent PalmOne handhelds come with the Palm Reader application on the installation CD (**Figure 12.1**). But you should update to the updated and newly renamed eReader application (`www.palmdigitalmedia.com/products/palmreader/free`), which adds a dash of color and a bit more functionality (**Figure 12.2**). You can purchase a wide variety of books that can be read by either application at the eReader site (`www.ereader.com`), including recent best sellers like *The Da Vinci Code* and Bill Clinton's memoir (for which you'll definitely need a large memory card).

Features of eReader

♦ Tap the Open icon (▣) to see all available ebooks stored in either the handheld's memory or on a memory card, or tap the Contents icon to view chapters within an open ebook (▣).

♦ Mark favorite sections by tapping the Bookmark icon (▣).

♦ Add notes to the text by tapping the Annotations icon (▢).

♦ Invert the screen for better readability on some models by tapping the Invert Screen icon (▣).

♦ Tap the Book Info icon (▣) to view the ebook's title, current page, and page total, as well as categorize and mark as private (**Figure 12.3**).

STEPHEN KING

RIDING THE BULLET

SCRIBNER/PHILTRUM PRESS

▢pg 1

Figure 12.1 The original Palm Reader, in all its two-dimensional glory.

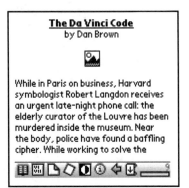

The Da Vinci Code
by Dan Brown

While in Paris on business, Harvard symbologist Robert Langdon receives an urgent late-night phone call: the elderly curator of the Louvre has been murdered inside the museum. Near the body, police have found a baffling cipher. While working to solve the

Figure 12.2 The eReader software updates the interface with colored 3D buttons and more options. Tap the image icon below the title to view the book's cover.

Book Info

Title: Winter 2004 Mini Catalog
Current Page: 34
Total Pages: ___
Category: | Biography
Private: | Fiction
| Sampler
| Unfiled
OK Cance | Edit Categories...

Figure 12.3 Categorize your ebooks to keep your library organized.

Figure 12.4 Highlight favorite quotes, look up a word in an installed dictionary, or add a note.

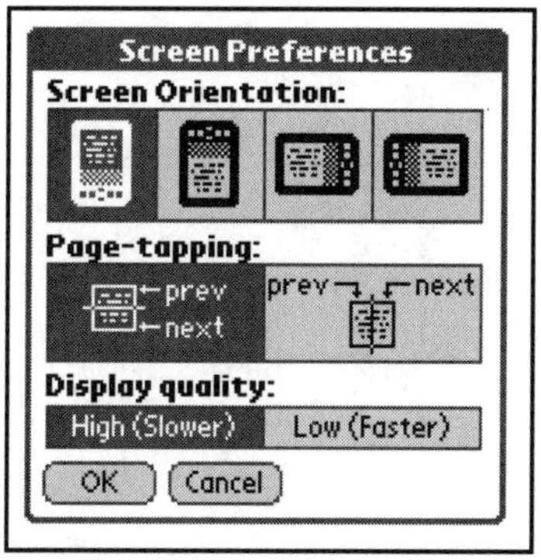

Figure 12.5 Use eReader's preferences to choose the best method of reading and navigating books on your handheld.

Figure 12.6 Easily jump around an eBook by using the navigation bar or entering a specific page.

◆ For those times when you get engrossed in a book, be sure to check the time and your battery level by tapping the Current Time icon (◉).

◆ Let eReader move through the ebook for you by tapping the Auto Scroll button (▣).

◆ Who says an ebook can't be a study aid? Select text, then choose Highlight from the pop-up menu to color the text. Open Selection Preferences under Options to configure the colors of up to four pens, or choose to look up a word in an installed dictionary, add a note, or copy a quote for pasting into another application (**Figure 12.4**).

◆ Change the screen orientation and the tapping control of the screen by choosing Screen Orientation from the Options menu (**Figure 12.5**).

To navigate an ebook:

◆ Tap the bottom or right of the screen to move to the next page; tap the top or left of the screen to go to the previous page (configure this in Screen Preferences) (**Figure 12.5**).

◆ Use the navigation buttons (right and down for next; left and up for previous).

◆ Tap the current page/status bar in the lower-right corner or choose Go To Page (✓-J) from the Go menu to choose a specific page or navigate the larger status bar (**Figure 12.6**).

✔ Tips

- If you already have Palm Reader installed onto your Palm, the eReader application will automatically replace it when you install it.

- Save battery power and increase page-turning speed by selecting Low display quality in Screen Preferences. This also reverts back to the original 2D icons.

- If you're a hands-free speed reader, you can adjust the Auto Scroll speed (which is measured by pixels) by selecting Auto Scroll Preferences under the Options menu (**Figure 12.7**). Choose from three preset speeds, or enter your own level.

- Palm Reader understands Doc files, so you can use it to swap between multiple text formats on your handheld (see "Reading Doc-Formatted Texts," later in this chapter).

- If you own a device that has a rectangular screen, such as the Tungsten T3, rotate the screen orientation to view more text while reading.

- For more reading options, buy eReader Pro ($15), which supports more fonts and includes a built-in dictionary.

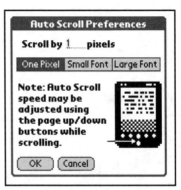

Figure 12.7 Satisfy your need for hands-free reading speed by adjusting the Auto Scroll Preferences.

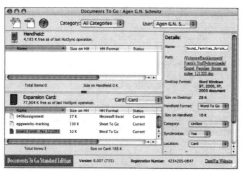

Figure 12.8 Simply drag Word or Excel files to the Documents To Go window to prepare them for installation at the next HotSync operation.

Figure 12.9 Quickoffice retains the native Office file format when moving the file to the handheld.

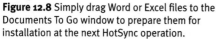

Figure 12.10 Documents To Go retains formatting from the word processor that created the original file.

Reading and Editing Microsoft Office Files

If you're like a lot of people, you may not want to read books or preformatted files on your handheld. Instead, wouldn't it be great to take some of your Microsoft Office documents with you and edit them on the road?

DataViz's Documents To Go (www.dataviz.com) and iGo's Quickoffice (www.mobl.com/software) enable you to do just that. Drag Microsoft Word or Excel files to Documents To Go (**Figure 12.8**) or Quickoffice (**Figure 12.9**) to convert them with styles and most formatting (including tables in Word and frozen panes in Excel) intact (**Figures 12.10** and **12.11**, next page).

✔ Tips

- For a faster method of specifying files to be converted by Documents To Go, select the file in the Finder (Mac) or Explorer (Windows), then either Control-click (Mac) or right-click (Windows) to select Take File to Go from the popup menu that appears. Under Windows, you can optionally select Documents To Go from the Send to submenu of the contextual menu.

- Just as data from Palm's applications are synchronized, so are files from Documents To Go. Each time you synchronize, Office files are updated on either your handheld or on the PC. If a file has been modified in both locations, a duplicate file will be created on both the handheld and the PC.

- You can use Quickoffice or Documents To Go as standalone word processors too: Create a new file on the Palm, then transfer it back to your PC at the next HotSync (a great use with an external keyboard).

✔ Tips

- Although much of the document's original formatting is translated to the handheld, keep in mind that the file is being converted, not just sent directly between the PC and handheld. So, some formatting (such as style sheets) may not be retained when you open the file again on the PC after editing it on the handheld.

- By default, Documents To Go and Quickoffice convert Microsoft Office documents to Palm OS-friendly files. But the latest versions of these applications also enable you to view native versions of Office documents, which is handy if you receive a document or spreadsheet via email or transfer via infrared or Bluetooth (or, conversely, if you want to easily share documents with others). Note that opening a native file requires a conversion within the handheld to view it; however, its native status is preserved once you close it (**Figure 12.12**).

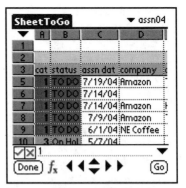

Figure 12.11 Documents To Go can even handle text formatting, cell highlighting, and frozen panes in Excel spreadsheets.

Figure 12.12 If you get a native Office file beamed to you, you can still open it without first converting it on your PC.

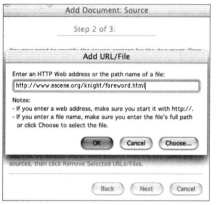

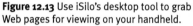

Figure 12.13 Use iSilo's desktop tool to grab Web pages for viewing on your handheld.

Figure 12.14 iSilo formats text defined by the underlying HTML, and includes links to other converted pages.

Viewing HTML Documents

iSilo (www.isilo.com) and HandStory (www.namo.com) take HTML pages and format them for viewing on a handheld. You can use them to read an individual HTML file, or point to a Web site and specify how many levels of links to follow. (We're using iSilo as the example below.)

To convert a file for viewing with iSilo:

1. Using the separate iSiloX application, select an HTML file you wish to convert (**Figure 12.13**). You can also provide a Web address that iSilo will connect to.

2. After the file has been converted, HotSync your organizer.

3. On the handheld, launch iSilo and choose the page(s) you installed. If you converted several pages of a Web site, you can tap the dotted-underlined words to bring up linked pages (**Figure 12.14**).

✔ Tip

- Most text readers for the Palm OS separate the screen into two areas, usually top and bottom, to control whether the text advances up or down when you tap it. iSilo wisely splits the screen into four equal areas, letting you control the amount of scrolling based on where you tap (**Figure 12.15**).

Figure 12.15 Control the page scroll rate by defining four screen regions.

Viewing PDF Documents

Adobe's Portable Document Format (PDF) began as a method of displaying print materials onscreen in a format that would retain the layout, fonts, and appearance of the original file, without requiring that the recipient own QuarkXPress, InDesign, or another page-layout application. Over time, PDF has become a way to view nearly any document on any computer, so it's only natural that you can now view PDF files on a Palm OS handheld.

A number of programs enable you to convert PDF files for viewing on the handheld, such as Adobe Reader for Palm OS (`www.adobe.com/products/acrobat/readerforpalm.html`). Other document applications, such as DataViz's Documents To Go Premium, can also convert and read PDF files.

To convert a PDF file:

1. Simply drag a PDF file to the main window of Adobe Reader for Palm OS; alternately, click the Add button (**Figure 12.16**). The PDF is converted to a format optimized for the handheld.

2. HotSync your handheld to transfer the file.

3. Launch the reader application to view the PDF document (**Figure 12.17**).

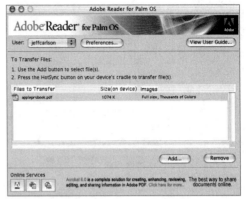

Figure 12.16 Adobe Reader for Palm OS prepares PDF files for your handheld.

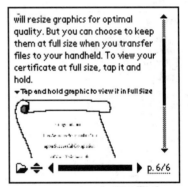

Figure 12.17 You won't forget you're viewing a document on a device with a small screen, but the information (including images) from a PDF is available on the handheld.

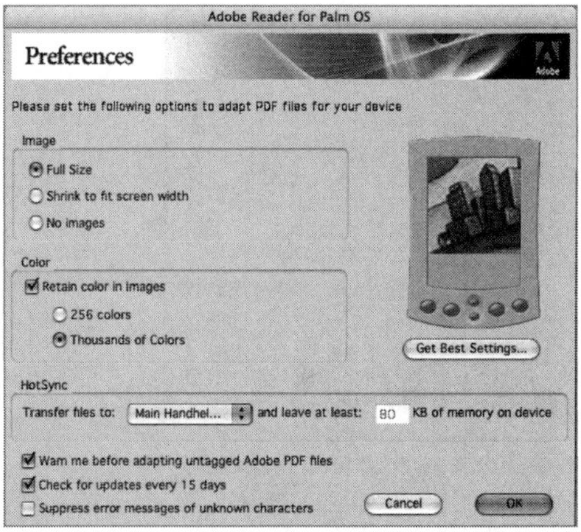

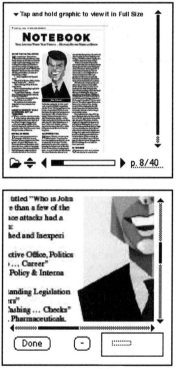

Figure 12.18 Optimize PDF files for viewing on your handheld by adjusting Adobe Reader for Palm OS preferences.

Figure 12.19 Some graphics-intensive PDF pages get converted into an image. Just tap and hold on the image to open the full version. Navigate the full-size image with your stylus or by tapping within the box at the bottom right.

Adobe Reader Preferences

The conversion process is easy peasy, but you might want to tweak the preferences, especially if storage space is at a premium (**Figure 12.18**).

◆ If you choose Full Size under Images, you can tap images to view them in their original size. Choosing Shrink to fit screen width saves on file size if you don't need close-up views of images.

◆ Shave off a few pixels by choosing 256 colors instead of Thousands of Colors, or go the old-school route with no color.

◆ If you have a Palm with an expansion slot, choose to send PDF files directly to your memory card instead of the handheld memory.

✔ Tip

■ Agen is a big fan of magazines offering a subscription that includes a full PDF download (Salon and The Nation are two examples). It's not as easily readable as a laptop screen, but he finds it easier to read from his Palm in confined spaces (such as when commuting on the bus). When converting PDFs, do some experimenting as some pages with a number of graphics get automatically turned into an image within the converted PDF file (**Figure 12.19**).

VIEWING PDF DOCUMENTS

Reading Doc-Formatted Texts

A number of applications are available for reading documents that you install on your handheld. An early document format, Doc, is read by most reader applications. For the sake of example, I'll focus on TealDoc (www. tealpoint.com).

Doc files can contain bookmarks that jump down to main sections of the document. Bookmarks can be preformatted (see "Converting Texts to Doc Format" later in this chapter), or created by the reader.

To open Doc files:

1. After installing a Doc file into the handheld, open TealDoc. You'll see a list of available Doc files that are stored in the device's memory (**Figure 12.20**).

2. Tap the Open button at the bottom of the screen, then tap the title of the document you want to read.

To navigate a document:

◆ Tap anywhere in the lower half of the screen to scroll down; tap the upper half to scroll up. You can advance through the files without having to be precise about tapping a scroll bar or arrow.

◆ You can also move to the top or bottom of the document by choosing Go Up Page (╱-U), Go Down Page (╱-D), Go to Top (╱-T), or Go to Bottom (╱-B) from the View menu.

◆ Tap the percentage indicator to display the Scroll panel (**Figure 12.21**). Drag the horizontal scroll bar at the bottom of the screen to scroll through the document; the percentage will change depending on the slider's location.

Figure 12.20 Any Doc-formatted files that you install show up in the Doc reader's list view.

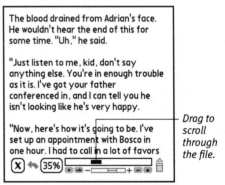

Drag to scroll through the file.

Figure 12.21 Move swiftly through your document by dragging the horizontal scroll bar in TealDoc.

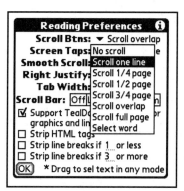

Figure 12.22 Control the scroll rate by choosing from the Scroll Btns and Screen Taps popup menus.

The blood drained from Adrian's face. He wouldn't hear the end of this for some time. "Uh," he said.

"Just listen to me, kid, don't say anything else. You're in enough trouble as it is. I've got your father conferenced in, and I can tell you he isn't looking like he's very happy.

"Now, here's how i » Edit Bookmarks...
set up an appointr » Add Bookmark...
one hour. I had to » Add Note...

Figure 12.23 Bookmarks can be set up before the file is installed, or you can add them to access your favorite passages.

✔ Tips

■ You can specify that tapping advances the text by screen (the default), partial page (a full screen minus one overlapping line), or line. Choose Reading Prefs from the Option menu (✓-P) and choose the degree of advancement from the Screen Taps popup menu. You can also specify scroll options for the physical scroll buttons on the handheld's case (**Figure 12.22**).

■ If you have the Scroll one line option selected above, tapping and holding the stylus to the screen will scroll the text until you lift the stylus. Depending on where you tap, the scrolling speed will be slower (closer to the middle) or faster (closer to the lower or upper edges).

■ If you want to be able to select and copy text with your stylus, choose Select word from the Screen Taps popup menu in the Reading Preferences screen.

To use bookmarks:

1. Tap the icon in the lower-right corner of the screen to view the bookmarks popup menu (**Figure 12.23**).

2. Tap the section name you want to access.

To add bookmarks:

1. Scroll up or down to display the section you wish to bookmark.

2. Choose Add Bookmark from the popup menu, or Add New Bookmark from the Marks menu (✓-1), and enter a descriptive title. Tap OK.

✔ Tip

■ To remove, rename, or scan the document for bookmarks, choose those options from the Marks menu.

To automatically scroll the document:

1. When AutoScroll is active, the screen advances automatically. Under the Special menu, choose AutoScroll Go (✓-G) to begin. AutoScroll Stop (✓-S) turns the feature off.

2. Tap the percentage indicator to display the Scroll panel, or choose Show Scroll Panel from the View menu.

3. The smaller horizontal bar at the botton of the page indicates the scrolling speed; tap the plus (⊕) or minus (⊖) buttons to the right of the bar to adjust the speed (**Figure 12.24**).

4. Tap the go button (⊕) to start, or the stop button (⊖) to stop scrolling.

✔ Tip

■ You can also control the scrolling speed using the application buttons on the front of the handheld's case. Choose Reading Prefs (✓-P), then tap one or both buttons under the heading App buttons control autoscroll on.

To perform a search within the current document:

1. Choose Show Font Panel (which also displays the search controls) from the View menu, or tap the percentage indicator.

2. To search, tap the magnifying glass icon, or choose Find from the Doc menu (✓-F) (**Figure 12.25**). Enter the text you want to find, and mark any of the four search options.

3. To search again for the same term, tap either of the arrows surrounding the magnifying glass icon; or, choose Find Next (✓-N) or Find Last (✓-L) from the Doc menu.

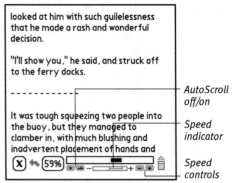

looked at him with such guilelessness that he made a rash and wonderful decision.

"I'll show you," he said, and struck off to the ferry docks.

It was tough squeezing two people into the buoy, but they managed to clamber in, with much blushing and inadvertent placement of hands and

AutoScroll off/on

Speed indicator

Speed controls

Figure 12.24 Configure the AutoScroll rate by tapping the controls at the bottom of the screen.

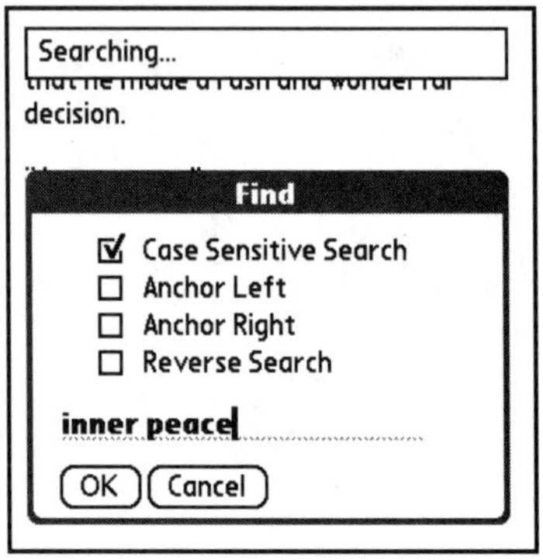

Searching...
that he made a rash and wonderful decision.

Find

☑ Case Sensitive Search
☐ Anchor Left
☐ Anchor Right
☐ Reverse Search

inner peace

(OK) (Cancel)

Figure 12.25 Tap the magnifying glass icon to perform searches.

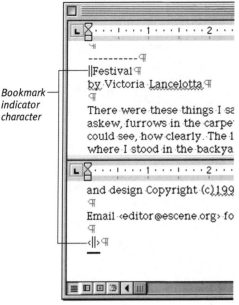

Bookmark indicator character

Figure 12.26 Specifying a unique character set at the end of the document (bottom) instructs Doc readers to add a bookmark where the characters are found within the text.

Converting Texts to Doc Format

You can create your own Doc files from existing text files using utilities such as MakeDocBatch (`www.freewarepalm.com/utilities/makedocbatch.shtml`) and QEX2 (`www.qland.de/qex2`). (Some Doc utilities, such as TealDoc, include a conversion program as well.)

To prepare the text file:

1. Your text is going to be viewed on the small screen, so strip out any long breaking lines of repeated dashes (----), or reduce them to about 20 characters.

2. Make sure there's a carriage return after each paragraph, not each line. This gives you more flexibility when viewing at different font sizes.

3. Save your document as a text-only file.

To specify bookmarks:

1. Choose a character combination that isn't likely to show up in your text (such as ||).

2. At the end of your document, put it between brackets (<||>) to define the file's bookmark notation.

3. Add the character combination (without brackets) before each section you wish to bookmark (**Figure 12.26**). When the Doc reader encounters the characters, it creates a new bookmark, using the text that follows as a bookmark label.

To convert the file:

◆ Drag and drop the text file onto the conversion utility, or open the utility and use the Browse button to locate the file.

✔ Tips

■ TealDoc offers the ability to embed pictures, links, and Web bookmarks into text files, similar to HTML markup. For this to be activated, though, the document needs to be converted to TealDoc format on the handheld. From the main list screen, select All to TealDoc format. To return the files to standard Doc state, select All to public format. See the documentation that comes with TealDoc for instructions on how to mark up your text to accommodate these features.

■ You can also edit Doc-formatted files directly on the handheld (**Figure 12.27**) using the editor/word processor QED (`www.qland.de/qed/`).

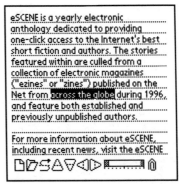

Figure 12.27 QED can edit Doc-formatted files, as well as open them.

GAMES AND ENTERTAINMENT

You're a working professional with a lot to accomplish in a limited time. Since purchasing your handheld, you've discovered new ways to squeeze your workload into the tight confines of your daily schedule, and finally carved out the quality time you've been dreaming about for months.

And yet, while on the bus or train, standing in line at the grocery store, or waiting at the airport—transitional time that would be ripe for reviewing the latest project outline—you just don't have it in you to *work*. These are the moments when a Palm device really shines, when you realize the full power of your investment.

These are the times to play games.

We couldn't hope to cover all the games that are available for the Palm OS platform, but we would feel remiss without extensively testing out a range of games that will tickle your fancy. As a friend of ours says, "The people have a right to know." The following programs are games we've become addicted to at one time or another, or are beguiling diversions that just deserve notice. But that's just the start. Check out Handango (www. handango.com) and Palmgear (www.palmgear. com) for a vast universe of titles.

Puzzles

Bejeweled!

Bejeweled! has a simple premise: Move jewels into rows of three or more to get rid of them and bring on new gems (**Figure 13.1**). Like its spiritual ancestor Tetris, Bejeweled! (`www.astraware.com`) will make you put off work to play for just one more minute...and then another, and another....

Bookworm

In Bookworm (`www.astraware.com`), tap letter tiles to create words and earn points; the longer the word, the more points (**Figure 13.2**). Watch out for burning tiles: If they get to the bottom of the screen, the library burns down.

Tetris Classic

Cultural anthropologists of the future will stumble upon Tetris one day, and either wonder at how backward our society was or marvel at how fast the human mind could move shapes into place in order to get rid of horizontal rows (`www.handmark.com`). We still have trouble getting the falling blocks out of our dreams.

Mahjong

The ancient Chinese game of mahjong (a tile-based matching game where you have to reverse engineer a pyramid) is very adaptable, as evidenced by a recent sighting of a Lord of the Rings version on Handango. We like the more traditional Mahjongg from Astraware, but our favorite is MahJong by Absolutist (`www.absolutist.com/palm/mahjong`), with one caveat—you need a 320 x 320 pixel screen (**Figure 13.3**). If you've got a compatible device, you'll dig the rich graphics and get caught up for hours.

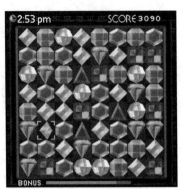

Figure 13.1 Bejeweled! is yet another classic battery-draining obsession.

Figure 13.2 Find words by connecting letters before the library burns down.

Figure 13.2 MahJong by Absolutist isn't just habit forming—its incredibly detailed 320 x 320-pixel graphics are gorgeous.

Figure 13.4 You may find yourself shouting "Yahtzee" at the most inappropriate times.

Figure 13.5 It's not Deep Blue, but Chess Tiger can easily make you realize that you're no Kasparov.

Figure 13.6 Blast away at your opponent's fleet in Battleship.

Classics

YahtChallenge

Who knew that Yahtzee could be entertaining for more than just a few minutes? At one time or another, YahtChallenge has occupied a lot of our collective brain power and spare time (home1.pacific.net.sg/~kokmun/yahtc/yahtc.htm). Roll dice and come up with combinations to score the most points against a friend or the Palm (**Figure 13.4**).

PocketChess Deluxe and Chess Tiger

This excellent chess program provides all the functions an average chess player needs (**Figure 13.5**). Chess geeks (a term we use affectionately) will appreciate PocketChess (www.handmark.com), which features a game synchronization tool under Windows as well as databases of famous games by the masters. Chess Tiger (www.chesstiger.com) features six board sizes, icon access to commonly used functions, and an opening book of 8,000 chess moves.

Klondike and FreeCell

No consumer electronic device should exist without a solitaire game installed. These two variations, the traditional Klondike and the more nefarious FreeCell (both at www.electronhut.com), can occupy your hours without the need for table space to set up real cards.

Battleship

"You just sunk my battleship!" Reproduced down to the look of the plastic ship pieces, Battleship (www.handmark.com) improves on the original board game (**Figure 13.6**). For more fun, find a buddy and play head-to-head over infrared, Bluetooth, or the Internet (if your Palm has Net access).

Notable Diversions

Zap!2000 and Zap!2016

Zoom through space blasting everything in sight in Zap!2000 (www.astraware.com). The game play is fast, the graphics are crisp, and the color version, Zap!2016, takes advantage of the thousands of colors available on some devices' screens (**Figure 13.7**).

DopeWars and Taipan

Are you a budding entrepreneur, looking for the high life? Does the thrill of making deals pump through your veins? Then perhaps you need to try your hand at DopeWars (www.palmtown.com/games/xgm105.php), a game geared toward making as much money as possible within a given timeframe (**Figure 13.8**). If you're uncomfortable with the DopeWars theme, install Taipan (find it at www.palmgear.com) instead and trade across the high seas of the Orient.

Scrabble

Agen's mother-in-law, an ardent Scrabble devotee for years, bought her first Palm handheld largely in order to play the game on her travels. The Palm OS version of Scrabble (www.handmark.com) includes both Friendly (where non-standard words are accepted) and Tournament modes and a built-in dictionary (**Figure 13.9**). But at nearly 1.5 megabytes, it will take a fairly hefty bite out of your memory.

✔ Tip

■ With the inclusion of an expansion card slot on just about every PalmOne device (including the Treo), you don't have to worry about filling up your handheld's memory with divertissements. Make sure to load a memory card into your device, then specify the card as the location before you install games via HotSync.

Figure 13.7 One of the best uses of color, Zap!2016 is beautiful and action-packed.

Figure 13.8 We don't want to run afoul of the law or common decency, but DopeWars is just too much fun. Think of it as an arbitrage training game for budding Wall Street traders—with a twist.

Figure 13.9 Lots of hot spots (i.e., squares with bonus points) are left on this virtual Scrabble board.

Managing Your Money

You've often heard the expression "time is money," but rarely do you hear the phrase, "money is sure a lot like time." As sayings go, it kind of stinks. Yet in our time working as freelancers, this nugget of wisdom has repeatedly proven itself true. As with time, you can burn through money without noticing it if you're not careful. Also like time (or rather, deadlines), bills have the uncanny ability to sneak up on you quickly.

Fortunately, you can use your handheld to keep track of finances as well as to help manage your time. Having that information at your disposal enables you to update your checkbook register while you're away from your computer, thus minimizing the number of faded receipts that are ballooning your wallet.

Track Your Personal Finances

If your spending seems out of control, or you just want to get a better idea of where your money is going, track your usage for a week or a month. (See Chapter 15 for tips on tracking how you spend your day.)

The built-in Expense application is all set up to make it easy for you to track your money's trajectory from wallet to the outside world.

To track your cash flow with Expense:

1. To create a new record, tap New or begin writing either the expense amount or the first letter of the expense type in the Graffiti area.

2. With the record still highlighted, tap the Details button to enter the Vendor, City, and any other information you want to store (**Figure 14.1**).

3. At the end of the tracking period, perform a HotSync and then tap the Expense button in Palm Desktop for Windows. You'll be able to open the data in an Excel spreadsheet and get an overview of where your money went (**Figure 14.2**).

✔ Tips

■ The Expense program is really geared for business travellers—it's not often we use the Hotels or Airfare types (though we'd like to). The other frustrating aspect is the fact that you can't modify the Expense types. Thus, it's important to create a wide assortment of categories that are relevant to both your life and how you use Expense on your handheld (**Figure 14.3**). For instance, Agen only includes items for expenses when he's out and about (but none for bills paid at home).

Figure 14.1 The more information you add to Expense items, the better you'll be able to track your money.

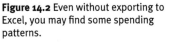

Figure 14.2 Even without exporting to Excel, you may find some spending patterns.

Figure 14.3 Make sure to create categories that are relevant to your spending patterns.

Figure 14.4 If you don't travel much, use the City field to keep brief notes about purchases.

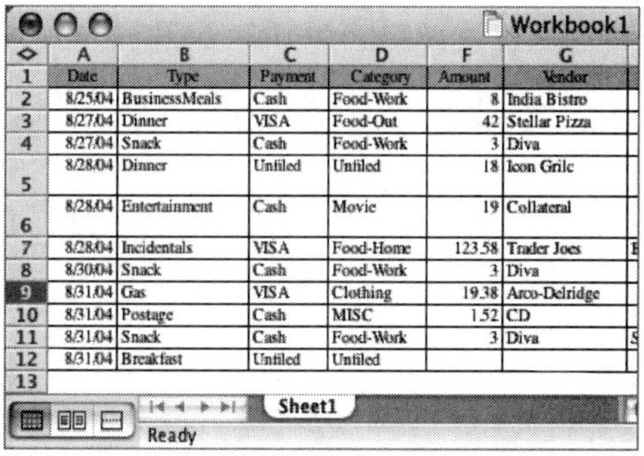

	A	B	C	D	F	G
1	Date	Type	Payment	Category	Amount	Vendor
2	8/25.04	BusinessMeals	Cash	Food-Work	8	India Bistro
3	8/27.04	Dinner	VISA	Food-Out	42	Stellar Pizza
4	8/27.04	Snack	Cash	Food-Work	3	Diva
5	8/28.04	Dinner	Unfiled	Unfiled	18	Icon Grilc
6	8/28.04	Entertainment	Cash	Movie	19	Collateral
7	8/28.04	Incidentals	VISA	Food-Home	123.58	Trader Joes
8	8/30.04	Snack	Cash	Food-Work	3	Diva
9	8/31.04	Gas	VISA	Clothing	19.38	Arco-Delridge
10	8/31.04	Postage	Cash	MISC	1.52	CD
11	8/31.04	Snack	Cash	Food-Work	3	Diva
12	8/31.04	Breakfast	Unfiled	Unfiled		
13						

Figure 14.5 With QueueSoft's freeware Expense conduit for the Mac, you can open your Expense log directly in an Excel spreadsheet after performing a HotSync. It even includes a column for attached Notes.

- If you don't do much travelling, disregard the title of Expense's City field and use it for making a brief note about a transaction (**Figure 14.4**). However, the field is limited to one line (about 20 displayed characters). And don't forget about attached notes, which can be handy for reminding yourself about complicated restaurant check splitting.

- As explained in Chapter 7, Palm Desktop for Macintosh includes neither a built-in Expense application nor a HotSync conduit. Luckily, QueueSoft provides a freeware conduit (www.queuesoft.jp/download-e.html), from which you can create either a tab- or comma-delimited output file or an Excel spreadsheet (**Figure 14.5**).

- Agen is a big fan of the book *Your Money or Your Life* by Joe Dominguez and Vicki Robin, of which tracking your every transaction is a component. But more than just seeing where your money is being spent, the book asks you to put a value on your time—your true hourly wage based on income as well as time and money spent on supporting your job. From this, you can then measure the worthiness of a purchase in "life energy" cost. For instance, you'll be able to figure out whether that new Benji movie is really worth a half hour of life energy ($10) plus two hours spent in the theater and another hour in transit.

- Jeff created a master list of the bills he pays each month, so that even if his income varies from month to month (one curse of freelancing), he'll know how much he needs to pay. The list originated as a Memo Pad entry on his Palm V, but can now be found as an Excel spreadsheet (which can be viewed using Documents to Go) on his Tungsten T.

TRACK YOUR PERSONAL FINANCES

Manage Your Financial Accounts

A checkbook was once a convenient place to record transactions in the paper register, as well as a handy storage folder for ATM withdrawal receipts, upcoming bills, parking tickets, etc. But now that we rely more and more on debit cards, it seems impractical to carry a checkbook anymore.

That's where Quicken (www.quicken.com) and its Palm OS companion, Pocket Quicken (www.landware.com), come to the rescue—especially if you're frustrated with the limits of the Expense application. Pocket Quicken syncs directly with Quicken on the PC or the Mac—where you'll keep your bank and credit card account ledgers—and includes the ability to configure your own transaction types and a budgeting calculator that shows how much has been spent on specific categories (**Figure 14.6**).

But Pocket Quicken isn't the only financial manager on the block. QMate (www.qmate.com), one of the first financial applications for the Palm OS, can take data from the handheld to be imported into Quicken, as can SplashMoney (www.splashdata.com). And there are others as well that don't need a desktop program, such as Personal Money Tracker (find it at www.palmgear.com).

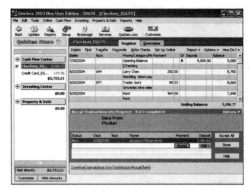

Figure 14.6 When you create transactions in Pocket Quicken, then perform a HotSync, you'll be given the opportunity to accept them (in the bottom pane) into the desktop Quicken software.

Figure 14.7 Pocket Quicken's transaction screen looks almost like the checks buried at the bottom of your purse or briefcase, without the paper.

Pick Category/Transfer	
abc def ghi jkl mno pqr stu v-z	
Household	Exp ↑
Insurance	Exp
Disability Insurance	Sub
Home Insurance	Sub
Life Insurance	Sub
Interest Exp	Exp
Interest Inc	Inc
Invest Inc	Inc
IRA Contrib	Exp ↓

(Use) (Cancel) (Transfers) ⬍

Figure 14.8 All of your Quicken categories transfer to the handheld.

Edit Split Transaction	
Category	**Amount**
▼ Groceries	18.41
▼ Wedding	13.99
▼ Household	6.31
▼	
▼	
Split Total:	38.71
Remainder:	0.00
Total:	**38.71**

(OK) (Cancel) (Edit...) (Adjust) ⬍

Figure 14.9 Splitting transactions in Pocket Quicken makes it easier to identify your expenses when you run reports in Quicken.

Getting started in Pocket Quicken

One of the great things about LandWare's Pocket Quicken is that all you need to do is install the desktop conduit and perform a HotSync operation. Your Quicken account names and balances are transferred to the handheld. Optionally, you can have your categories transferred as well.

✔ Tips

- A maximum of 15 accounts will be transferred. Unfortunately, if you have any inactive or hidden accounts in Quicken, those get sent over as well. However, you can delete an account from Pocket Quicken and still keep it in Quicken.

- You can add accounts on the handheld if you want, but they won't be created on the desktop after you HotSync.

To enter a transaction in Pocket Quicken:

1. In the Accounts screen, select the account from which the transaction will be debited. Then tap the Register button.

2. Tap the New button and choose the type of transaction from the popup menu that appears: Payment, Deposit, or Transfer. The transaction looks like Quicken's check format (**Figure 14.7**).

3. Write the information in the fields provided, or tap the field titles to access more information like categories (**Figure 14.8**).

4. Pocket Quicken supports split transactions. Tap Split to break out individual components (**Figure 14.9**).

5. Tap Done to apply the transaction, or Cancel to delete it.

MANAGE YOUR FINANCIAL ACCOUNTS

✔ Tips

- Start writing the payee's name in the Graffiti area to create a new transaction. You'll just assign the debited account by tapping the dotted Account box at the top of the screen.

- In the Transaction Categories screen, tap the shortcut letters at the bottom to take you to that block of categories. Tapping each one repeatedly cycles through the letters; for example, tapping mno once takes you to the top of the "m" list, but tapping it again jumps down to the "n" categories.

- Pocket Quicken also supports features like memorized, cleared, and voided transactions. Plus, if a payee isn't in your list of memorized transactions, you can look up a name from Contacts (**Figure 14.10**).

To set up accounts in SplashMoney:

1. From the main Accounts screen, select New Account from the Account menu, or write ∕-N.

2. Give it a name and select an account type from the Type menu (**Figure 14.11**).

3. Enter the account's current balance in the Beg. Bal. field. Tap OK to save the account's information.

✔ Tip

- You can also fill in your bank name and account number. If you feel squeamish about this, choose Set Password from the Options menu to create a mandatory password entry when you open SplashMoney (**Figure 14.12**).

Figure 14.10 Tap the Lookup button to find a payee's name in Contacts.

Figure 14.11 SplashMoney accounts need to share the same names of related accounts in Quicken.

Figure 14.12 Entry into SplashMoney can be protected by a password.

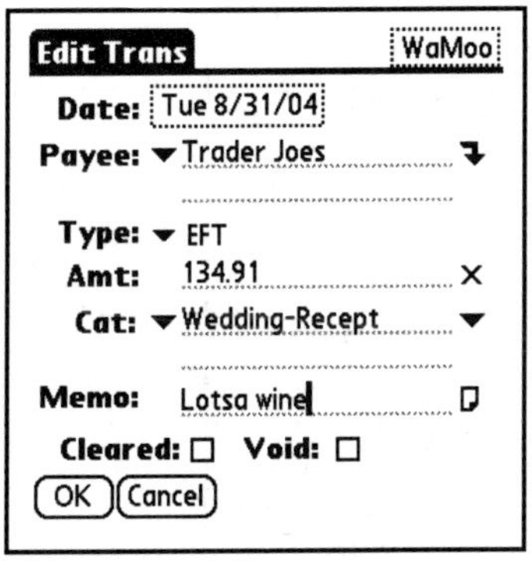

Figure 14.13 The Edit Trans screen includes many of the same fields found in Pocket Quicken as well as checkboxes for Cleared and Void.

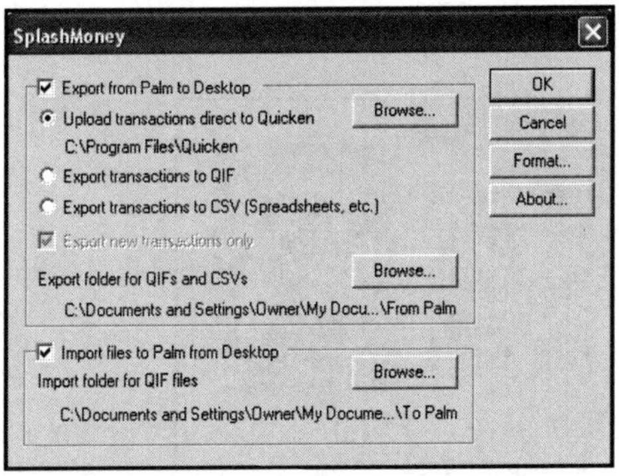

Figure 14.14 Configure your HotSync preferences for the SplashMoney conduit in Palm Desktop for Windows, including uploading transactions directly to Quicken.

To enter a transaction in SplashMoney:

1. Once your account is set up, select it from the Accounts screen to enter its Register view.

2. Tap the New button, or write ╱-N.

3. Tap the Date, Payee, or Cat (category) button to view a list of memorized transactions; or, write in the fields provided (**Figure 14.13**). Tap OK to apply the transaction, or Cancel to get rid of it.

✔ Tips

- Personalize your account and transaction settings by selecting Edit Categories (╱-C) and Edit Transaction Types from the List menu.

- You can also set up Classes, a secondary set of categorization to help differentiate between, say, business and personal transactions. Tap the popup to the right of the Cat field to select a class.

- The Memo displays just the beginning of your notation—if you run on, tap the note icon to see your memo in full.

To transfer data to Quicken:

1. In Palm Desktop for Windows, choose Custom from the HotSync menu.

2. Select the SplashMoney conduit from the list, then click the Change button (**Figure 14.14**).

3. Choose to upload transactions directly to Quicken (you may have to browse for the Quicken folder), or export to either a Quicken .qif or .csv (spreadsheet) data file.

4. Perform a HotSync.

Other Tools

Several solutions exist to track one's investments on your PalmOne handheld. Personal Stock Tracker (find it at www.palmgear.com) enables you to enter your stocks and trades manually. Stock Manager goes a step further, enabling you to not only update stock prices when you perform a HotSync, but also retrieve updates when using a Treo or connecting to the Internet via a Bluetooth-enabled cellphone (**Figure 14.15**).

If you go out to lunch with folks from the office, your handheld's calculator is ready to help you figure out how to divide the bill and how much of a tip to leave. But for those of us who are mathematically challenged, CheckSplit's $10 shareware fee is worth it (find it at www.handango.com). Just enter the sales tax, what percentage you want to tip (pre- or post-tax), and how many people the bill is being split among (**Figure 14.16**).

✔ Tip

- Of course, if you have a Treo and an Internet package as part of your wireless subscription, you can simply use the Blazer Web browser to check your favorite financial Web site for stock updates.

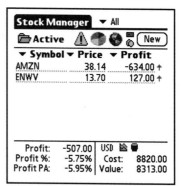

Figure 14.15 Enter your stocks and trades into Stock Manager, then update stock prices via a HotSync or connecting to the Internet using a Treo or a connection with a Bluetooth-enabled cellphone.

Figure 14.16 My brain hurts—how much do I owe for lunch?

OTHER TOOLS

MANAGING
YOUR TIME

Believe us, we're not slick-suited time management gurus, masters of every minute and second. The truth is, neither of us has ever really been *great* at time management. This is what led us to buy handhelds in the first place.

We are full-time freelancers/free agents/ independent contractors (pick your favorite term) who have managed to wrestle control of schedules and tasks with the help of a remarkable pocket-sized gadget. When we started using our handhelds, we were amazed to discover that they were not tools people used only during business hours. Organizers soon become integrated into their owners' lives, instead of gathering dust on the corner of their desks.

Everyone is trying to manage his or her time, whether that means setting up an efficient workflow system at work, or keeping track of where to take the kids throughout the week. It's likely you carry your Palm device everywhere—so use it to help take control of your time.

Chapter 15

Track Your Time

Have you ever read stories where the hero has to track something through an impenetrable jungle? In these scenes, the star is the Expert Guide who inspects every branch, leaf, and mismatched clump of dirt to divine the path of his or her prey. It's that attention to detail that fascinates him, of looking at the same thing everyone else is viewing, but seeing something different.

If ever an impenetrable wilderness was to be explored, it's the schedule that many of us live with every day. Your desire to tame it may have led you to buy a Palm organizer in the first place. Like the Expert Guide who notices all details, it's important that you do some tracking before you can reach your goal of personal organization.

Many people have a natural aversion to tracking their time, ourselves included. If you're recording all the minutiae of your daily life, you tend to feel more focused on tracking than on accomplishing. However, it's important that you know where your time is going before you can redefine where you want it to go. Keep track of where (or when) you spend your time for a week or a month.

For a visual approach that's built in to your handheld, consider using Calendar to track your time (**Figure 15.1**). Instead of scheduling only upcoming events, mark things as you do them.

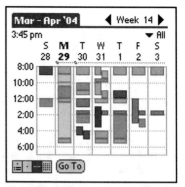

Figure 15.1 Your calendar will start to fill up, but by tracking everything you do plus your appointments, you can see how much time your tasks are taking.

Figure 15.2 To make it easier to differentiate between appointments and tracked items, use a special character (such as ~) to indicate your tracking.

To track your time using Calendar:

1. Launch the program by pressing the plastic Calendar button on the front of the case. This also displays today's events in the Day view.

2. Tap New, or tap the current time to create a new event. Write your activity on the event's title line.

3. If you know how long the activity will last, tap the Details button and enter an end time. If not, just stick with the default one-hour time span.

4. When you've finished, go back into the record and adjust the end time, then start a new record for your next activity.

✔ Tips

- To keep scheduled events and tracked events separate, mark the title with a unique character or word; you can set up a ShortCut (see Chapter 2) to quickly enter the notation (**Figure 15.2**).

- This also can be a good opportunity to add notes about your activity for reference later. Tap the Note button in the Event Details screen, or select Attach Note (✓-A) from the Record menu.

- If you don't want your Calendar screens cluttered with appointments *and* tracking information, mark the tracking events Private (see Chapter 4). They won't be visible, but they will be stored.

- Don't purge the old records from your Calendar until you've finished your time-tracking period.

Use a Tracking Program

A few applications have been designed specifically to track time. One application Jeff uses is HourzPro (www.zoskware.com), which lets him record his billable hours as well as non-billable time that he wants to keep tabs on. Other similar applications include Timesheet (www.seatechnology.com.au/timeSheet.html) and TEAK (www.eb7.com).

To track your time using HourzPro:

1. Launch HourzPro (**Figure 15.3**). Tap one of the view icons at the lower left to choose between the project view (▦) and the day view (⬚). Tap the New button to create a new record.

2. From the Project popup menu, choose Edit Projects to set up a new activity; if this is a business-related project, enter the client name and rate. Tap OK and then select the activity from the popup menu.

3. The timer begins when you create a new record, which will be shown on the HourzPro Entry screen (**Figure 15.4**). Tap Done to return to the main screen.

4. When finished with the activity, tap the stopwatch icon to the right of the description to stop the timer; the duration (and charge, if you entered a rate) is automatically calculated.

✔ Tip

■ If you're interrupted by something that you don't necessarily need to track, open your record and enter the amount of interrupted time in the Break field.

Figure 15.3 HourzPro offers advanced options for tracking your time.

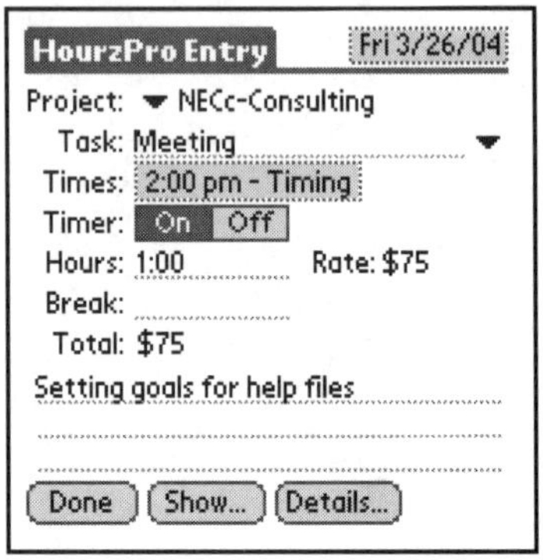

Figure 15.4 When you create a new record, the timer begins tracking. Specify a project and task for later reference.

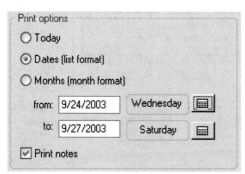

Figure 15.5 Specify Dates (list format) when printing your Calendar entries to see your events' details and save some paper.

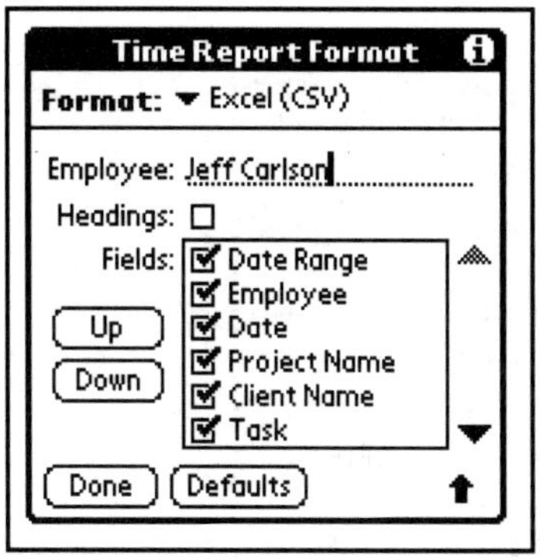

Time Report Format ℹ️

Format: ▼ Excel (CSV)

Employee: Jeff Carlson|
Headings: ☐
Fields: ☑ Date Range
        ☑ Employee
[Up]   ☑ Date
[Down] ☑ Project Name
        ☑ Client Name
        ☑ Task   ▼
[Done] [Defaults]   ↑

Figure 15.6 Set up the contents of your reports for when you export them.

Reportz List
- ⏱ 9/24 Hourz-Report $0
- ⏱ 9/24 filing $0
- ⏱ 9/24 lunch $0
- ⏱ 9/24 meetings $0
- ⏱ 9/24 proj mgmt $0

[Time Report]   [⏱]
[Expense Report] [$]

Figure 15.7 Generate comma-delimited time reports that can be opened in Excel on your PC.

Review Your Tracks

When you're finished recording your moves, you will have a wealth of raw data. Seeing where your time actually goes isn't always heartening, but at least you'll have a basis to build upon and improve. The next step is to analyze that data.

If you used the Calendar method mentioned earlier, go back and review where you spent your time. One easy method of doing this is to make a printout of the time period you spent tracking. If you're using HourzPro, a companion application, Reportz, makes it easy to create reports.

To generate a Calendar report:

1. Perform a HotSync to update your Palm Desktop records.

2. Choose Print from the File menu, or press Control/Command-P.

3. Under Print Options, choose Dates (list format) (**Figure 15.5**). Only days with an event on them will print. Click OK.

To generate an HourzPro report:

1. From the HourzPro screen, tap the Reportz icon (📄), or choose Go To Reports from the Options menu.

2. Tap the Time Report button to create a new report. You'll have to specify an employee (you) and default export format the first time you run Reportz (**Figure 15.6**). Tap Done when finished.

3. Name the report in the Title field, then select criteria from the Project, Period, Status, and Action popup menus.

4. Tap Create to generate the report. It will be added to the Reportz List (**Figure 15.7**). At your next HotSync, the report will be transferred to your PC.

Fine-Tune Your Time Management

Now that you have your data, look it over carefully. Are you spending too much time preparing for meetings? Too little? Do phone calls routinely interrupt your workflow? Examining this type of schedule overview tends to make previously minor annoyances or hidden successes stand out.

Know your own schedule

Most people have an internal clock that seems to pay no attention when they need to crunch on a deadline or be awake for a poorly scheduled important meeting. Look at how you space your activities throughout the day, then restructure accordingly.

If you're a walking corpse at 3 p.m., don't plan meetings, appointments, or important tasks; high doses of caffeine can sometimes overcome mid-afternoon sluggishness, but not always. Set up a repeating event ("Siesta" perhaps?) that spans 3:00–4:00 each business day (**Figure 15.8**).

Be alarming

Have you ever been so involved in a project that several hours can slip by without notice? Calendar's alarm features help keep Jeff focused when he needs to shift gears.

He's set up his Calendar preferences so that every event is assigned a 10-minute alarm. Select Preferences from the Options menu (/-R) and mark the Alarm Preset checkbox (**Figure 15.9**). Make sure you're being realistic about the alarms—adjust each event's alarm preset to account for things like travel time and preparation (yes, you should shave before dinner with the boss).

Another option is to use reminder software like BugMe! (www.electricpocket.net) (**Figure 15.10**).

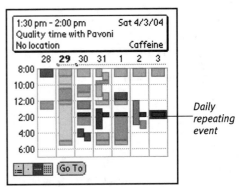

Daily repeating event

Figure 15.8 A scheduled break can help you get through the most unproductive time of the day.

Figure 15.9 I'd rather endure multiple alarms during the day than miss an appointment. Each new event is assigned an alarm when you activate the Alarm Preset option.

Figure 15.10 Think of BugMe! as a helpful Post-it note that's stuck to you.

FINE-TUNE YOUR TIME MANAGEMENT

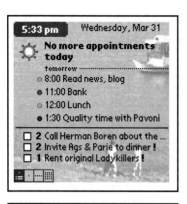

Figure 15.11 Don't forget about the improvements to your favorite Palm applications. A quick glance at the Agenda view shows you tomorrow's schedule, while the tabbed views in Tasks help you zero in on what's most pressing.

Prioritize events and tasks wisely

Is every task really a number-one priority? We occasionally enter tasks without considering their priority settings—as long as they're on the list, that should be good enough, right?

Maybe that works for some people, but being smart about prioritizing items generally improves the ability to deal with them in a timely manner. If you have to manually scan through the list each time you finish a task, you may be wasting valuable time. If, on the other hand, you figured out each item's priority ahead of time, you can jump through the list quicker.

See the bigger picture

The Palm OS is great at taking lots of little scraps of information and organizing them in one place. The problem is that your information is then all "hidden" behind the current application—you can't see what's coming up if you don't look at your schedule or Tasks list. The saying "out of sight, out of mind" can be apt, but not beneficial, for Palm owners. (We've seen people with handhelds in larger carrying cases that are festooned with sticky notes.) Don't forget to utilize the biggest improvements in Palm's organizer applications: the Agenda view in Calendar (which includes a peek into your tasks) and the tabbed, sortable views in Tasks (**Figure 15.11**).

✔ Tip

■ Give yourself some breathing room between appointments. A common scheduling mistake is to run meetings together, made all the easier because the Calendar defaults to hourly blocks of time. Use the alarm preset option to give you a breather before the next appointment.

Mark items for quick scanning

Don't start a memo with "Memo" or "Important Note," or list a task as "business stuff." Launch right into the meat of it, and explain later. Assume that you're going to be quickly scanning through the items most of the time—you don't want to waste time with two or three taps just to decipher something you wrote two hours ago. You should be able to identify the memo, task, or event just by looking at its title in a list.

Use ShortCuts

The ShortCuts feature is one of the most underutilized aspects of the Palm OS (see Chapter 2). ShortCuts are great for saving several Graffiti strokes when writing long words, and they're also ideal for frequently used items.

Look back at your time report and mark which events or keywords are most often repeated. Then go to the Prefs application, choose ShortCuts from the popup menu in the upper-right corner, and create ShortCut strokes for those items (**Figure 15.12**).

Figure 15.12 Figure out which tasks and events you write often, and create ShortCuts for them.

The Palm OS's Personal Touch

Another amazing thing about Palm devices is that they aren't just business devices. People schedule birthdays, anniversaries, reminders to watch favorite TV shows, etc. Your schedule is your life's schedule, which is why many more "non-business" people are buying handhelds.

However, some people think that if you enter a personal appointment (such as "dinner with Kim") into your impersonal gadget, then somehow that person has been "impersonalized." Not true—scheduling personal and family time is just as important as scheduling a meeting with the boss (if not more important).

Build Your Time Management Skills

Now that you have a better idea of where your time has gone and how to get more of it in the present, you can begin taking steps to shape where it will go in the future.

Notes: your secret workhorses

They seem so inconsequential, making an appearance only when the little note icon shows up to the right of a Calendar item or task. However, notes can be one of the most useful features you'll find. We attach notes to everything: alternate addresses, driving directions, and miscellaneous data (such as spouse and children's names to Contacts items). Meeting notes, flight schedules, and even people notes get added to records in handhelds ("Andrea: wore cream-colored suit and cool glasses; quick responses, good ideas, but poked fun at my good-luck teddy bear"). In the Calendar, Contacts, and Tasks applications, select Attach Note from the Record menu ($\diagup$-A).

Categorically speaking

One of the first things Jeff did when he started using his organizer was to reassign the categories (see Chapter 2). "Business" and "Personal" are just too broad for practical use, and invite catch-all disorganization (it's similar to creating a folder called "Misc" on your desktop—everything ends up there).

Try to be as precise as you can: "Office Phone Calls," "Kids," "Chicken Coop," etc. That way, you've started creating an organizational system before there's anything to organize (the piles of unfiled bills and receipts on both of our desks are a testament to the benefits of setting up categories prior to accumulating stuff).

The Power of Motion

One of the more important aspects of time management is being able to stick to the schedule you've created. Yet, there are times when an effectively plotted out day gets bogged down: phone calls, fatigue, a difficult project, whatever. These are the times to get off one's posterior and move around a little.

Take a break. If you're pressed for time, create a Calendar event that signals an alarm in 10 minutes. Better yet, if you find yourself working for long stretches of time without resting (a practice that looks good from management's viewpoint, but can quickly lead to health problems and burnout), set up several repeating events that signal alarms every two hours or so. If you're using DateBk5 (see later the next page), create a floating event that you can dismiss until later if you absolutely can't get away at that moment.

Or, set up a task that reminds you to take a break, get some coffee, or step outside for two minutes of fresh air. Position its priority so that after you complete the first one or two items on your list, you feel compelled to take a break in order to mark it off your list.

Motion has power, so it's in your best interest to keep moving, even if you spend most of your day in front of a computer. Remember that this type of motion is not counterproductive to "real work."

Linking Records with DateBk5 and Actioneer

One of the most frequently voiced complaints about the built-in applications is that they aren't tied together well. Although you can perform phone lookups within other applications, you can't create a task and have it show up on your schedule, for example. Two developers have come up with methods that bypass this limitation.

DateBk5 (www.pimlicosoftware.com) adds "floating" appointments, which get copied to successive days until marked Done.

To create a floating appointment in DateBk5:

1. Create a new event at the time and date you want to work on it, then tap Details.

2. In the Type category, tap the Float button (**Figure 15.13**). In DateBk5 you can also set up categories for events using the Category popup menu.

3. Tap OK. When you return to the Day view, you'll notice a circle icon at the far right of the event's name. After completing the task, tap the circle to checkmark it, or go to the Event Details screen and select Done from the Type popup menu.

Actioneer (www.actioneer.com) works ahead of the built-in applications by scanning what you write for keywords (such as times, days of the week, names, and others that you can set up).

To create new events and tasks using Actioneer:

1. Launch Actioneer and write your event or task. As you write, the icons on the right will become highlighted if a matching keyword is found (**Figure 15.14**).

2. If you want to refine Actioneer's matches before exiting, tap the icons to view options that can be added to your event.

3. When you're satisfied, tap OK. The record will appear in each application that Actioneer highlighted.

Figure 15.13 DateBk5 adds the concept of "floating" events to the normal Calendar features (top). When the mission is accomplished, check the circle in DateBk5's Day view (bottom).

Figure 15.14 Actioneer looks for keywords in what you write, then creates new records in the built-in applications.

Managing Your Data

We've gone on and on about how simple the Palm OS platform is, how its design is based on the idea that an *extension* of one's PC is better than an attempt at a miniaturized PC, and how this "less is more" approach is one key to the Palm OS's lead in the market.

"Yes, okay, fine, understood, *enough* already."

And yet, after owning a handheld for only a few weeks, many of us find it crammed with information other than what the built-in applications support. With thousands of programs available for downloading, and up to 64 MB of memory available in off-the-shelf devices (and an almost limitless amount of storage via optional memory cards), we can't help but store and manipulate all sorts of data. Our Palm handhelds are stuffed to the gills with outlines, ideas, sketches, spreadsheets, stories to read, groceries to buy, family photos, and important numbers—and that pales compared to some other people's organizers we've run across in the past.

A Palm OS-based organizer is ideal for storing all sorts of data, anything that you need to access or edit without opening a laptop computer or driving to the office late at night. Despite the volume of data, the resources for organizing it all are able to do more with less.

Outlining and Brainstorming

Jeff never liked outlining in school, preferring instead to just begin writing and see what he ended up with. But after a few less-than-encouraging grades, he realized that perhaps some advance planning and structure might help after all. Now, Jeff does quite a bit of outlining; not only for writing, but also to organize thoughts, plans, and even which videos to rent. (On the other hand, Agen, who comes from project planning lineage, is known for databasing his own wedding.)

We recommend Ultrasoft's BrainForest (`www.ultrasoft.com/brainforest`), which is what we'll use as an example in this chapter; other good outliners include Hi-Note (`www.cyclos.com/hi-note.htm`) and ThoughtManager (`www.handshigh.com/html/thoughtmanager.html`). You can achieve similar, though significantly limited, results with the Memos application.

To understand how BrainForest works, you have to think hierarchically in terms of trees and branches: An outline is the tree, the main entries are branches, and entries filed under the branches are leaves (**Figure 16.1**).

To create outlines with BrainForest:

1. Launch BrainForest, then tap the Create button, or choose Create Tree (/-U) from the Tree menu. An empty tree is created.

2. To create a branch, tap the New button or choose New Branch from the Tree menu (/-N). Write the branch's title in the new text field that appears (**Figure 16.2**).

3. You can either create more branches, which exist at the same level of importance as the first, or add leaves (subsidiary information) to the branch. Select New Leaf from the Tree menu (/-1).

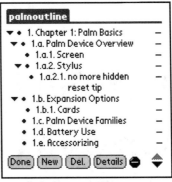

Figure 16.1 BrainForest makes it easy to create and edit hierarchical outlines.

Figure 16.2 Adding a new branch or leaf is easy—just tap the New button. Note that this outline uses BrainForest's action, becoming a super-sized to-do list.

OUTLINING AND BRAINSTORMING

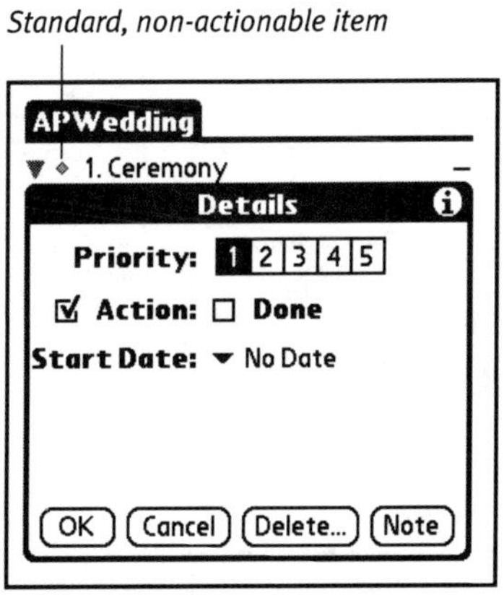

Standard, non-actionable item

Figure 16.3 If you don't want a tree, branch, or leaf to have a checkbox, deselect Action in the Details dialog to turn it into a standard item (denoted by a bullet).

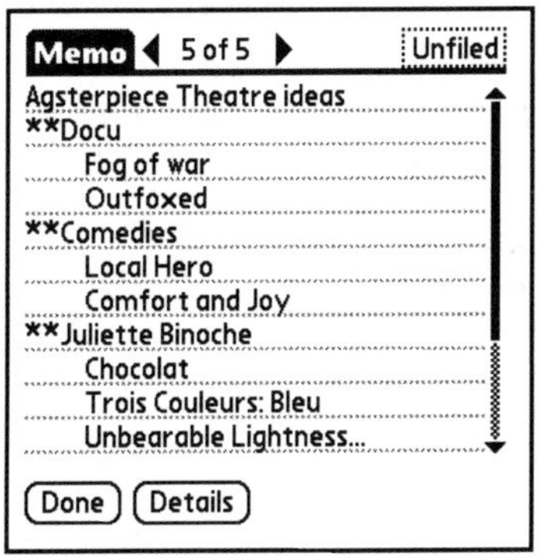

Figure 16.4 Tabbed lines in Memos are read as lower-level items when imported into BrainForest.

4. By default, trees are set up as actions (to-do items), with checkboxes running down the left side of the screen for each entry. To turn a tree, branch, or leaf into a standard item (identified by a black dot to the left), choose Toggle Action from the Edit menu (✓-T); or, tap Details, then deselect Action (**Figure 16.3**).

To edit outlines with BrainForest:

1. At the main screen, select the outline you want and tap the Open button, or choose Open Tree from the Tree menu (✓-L).

2. Tap and drag items to reposition them within the tree; a horizontal line appears to indicate where the item will end up when you lift your stylus.

To place an item under another item in the hierarchy (reducing its importance, as opposed to moving its position), drag and drop it onto the branch you wish to use as a parent item; the indicator line will disappear, and the parent will be highlighted before you drop the item.

3. To rename a branch or leaf, double-tap its title to display the popup text field.

✔ Tips

- If you're brainstorming and don't want to tangle with BrainForest's trees and branches, go ahead and write your ideas in Memos. Later, when you have more time, choose Import from the Tree menu (make sure the plug-in "BF Text Plug.prc" has been installed) to bring your notes into BrainForest.

- If you do write a note using the Memos application, add tab characters (↱) at the front of each line based on the level in the hierarchy where the item will reside (**Figure 16.4**).

Making Lists

Thanks to the Palm handheld, hastily scrawled shopping lists on scraps of paper and post-it notes are things of the past. Now, in addition to saving some paper, we have shopping lists that remember the usual staples so we don't have to start from scratch every time.

Lists, of course, go beyond noting the things needed at the store. You can create reusable checklists of procedures, clothing to pack when you travel, music you want to buy...the list of lists is practically unending. For generating lists of all kinds, try ListMaker (find it at www.handango.com). JShopper (www.land-j.com) is an advanced list tool tailored for shopping, with support for 15 stores, item lookups, and even the ability to track prices and coupons. SplashShopper (www.splashdata.com) does all that and ups the ante with a good range of built-in lists (from CDs and videos to calorie counting and Chinese take-out), the ability to create your own topics, and conduit support for a desktop application (**Figure 16.5**).

For Palm OS purists, the new and improved Tasks application can also expand its usefulness to include other types of lists.

To create lists using Tasks:

1. Open Tasks.

2. Tap the Category popup menu in the upper-right corner of the screen and choose Edit Categories.

3. Each built-in application can support up to 15 categories, but there's no rule saying that they all have to be related (**Figure 16.6**). Tap the New button and name your category (such as "Grocery store").

Figure 16.5 SplashShopper offers one-stop shopping for all your list needs. It includes a selection of pre-made lists (top) as well as the ability to customize your own. Within a list, simply check off an item once it's been procured (bottom).

Figure 16.6 Tasks can be used for other purposes in a pinch. Set up a new category representing your topic.

Figure 16.7 Turning on the Show Completed Tasks option lets you go back and unmark the items you've completed to "reset" the list.

Figure 16.8 Priorities and due dates can be used to sort your lists.

4. When you want to access your list, simply launch Tasks, go to the Category tab, and select the list's category from the popup menu. You may want to mark the Show Completed Tasks checkbox in the Tasks Preferences screen (✓-R), so you can uncheck items when you need them again (**Figure 16.7**).

✔ Tips

- Attach notes to items that require more explanation. In a grocery store list, you could include specific brand names in the note. Agen, always the Midwesterner, likes to track prices for list items at different stores.

- If you already use several categories, things might get confusing if you choose to display them all at once; mark the non-task records Private to hide them during everyday use.

- To reorder items in your list, assign priorities or set varying due dates to the records (**Figure 16.8**).

A Spirited Use of Contacts

While visiting California, I ran into Doug Wilder, a wine expert for Dean & DeLuca. To easily keep track of the wines he tastes and sells, he stores the information in his Contacts under a Wine category. When a question comes up, he can check the Palm for details, and frequently beams the information to folks who also have Palm handhelds. (Email dougwilder@ wildernapavalley.com to subscribe to his electronic wine newsletter.)

Databases and Spreadsheets

It's always been the job of database and spreadsheet software to elevate computers above the "toy" stage into the realm of "serious business." The next time someone asks you if your Palm device is some sort of handheld gaming device, show them how you can crunch data with one of these programs (*then* you can get back to that game of Bejeweled—see Chapter 13).

JFile, MobileDB, HanDBase, and FileMaker Mobile

For actual database functionality, turn to JFile (www.land-j.com), MobileDB (www.handmark.com), or HanDBase (www.ddhsoftware.com). If you use FileMaker on your PC, FileMaker Mobile (www.filemaker.com) can read, edit, and create FileMaker databases (**Figure 16.9**). A number of existing databases are available to download, ranging from subway schedules to medical references.

To create a database:

1. Tap the New DB (JFile) or the New (MobileDB and HanDBase) button.

2. Write the name of the database, then enter the field names in the lines provided. Click Done.

3. Within your new database, tap the New button (MobileDB and HanDBase) or Add button (JFile) to create a new record.

4. Enter the field data for that record (**Figure 16.10**). Tapping New on this screen creates a new blank record.

5. Tap Done (or OK) to go back to the list of records, where you can sort the records, perform searches, or choose other options (**Figure 16.11**).

Figure 16.9 Agen uses FileMaker Mobile to keep track of his music library (so he doesn't double up).

Figure 16.10 Once you're in a database (JFile shown here), you can enter your data next to the field titles you set up.

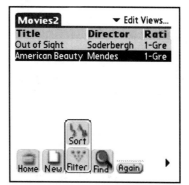

Figure 16.11 View, sort, and find the records from the database's main screen (HanDBase shown here).

DATABASES AND SPREADSHEETS

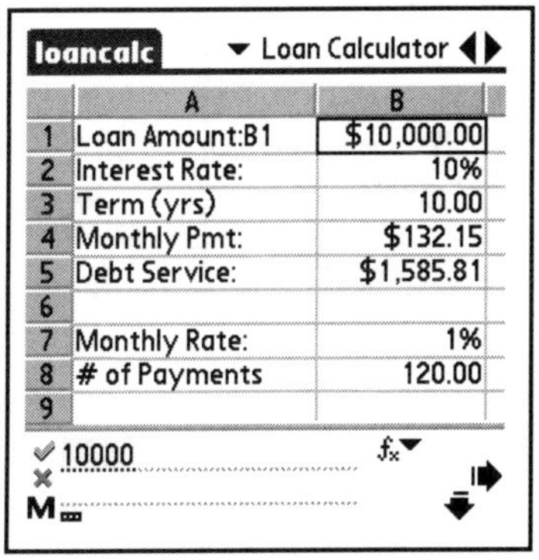

Figure 16.12 Quicksheet looks and acts like a desktop spreadsheet program.

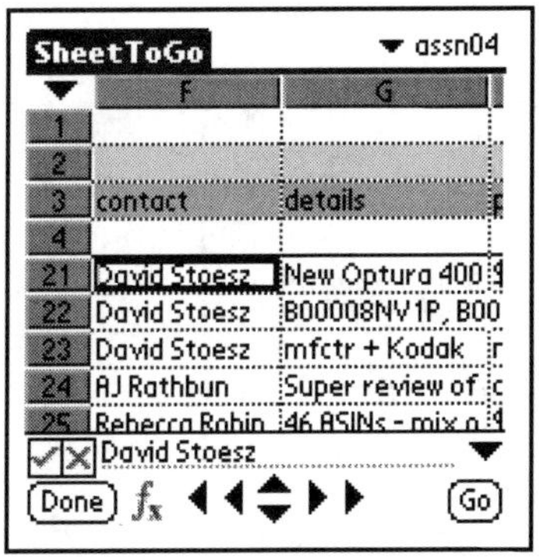

Figure 16.13 The SheetToGo component of Documents To Go displays and edits Excel spreadsheets.

Figure 16.14 Spreadsheets become more useful on devices with high-resolution screens.

✔ **Tip**

- You can also get a variety of programs that let you interface your handheld database with one on your PC. Check the Web sites of each database application for links.

Quicksheet, TinySheet, and Documents To Go

If you spend much of your time locked in Microsoft Excel's data cells, you'll be happy to know that Quicksheet (www.mobl.com/software), TinySheet (www.iambic.com), and Documents To Go (www.dataviz.com) put a true spreadsheet onto your handheld's small screen, complete with built-in functions, linking of named spreadsheets within workbooks, and a surprisingly easy method of maneuvering lots of data within a small space (**Figures 16.12** and **16.13**).

All three spreadsheets include conduits that synchronize the data on your device with the data on your hard disk.

✔ **Tip**

- If you're a regular spreadsheet user, you might seriously consider getting a high-resolution organizer such as a Palm Tungsten. The high-resolution screen can display more cells (**Figure 16.14**). Even better, get a Tungsten T3: The Graffiti area can be hidden to make full use of the screen, and with some applications you can rotate the screen to view more columns.

Printing from Your Palm

Remember all the hoopla about paperless offices? A Palm device would seem to be the perfect antidote to mass paper consumption, but every now and again it would be handy to print something from your handheld. A few utilities will do just that: TealPrint (www.tealpoint.com) and PalmPrint (www.stevenscreek.com/palm) enable you to connect to a variety of printers using a special cable or, better yet, via infrared. PrintBoy (www.bachmannsoftware.com/pbprem.htm) is even more wireless-friendly—in addition to infrared, it supports Bluetooth and wi-fi connectivity.

To print from your Palm device:

1. Launch your printing utility (we're using PrintBoy as an example), and select the type of document you wish to print, or choose which application to print from (**Figure 16.15**).

2. If the printer is equipped with an infrared port, aim your handheld at the printer and tap the Print button (**Figure 16.16**).

✔ Tips

■ If your printer doesn't have a built-in infrared port, consider buying the InfraReady adapter, an IR adapter that plugs into a printer's serial port (www.bachmannsoftware.com).

■ Sometimes it's just easier to print out a portion of your schedule and share it with someone. If you're not near your PC, use one of these printing programs to output your appointments over a span of time (**Figure 16.17**).

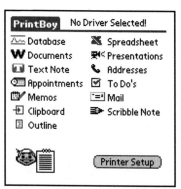

Figure 16.15 Don't wait to HotSync before printing something. Most document types can be printed directly from your handheld.

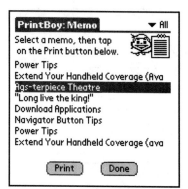

Figure 16.16 Printing from Memos is as simple as reading a memo.

Figure 16.17 If you want to share a week's schedule, it may be easier to simply print the week's appointments.

PROTECTING YOUR DATA

At a conference we attended, one of the keynote speakers, a pioneer in the Web marketing field, lost his handheld during the event. Tragic, yes, but not because he was missing a cool gadget. As a colleague mentioned, "There are people in this room who would *kill* for the phone numbers in that PalmPilot."

Most of us probably don't carry the private contact information of industry leaders and heads of state in our organizers, but we store plenty of phone numbers, appointments, and memos that we'd rather not share with just anyone. And with the ever-growing problem of identity theft, it's vitally important to implement a security system to safeguard your data.

We'll cover the built-in basics within the Palm OS and Palm Desktop, as well as several third-party applications to help you keep your identity your own.

Built-in Security

The Palm OS provides two methods of securing the data on your handheld, accessible through the Security Preferences (or the Security application on the Treo). See Chapter 2 for instructions on configuring specific Security settings.

Show/Hide/Mask private records

Using the Current Privacy popup menu in the Security preferences, you can choose to completely hide private records or to mask them with a dark gray band, so that you don't forget about private records entirely (**Figure 17.1**). (You don't want to know how many times we've recreated an appointment or contact that already existed but was hidden.)

If you select Hide Private Records and want to view them, you need to return to the Security Preferences (or application in the Treo), tap the Show button, and enter your password. When Mask Private Records is selected, you'll be asked for your password when you tap a masked record.

This system is simple and, for the most part, effective. A password-protection scheme won't keep out someone intent on getting your data, but it will likely deter most people.

✔ Tips

- With Palm OS 3.5 and later, you don't have to continually return to the Security Preferences to change the settings. Just select Security from the Options menu (✓-N) in one of the built-in applications to change the Show/Hide/Mask level (**Figure 17.2**). (Note that this makes a global change, not one just for the application you are in.)

- If you make records visible, don't forget to hide them again. Even your most ingenious password won't make the data secure.

Figure 17.1 The Security Preferences uses password protection to hide or mask private data and lock the device.

Figure 17.2 Don't forget that you can access the Security settings in any built-in application via the Options menu.

Figure 17.3 The Owner screen (which you set up in the Preferences program) is used when powering on your handheld after locking it.

Figure 17.4 The freeware LockMe! provides a bit more control over the Palm OS lock feature.

Locking it down

The other built-in security feature is the ability to lock your device by requiring users to enter the Security password before they can access anything (**Figure 17.3**). This is invoked by tapping the Lock & Turn Off button in the Security Preferences/application. Additionally, you can set your handheld to automatically lock itself. Tap the box below Auto Lock Handheld, enter your password, and choose Never, On power off, At a preset time, or After a preset delay (such as 5 minutes).

However, like the Show/Hide private records setting, this feature's usefulness is somewhat diminished by the number of taps it takes to actually activate it. Again, third-party software saves the day. Most of the "launcher" utilities that replace the Applications program (see Chapter 2) include an option to power off and lock the handheld.

For more control, turn to LockMe! (www.pilotzone.com/palm/preview/34342.html), a small freeware utility that lets you specify a time to periodically engage the locking mechanism; tap the Lock every popup menu to choose the duration, and then choose a beginning time from the Starting at popup menu (**Figure 17.4**).

✔ Tip

- Even if you use Lock & Turn Off... on a Treo smartphone, you can still make an emergency phone call to 911 without having to enter your password (**Figure 17.5**).

System Lockout

This handheld computer is owned by:

Jeff Carlson

Enter password to access this handheld computer:

OK   Make Emergency Call

Figure 17.5 You can still dial 911 without entering a password on your Treo when in System Lockout mode.

BUILT-IN SECURITY

Custom Security Options with TealLock

TealLock (www.tealpoint.com) adds steroids to the Palm OS's security capabilities, making them seem rather puny in comparison. At the same time, it centralizes many of the functions offered by other utilities in one application.

To set up and activate TealLock:

1. Launch TealLock from the Applications screen (**Figure 17.6**).

2. Tap the Password button to assign a full password, or an optional quick password (see Tip below). Enter the full password again when prompted to confirm your choice.

3. Tap the TealLock Status On button to activate TealLock. Your handheld will reset to load TealLock's features at startup.

Tapping the Lock and Off button turns off the device; when you power it on again, you're presented with a customizable screen where you enter your password to gain access to the device (**Figure 17.7**).

✔ Tip

■ TealLock gives you the option of using a Quick Password, which is only used when unlocking your handheld (enabling you to use a longer, more complex password for securing your data). You can map numbers and letters to the hardware buttons; tap Change Settings, select Lock Screen, Password Key entry, and enter mappings (**Figure 17.8**). Or, you can choose to use an onscreen keypad; go to TealLock's settings, select Lock Screen, Additional Display Options, and choose a style from the Number keypad popup menu (**Figure 17.9**).

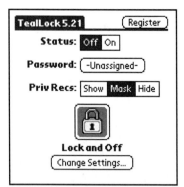

Figure 17.6 Similar to the Security Preferences, TealLock offers more settings by tapping Change Settings.

Figure 17.7 TealLock's Lock Screen includes the date and time, a custom image, and the option to show, mask, or hide private records.

Figure 17.8 With Quick Password enabled, you can map numbers and letters to your device's hardware buttons.

Figure 17.9 You can also turn on a keypad to enter the Quick Password if you're all thumbs.

Figure 17.10 Enter the text that you would like to be displayed on TealLock's Lock Screen.

Figure 17.11 TealLock's activation settings are the heart of its usefulness.

To change the Lock Screen image:

1. From TealLock's main screen, tap the Change Settings button (and enter your password) to display the TealLock Settings window.

2. Tap the Lock Screen box, then Background Image from the list below.

3. Tap the Select button or write the name of a TealPaint database containing images you'd like to use for the Lock Screen (the "LockImgs" database comes preloaded). (See Chapter 11 for information about TealPaint.)

4. Mark the Use Image checkbox to activate the custom screen feature. Tap OK.

To change the Lock Screen text:

1. From the TealLock Settings window, tap Lock Screen box, then Owner Text.

2. Write the text as you'd like it to appear. Use carriage return characters (/) to move the text down the screen and avoid overlapping your image (**Figure 17.10**).

3. Mark the checkboxes below the text field to specify the text style and placement. Tap OK.

To configure when to hide or mask private records:

1. From the TealLock Settings screen, tap the Activation box, then Automatic Hiding/Masking.

2. Tap the Hide/Mask Private Records popup to configure settings for either state.

3. Mark the checkboxes of the features you'd like to use. You can choose to hide records depending on a time range, or when your device turns off; specify the character to use by writing it in the ShortCut field (**Figure 17.11**). Tap OK when you're done.

CUSTOM SECURITY OPTIONS WITH TEALLOCK

To set up a locking schedule:

1. From the TealLock Settings screen, tap the Activation box, then Automatic Locking. You'll find the same variables here as in the Hiding/Masking settings (see previous page).

2. Specify a time period to automatically lock the handheld or set the lock to engage when the power shuts off.

3. Tap OK when you're done.

To configure when to show private records:

1. From the TealLock Settings screen, tap the Activation box, then ShortCut Strokes.

2. Specify a ShortCut character that will display hidden records by writing it in the ShortCut field (**Figure 17.12**). Tap OK when you're done.

Advanced TealLock Security settings

TealLock includes more security settings than we have room to detail here. From the TealLock Settings screen, tap the Security box, then Password Controls to set options such as specifying a time to expire the current password, enabling a guest password (which can open TealLock, but not reveal private records), and others (**Figure 17.13**). By selecting Data Encryption or Card Encryption from under the Security box, you can encrypt applications and certain record databases when the device is locked for yet more security (**Figure 17.14**).

Figure 17.12 Use Graffiti ShortCuts to access/hide records or to lock your handheld.

Figure 17.13 Specify a number of days before TealLock automatically prompts you to change your password.

Figure 17.14 TealLock enables you to encrypt both applications and certain record databases.

Figure 17.15 Spock! The Klingons have trapped us! Hit TealLock's self-destruct button.

Figure 17.16 The Locking/Unlocking setting enables you to open any application after a System Lockout.

✔ Tips

- Just like the Starship Enterprise, TealLock provides its own self-destruct sequence (minus the red flashing lights and Klaxon horns). In TealLock Settings, tap the Security box, then Data Self-Destruct to choose a "booby trap" password or configure destruction of data after a certain number of password attempts (**Figure 17.15**).

- By default, you're brought to the TealLock application when you enter your password after being locked out. In TealLock Settings, tap the Security box, then Locking/Unlocking options. Mark Launch app on unlock, then tap the box below to select the application (such as "Launcher") to start at the Palm OS Applications screen (**Figure 17.16**).

- A security flaw was found in Palm OS 3.5 and earlier that lets someone access a locked handheld using a serial cable and debugging commands. If you have an older Palm device, enable the Lock out serial port checkbox in TealLock's Security, Advanced Options screen.

- If TealLock doesn't provide the peace of mind you're looking for, consider PDADefense Professional (`www.pdadefense.com`), which boasts usage in the FBI, military, *and* White House. PDADefense provides 128-bit encryption, Administrator settings, and more.

When the Palm OS Security Isn't Necessarily Secure

The Palm OS's built-in security features are good enough for most of us. If you're concerned about having your handheld lost or stolen, setting up a lock screen and private records will probably keep unwanted eyes away from your data. Unfortunately, anyone with access to your desktop computer can easily read your records, whether they're marked private or not.

Figure 17.17 You can access your records using a standard text editor or word processor.

As mentioned in Chapter 2, your data is stored in a number of folders within a user folder that resembles your organizer's device name. The bad news is that those files are not encrypted, scrambled, or otherwise protected. Try the following steps.

To read your "private" data:

1. Make sure you have some records marked private, and that Hide Private Records is selected under the View menu in Palm Desktop.

2. Open a text-editing application such as Notepad (Windows) or TextEdit (Mac).

3. Choose Open from the File menu and navigate to your user folder.

4. Open your user folder (still within the text editor's Open dialog box). In Windows, open one of the folders corresponding to the built-in applications (**Figure 17.17**).

5. In Windows, make sure Files of type is set to All Files (*.*), and select a .dat file (such as memopad.dat). On the Mac, open User Data. (The Palm Desktop for Macintosh stores all of its records in one file.)

6. All of your memos will be viewable, interspersed with a bit of garbage characters. Scroll down to read the "private" information from a contact marked Private (**Figures 17.18** and **17.19**).

Figure 17.18 The so-called "private" record in the figure below is quite visible in both Windows (top) and Mac (bottom).

```
Contact Edit                    Unfiled

Last name: ...........................
First name: Private eyes, they're
            watching you..............
Company: They see your every
         move (and file)..........
         Contact Details        ℹ

Show in List: ▼ Mobile
   Category: ▼ Unfiled
     Private: ☑

( OK ) ( Cancel ) ( Delete... ) ( ◻ )
```

Figure 17.19 This record was, indeed, marked Private in our handheld.

Figure 17.20 Consider the desktop password access option if your computer is publicly available to others, or if you synchronize Palm Desktop with multiple handhelds. Checking this option (bottom) requires password entry (top) each time you launch Palm Desktop.

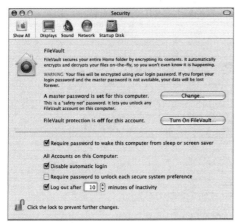

Figure 17.21 Mac OS X Panther provides on-the-fly encryption/decryption with the FileVault System Preference.

Palm Desktop Security

So what can you do to protect your data on the desktop? In addition to optionally hiding and showing private records, Palm Desktop can also require a user to enter her password to gain access to her data.

To keep people from snooping on your hard drive, you may want to look into purchasing a professional security program that lets you encrypt your handheld files (or folders). You would have to decrypt them before you launched Palm Desktop or performed a HotSync, but that may be a fair trade-off if you're particularly concerned about security.

To set up Palm Desktop password access (Windows):

1. From the Tools menu, choose Options. The Options dialog box appears.

2. Click the Security tab and mark the Require password to access the Palm Desktop data checkbox (**Figure 17.20**). Click OK.

✔ Tip

■ Macintosh Palm Desktop offers no such access security, but you do have two options under Mac OS X Panther. If you share your computer with other user accounts, the easiest method is to change Ownership & Permissions. Select the Palm Desktop application icon and choose Get Info from the File menu (Command-I), then adjust permissions for other individual users and groups. Or, you can go on the offensive with Panther's FileVault System Preference, which encrypts/decrypts on the fly and lets you configure settings for when the computer goes to sleep or initiates a screen saver (**Figure 17.21**).

Record-Level Encryption

Another option on the handheld is to encrypt your information on a record-by-record basis. The Babel Encryption Utility (www.wangner.net/babel.html) provides basic, but effective, cryptography. CryptoPad (find it at www.palmgear.com) encrypts information in a Memos-like listing.

To secure information using Babel:

1. Go to a record that you want to secure, and copy the sensitive text (such as a memo or part of a Contact record).

2. Highlight the text and choose Copy from the Edit menu (✓-C).

3. Switch to Babel, then enter a three-digit passcode. Tap the Encrypt button to continue (**Figure 17.22**).

4. Switch back to your source application (Memos, in this case), and paste the encrypted information over the existing data by choosing Paste from the Edit menu (✓-P). You'll see a string of garbage representing your data (**Figure 17.23**).

5. To unscramble the encrypted text in the future, reverse the process, this time tapping the Decrypt button and pasting the normal text over the encrypted text.

To secure information using CryptoPad:

1. In the CryptoPad application, open an existing Memos record; or, choose New Memo from the Record menu (✓-N), or tap the New button.

2. Choose Encrypt Memo from the Record menu, or write ✓-Y (**Figure 17.24**). A Password dialog appears.

3. Enter a password for this record. Each encrypted record can have its own unique password. Tap OK.

Figure 17.22 Babel encrypts and decrypts the contents of the Clipboard.

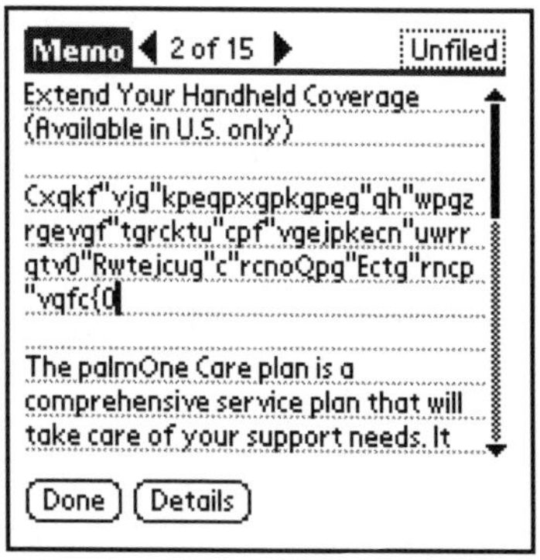

Figure 17.23 This garbage (admittedly useful garbage) results when you paste encrypted contents over the original.

Figure 17.24 CryptoPad replaces the Memos application, adding the option to encrypt individual records.

Storing Secure Account Information

It's amazing that we're able to keep track of all the important phone numbers, credit card numbers, and passwords that go into our heads—so amazing, in fact, that most of us can't do it. Numerous applications let you store your most important information in one secure place.

Both SplashID (`www.handmark.com`) and TurboPasswords (`www.chapura.com`) store information for credit cards, product serial numbers, access numbers, bank accounts, and more. Both provide password security to enter the application, configurable fields, and the ability to add longer notes.

To store information in SplashID and TurboPasswords:

1. From the application's main window, tap New to create a record. Tap the type of entry you want from the list that appears.

2. Enter your information in the fields provided. Each record type has prespecified field labels, but you can choose other labels that reflect your data by tapping the named popup menus or any empty fields.

✔ Tips

- Both applications have a maximum of six fields. TurboPasswords has only 11 category types, while SplashID has 18 built-in types as well as the ability to edit and create new categories.

- SplashID also enables you to mask certain fields when viewing from the main or details screen to protect your data from wandering eyes (though the field is never masked on the Edit screen).

Security Risks Most People Don't Consider

It's tempting to install some sort of security program and then rest easy. However, there are other security weaknesses you should keep in mind if you're serious about protecting your data.

Passwords

Don't use your name, birthdate, or anything else that's fairly obvious to guess as a password. Try to mix and match numbers and letters, or substitute numbers for letters (such as "s1ngs0ng"). Another technique is to think of a phrase and use the first letters of each word to create a password (such as "w2fm1" for "watch two funny movies first").

Social engineering

Gaining access to your computer or handheld doesn't have to happen over a network or via software. A colleague of mine with data security consulting experience told me about one act of "social engineering," a method of circumventing a security system's encryption, passwords, or firewalls. To test a client's security setup, he donned a telephone repair man's uniform and went to the company's headquarters. The helpful staff directed him to the phone closet, where he was able to install a device that monitored all of their network traffic, rendering their external security measures useless.

Basic Troubleshooting

A PalmOne handheld is one of the most trustworthy electronic devices we've ever encountered, but that doesn't mean it doesn't act up on occasion. Often the cause of problems and error messages is a conflict among the installed applications (sometimes applications or system extensions can be picky neighbors with other programs' code). Occasionally the problem is hardware-related, ranging from the components of the device itself, to batteries, to third-party accessories. Knowing how to deal with possible problems goes a long way toward reducing that first moment of panic when something isn't working.

Back Up Your Data

When you perform a HotSync, the data on your handheld gets copied to your user directory on your PC or Macintosh—or rather, *most* of it gets copied. The data from third-party applications may get backed up at HotSync, but the applications themselves sometimes don't, depending on which version of the Palm OS you're running (versions prior to Palm OS 3.3 can be problematic in this respect). In the event of a hard reset, where all data on the device is lost (see next section), it's great to be able to restore everything to the state it was in before the reset. To ensure that you're getting a full backup, we recommend the essential BackupBuddy (`www.bluenomad.com`), which is available for both Windows and Mac.

It allows you to back up and restore your full data, as well as perform incremental backups. If you have to do a complete restoration of your data, simply perform a HotSync. BackupBuddy VFS can back up your data to a memory expansion card in the device.

Broken Screen

If a screen problem requires you to send it back to the manufacturer, the situation is actually rather good. Agen recently had to send his new Zire 72 back to PalmOne after the screen fizzled out (due to a pratfall gone wrong). Luckily, it occurred within the 90-day warranty period and it wasn't cracked (which wouldn't have been covered). He sent it overnight to the service depot in Laredo, Texas, and received it back within seven days.

Based on this experience, Agen is a firm believer in the PalmOne Care extended warranty (and promises to end the pratfalls). It's $50 for a 12-month extension to the original 90-day warranty, but it also covers a one-time screen replacement during this time period.

Technical Support and Helping Hands

PalmOne, Inc. support

- Web site:
  `www.palmone.com/support/`
- Technical Support (847-262-7256) can answer your software questions.

PalmSource, Inc. support

- All operating system-related questions should be handled by your device's manufacturer.

Resetting Your Handheld

Like turning your desktop computer off and on, a Palm organizer occasionally needs to be reset (though infrequently). Three methods of resetting the device are available.

A *soft reset* is like rebooting a computer, initializing its internal system files and libraries. All of your data remains intact.

If something is giving you errors as your device starts up from a soft reset (such as a system update patch, for example), try doing a *warm reset*. This is analogous to booting Windows in Safe Mode or starting a Mac with extensions turned off.

A *hard reset* is the action of last resort, erasing all of your data and taking the handheld back to its original state. Be sure you have a recent backup of your information!

To perform a soft reset:

◆ Insert a thin, straight end (such as a straightened paper clip) into the reset hole on the back of the device.

To perform a warm reset:

1. Hold down the plastic Scroll Up button on the front of the device case.

2. Insert a straight end into the reset hole on the back of the device, then release the button. The screen should flash, then restart normally.

To perform a hard reset:

1. Hold down the power button.

2. With the power button still held down, insert a straight end into the reset hole on the back of the device, then release the power button.

3. A confirmation message appears on the screen. Press the Scroll Up button to erase the memory, then restore your data.

The Evolution of the Stylus

In ye olden days of the PalmPilot, the stylus that came with the handheld had a rather James Bondian double duty. By unscrewing the stylus's tip from its metal barrel, you'd reveal a thin, plastic reed—a reset pin at the ready. Unfortunately, progress (and economic consideration) has brought about more and more uni-body plastic styli with today's PalmOne handhelds, which can cause a bit of a scramble during an emergency need for a hard reset.

The good news is that some new models (like the Zire 72) have a slightly inset, pressure-sensitive reset button. But if you have a model with a traditional reset hole (like the Zire 31), be sure to keep our favorite tool on hand: a straightened paper clip.

RESETTING YOUR HANDHELD

Deleted applications return after a hard reset (Mac)

We performed a fair share of hard resets during testing for this book. And on our initial post-reset HotSync from our Macintosh, we were continually frustrated with the reappearance of many third-party applications and files that had been previously deleted from the handheld—even after we'd performed a HotSync after deleting them on our handhelds.

As a reminder, the majority of applications that you add to your PalmOne device are stored in the Backups folder within the folder bearing your HotSync name (accessed at [home] > Documents > Palm > Users > [HotSync name] > Backups). When you delete an application, it should be automatically moved to the Archive folder within Backups—but this doesn't seem to be the case.

Unfortunately, there seems to be only a manual solution. First, drag unwanted application (.prc) and database (.pdb) files to the Archive folder. Then, perform another hard reset followed by a HotSync to restore your user data.

✔ Tips

- You could drag files to the Archive folder *and* delete them on your handheld, but that's double the work.

- If you move files to the Archive folder, then perform a HotSync without performing a hard reset, the files will regenerate in the Backups folder since they were found on your handheld.

- If you delete applications on your handheld, it's a good idea to do some of this maintenance in the Backups folder from time to time so you won't be faced with this problem at a hard reset.

Handheld Won't Turn On

Most likely, your handheld's rechargeable battery has drained to the point where it's passed all of the low battery warnings. Plug in the AC adapter to feed it a little power. Perform a soft reset, then let it charge for at least three hours.

HotSync Troubleshooting

If you have any troubles at all, they're likely to be related to HotSync. Although in practice HotSync is a simple process, it relies on several factors that control the communication with your computer.

Common HotSync fixes

◆ In Palm Desktop, check that your settings in the HotSync Setup screen are correct.

◆ Under Windows, exit HotSync Manager, then launch it again. On a Macintosh, make sure Local HotSync is enabled; if it is already on, disable it manually, wait a few seconds, then re-enable it.

◆ Verify that the HotSync cable or cradle is plugged into the correct port on your computer.

◆ Reduce the port speed in the Setup screen.

◆ Disable any software that might be sharing the communication ports. Fax software is often the culprit, because it's always monitoring for incoming faxes.

◆ If you're using a USB hub, try plugging the HotSync cradle or cable directly into the USB connection on the computer.

HOTSYNC TROUBLESHOOTING

Windows COM port conflicts

If the previous suggestions don't produce a successful HotSync, your COM ports may be misconfigured or confused. COM ports are the physical ports used to hook up devices such as modems and mice to the back of your computer. Some machines also use COM ports for internal devices.

To work together, these ports communicate with the computer's processor over Interrupt Request (IRQ) channels. Often, one IRQ channel is shared by two COM ports, which means they can both be vying for attention (COM 1 and COM 3 usually share an IRQ, while COM 2 and COM 4 share another IRQ). If you have the option of doing so, move your HotSync cable to a different COM port. If not, and if you're skilled in complex computer configuration, try reassigning the port settings.

Keep in mind that tinkering with IRQ settings has the potential to cause conflicts where none existed before. Make changes one at a time; if they don't fix the problem, undo the change and reboot your computer before making any more changes.

To modify Windows COM settings:

1. Double-click the System icon from the Windows Control Panel.

2. Click the Device Manager tab, then click the plus sign next to Ports (COM & LPT).

3. Double-click the Communications Port you want to change.

4. Click the Resources tab. If the Use automatic settings checkbox is on, click to unmark it.

5. Choose an alternate configuration from the Settings based on popup menu.

6. When finished, click OK, then restart your computer.

INDEX

INDEX

INDEX

log files, 56, 91, 235, 250
Logic Calculator, 214
login scripts, 57
long documents. *See* documents
Look Up field, 154
lost data, 92, 103
lost passwords, 44
low display quality, 312
lowercase characters, 33

M
.Mac accounts, 98, 99, 103
Macintosh software.
    See Palm Desktop (Macintosh)
Macintosh systems.
    See also Palm Desktop (Macintosh)
    Bluetooth clicker software, 63
    Mac OS 9 *vs.* Mac OS X, 23
    OS 8 and OS 9, 269
    remote control using Bluetooth, 63
    synchronizing email, 248
magnifying
    photos, 292, 297
    Web page content, 277
Mahjong game, 324
mail. *See* email and email messages
Mail application (Treo), 242, 247, 261
mail server setup, 260, 262
mailboxes, 253, 261
MakeDocBatch application, 321
managing time. *See* time management
    and tracking
manually assigning IP addresses, 65
mapping numbers to hardware buttons, 356
maps, 226
Mark/Space company, 23, 100–102
marking records
    built-in security settings, 354–355
    email messages, 257
    marking tasks complete, 187, 207
    for printing or filtering, 178
    private contacts, 168
    private memos, 193
    security settings, 169, 186
    TealLock security, 356
masking private records, 354–355, 356
    built-in security for records, 354–355, 356
    fields, 363
    private contacts, 168
    private events, 129
    security settings, 43, 169, 186
Math Calculator application, 214
mathematical symbols, 210
Media application, 69, 282, 284, 291
meeting attendees, 220
Memo List (Palm Desktop), 204
Memo Pad. *See* memos and Memos application
Memo Pad (Apple), 102
memopad folder, 78

memorized calculation results, 211
memorized transactions, 332, 333
memorized views, 179, 205
memory. *See also* expansion cards; purging
    background images and, 109
    beaming and, 70
    Blazer management, 276
    calculation results in, 213
    completed tasks and, 192
    downloading Web pages to, 278
    expansion cards, 72
    free memory, viewing, 70
    photos in, 241
    photos on expansion cards, 285
    video capture and, 290
memory cards. *See* expansion cards
Memory Stick modules, 17.
    See also expansion cards
memos and Memos application. *See also* notes and
        Note Pad application
    Alphabetic sort option, 194
    attaching memos to records, 146–147, 206
    attaching notes to contacts, 166
    attaching records to memos, 206
    beaming memos, 200
    categories, 198–199
    creating, 204
    creating memos, 193, 204
    display fonts, 201
    editing Calculator views in, 214–215
    editing memos, 193
    effective titles, 342
    exporting memos to BrainForest, 347
    filtering memos, 205
    Graffiti and repetitive strain injuries, 195
    Manual sort option, 194
    memorized views, 205
    navigating memos, 195
    Note Pad, 196
    Palm Desktop modules, 202–207, 204–207
    printing memos, 203
    private memos, 193
    reordering items, 194
    sharing memos with desktop
        applications, 202–207
    sorting, 205
    sorting memos, 27, 194, 205
    Voice Memo application, 197
Menu button (Treo), 36
Menu icon/button, 11, 12, 26, 28
MenuHack extension, 28
menus, 26, 28, 29, 35
merging categories, 199
messages
    chatting, 238
    default applications, 53
    email. *See* email and email messages
    GSM phones, 230
    instant messaging, 161, 236–237
    MMS messaging, 239–241, 242, 289

Q

QED application, 322
QEX2 application, 321
QIF files, 333
QMate application, 330
Query DNS setting, 57
QueuSoft application, 329
Quick Connect feature, 161
Quick Install feature, 67, 77
Quick Key shortcuts, 232
Quick Password feature, 356
Quick Unlock feature, 45
Quicken, 330–332, 333
QuickInstall folder, 78
Quickoffice application, 313
Quicksheet application, 351
QuickText application, 236
quotations, highlighting in eBooks, 311
Qwerty keyboard, 31

R

radio shows, playing, 303
RAM, applications in, 66
random play feature, 306
RC4 encryption, 46
reading
    email messages, 255
    private records, 360
Real Music Store, 303
Real Networks, 303
RealOne Player, 294
RealOne Player for Palm, 303, 304, 306
receipts
    creating, 224
    editing, 223–224
    Expense application, 217–224
    faded, 327
receiving
    beamed applications, 71
    beamed data, 42, 130, 171
    calls, 235
    MMS messages, 240
    SMS messages, 237
recent calculations, viewing, 211
rechargeable batteries, 18, 368
recording
    video, 290
    voice memos, 5, 9, 197
records
    address records. See contacts and Contacts
        application
    archiving deleted records, 95–96, 121, 132
    attaching notes, 146–147
    beaming a category of, 131
    command bar actions, 29
    copying vs. synchronizing data, 76
    deleting duplicate records, 160
    deleting with lost password, 44–45
    duplicating, 160

encrypting, 46, 358, 362
exporting or importing, 96
linking, 177, 206, 344
private records, 168, 169, 186, 193, 355–355, 356,
    357, 358. See private records
restoring archived records, 95–96
security on desktop, 360–361
self-destruct feature, 46
specifying for transfer to new Palm devices, 97
synchronizing, 80
transferring with Bluetooth, 62
Records button, 70
recurring events. See repeating events
Red-eye tool, 297–298
red time bars, 111
reimbursal records. See Expense application
relational links between records, 177, 206, 344
remapping application buttons, 14
Remember Last Category option, 68, 167
reminders
    alarms, 122
    birthdays, 126, 156
    software, 340
    to synchronize, 102
    tasks, 133, 185, 189
remote access HotSyncing, 89
remote control using Bluetooth, 63
rendering photos, 296
repeating events
    banners, 114, 145
    changing, 126
    creating, 125
    deleting text, 120
    in Month view, 115
    repeating event icon, 110, 125
    time management and, 343
    in Week view, 113
repeating tasks, 190
repetitive strain injuries and Graffiti, 195
replaceable batteries, 18, 19
replacing batteries, 19
replying to email messages, 256
reports, printing, 339
Reportz application, 339
reset pins, 16, 367
resetting devices, 16, 367, 368
resizing images or photos, 241, 295, 296, 317
resolution
    file size and, 288
    images, 278
    matching handheld screen resolution, 296
    photos, 286, 287
    screen resolutions, 10, 351
    video, 290
responding to alarms, 122
restaurant bills, splitting, 334
restoring data
    after hard reset, 368
    archived records, 95–96
    backed up data, 366

INDEX

INDEX

INDEX